REMINISCENCES

OF

LEVI COFFIN,

The Reputed President of the Underground Railroad;

BEING

A BRIEF HISTORY OF THE LABORS OF A LIFETIME IN BE-
HALF OF THE SLAVE, WITH THE STORIES OF NUMER-
OUS FUGITIVES, WHO GAINED THEIR FREEDOM
THROUGH HIS INSTRUMENTALITY, AND
MANY OTHER INCIDENTS.

———

AMS PRESS
NEW YORK

102713

Reprinted from the edition of 1876,Cincinatti

First AMS EDITION published 1971

Manufactured in the United States of America

International Standard Book Number :0-404-00143-2

Library of Congress Number:79-113578

AMS PRESS INC.
NEW YORK, N.Y. 10003

PREFACE.

————o————

I HAVE been solicited for many years to write a history of my anti-slavery labors and underground railroad experiences, and although I had kept a diary the most of my life, it was without any prospect of ever putting it into book-form. I had no desire to appear before the public as an author, having no claim to literary merit. What I had done I believed was simply a Christian duty and not for the purpose of being seen of men, or for notoriety, which I have never sought. But I was continually urged by my friends to engage in the work, believing that it would be interesting to the rising generation; but being so fully occupied with other duties, I seemed to find no time that I could devote to this work, so that it was put off from year to year. I also often received letters from different parts of the country, desiring me to write the history of my life and labors in the anti-slavery cause, reminding me that the most of my co-laborers had passed away, and that I must soon follow, and that these stirring anti-slavery times in which I lived and labored were a part of the history of our country, which should not be lost. But still I deferred it until now, in the seventy-eighth year of my age. And although I feel the infirmities of that period of life fast gathering around me, I have gathered up my diaries, and other documents that had been preserved, and have written a book. In my own plain, simple

(i)

style, I have endeavored to tell the stories without any exaggeration. Errors no doubt will appear, which I trust the indulgent reader will pardon, in consideration of my advanced age and feebleness. It is here proper also to acknowledge the valuable services of a kind friend, for aid received in preparing these pages for the press. I regret that I have been obliged to leave out many interesting stories and thrilling incidents, on account of swelling the size and cost of the book beyond what was agreed upon with the publishers. Among the stories omitted is the account of the long imprisonment and sufferings of Calvin Fairbank, of Massachusetts, in the Kentucky penitentiary, for aiding fugitives, and of Richard Dillingham, of Ohio, who suffered and died in the penitentiary at Nashville, Tennessee, for a similar offense.

Some time ago I requested my dear old friend and co-laborer in the cause of the slave, Dr. Wm. Henry Brisbane, to write a few introductory words for my book, which I here introduce as part of the preface :

My very dear old friend has requested me to write some introductory words, or preface, for his book ; and I can not do justice to my own most affectionate feelings toward him and his amiable wife, dear "Aunt Katy," without complying with his request and accepting the honor thus conferred upon me.

I have in my possession a picture, executed by Mr. Ball, a colored man from Virginia. The central figure is a native of South Carolina, a representative of the old planter class of that State, who manumitted his slaves many years before the Emancipation Proclamation of President Lincoln. On each hand sits with him a friend and Christian brother—the one, a sedate, benevolent-looking Quaker, a native of North Carolina, and a faithful representative of that class known as Orthodox Friends ; the other, with a countenance full of humor and amiable mischief, a native of Rhode Island, and a true representative of the old Roger Williams class of Soul-Liberty Baptists. The cause of the slave brought into a most intimate and happy friendship these three men of diverse origin, training, habits of life, temperament, disposition and other personal characteristics. For many years they labored and suffered together for those in bonds as bound with them. In Christian love they bowed themselves before their Heavenly Father and prayed together for the oppressed race; with a faith that knew no wavering they worked in fraternal union for the enfranchisement of their despised colored brethren, and shared together the odium attached to the name of abolitionist, and finally they rejoiced together and gave thanks to God for the glorious results of those years of persevering effort. The youngest of these has gone to his reward in heaven, and those who knew Edward Harwood can not wonder that the other two loved him with a love that was more than a brother's. The oldest—the placid, the benevolent, the kind-hearted and devoted friend of the slave, and of all mankind— Levi Coffin, still lives to give, for the benefit of humanity, the reminiscences of his experiences, so full of interesting incidents and touching pathos. The other survivor thanks God with all his heart that his dear brother has been spared to leave this valuable record as a legacy to his thousands of friends, white and black, in this our beloved country, redeemed from the curse of slavery with the atoning blood of many a battle-field.

And now, with no more fugitives to hide, and no clanking chains to disturb our peaceful old age, I subscribe myself,

Fraternally and lovingly his,

WM. HENRY BRISBANE.

CINCINNATI, OHIO, *June* 17, 1876.

Trusting that this volume will accomplish something toward the eradication of the spirit of caste, which still exists in our land— though, in the providence of God, slavery itself has been removed— and in the acceptance and practice of that command, which reads: "Love thy neighbor as thyself," I now commend it to the reader.

LEVI COFFIN.

CINCINNATI, *Eighth Month*, 1876.

CONTENTS.

INTRODUCTORY CHAPTER.

CHAPTER I.

CHAPTER II.

CHAPTER III.

CHAPTER IV.

CHAPTER V.

CHAPTER VI.

CHAPTER VII.

CHAPTER VIII.

CHAPTER IX.

CHAPTER X.

CHAPTER XI.

CHAPTER XII.

CHAPTER XIII.

CHAPTER XIV.

CHAPTER XV.

CHAPTER XVI.

CHAPTER XVII.

CHAPTER XVIII.

CHAPTER XIX.

CHAPTER XX.

INTRODUCTORY CHAPTER.

GENEALOGY.

THE following brief sketch of the Coffin family is gathered from the first number of the American Historical Record, published at Philadelphia, and from private records copied from those kept at Nantucket. The earliest account of the name we have dates back to 1066. In that year Sir Richard Coffin, knight, accompanied William the Conqueror from Normandy to England, and the manor of Alwington, in the county of Devonshire, was assigned to him. The authorities respecting the county of Devonshire make honorable mention of Sir Elias Coffin, knight of Clist and Ingarby, in the days of King John; of Sir Richard Coffin, of Afwington, in the time of Henry II.; of Sir Jeffrey Coffin and Combe Coffin, under Henry III., and of other knights, descendants of these, until the time of Henry VIII., when we find Sir William Coffin, sheriff of Devonshire, highly preferred at Court, and one of eighteen assistants chosen by the king to accompany him to a tournament in France, in 1519. He was also high steward of the manor and liberties of Standon, in Hertford. By his will he bequeathed his horses and hawks to the king, and devised the manor of East Higgington, Devonshire, to his nephew, Sir Richard Coffin, of Portledge. His monument in

(3)

Standon Church is mentioned in Weever's "Funeral Monuments," at page 534.

Nicholas Coffin, of Butler's parish, in Devonshire, died in 1603. His will, which was proved at Totness, in Devonshire, November 3, 1603, mentions his wife and five children, viz: Peter, Nicholas, Tristram, John and Anne. Peter married Joanna Thimber, and died in 1627, leaving four daughters and two sons. One of these sons was the famous Tristram Coffin—or Coffyn, as he spelled it—the ancestor of the numerous families of that name in this country. Nearly all his descendants are enabled, by means of the accurate genealogical records in existence, to trace their lineage back to him, although nearly two centuries have elapsed since his death. He was born at Brixton, near Plymouth, in the county of Devonshire, England, in the year 1605. He married Dionis Stevens, and in 1642 came to New England, bringing with him his wife and five children, his mother and his two sisters. He first settled at Salisbury, Massachusetts, where he lived a number of years, and in 1660 removed, with his family, and settled upon the island of Nantucket. He was one of a company of nine who first purchased Nantucket from the Indians, which fact appears in a conveyance from the Sachems, Wanackmamack, and Nickanoose. Prior to this purchase from the natives, the English title to the greater portion of the island had been obtained from Thomas Mayhew, who held the same under a conveyance from Lord Stirling. Tristram Coffin and his sons at one time owned about one-fourth of Nantucket, and the whole of the little island adjacent to it on the west, called Tuckernuck, containing one thousand acres, which was purchased of the old sachem, Potconet. He appears to have been a leading spirit among the first settlers, and was frequently selected by the inhabitants to transact important public business.

The children of Tristram Coffin were Peter, Tristram, Elizabeth, James, John and Stephen. We trace our line of the family from John. He married Deborah Austin; their son Samuel married Miriam Gardner; their son William married Priscilla Paddock; their son Levi married Prudence Williams. These last were my parents, and this places me in the fifth generation from the first Tristram Coffin, of Nantucket. The different branches of Tristram Coffin's family have increased and scattered, until there are representatives in nearly every part of the United States.

The island of Nantucket being small, and its soil not very productive, a large number of people could not be supported thereon, and as the population increased, a number of the men engaged in the whale fishery and other maritime pursuits, in order to gain a livelihood. Others turned their attention to other parts of the country, and were induced to remove and settle elsewhere, with a view to better their condition, as to providing for their children, etc. Awhile before the Revolutionary War a considerable colony of Friends removed and settled at New Garden, in Guilford County, North Carolina, which was then a newly settled country. My grandfather, William Coffin, was among those who thus emigrated. His removal took place in the year 1773. My grandparents, William and Priscilla Coffin, had ten children—eight sons and two daughters—all of whom lived to have families of their own. They settled at New Garden, North Carolina, and were all members of the religious Society of Friends. My father, Levi Coffin, was the youngest of eight sons and next to the youngest child. He was born on the island of Nantucket, 10th month, 10th, 1763, and was about ten years old when the family moved to North Carolina. My grandfather Coffin lived to be eighty-three, and my grandmother eighty-one years old. Both died in the year 1803, at the place where they first settled in North Carolina. I remember them well, though I was young at the time of their death. Both were valuable elders in the religious Society of Friends, and were highly esteemed in the community. Their house had long been a resort and a place of entertainment for Friends who came into the neighborhood to attend religious meetings, and for traveling ministers. They lived on a farm, a short distance from New Garden Meeting-House. My father was brought up as a farmer, but managed to get a fair education, considering the limited advantages at that day, and, when a young man, engaged during the winter season in teaching school in the neighborhood. After the marriage of my parents, they settled on a farm in the neighborhood of New Garden, and I was brought up as a farmer, until I reached my twenty-first year. My parents had seven children. I was the only son and next to the youngest child. I could not well be spared from the farm to attend school, and the most of my education I obtained at home. My father took pains to instruct me and my sisters during his hours of leisure from out-door work, so that I kept about even with my associates in the neighborhood who had better opportunities for gaining an education, and during the short intervals that I attended school, I was classed with them, and often stood at the head of my class. But our schools then were very inferior, compared with those at the present. I thirsted for a better education, and as soon as I was of age I sought a better school than we had in our neighborhood.

I remained there one session, then engaged as assistant teacher during the winter session, and the following winter attended another good school. I then taught, at intervals, for several years. In the year 1816 my sister Sarah died. She was in her twentieth year and two years my senior. This was a heavy stroke upon me. She was a kind and affectionate sister, and we had been inseparable companions in our childhood. Although she died rejoicing in her dear Redeemer, with a bright and glorious prospect before her, I could not for a long time be resigned sufficiently to say concerning her loss, "Thy will, O Lord, not mine, be done." My older sisters were married, and I and my youngest sister Priscilla were all that were left at home with our parents. Priscilla was three years my junior. She was a sweet and attractive child, and we were warmly attached to each other. When she was about twelve years old she was converted, and at the age of fifteen she appeared in public testimony. She appeared to have a remarkable gift in the ministry, and her words impressed all who heard her and touched the hearts of many. Her mission and labors for several years seemed to be mostly confined to family circles and to social gatherings of young people. On such occasions she was frequently prompted to speak in a most remarkable manner, and her words seemed to have great effect on her young associates and others who heard her. For some years after her first appearance in the ministry, she spoke but seldom in public assemblies, but when she did, it was to the edification of her hearers. A few years afterward she was recorded as a minister of the religious Society of Friends.

In the spring of 1825 my parents and sister moved to the State of Indiana, where my married sisters had all located. I was then engaged in teaching, but expected soon to follow with my own little family, which I did the next year. My sister Priscilla married a short time before I removed to Indiana. My parents were now left alone, and being old and feeble, I took charge of them and located them near me, in the village of Newport. My father died in 1833, in his seventieth year. We then took my mother into our house and cared for her until the close of her life. She died in 1845, in her eighty-eighth year.

My mother's family, the Williamses, were of Welsh extraction. I have understood that my great-grandfather, George Williams, came from Wales to America, and settled in Prince George County, Maryland. My grandfather, Richard Williams, married Prudence Bales, and their oldest two children were born in Maryland. Afterward they emigrated to North Carolina and settled in Guilford County, about the year 1752. They located near the place where the old New Garden Meeting-House now stands, and where the yearly meeting of the religious Society of Friends has been held for many years. At the time of their removal to that neighborhood, it was thinly settled, but it grew in time to be a large and prosperous settlement, the members of which were mostly Friends. My grandparents had many hardships to encounter and privations to undergo, such as the first settlers of a new country always have to experience. When the stock of provisions which they had brought with them gave out, they had to go to an older settlement, about fifty miles distant, to get a new supply. The first winter they cleared a small piece of land, and in the spring planted corn and garden seed. Provisions again became scant, and they had to live on roasting-ears and vegetables till the corn ripened, being entirely deprived of bread. As soon as the corn was ripe enough to shell, they dried it by spreading it on the ground in the sun, and then took it on horseback to a mill about thirty miles distant, on Cane Creek, now in Chatham County. My grandfather Williams donated the ground on which New Garden Meeting-House was built, besides several acres of land, covered with timber sufficient for all building purposes. The battle of Guilford Court-House, fought about the close of the Revolutionary War, commenced near New Garden Meeting-House and continued along the old Salisbury road, a distance of about

three miles, to Martinsville, the old Guilford Court-
House, near where the main battle was fought. A
number of soldiers were killed near the meeting-
house and along the road, and were buried by the
roadside and in the Friends' burying ground near
the meeting-house.   I have often seen their graves.
After the battle the meeting-house was used as a
hospital for the wounded soldiers, and my grandfather Williams' house was occupied by the wounded
British officers.   My grandfather Coffin's house was
used by the American officers as a hospital for their
sick and wounded.   The two farms joined, and the
headquarters of the different forces were thus in
close proximity.

The small-pox broke out among the British officers, and my grandfather Williams caught the disease
from them and died.   My grandmother was left with
twelve children, five sons and seven daughters.   She
was sister to Thomas Bales, who is said to have been
the first white emigrant that settled in Ohio.   At his
death he was buried in a coffin dug out of a log,
there being no dressed timber available and no saw-
mill within hundreds of miles.   His descendants are
quite numerous in the Western States.   My grandmother remained a widow for the rest of her life.
She lived to a good old age, and died respected by
all who knew her.   She was an elder in the religious
Society of Friends for many years, and was highly
esteemed as a " Mother in Israel."   The date of her
death and her age are not in my possession, but I
can remember her well.   Most of her children lived

to a good old age, and, with the exception of one son, all had large families, so that my connections, on my mother's side, as well as on my father's, are quite numerous.

Both my parents and grandparents were opposed to slavery, and none of either of the families ever owned slaves; and all were friends of the oppressed, so I claim that I inherited my anti-slavery principles.

CHAPTER I.

CONVERSION TO ABOLITIONISM—INCIDENTS OF THE
CRUELTIES OF SLAVERY—FIRST EFFORTS ON BE-
HALF OF THE SLAVES—STEPHEN, THE KIDNAPPED
NEGRO—THE CAPTURED SLAVE—SERVICES OF VES-
TAL COFFIN—THE STORY OF EDE—THE WHITE
SLAVE.

I DATE my conversion to Abolitionism from an incident which occurred when I was about seven years old. It made a deep and lasting impression on my mind, and created that horror of the cruelties of slavery which has been the motive of so many actions of my life. At the time of which I speak, Virginia and Maryland were the principal slave-rearing States, and to a great extent supplied the Southern market. Free negroes in Pennsylvania were frequently kidnapped or decoyed into these States, then hurried away to Georgia, Alabama, or Louisiana, and sold. The gangs were handcuffed and chained together, and driven by a man on horseback, who flourished a long whip, such as is used in driving cattle, and goaded the reluctant and weary when their feet lagged on the long journey. One day I was by the roadside where my father was chopping wood, when I saw such a gang approaching along the new Salisbury road. The coffle of slaves came first, chained in couples on each side of a long chain which extended between them; the driver was some distance behind, with the wagon of supplies. My father addressed the slaves pleasantly, and then asked: "Well, boys, why do they chain you?" One of the men, whose countenance betrayed unusual intelligence and whose expression denoted the deepest sadness, replied: "They have taken us away from our wives and children, and they chain us lest we should make our escape and go back to them." My childish sympathy and interest were aroused, and when the dejected procession had passed on, I turned to my father and asked many questions concerning them, why they were taken away from their families, etc. In simple words, suited to my comprehension, my father explained to me the meaning of slavery, and, as I listened, the thought arose in my mind—"How terribly we should feel if father were taken away from us."

This was the first awakening of that sympathy with the oppressed, which, together with a strong hatred of oppression and injustice in every form, were the motives that influenced my whole after-life. Another incident of my boyhood is indelibly engraved on my mind. I accompanied my father one spring to the famous shad fishery at the narrows of the Yadkin River, a spot of wild and romantic scenery, where the stream breaks through a spur of the mountains and goes foaming and dashing down its rocky bed in a succession of rapids. Every spring, when the shad ascended the river, many people resorted to the place to obtain fish. They

brought with them a variety of merchandise, sad-
dlery, crockery-ware, etc., and remained in camp
some time, buying and selling. The fishery was
owned by two brothers named Crump. They were
slaveholders, and sometimes allowed their slaves the
privilege of fishing after night and disposing of the
fish thus obtained, on their own account. A slave,
who had availed himself of this privilege, disposed
of the fish he caught to my father. Next morning
he came to the place where we were preparing
breakfast, and entered into conversation with my
father, speaking of the fish he had sold him, and
asking if he would take more on the same terms.
Noticing this, and thinking it a piece of presuming
familiarity and impertinence, on the part of the
negro, a young man, nephew of the Crumps, seized
a fagot from the fire and struck the negro a furious
blow across the head, baring the skull, covering his
back and breast with blood, and his head with fire;
swearing at the same time that he would allow no
such impudence from niggers. My father protested
against the act, and I was so deeply moved that I
left my breakfast untasted, and going off by myself
gave vent to my feelings in sobs and tears.

A few such instances of "man's inhumanity to
man" intensified my hatred of slavery, and inspired
me to devote myself to the cause of the helpless
and oppressed, and enter upon that line of humane
effort, which I pursued for more than fifty years. I
would still be engaged in it had not Abraham
Lincoln broken up the business by proclamation in
1863.

STEPHEN, THE KIDNAPPED NEGRO.

The first opportunity for aiding a slave occurred when I was about fifteen years old. It was a custom in North Carolina, at that time, to make a "frolic" of any special work, like corn husking, log-rolling, etc. The neighbors would assemble at the place appointed, and with willing hearts and busy hands soon complete the work. Then followed the supper and the merry-making, and the night was in

"The wee sma' hours ayant the twal,"

before the lights were out and the company gone.

At a gathering of this kind, a corn husking at Dr. Caldwell's, I was present. The neighbors assembled about dark, bringing their slaves with them. The negroes were assigned a place at one end of the heap, the white people took their place at the other, and all went to work, enlivening their labor with songs and merry talk.

A slave-dealer, named Stephen Holland, had arrived in the neighborhood a short time before, with a coffle of slaves, on his way to the South, and as this was his place of residence, he stopped for a few days before proceeding on his journey. He brought with him his band of slaves to help his neighbor husk corn, and I was much interested in them. When the white people went in to supper I remained behind to talk with the strange negroes, and see if I could render them any service. In conversation I learned that one of the negroes, named Stephen, was free born, but had been kidnapped and sold into slavery. Till he became of age he had been indentured to Edward Lloyd, a Friend, living near Philadelphia. When his apprenticeship was ended, he had been hired by a man to help drive a flock of sheep to Baltimore. After reaching that place he had been seized one night as he was asleep in the negro house of a tavern, gagged and bound, then placed in a close carriage, and driven rapidly across the line into Virginia, where he was confined the next night in a cellar. He had then been sold for a small sum to Holland, who was taking him to the Southern market, where he expected to realize a large sum from his sale. I became deeply interested in his story, and began to think how I could help him to regain his freedom. Remembering Dr. Caldwell's Tom, a trusty negro, whom I knew well, I imparted to him my wishes, and desired him, if it could be arranged, to bring Stephen to my father's the next night. They came about midnight, and my father wrote down the particulars of Stephen's case, and took the address of the Lloyds. The next day he wrote to them, giving an account of Stephen and his whereabouts. In two weeks from that time, Hugh Lloyd, a brother of Edward Lloyd, arrived by stage in Greensboro. Procuring conveyance, he came to my father's, and there learned that Stephen had been taken southward by the slave-dealer Holland. Next day being regular meeting-day at the Friends Meeting-House, at New Garden, the case was laid before the men after meeting, and two of them, Dr. George Swain and Henry Macy, volunteered to accompany Hugh Lloyd in search of Stephen.

A sum of money was made up for the expenses of their journey, and Lloyd was furnished with a horse and saddle and the necessary equipments. The party found Stephen in Georgia, where he had been sold by Holland, who had gone farther South. A suit was instituted to gain possession of him, but the laws of that State required proof, in such instances, that the mother had been free, and Hugh Lloyd was too young to give this proof. So the matter was referred to the next term of court, security being given by Stephen's master that he should be produced when wanted. Lloyd returned North, and sent affidavits and free papers giving proof in the case, and in six months Stephen was liberated and returned home. The man who had hired him to drive the sheep to Baltimore had, in the meantime, been arrested on the charge of kidnapping, but as Stephen was the only prosecuting witness, the suit could not go on while he was absent. The man's friends took him out of jail on a writ of *habeas corpus* and gave bond for his appearance at court, but he preferred forfeiting his bond to standing the trial, and fled the country before Stephen returned.

THE CAPTURED SLAVE.

But I was not always so fortunate as to be able to render assistance to the objects of my sympathy. Sometimes I witnessed scenes of cruelty and injustice and had to stand passively by. The following

2

is an instance of that kind: I had been sent one day
on an errand to a place in the neighborhood, called
Clemen's Store, and was returning home along the
Salem road, when I met a party of movers, with
wagons, teams, slaves and household goods, on
their way to another State. After passing them I
came to a blacksmith's shop, in front of which were
several men, talking and smoking, in idle chat, and
proceeding on my way I met a negro man trudging
along slowly on foot, carrying a bundle. He inquired of me regarding the party of movers; asked
how far they were ahead, etc. I told him " About
half a mile," and as he passed on, the thought
occurred to me that this man was probably a runaway slave who was following the party of movers.
I had heard of instances when families were separated—the wife and children being taken by their
owners to another part of the country—of the husband and father following the party of emigrants,
keeping a short distance behind the train of wagons
during the day, and creeping up to the camp at
night, close enough for his wife to see him and bring
him food. A few days afterward I learned that this
man had been stopped and questioned by the party
of men at the blacksmith's shop, that he had produced a pass, but they being satisfied that it was a
forgery had lodged him in jail at Greensboro, and
sent word to his master concerning him. A week or
two afterward I was sent to a blacksmith's shop, at
Greensboro, to get some work done. The slave's
master had, that very day, arrived and taken possession of him, and brought him to the blacksmith's shop

to get some irons put on him before starting back to his home. While a chain was being riveted around the negro's neck, and handcuffs fastened on his wrists, his master upbraided him for having run away. He asked:

"Wer'n't you well treated?"

"Yes, massa."

"Then what made you run away?"

"My wife and children were taken away from me, massa, and I think as much of them as you do of yours, or any white man does of his. Their massa tried to buy me too, but you would not sell me, so when I saw them go away, I followed." The mere recital of his words can convey little idea of the pitiful and pathetic manner in which they were uttered; his whole frame trembled, and the glance of piteous, despairing appeal he turned upon his master would have melted any heart less hard than stone.

The master said, "I've always treated you well, trusting you with my keys, and treating you more like a confidential servant than a slave, but *now* you shall know what slavery is. Just wait till I get you back home!" He then tried to make the negro tell where he had got his pass, who wrote it for him, etc., but he refused to betray the person who had befriended him. The master threatened him with the severest punishment, but he persisted in his refusal. Then torture was tried, in order to force the name from him. Laying the slave's fettered hand on the blacksmith's anvil, the master struck it with a hammer until the blood settled under the finger nails. The negro winced under each cruel blow, but said not a word.   As I stood by and watched this scene, my heart swelled with indignation, and I longed to rescue the slave and punish the master.   I was not converted to peace principles then, and I felt like fighting for the slave.   One end of the chain, riveted to the negro's neck, was made fast to the axle of his master's buggy, then the master sprang in and drove off at a sweeping trot, compelling the slave to run at full speed or fall and be dragged by his neck.   I watched them till they disappeared in the distance, and as long as I could see them, the slave was running.

FUGITIVES IN CONCEALMENT.

Runaway slaves used frequently to conceal themselves in the woods and thickets in the vicinity of New Garden, waiting opportunities to make their escape to the North, and I generally learned their places of concealment and rendered them all the service in my power.   My father, in common with other farmers in that part of the country, allowed his hogs to run in the woods, and I often went out to feed them.   My sack of corn generally contained supplies of bacon and corn bread for the slaves, and many a time I sat in the thickets with them as they hungrily devoured my bounty, and listened to the stories they told of hard masters and cruel treatment, or spoke in language, simple and rude, yet glowing with native eloquence, of the glorious hope of freedom which animated their spirits in the darkest hours, and sustained them under the sting of the lash.

These outlying slaves knew where I lived, and,

when reduced to extremity of want or danger, often came to my room, in the silence and darkness of night, to obtain food or assistance. In my efforts to aid these fugitives I had a zealous co-worker in my friend and cousin, Vestal Coffin, who was then, and continued to the time of his death—a few years later —a stanch friend to the slave.

Vestal was several years older than I, was married and had the care of a family, but, in the busiest season of work, could find time to co-operate with me in all my endeavors to aid runaway slaves. We often met at night in a thicket where a fugitive was concealed, to counsel in regard to his prospects and lay plans for getting him safely started to the North. We employed General Hamilton's Sol, a gray-haired, trusty old negro, to examine every coffle of slaves to which he could gain access, and ascertain if there were any kidnapped negroes among them. When such a case was discovered, Sol would manage to bring the person, by night, to some rendezvous appointed, in the pine thickets or the depths of the woods, and there Vestal and I would meet them and have an interview. There was always a risk in holding such meetings, for the law in the South inflicted heavy penalties on any one who should aid or abet a fugitive slave in escaping, and the patrollers, or mounted officers, frequently passed along the road near our place of concealment. When information had been obtained from kidnapped negroes regarding the circumstances of their capture, Vestal Coffin wrote to their friends, and in many cases succeeded in getting them liberated. In this way a negro man of family and means, who

had been abducted from Pennsylvania and taken to
New Orleans and sold, was finally restored to his
friends. Obtaining through Vestal Coffin a knowledge of his whereabouts, they° brought suit against
his owners and gained his liberty.

SERVICES OF VESTAL COFFIN.

Another negro was kidnapped from Delaware, and
brought to Guilford County, North Carolina, by a
man named John Thompson. Learning the particulars of his case, Vestal Coffin went to Hillsboro, a
neighboring town, and obtained a writ, which he
placed in the hands of the sheriff to be served on
Thompson, requiring him to produce the negro in
court, for investigation regarding the unlawfulness
of his being held in bondage. Thompson, disregard-
ing the writ, sent the negro South, and sold him.
Vestal Coffin went back and procured another writ,
causing Thompson to be arrested on charge of kidnapping, and thrown into prison till the negro should
be produced. This proceeding greatly enraged
Thompson, but he was obliged to send for the
negro, who was delivered to the charge of Vestal
Coffin. When the case went into court, Thompson
secured the best lawyers, but Vestal Coffin had right
on his side, and finally triumphed. As the poet
says:

"Thrice is he armed who hath his quarrel just."

The case was delayed nearly a year, and in that
time Vestal Coffin procured affidavits and other documents establishing the negro's freedom, and he was

set at liberty.　These are some of the results of the consultations held by night in the pine thickets.

EDE.

As I was always interested in the work and ready to engage in it, I found opportunities to be of service to the slaves in various ways.　The following is an account of one of my efforts in this line:

Dr. Caldwell, whose name has been mentioned before, was one of our near neighbors.　He was a learned clergyman and physician, founded a college —said to be the first in North Carolina—and numbered among his pupils many of the prominent men of that State.　His son Samuel was a Presbyterian minister, and was located in the southwestern part of the State, in charge of a church there.　At one time, when on a visit to his relatives in Guilford County, he told his father that his wife very much needed a good house servant, and, after some deliberation, the old Doctor concluded to make him a present of one.

The question thus was, Which one of the negro women should it be?

The mistress was a humane Christian lady, and did not like the idea of separating husband and wife, but all the negro women that were grown had husbands, and the girls were too young to fill the place, so it was finally decided that a woman named Ede should go.　She was strong and healthy, and in the prime of life, and would be the most suitable.　She had four children, three of whom were to be left behind; the youngest, being a babe a few months old, was to go with its mother. To satisfy the scruples of his wife against separating husband and wife, the old Doctor told her that Ede's husband—who belonged to another master—was a trifling negro, and that his master would probably sell him before long; that slave marriage was not legal; and that perhaps Ede would soon get a better man for a husband.

When Ede learned that she was to go and live with her young master, more than a hundred miles distant from her husband and children, she was filled with grief and dismay, and studied how she might avert the threatened calamity.

The night before the time fixed for her start to her new home, she decided to flee to the thickets and hide herself for a week or two, hoping that in this time her master and mistress would change their mind about sending her away, and consent to let her remain. Preparing a little store of provisions, and taking her baby in her arms, she fled to the woods, and found a hiding place in a dense thicket, about a mile from my father's house. As it was some distance from the road, she ventured to kindle a little fire by the side of a log, for the weather was cool and chilly, and both she and her child suffered from the cold. She made a bed of leaves, by the side of a large log, and sheltered herself as well as she could from the wind. She had remained in this hiding place for several days and nights, when her child became ill, from cold and exposure. Filled with fresh anguish at the sight of its sufferings, and unable to alleviate them, she determined to leave her place of concealment. Her little stock of provisions had by this time given out, and she was beginning to suffer with hunger. She was acquainted with my father's family, and knew us to be friends to the fugitive, and resolved to apply to us for help. She made her way to our house, at night, and was kindly received, though we knew we laid ourselves liable to a heavy penalty by harboring a fugitive slave. A hot supper was prepared for her, and then we heard her story, and consulted together in regard to what should be done. Father was liable to fine and imprisonment **if** she was discovered at our house, yet we could **not** turn her away. The dictates of humanity came **in** opposition to the law of the land, and we ignored **the** law. My mother said, "The child is sick, and **may** die before morning ; we can not turn them from our doors." My father said he would risk the penalty, and Ede was given a comfortable resting place for the night. My mother did all that she could for the sick child. She spent the night trying to relieve its sufferings, and, at daylight, had the satisfaction of seeing it free from pain and in a quiet sleep.

When morning came, the question arose, What should be done with Ede ? We could not turn her out in the cold with her sick child, to return to her hiding place in the woods, and she begged us not to send her back to her master's. As she repeated her sad story, the tears streamed down her cheeks, and she said she would rather die than be separated from her family.

I volunteered to go and plead her case with her master and mistress, as I was acquainted with them, and thought I could persuade them not to send her

3

away. I also hoped to save my father from the penalty he had incurred by harboring a fugitive. Leaving Ede and the child at my father's, I made my way to the mansion of the aristocratic gentleman of the old school. I felt some misgivings as to the success of my mission when I entered the house, and was at first embarrassed when I was shown into the room where the Doctor was sitting. He received me kindly, as was his custom, and entered into conversation. Among the solid qualities of his character was a rich vein of humor, and he always made himself attractive to young people, entertaining them with some droll story, or puzzling them with knotty questions. He inquired about our school at New Garden, where Jeremiah Hubbard, a well-known Quaker preacher, was then teaching, and said, "You ought to pay Mr. Hubbard double price for your tuition, for I hear that he has taught his pupils the art of courting, beside the common branches of a school education. I hear that two of his pupils have made known their intentions of marriage, or given in meeting, as you call it. How do you suppose those young Quakers feel now that they are half married?"

"Like they intended to be wholly married soon, I suppose," I replied.

He continued, "Now, we Presbyterians do up such business sooner than you Quakers do"—and was going on in this strain when his wife entered the room. My diffidence had vanished by this time, and I longed for an opportunity to introduce the subject which occupied my thoughts. After the mistress of

the house had greeted me and taken her seat, I said
that I had come to speak with them on an important
matter, and inquired if their slave woman Ede had
run away.

The Doctor replied, "Yes, she ran off several days
ago, to keep from going home with our son Sam, I
suppose. She needs a good flogging for her foolish-
ness—she would have a good home at his house. Do
you know where she is hiding?"

I related the incident of her coming to our house
and what had been done for her, and then pleaded
her case with all the earnestness and eloquence I was
master of, quoting all the texts of Scripture bearing
on the case that I could remember, and bringing the
matter home to ourselves, putting ourselves in her
place, etc. I soon saw that I had touched the old
lady's feelings. She said she thanked my mother for
taking such good care of the sick child, and that
she had very reluctantly given her consent for Ede to
be separated from her family. I told them that Ede
said she wished to come home if they would let her
stay, but that she had rather die than be sent away
from her husband and children. The old Doctor had
listened attentively to my pleading, but had made no
reply. I now asked him if my father had done right
in taking in Ede and her child in violation of the law,
thus laying himself liable to a heavy penalty, if he
was disposed to prosecute.

He replied, "Your father has done right; I shall
not trouble him, and I thank your mother for her
kindness to the sick child. As for you, you have
done your part very well. Why, Mr. Coffin, you

would make a pretty good preacher; if you will come to me I will give you lessons in theology without charge."

I thanked him for his offer, but said I had not come to talk about theology that morning; I wanted to know what word I should carry back to poor Ede, who was waiting at our house, in anxious suspense.

He said, ''Well, this is no doubt your first sermon, and you would be disappointed and might give up preaching if you are not successful; you may tell Ede to come home, and I will not send her away."

I took my leave, and went home rejoicing. I gave an account of my visit and the success that had attended my efforts, and Ede shouted for joy. In the middle of the day, when it was warm and sunny, she started home, carrying her child, which my mother had wrapped comfortably in a small blanket.

The Doctor kept his word, and she was allowed to remain at home with her family.

THE WHITE SLAVE.

In the following story I was no way concerned, but the incidents came under my observation, and I can well remember the feelings of deepest sympathy and indignation which it aroused in our neighborhood at the time of its occurrence. It shows one of the cruelest phases of slavery, and gives one of the many instances in which the deepest suffering was inflicted on those who merited it by no act of their own, but received the curse by inheritance.

A slaveholder, living in Virginia, owned a beautiful slave woman, who was almost white. She became the mother of a child, a little boy, in whose veins ran the blood of her master, and the closest observer could not detect in its appearance any trace of African descent. He grew to be two or three years of age, a most beautiful child and the idol of his mother's heart, when the master concluded, for family reasons, to send him away. He placed him in the care of a friend living in Guilford County, North Carolina, and made an agreement that he should receive a common-school education, and at a suitable age be taught some useful trade. Years passed; the child grew to manhood, and having received a good common-school education, and learned the shoemaker's trade, he married an estimable young white woman, and had a family of five or six children. He had not the slightest knowledge of the taint of African blood in his veins, and no one in the neighborhood knew that he was the son of an octoroon slave woman. He made a comfortable living for his family, was a good citizen, a member of the Methodist Church, and was much respected by all who knew him. In course of time his father, the Virginian slaveholder, died, and when the executors came to settle up the estate, they remembered the little white boy, the son of the slave woman, and knowing that by law—such law!— he belonged to the estate, and must be by this time a valuable piece of property, they resolved to gain possession of him. ·After much inquiry and search they learned of his whereabouts, and the heir of the estate, accompanied by an administrator, went to Guilford County, North Carolina, to claim his half-brother as a slave. Without making themselves known to him, they sold him to a negro trader, and gave a bill of sale, preferring to have a sum in ready money, instead of a servant who might prove very valuable, but who would, without doubt, give them a great deal of trouble. He had been free all his life, and they knew he would not readily yield to the yoke of bondage. All this time the victim was entirely unconscious of the cruel fate in store for him.

His wife had been prostrated by a fever then prevalent in the neighborhood, and he had waited upon her and watched by her bedside, until he was worn out with exhaustion and loss of sleep. Several neighbor women coming in one evening to watch with the invalid, he surrendered her to their care, and retired to seek the rest he so much needed. That night the slave-dealer came with a gang of ruffians, burst into the house and seized their victim as he lay asleep, bound him, after heroic struggles on his part, and dragged him away. When he demanded the cause of his seizure, they showed him the bill of sale they had received, and informed him that he was a slave. In this rude, heartless manner the intelligence that he belonged to the African race was first imparted to him, and the crushing weight of his cruel destiny came upon him when totally unprepared. His captors hurried him out of the neighborhood, and took him toward the Southern slave markets. To get him black enough to sell without question, they washed his face in tan ooze, and kept him tied in the sun, and to complete his resemblance to a mulatto, they cut his hair short and seared it with a hot iron to make it curly. He was sold in Georgia or Alabama, to a hard master, by whom he was cruelly treated.

Several months afterward he succeeded in escaping, and made his way back to Guilford County, North Carolina. Here he learned that his wife had died a few days after his capture, the shock of that calamity having hastened her death, and that his children were scattered among the neighbors. His master, thinking that he would return to his old home, came in pursuit of him with hounds, and chased him through the thickets and swamps. He evaded the dogs by wading in a mill-pond, and climbing a tree, where he remained all night. Next day he made his way to the house of Stanton White (afterward my father-in-law), where he remained several days. Dr. George Swain, a man of much influence in the community, had an interview with him, and, hearing the particulars of his seizure, said he thought the proceedings were illegal. He held a consultation with several lawyers, and instituted proceedings in his behalf. But the unfortunate victim of man's cruelty did not live to regain his freedom. He had been exposed and worried so much, trailed by dogs and forced to lie in swamps and thickets, that his health was broken down and he died before the next term of court.

CHAPTER II.

THE STORY OF JACK BARNES—MY JOURNEY WITH A
SLAVE-OWNER—A MISSION FULL OF ANXIETY—
THE STORY OF SAM—I TURN SLAVE-HUNTER—NAR-
ROW ESCAPE FROM ARREST—PENALTY OF AIDING A
SLAVE—FATE OF POOR SAM.

I NOW come to the relation of an occurrence in which, strange as it may seem, I turned slave-hunter. A gentleman by the name of Barnes, who lived in the eastern part of the State, had a body servant named Jack, to whom he was much attached.

Barnes was a bachelor, with no direct heirs, and being in ill-health, he made his will, in which, as was allowed by a provision of the law, he bequeathed to Jack his freedom for faithfulness and meritorious conduct, also a considerable portion of his estate. At his death, distant relatives flocked to the scene, seized upon the property and entered suit to contest the will. Jack knew very well that from Southern courts of justice he could expect no favor; so procuring a copy of the will, and a certificate of good conduct, signed by several leading white men of the place, who were friendly to him, he sought a more secure place in which to await the decision of the court. He had heard of a settlement of Quakers at

New Garden, near Greensboro, Guilford County, who were opposed to slavery and friendly to colored people. He obtained directions to aid him in finding this place, and left home privately, that it might not be known where he was if the case should go against him. He reached New Garden safely, was introduced to me, and I took him to my father's house.

Jack remained in our neighborhood for some time, employed on the farms of my father, of Vestal Coffin, and others, and proved himself to be an industrious and faithful servant. He won the esteem and sympathy of all who knew him and his story, by his steady habits, intelligent character and manly deportment. He came to New Garden in the fall of 1821, and in the following March received the news that the case in court had been decided against him. The property that had been willed to him was turned over to the relatives of his master, and he was consigned again to slavery. The judge decided that Barnes was not in his right mind at the time he made the will; this was apparent from the nature of the will. The heirs took possession of the property, but where was Jack, the able-bodied valuable servant, who also belonged to them? He was not to be found, and they advertised in the papers, offering one hundred dollars reward to any one who would secure him till they could get hold of him, or give information that would lead to his discovery.

This advertisement appeared in the paper published at Greensboro, and when Jack saw it he was greatly alarmed. The questions which occupied his mind and with which he greeted his friends were, "What shall I do? can I get to a free State, or any place, where I can enjoy liberty in safety?"

It was decided that for the present he must be concealed, and he was secreted among his friends, part of the time at our house, and part at the house of Vestal Coffin. A council was held by Jack's friends to devise some plan to get him to a free State. Bethuel Coffin, my uncle, who lived a few miles distant, was then preparing to go to Indiana, on a visit to his children and relatives who had settled there. He would be accompanied by his son Elisha, then living in Randolph County, and by his daughter Mary. They intended to make the journey in a two-horse wagon, taking with them provisions and cooking utensils, and camp out on the way. This was the usual mode of traveling in those days. The road they proposed to take was called the Kanawha road. It was the nearest route, but led through a mountainous wilderness, most of the way. Crossing Dan River, it led by way of Patrick Court-House, Virginia, to Maberry's Gap, in the Blue Ridge mountains, thence across Clinch mountain, by way of Pack's ferry on New River, thence across White Oak mountain to the falls of the Kanawha, and down that river to the Ohio, crossing at Gallipolis.

This was thought to be a safe route for Jack to travel, as it was very thinly inhabited, and it was decided that my cousin Vestal and I should go to see our uncle, and learn if he was willing to incur the risk and take Jack with him to Indiana. He said he was willing, and all the arrangements were made, and the time for starting fixed. The night after they started, Vestal Coffin took Jack, on horseback, to Dan River, about twenty miles distant, where they camped the first night, and where the fugitive joined them.

Here we will leave his story for a time, and turn to the trials and persecutions of another slave, named Sam, who lived in the neighborhood of New Garden. Osborne, his master, who might have represented the character of Legree in "Uncle Tom's Cabin," took particular delight in whipping and abusing poor Sam, till he was compelled to take to the thickets or the premises of his friends for safety. Even the slave-holders in the neighborhood sympathized with him. After living in this manner for several months, and finding no opportunity to escape to the North, Sam went to Robert Thompson, a slave-dealer, and asked him to buy him. He was willing to take the chance of getting a better master, even if he was sold to the rice swamps of the far South. Thompson went to Osborne, and offered him six hundred dollars for Sam, "as he ran," taking the chances of his capture.

Osborne replied, "I'll not take less than $999.99 for him until I have caught him; then, after I have settled with him, you may have him for $550."

Thompson swore at Osborne, and told him he hoped he would never get Sam, then returned home, and giving Sam a pair of good pantaloons, told him to clear himself and never let his master get possession of him again.

A few days after my uncle had started on his

journey to the West, Osborne was out looking for his slave. Meeting a man whom he knew, who was returning from a journey near the mountains, Osborne asked him if he had met any movers on that road accompanied by a negro.

"Yes," was the reply; "I met an old Quaker man with a two-horse wagon, who said he was going to Indiana, and there was a negro man walking a short distance behind the wagon."

He described the negro, and Osborne said, with an oath:

"That's my nigger Sam, I'm sure. The rascal has been lying out for several months, and I heard that he got the papers of some free nigger, and said he intended to follow the first movers he could meet with going to the West. It is old Mr. Coffin and his son Elisha; I know them. I suppose that rascal Sam has met with them somewhere on the road, and made them believe he is a free man, and is now traveling with them. I think they are both gentlemen and would not steal my nigger. Well, I will follow them and get that rascal Sam."

As I was returning from Fourth-day meeting at New Garden, the third day after my uncle started, I met a man who had heard this conversation between Osborne and the traveler, and who informed me that Osborne had gone directly home, got a fresh horse and started in pursuit that very morning. I hastened home and told my father the story. We decided that something must be done immediately. We knew that if Osborne should come up with the party and find that the negro was not his Sam, but

Jack Barnes, he would capture him all the same, for he knew that Jack had been in the neighborhood, and that a reward was offered. He would recognize Jack by the description in the advertisement, and would secure him, and bring him back for the sake of the one hundred dollars reward. It was decided that I should go at once to my Cousin Vestal, a man several years older than I was, and a faithful worker in the cause of liberty, and see if he could not suggest a plan by which Jack might be saved. I laid the matter before Vestal, who felt, as we did, that something must be done, and that quickly, to rescue Jack from Osborne's clutches. We came to the conclusion, that the only thing to be done was for some person to start at once on a good traveling horse, and go far enough ahead of Osborne to warn Jack of his danger. Vestal was so situated that he could not go, but he accompanied me to his brother Elihu's, to see what arrangements could be made there. We laid the matter before him, knowing that he would be a suitable person to go, but he could not leave his business then. He insisted that I should undertake the trip, and Vestal uniting with him, I decided to go, though I was young and had never been on such a responsible journey before.

Elihu offered me his fine traveling mare and all the necessary equipments. I told him I had no money with me and no overcoat — was entirely unprepared for traveling, as I had no such prospect in view when I left home. But they agreed to furnish everything needful, and to inform my parents of my mission, that they might not be uneasy at my long absence. Elihu had the horse brought out and freshly shod, and prepared a wallet of oats that I might feed it when necessary during the night. His wife prepared some provisions for me to eat on the journey, which were placed in the saddle-bags. I put on Elihu's warm overcoat, and with enough money in my pocket to take me to the Ohio River and back, I felt fully equipped. I ate my supper, mounted my beautiful traveling mare, and started, between sunset and dark. There was no moon, but the night was clear and the stars shone brightly. The first ten miles of the way was familiar to me, and I had directions as far as Dan River ford; beyond that, all was new and strange. I traveled at a steady but moderate pace the first twenty miles, and reached the ford about midnight. Dan River at this place is a wide, shallow stream, with a swift current, perfectly safe to cross if one is acquainted with the ford. There were piles of stones placed at intervals across it, to guide the traveler, but it was difficult to see them by starlight, and when I got to the middle of the river I lost sight of them. I thought I had got into deep water and that my mare was swimming—I seemed to go so swiftly and easily—but I soon discovered it was my head that was swimming, and that the animal was standing still. I had involuntarily checked her by my tight hold on the reins. Casting my eye across the river I pushed ahead, and in a few moments was below the ford and in deep water. My animal swam out with me nicely, but I got a good wetting. Reaching the opposite shore, I alighted, and pulling off my shoes, wrung the water from my stockings and pantaloons as well as I could. I then rubbed the limbs of the mare, and after giving her some oats on a smooth stone, and partaking of some food from my store in the saddle-bags, I mounted again, and set off at greater speed. Now and then I drew rein in front of a house by the way-side, and calling somebody out of bed, inquired the road to Patrick Court-House. After receiving direc-tions, I rode on before the people had time to question me. Just at daybreak I came to a log-house with a tavern sign. Calling the man out, I inquired about the road and found I had traveled forty-seven miles. The man told me if I would stop an hour or two, I would have company on my journey, a gentleman who had stopped with him that night and was going the same road, adding:

"He is in pursuit of some movers who have one of his negroes with them."

I made some excuse and pushed on. I knew that it was Osborne and that I was now ahead of him, but the next thought was—can I keep ahead of him? I was satisfied that I could not; I had traveled all night and my animal was tired, while his had rested through the night and would be fresh for the journey. I had taken good care of my mare, giving her a light feed of oats several times during the night and rubbing her legs frequently; she seemed in good condition, but I did not think it would be possi-ble to push ahead and reach my uncle's wagon before Osborne overtook me.

Many anxious thoughts passed through my ex-cited mind, and finally I fixed on a plan. I would stop at the next tavern, which was a few miles ahead, feed my mare, get breakfast and rest a few hours, thus allowing Osborne to overtake me. I knew him by sight but did not think he knew me, as we had never had any acquaintance. I intended to.travel awhile in his company and find out his plans, then make an excuse for taking another road, and fall back while he went on, then pass him in the night when he was at some tavern. Public houses were scarce in that poor and thinly settled part of Virginia, and private houses would not take in travelers, because the law of the State did not allow them to charge for entertainment without obtaining license. It was half past eight o'clock when I halted at the next tavern, and called for breakfast, and food for my horse. About nine o'clock Osborne rode up and stopped for the same purpose. It was the custom then, in traveling on horseback, to make an early start, and stop about nine o'clock for breakfast.

Osborne went to the bar and called for liquor and invited me to drink with him—though I was a stranger to him—but I declined. After breakfast he inquired which way I was traveling. I told him that I was going west, would cross the mountain at Maberry's Gap, then take the left-hand road, leading to Burk's Forks. At that place my Uncle Samuel Stanley had a stock farm where he kept a number of cattle through the winter, allowing them to fatten on the range during the summer. I said:

"Last fall I went over there and helped my Cousin Jessie Stanley drive a drove of beef cattle home to Guilford County, then we crossed the mountain at Bell Spur, but I thought I would cross this time at Maberry's Gap."

Osborne inquired: "Is your name Stanley?"

"No, it is Coffin."

"Are you any relation to old Mr. Bethuel Coffin?"

"Yes, he is my uncle."

"Well, I am in pursuit of him."

"What is the matter?"

"Why, he has one of my niggers with him, taking him to Indiana, I suppose."

"How is that?" I asked, assuming great surprise; "how did he get the negro? I saw him start and there was none with him then."

" Oh, I don't think he stole the nigger," said Osborne; then he went on to relate the story that has been told before, how he supposed his negro had got free papers, and imposed on my uncle.

Osborne now supposed my only business was the journey to Burk's Fork; I had certainly deceived him, but told no untruth. He had taken several drinks, and now became very jovial and familiar with me, expressing great satisfaction that I was going the same road; it was lonesome traveling through that rough, thinly settled country, and he was glad to have my company. His pocket-bottle was filled with whisky; then our horses were brought to the door, and we started off together. As we traveled along he talked and joked in great good humor, but I hardly heard what he said, for my mind was still full of plans and anxious thoughts. He had frequent recourse to his whisky bottle, and

4

pressed me to drink; I turned it up to my mouth several times, but took care that no liquor passed down my throat.   I wanted to encourage his drinking and keep my own head clear, thinking that if he became stupefied with liquor I could more easily gain ground upon him, reach the camp that night before him, and warn poor Jack of his danger.

Osborne communicated all his plans to me, saying that he did not intend to go upon them in the day-time, but to keep back, when he came near them, till they had camped for the night; then he would gather a company of armed men, surround the camp and take Sam, dead or alive, shooting him down if he attempted to escape.   He said:

"See here, young man, I want you to go with me, and help capture the nigger; I will pay you well.   If it proves not to be Sam, I think I know who it is.   There was a nigger man working about last winter in the Quaker settlement, who was willed free by a crazy master, but the heirs broke the will and have advertised for him, offering a hundred dollars reward to any one who will secure him and give them notice.   His name is Jack Barnes, and he is so well described in the advertisement I think I would know him.   If it is not my nigger with your uncle, it must be that fellow, and I will land him in Greenboro jail, sure.   If you will go along and help me I will divide the reward with you; that will be fifty dollars apiece, and will pay us well these hard times."

I made several excuses: said it would consume too much time, my business was urgent, etc.

"Now, see here, my good fellow," continued Osborne, "you will lose nothing. I will return with you through the Burk's Fork settlement, and spend a day or two there, giving you time to do your business. Come, what do you say?"

I still made excuses, though I had fully made up my mind to go with him, having come, by this time, to the conclusion that my first plan would not do. Osborne had inquired of every person we met in regard to the party of movers, asking how far they were ahead and if there was a negro man with them. The answer to the last question was always "Yes;" then Osborne would ask them to describe the man, and when they did, he would exclaim, with an oath, "That's my nigger, sure."

He made similar inquiries at every house, and the statements he received confirmed him in the belief that the fugitive was his slave. Jack answered the description of Sam pretty well in regard to personal appearance. All this made it plainer to me that my original plan would not do: if I were to get ahead of Osborne, overtake my uncle and get Jack out of the way before Osborne came upon them, and try to keep him out of the way, Osborne, on coming to the wagon and not finding the negro, could easily prove that he had been with the party at the last camping place, and might harass and perhaps detain my uncle. Then it would be difficult for me to keep Jack secure in the mountains till Osborne gave up the search and returned home, and then try to place him with my uncle again. This arrangement, therefore, was abandoned, and I resolved to travel on with Osborne till we reached the movers, hoping that the influence of the liquor, which he had partaken of freely during the day, or some other influence, would aid me in effecting Jack's escape. We were now nearing the top of the Blue Ridge, and in the afternoon passed the spot where my uncle had camped the night before. A short distance beyond the mountain ridge was the road that led to Burk's Forks. When we reached it, I halted and allowed Osborne to renew his urgent solicitations and offers of money. Finally, and in an apparently reluctant manner, I agreed to keep him company, just to oblige him, he thought— and we went on together. By this time we were seemingly much attached to each other. Osborne's pocket bottle had been refilled, at my expense, and to gain still further his favor, I exerted myself to entertain him, telling him stories and recounting jokes that kept him constantly laughing. It is needless to say that this gayety was all assumed on my part, for I was still weighed down with the heavy responsibility of my mission. Toward nightfall we learned that the wagon was only twelve or fifteen miles ahead of us. I was anxious to press on and accomplish our work that night, pleading the urgency of my business at Burk's Forks. Osborne, on the contrary, wished to stop for the night at the first house that afforded entertainment. I said, " Let us stop and get our horses fed, allow them to rest an hour or two and take some refreshment ourselves, then press on and finish our work to-night."

"No," said Osborne, "that will not do. I want to collect a company of eight or ten men, well armed, to surround the camp, and it is too late to rally them to-night."

We stopped at a little log-house, where a sign indicated entertainment for man and beast, and called for refreshments. I was now getting into a part of the country I had seen before, Montgomery County, Virginia. I had spent two weeks in that county the previous fall, collecting cattle, as I had told Osborne. I knew that one Squire Howells kept a tavern on that road, not far ahead; that he owned no slaves, and was a popular man among the mountaineers. I inquired the distance to his house, and was informed that it was eight miles. I also learned that my uncle's party had passed a few hours before, and would probably camp near Squire Howells', as it was a favorable spot, on account of water, etc.

I now renewed my persuasions to induce Osborne to go on; told him that the poor cabin where we then were afforded little accommodation or comfort; that if we went on to Squire Howells' we would be near the camp, and as that neighborhood was more thickly settled, we could collect the men he wanted and accomplish our work without spending another day. He finally yielded, and called for our horses. He invited me to drink with him at the bar, and I sipped the liquor lightly, wishing to promote his drinking. It was now dark, but the stars shone brightly, and we made our way along the road without difficulty.

We arrived at Squire Howells' tavern before the inmates had gone to bed. Riding up to the gate, we hallooed, and the landlord came out. Osborne inquired if a two-horse wagon with movers had passed that evening, and where they would be likely to camp. Howells replied, "They passed this evening; bought some horse feed of me, and inquired for a good camping place. I directed them to the Six-Mile Branch, as we call it, a stream about six miles from here, where they would find good water and every accommodation for camping."

"Was there a nigger with them?" asked Osborne.

"Yes," answered Howells, and gave his description.

"That's my nigger," said Osborne; "and I am after him, bound to have him, dead or alive. I want you to raise a company of men and help me capture him. I will pay you well for it."

"I don't much like that kind of business," said Howells.

"Oh, I'll make you like it," added Osborne; "I have plenty of money."

A glow of hope and comfort warmed my heart. I liked Howells' expression, and thought perhaps he might aid me if I could enlist his sympathy for the fugitive. I dismounted and said: "Well, we will have our horses fed, get some refreshment, and talk the matter over." Howells invited us to walk into the house while he and his son took our horses to the stable. I told Osborne to go in and I would go to the stable to give directions about feeding our horses. I was all excitement, for I felt that the crisis was near. Now was the time to act, if I succeeded in saving Jack. It would be difficult to describe my feelings, my intense anxiety. I had traveled one hundred and twenty miles without sleep or rest, yet I felt no symptoms of sleepiness or fatigue. After giving directions to the young man about feeding our horses, I took Squire Howells to one side and ventured to make a confidant of him. I told him that Osborne and I were from the same county in North Carolina, and that I fell in company with him that morning as I was traveling in this direction on business; that Osborne was in pursuit of my uncle — the man with the wagon, who was going to Indiana—believing that he had one of his negroes with him. I gave him Osborne's story, about hearing that his slave had got hold of free papers; then pictured Osborne's character. I said that the master was a cruel tyrant, and that the slave was a faithful servant who ran away on account of the inhuman treatment he received, and lay out in the woods and thickets for several months. Osborne bore such a character for cruelty in the neighborhood, that even the slaveholders would not aid him in capturing his negro. After relating this, I went on to say that I did not believe the negro with my uncle was Osborne's slave, but another fugitive, and then gave the story of Jack Barnes. I said that before reaching the road, on top of the mountain, leading to Burk's Fork settlement, which I had intended to take, Osborne had insisted on my coming with him to help him capture his slave, and feeling pretty certain that the negro in question was not his Sam, but Jack Barnes, I had come on hoping to be of use in another way. Jack, in my opinion, was entitled to his freedom, having been willed free by his master, and if this were he, I would have nothing to do with recapturing him. But if it proved to be Osborne's negro, I would do what I could in aiding the master to recover his property. I did not tell Howells all I knew; I did not tell him that Sam, Osborne's slave, was lying in the hay-mow in my father's barn when I left home, nor that I knew to a certainty that the negro with my uncle was Jack Barnes.

Howells said at once: "If it is the negro you describe, he ought to be free; I would not detain him a moment, but would much rather help him on his way."

I told him Osborne's plan was to raise a company of armed men, surround the camp and take the fugitive, dead or alive. If it proved to be Jack Barnes, Osborne would drag him back to slavery for the sake of the reward offered.

I said: "I hope you will go with us, and help me in my efforts to save Jack from such a fate."

He replied: "Since hearing your statement I have concluded to go with you. In regard to the other part, it will depend entirely on the class of men Osborne gets to go with him. However, I think I can manage that. I will take my son for one, and send for one of my near neighbors, and we will pick up a few more on the way."

Some relief came to my overburdened mind, and I felt quite hopeful. We went into the house and found Osborne dancing in the bar-room; he had been drinking, and was quite jubilant over the pros-

pect of soon having his negro secured with the handcuffs and rope he had in his saddle-bags.

I told him that Squire Howells had agreed to go
with us, and would collect a company of men to
surround the camp.

"How many do you want?" asked Howells.

"A half dozen or more, beside Mr. Coffin and
myself, and all must be armed, for if the rascal attempts to escape, I want him shot down. I would
much rather kill him than let him get away; he has
been too much trouble to me already. I will give
Mr. Coffin one of my pistols; he says he has none."

Howells' neighbor came, bringing his gun, Howells and his son took their guns, and mounting our
horses we started for the camp, six miles distant. It
was now about midnight. As we traveled on, Howells called at several houses a little off the road, leaving us in the road till he returned. He thus gained
time to talk with the men and give them the right
side of the story. Three more joined us, increasing
our party to eight. All were armed but myself; I
declined accepting a pistol from Osborne, telling
him I did not believe in killing folks. We were
now getting very near the Six-Mile Branch, and
my heart throbbed with intense excitement. A
few minutes more would decide it all. We soon
espied the camp-fire and retreated a little way to
hold a consultation, and settle the plan of operation.

Howells struck a match and looked at his watch;
it was near daylight. Now was my time, and I
nerved myself to the effort, feeling that I needed
the eloquence of the most gifted orator to aid me

5

in making the appeal in behalf of poor Jack. I told the men that before we formed our plan of attack, I had something to say to them, and then went on to state: "If the negro in camp with my uncle is Osborne's Sam, I will do all I can to secure him, but I am inclined to think it is another man, a negro who was willed free by his master for his meritòrious conduct." Then I gave the circumstances of the will case, and described Jack's character in glowing terms, adding the testimony of the recommendation signed by the leading white citizens of his own neighborhood. I said that Jack had worked in our settlement all winter, but since learning the news that the will had been broken and he was consigned to slavery, he had disappeared, and I presumed he was with my uncle trying to make his way to a free State. If this is the man we find in camp, I further said, I will have nothing to do with capturing him.

Howells said: "Mr. Coffin appears to act from principle, and I think he will find us men of principle too. If it should be the negro described, he ought to be free, and I would much rather aid him on his way to liberty than detain him."

The rest of Howells' company joined with him, and Osborne seeing them all agreed, turned clever fellow too, and said if it were not his negro he would have nothing to do with him. But he still thought it would prove to be Sam. I now told them I had another proposition to make:

"If we were to surround the camp and break in suddenly upon the sleepers, it would be a great

shock and alarm to them. They would find themselves attacked by armed men, and seeing me in the
midst would be greatly bewildered. The fright
might prove an injury to the young lady, my cousin,
who is with her father. As it is now near daybreak,
I propose that we wait till daylight, when I will go
up to the camp alone, leaving you concealed in the
woods and thick underbrush. I will introduce myself to my uncle and give him privately to understand what is going on, and if the negro with them
is Sam, I will make some excuse in his hearing, pass
on a little way, then take a circuit through the
bushes, and return to you. Then we will hitch our
horses here, slip up through the thick bushes, and,
surrounding the camp, pounce upon Sam and secure
him. But if I find that it is Jack, I will soon ride
back in sight of you and give a signal for you to
come up to camp."

All agreed to this but Osborne, who objected to
the plan, fearing he should lose his negro. I argued
the matter with him and told him if his negro escaped by that plan, I would obligate myself to pay
for him. The rest thought this was a fair offer, and
Osborne, seeing they were against him, finally submitted. When daylight had fully appeared, I rode
up to camp. They were greatly surprised at my
unexpected appearance in the wild mountain regions
of Virginia at such an hour. I hastily informed them
of my errand. Jack was much alarmed and wanted
to flee to the bushes, but I assured them there was
no danger and induced him to remain where he was.
I then rode back in sight of the company and gave

them the signal to come forward. They advanced to the camp, presenting a formidable appearance with their guns, enough to strike terror to poor Jack's heart. My uncle and cousin knew Osborne and shook hands with him heartily. There was a general greeting for the rest of the party, then my uncle got out a jug of old peach brandy from his wagon, and passed the contents freely around. We all drank, and had a hearty laugh, which made the woods and rocks around us ring and echo. The morning was clear and bright, the load of care was off my heart, and I was jubilant.

But poor Jack did not partake of our merriment. He still feared danger, and thought that the party of armed men had come to take him back to slavery. When brought face to face with him, Osborne acknowledged that it was not his negro, but said, "He looks a d—— sight like that rascal Sam."

After some time spent in talking, joking, and partaking of my uncle's good peach brandy, I told Osborne that I would stay and breakfast with my uncle's party and see them off. He might return to the tavern with friend Howells and get breakfast and have his horse fed, and I would join him there.

This gave me an opportunity to explain matters more fully to my uncle's party, and to remove Jack's doubts and fears. He expressed heartfelt thanks to me for my efforts in his behalf, and I felt repaid for my long fatiguing journey and intense mental anxiety. I spent an hour or two with them, then bade them good-by, wishing that they might have

a safe and pleasant journey, and land Jack in Indiana, beyond the reach of the cruel task-master.

I now turned my face homeward. The excitement
was over, the anxiety was gone. In looking back
over the work of the past few days, I felt that the
hand of God was in it. He had blessed my efforts;
he had guided my steps; he had strengthened my
judgment. My heart was full of thankfulness to
my Heavenly Father for his great mercy and favor;
my eyes filled with tears, and I wept for joy. Then,
as I rode along slowly through the thick woods, I
reflected on what I should do next. Osborne was
waiting for me at Squire Howells' tavern, and I must
soon join him. I did not want his company on the
homeward journey, but knew not how to get rid of
it. He had promised to accompany me to Burk's
Fork, where he understood I had business. That
would be ten or fifteen miles out of our way, but I
saw no other way to make my story good and keep
him blinded in regard to my real mission. While
pondering on this dilemma, I arrived at Howells',
and soon saw a way out of my difficulties. In that
State, magistrates had certain days to attend to law
business, and this was one of Squire Howells' days.
Several men had already come, on law business, and
as Osborne and I were talking about our route, I saw
a man whom I knew ride up and dismount from his
horse. He lived in Burk's Fork settlement, near my
Uncle Stanley's farm. · I had had some acquaintance
with him the previous fall, and when I went out and
met him, he recognized me. I told Osborne to
have his horse got out and we would be off; mean-

while I took this man apart and entered into conversation with him. I asked him all the questions I
could think of about my uncle's cattle, and his grass
farm and the man who lived on it, inquiring if he
gave proper attention to the cattle out on the range,
salting them frequently to keep them tame and gentle, etc., etc,

I then went to Osborne and told him that I had
been quite fortunate; I had met a man right from
Burk's Fork, a reliable person to whom I committed
my business, and now we were saved the time and
trouble of going out of the way—we could go directly home. This seemed to please him, and it
was certainly a relief to me. He got his bottle filled
at the bar, then we mounted our horses and set our
faces homeward. My fleet mare kept up wonder-
fully; she traveled well, though for two days and
nights she had had little rest. As for myself, I was
exceedingly weary; the sharp tension of mind and
body was relaxed, and I felt the need of sleep and
rest. When night overtook us, we were in a poor,
thinly settled region, and though we asked for entertainment at all the private houses—some of them
mere huts—which we passed, we were not taken in,
and had to travel till eleven o'clock before we reached a tavern. We had our horses put up and called
for supper, and it was after midnight when we got
to bed. I felt worn out and fell into a hard sleep;
arising in the morning but little refreshed. After an
early breakfast, we started again, and pursued our
journey together very pleasantly. The next day we
arrived at home, and Osborne and I parted on good

terms; he lived eight or ten miles from my father's.

I was warmly greeted by my parents and friends; they had felt anxious about me and were elated with my success. The night after my return Sam slept in the hay-mow of my father's barn. I carried victuals to him and told him the story of my journey with his master. He evinced his emotion during the recital by various exclamations in a subdued tone. We dared not speak aloud, not knowing who might be lurking around in the dark, watching for him or some other fugitive.

About two weeks afterward, Osborne came to my father's house to get me to go with him to hunt his negro. He said he thought Sam was skulking about in that neighborhood, probably hiding during the day in the thickets between our house and old Dr. Caldwell's. • He thought Dr. Caldwell's negroes fed him, for he heard that runaways often lay in those thickets and were fed by those d——d niggers. My father reproved him for using profane language, and he replied:

"It's enough to make anybody swear. I have lost time and money looking after that rascal. I can hear of his skulking around Dr. Caldwell's nigger huts, but can't find him. I have got acquainted with your son, Mr. Coffin, and think him a fine young fellow; I had rather trust him than anybody in this neighborhood. I don't know the woods among these thickets, and want him to go with me."

I said I would go, as I was well acquainted with all the paths and byways through the woods, having often traversed them when hunting for deer and wild turkeys, or looking after our out hogs. Father then invited Osborne to eat dinner with us and have his horse fed. He accepted the invitation, and my father was very social and friendly with him, but reproved him if he used profane language, as he frequently did in common conversation. After dinner I got out my horse and his, and we started off slave-hunting. Rather novel business for me, I thought, but I guess I knew what I was about. Old Dr. Caldwell lived a mile and a-half east of my father's place. The space between the two farms was densely overgrown with small trees, shrubs and vines — the large timber having been destroyed by fire some years before. These thickets were the resort of wild game of different kinds, and formed also good hiding-places for fugitive slaves. In some of these, near Dr. Caldwell's, Osborne supposed Sam to be lurking, but I knew that he was then sitting in a thicket, half a mile northeast of my father's, weaving baskets. Caldwell's slaves were frequently permitted to go to the neighbors after night to sell the baskets which they had woven during spare hours, and in this way they disposed of Sam's baskets for him. Only that morning I had taken him some victuals when I went to feed some of our out hogs that ranged in that direction. I guided Osborne toward the southeast, to a dense thicket not far from Dr. Caldwell's. Dismounting from our horses, we hunted through this thoroughly, and followed a spring branch to its source in another thicket looking for tracks made by Sam's feet when he came to get water. We then searched in neighboring thickets but found no trace of Sam. I guided Osborne farther to the south all the time, widening the distance between him and the object of his search. Quite discouraged at finding no track of Sam, Osborne finally gave up the hunt, and we rode out of the bushes into the Greensboro road. Osborne offered to pay me for my time and trouble, but I refused to take anything; then he thanked me for my services and we parted. I reached home about sunset, feeling that I should be well satisfied if that was my last slave hunt. Osborne afterward remarked to some one that there was not a man in that neighborhood worth a d——n to help him hunt his negro, except young Levi Coffin.

About this time one of our neighbors, named David Grose—a man respected by all who knew him—sold his farm, and prepared to move with his family to the State of Indiana. Vestal Coffin and I held frequent consultations about Sam, knowing that he was liable to be captured so long as he remained in the neighborhood, and we thought this was a good opportunity to get him to a free State, if David Grose was willing to assume the risk. We knew Grose to be a kind-hearted, benevolent man, of anti-slavery sentiments, but whether he would be willing to undertake anything so hazardous was a question to be decided. We concluded to go to his house and lay the matter before him. He seemed deeply interested in Sam's case, and said he would consult his wife and consider the subject. Having never seen Sam, he expressed a desire to see and talk with him, and ascertain if he was a bright, shrewd fellow, who could be relied on to act up to arrangements, and carry out plans for traveling, etc. Vestal and I agreed to bring Sam to Grose's house between twelve and one o'clock on a night appointed. It was unsafe to come at an earlier hour, for there might be persons passing about who would betray us. It was death, by the law of North Carolina, to steal negroes, and a heavy penalty to feed or harbor a runaway slave. At the time appointed, and on several subsequent nights, we accompanied Sam to Grose's house and held conferences in a private room, maturing our plans and fixing the time for starting. One night we narrowly escaped being detected by the patrol, a body of armed men who acted as watchmen or mounted police. They acted chiefly in the interest of the slaveholders, arresting all slaves they found out at night without passes from their masters, and administering to them severe whippings, and keeping a sharp look-out for fugitives.

On the occasion referred to, Vestal and I, in company with Sam, were going along the main road, about twelve o'clock at night, on our way to Grose's house. Suddenly hearing the sound of horses' feet coming toward us, we sprang out of the road and threw ourselves down behind a large log in the woods. We had no time to get further away, and lay close to the ground, hoping to escape detection, while our hearts throbbed with excitement, and the sound of horses' feet came nearer and nearer. When the party passed us, we heard the riders talking, and learned from their conversation that they were the patrol. They were talking about capturing runaway slaves, telling of their exploits in that business, and boasting of how many niggers they had whipped. Their conversation was plentifully interlarded with oaths. I well remember the thoughts that passed through my mind as I lay behind that log. I felt that I could fully realize the sensation of the poor hunted fugitive as he lay in woods or thickets, trembling lest any sound that greeted his ear should prove to be the step of a pursuer, come to drag him back to cruel bondage. I could appreciate the anxiety and distress that filled his mind as he wandered about in search of food, perhaps bearing on his back, in marks that were bleeding and sore, the cruel cuts of his master's lash. I could realize vividly his forlorn situation, exposed to the rain and cold and obliged to suffer from hunger, unless he could steal food or find some person who would venture to violate the laws of the land and give him something to eat, and allow him to seek shelter in the hay-mow of his barn. When the patrol had passed, and we heard the sound of their horses' feet dying away in the distance, we arose from our hiding-place, speaking to each other in whispers, and slipped silently through the woods in the darkness. Finally, we ventured to return to the road, and hearing no sound of horseman or foot traveler, we resumed our journey, stepping as lightly as we could. We approached David Grose's house cautiously, not knowing what enemy might be lying in wait. The dog, which was fast in his kennel, gave a short bark, but soon became quiet, and we passed around to the kitchen, where David was waiting for us.

The windows were darkened, and a dim light was burning inside. David admitted us, and we soon completed the arrangement for Sam to accompany him to Indiana. He had a large wagon, drawn by four horses, and intended to take what was called the Kentucky road, crossing the Blue Ridge at Ward's Gap, crossing New River near Wythe Court-House, Virginia, thence by way of Abingdon, crossing Cumberland River near Knoxville, thence over the Cumberland mountains and through Kentucky to Cincinnati, Ohio. He agreed to take the bundle of clothing we had prepared for Sam, in his wagon ; Sam was to travel at night, and come up to the camp each morning before daylight to get his breakfast and enough provisions to last him through the day, while hiding in the bushes. The road was rough, and led over hills and mountains the greater part of the way, and the movers would not be able to make more than twenty miles a day; so Sam could easily keep up with them.

Where the road forked, Grose was to leave a green bush or some other sign in the road he had taken, in order to guide Sam, and when he approached rivers that must be crossed by ferries, he would camp near the bank and wait for Sam to come up, then conceal him in the wagon, and thus convey him to the other side.

Matters were now all arranged, and understood by both parties. Our conference closed, and as it was near daylight we hurried away, Vestal and I to our separate homes, Sam to our hay-mow.

Some shrewd young men, not over-conscientious about violating the slave laws of the State, believing that every man was entitled to liberty who had not forfeited that God-given right by crime, managed to get hold of free papers belonging to a free colored man in the neighborhood, and copied them, counterfeiting the names of the signers as well as they could, not stopping to consider the severe penalty attached to such violations of the law.   It was so managed that the papers were given to Sam by a slave, and he was instructed not to use them unless he should get into a tight place—even then they might not save him.

The night after Grose and his family started on their journey, we sent Sam on horseback, with a trusty young man, to my Uncle Samuel Stanley's, about ten miles on his route.   According to arrangements, previously made, he was to remain there that night and the next day, then, on the following night, overtake the movers.

But next day, my cousin, Jesse Stanley, being about to start on a short business journey to the west, concluded to give Sam a lift by taking him to drive his carriage as far as he traveled on Sam's road.   He thought that he would incur no risk, as Sam was now out of the neighborhood where he was known.   But it was a daring venture, and afterward involved my cousin in trouble, for, while traveling the main road, they met a man living near Greensboro, who was returning from Salem, Stokes County, to his home.

He did not know my cousin, but recognized Sam at once, though he did not speak. We will refer to this again.

Sam overtook the movers that night and traveled on, as arranged, lying by in the daytime and pursuing his journey at night. He got along all right for more than a week, having in this time crossed the Blue Ridge, and traveled some distance in Virginia. One morning he came up to the party, then camped on the Abingdon road, some distance beyond Wythe Court-House, but still in Wythe County. He got his supply of food as usual, then retired some distance from the road to find a safe hiding-place among the hills. He remained in a dense thicket during the day, and at night attempted to make his way into the main road. But he heard wolves howling near him, and suddenly found himself surrounded by a hungry pack, their eyes glaring like balls of fire in the darkness. He had no weapon but a pocket-knife, and that was useless against such enemies. Seizing a club, he beat his way through them and reached a by-road, but was so frightened and bewildered that he knew not which way to turn to reach the main road. Running as fast as he could to escape the wolves, he heard dogs barking, and guided by the sound, made his way to a cabin. It was inhabited by the class of people known down South as poor white trash. He ventured in and inquired the way to the main road, saying he belonged to a party of movers, going to Tennessee, who had camped a few miles ahead on the Abingdon road. He said he had been sent back to look for something left behind, and had lost his way. The people seemed friendly and invited him, saying that they would send for one of the neighbors to go with him and show him the way. Sam suspected no danger and came into the cabin, to rest from his hasty run and his fright. In a short time the boy who had been sent to the neighbors returned, accompanied by two men. Poor Sam now saw that he was in a trap. There was but one door to the cabin, and the men stood in that, looking at him fiercely and questioning him closely. They accused him of being a runaway slave, which he denied, but could produce no free papers to prove his assertion—the papers furnished him being with his bundle of clothes in the wagon. The men seized him and tied him fast, believing him to be a runaway slave, and hoping no doubt to receive a large reward for capturing so valuable a piece of property. Next day he was taken back to Wythe Court-House and put in jail, no camp of movers being discovered in the neighborhood where he was captured.

In slave States every negro was regarded as a slave unless he could produce evidence that he was free, and when one was captured and it could not be ascertained who his master was, he was advertised in the county newspapers. A full description of him was given, and if no owner applied for him within the time fixed by law, he was sold to the highest bid-der; part of the money being used to pay jail fees and other expenses, the rest going into the county treasury. Sam would not give his master's name, still claiming that he was free, and he was adver-tised. The advertisement was copied in the Greens-

boro *Patriot*, and Osborne saw it. Believing the
person described to be his slave Sam, he went to
Wythe Court-House, Virginia, and claimed him.
He put poor Sam in irons and started homeward,
but never brought him back to Guilford County.
The story he told afterward was that he had returned by way of Salisbury, North Carolina, and
there sold Sam to a slave-trader. We only had Osborne's statement for this, and some thought that he
was wicked and revengeful enough to have whipped
poor Sam to death in some wild spot in the Virginia
mountains; others thought, however, that even his
desire for revenge would not lead him to sacrifice so
valuable a piece of property. At any rate, that is
the last we ever heard of poor Sam.

Some time after Osborne returned from Virginia,
he learned that Sam had been seen driving my
Cousin Jesse Stanley's carriage, just before he
started for the Northwest. After getting all the
necessary evidence, he set about procuring a writ to
arrest Stanley for negro stealing. This crime, it will
be remembered, was punishable by death according
to the laws of that State. I received intelligence of
Osborne's intentions while at my school. I was
then teaching near Deep River Meeting-House,
about eight miles from my home. During the
week I boarded with a family near by, riding home
at the last of the week. The news reached me
about noon one day, and I immediately adjourned
my school till the next week, telling my pupils that
special business claimed my attention.

I kept my horse at my boarding-place, and it

did not take long for me to saddle and bridle it, mount, and be off. My Uncle Samuel Stanley lived ten miles away, near the western line of Guilford County. I made the distance in a short time, and informed my uncle's family of the threatened danger. They were of course greatly alarmed, and immediately began to ask what should be done. My Cousin Jesse was about my own age, and we were much attached to each other, seeming more like brothers than cousins. I entered fully into the feelings of the family, and advised Jesse to flee from the State at once. It was decided that he should go to Philadelphia, Pennsylvania, where he had relatives. The distance was fully six hundred miles, and there was no public conveyance by the route he must go. He must travel on horseback and start immediately; there was no time for deliberate preparation or leave-taking. He needed a new coat and hat, and as I happened to have on a good coat and a new hat, I exchanged with him. We fitted him out as well as we could on such short notice, and his horse was brought to the door. I agreed to travel with him that night, for company, and see him safely out of the State.

We started about sunset and traveled a by-way till dark—then came out into the main road. We made good progress and soon got out of Guilford County, and into Rockingham County, which bordered on Virginia. I continued with him until we crossed into Virginia, then bade him good-by and returned to my father's house, much fatigued with

6

my journey, but rejoiced to know that my cousin was safe from the clutches of the law.

He arrived safely in Philadelphia, where he soon engaged in teaching. He continued in that profession about twelve years, marrying in the meantime an excellent woman with whom he lived happily. After an absence of nearly twenty years he paid a visit to his friends in North Carolina, but heard nothing of Osborne's writ for negro stealing. I might relate here that after my cousin left the country, Osborne searched for evidence that might implicate others for harboring his slave. He finally learned that Sam had been seen at Abel Stanley's, Jesse's uncle. Abel at that time had sold his farm, intending to move to Indiana. Hearing that Osborne was preparing to have him arrested, he fled from the State, leaving his family to complete the arrangements for moving and join him in Indiana. The rest of us, who were more deeply involved in the crime of harboring and feeding the fugitive slave, than either of the Stanleys, escaped detection, and were never troubled by Osborne.

In the fall of 1822, the year after David Grose had left North Carolina, I accompanied my brother-in-law, Benjamin White, and his family to Indiana. We traveled the same road that David Grose had traveled, camping out every night as was the custom of movers at that day. While passing through Wythe County, Virgina, we camped near the place where Sam had been taken, and there learned all the particulars of his being chased by wolves, his capture and imprisonment. When we reached Richmond, Indiana—near which place my brother-in-law located for the winter—I inquired for Jack Barnes and learned that he lived at Milton, about fifteen miles to the west. Having relatives at that place, I went there, in a few days, traveling on horseback. As I rode into the village, almost the first man I saw was Jack Barnes. As soon as he recognized me, he hastened to me and clasped me in his arms, uttering exclamations of joy and gratitude that attracted the passers-by. A little crowd of people gathered, and Jack told them that I had saved him from slavery, that if it had not been for me, he would have been dragged back to prison and perhaps sold to the rice swamps of Georgia, or the cotton fields of Alabama, where his only allowance of food would have been a peck of corn a week. When his first excitement was over, he wanted to give me some money, to repay me for my trouble and exertion on his behalf. I told him that I was amply repaid and would not receive a cent. Jack had got employment at good wages, had been industrious and frugal, and had accumulated property. Milton was a new place then; Jack had bought a lot and built the first cottage in the village. He had many friends in the place, and it would have been a difficult task for Osborne, Barnes' heirs, or anybody else, to have captured Jack and taken him away from Milton.

Early in the following spring, I went to Terre Haute, Vigo County, to enter land for my brother-in-law, and finding that David Grose had settled in that county, several miles below, I went to visit him, receiving a warm welcome. He still had Sam's bundle of clothing, but had not heard a word about him since the morning he left their camp in Wythe County, Virginia, to hunt a place of concealment during the day among the thickets. On the follow-lowing morning, when he did not join them as usual, they felt much anxiety about him, fearing that he had got lost or been captured, or that some accident had befallen him. They still hoped that he might over-take them the following night, but when the next night came and no Sam appeared, they gave him up. Since locating in Indiana they had seen no person from North Carolina, of whom they could inquire, and until I arrived they were in the dark regarding the fate of poor Sam.

CHAPTER III.

TEACHING SLAVES TO READ—SABBATH-SCHOOL WORK—
AGITATION OF THE ANTI-SLAVERY CAUSE—MANU-
MISSION SOCIETIES—TRIP TO INDIANA—INCIDENTS
ON THE WAY—THE EARLY SETTLEMENTS OF IN-
DIANA—I ENGAGE IN SCHOOL LABORS—ORGANIZA-
TION OF THE FIRST SABBATH-SCHOOL IN WESTERN
INDIANA—A VISIT TO ILLINOIS—LOST ON THE
PRAIRIE—SPRINGFIELD, ILLINOIS, FIFTY YEARS AGO
—CONCLUSION OF SCHOOL LABORS IN INDIANA—
RETURN TO NORTH CAROLINA—SHORT TRIP TO
VIRGINIA.

IN the summer of 1821, my cousin, Vestal Coffin, suggested to me that we should organize a Sabbath-school for the colored people, and endeavor to obtain the consent of the slaveholders in the neighborhood to teach their slaves to read. We knew that the Caldwell family—the old doctor, and two or three of his sons who lived on their own plantations—and a few other slaveholders, were lenient and would have no objection to our teaching their slaves to read the the Bible. I heartily united with my cousin in this project, and we visited the Caldwells, the Dokes, and a few other slaveholders, and obtained the desired permission. It was arranged that the slaves should come one Sabbath afternoon to the brick school-house, near New Garden Meeting-House. They collected at the time appointed, wondering at the new and unexpected privilege which had been accorded them. Among them was one of Thomas Caldwell's slaves, called Uncle Frank. He was a gray-haired old negro who had all his life been kept in ignorance, but his heart was full of love for God, and he was thankful for this opportunity of learning to read the Bible. He was quite a preacher in his way, and frequently exhorted the slaves in the neighborhood. On this occasion, he made a long and fervent prayer. He said: "I pray dat de good massa Lord will put it into de niggers' hearts to larn to read de good book. Oh, Lord, make de letters in our spellin' books big and plain, and make our eyes bright and shinin', and make our hearts big and strong for to larn. Make our minds sharp and keen; yes, Lord, as sharp as a double-edged sword, so dat we can see clean through de book. Oh, Hebbenly Fader, we tank De for makin' our massas willin' to let us come to dis school, and oh, Lord, do bress dese dear young men you has made willin' to come heah and larn us poor slave niggers to read de bressed word from de mouf of God. Oh, Lord, teach us to be good sarvents, and touch our massas' hearts and make 'em tender, so dey will not lay de whips to our bare backs, and you, great Massa, shall have all de glory and praise. Amen."

Then the negroes broke out with one of their plantation songs or hymns, led by Uncle Frank; a sort of prayer in rhyme, in which the same words occurred again and again.

After this was over, we arranged them in separate classes, and began to teach them the alphabet. It was new business to them, and they were so excited with the novelty of the situation that they accomplished little that day. The next Sabbath they made better progress, and in a short time some of them had mastered the alphabet and began to spell words of two or three letters.. Others, mostly adults, were dull, and hard to teach, though they tried hard. After we had continued the school every Sabbath for the most of the summer, and had been encouraged by the progress of some of our pupils, we found that we would be obliged to give it up. Some of the neighboring slaveholders, who were not friendly to our work, threatened to put the law in force against us, and visiting those who had let their slaves attend our school, told them they were guilty as well as the teachers, and that the school must be discontinued. They said that it made their slaves discontented and uneasy, and created a desire for the privileges that others had.

Our pupils were kept at home, and we were obliged to give up our school and succumb to the influence of the slave laws. Thus ended our slave teaching.

SABBATH-SCHOOLS.

Strange as it may seem to us now, there were then no Sabbath-schools in that part of the country, either among Friends or other religious denominations. I think it was about 1818 when a few of the young people of our society, at New Garden, met together to consult about organizing a Sabbath-school. I was among the number, and took an active part, for it was a subject in which I was deeply interested. Our conference resulted in opening a Sabbath-school in our new brick school-house, at New Garden. With few exceptions, we had no encouragement from parents and older Friends. On the contrary, we had much opposition to contend with. The school was small at first, but increased in numbers, and was soon large and interesting. It was the first Sabbath-school that I have any knowledge of in that part of the country. My cousin, Elijah Coffin, and my sister Beulah, afterward the wife of Daniel Puckett, a noted minister among Friends, were our ablest instructors. The results of the school were very satisfactory to all engaged in it, and instilled into my heart a love for Sabbath-school work that increased as I grew in years, and has continued with me even to the present time.

In the spring of 1822, I opened my first school, having previously served as assistant teacher.

I continued this business for more than three years, in different neighborhoods, and assisted in organizing Sabbath-schools in various places.

When I opened my first school, I had no prospect of continuing in the business long, for I felt that my qualifications were not sufficient for so responsible a work, but meeting with success in my school, gaining the affection of the pupils and the approbation of their parents, I felt encouraged to continue. I had a deep concern for the moral and religious welfare of my associates, for though young in years, I had experienced a change of heart. I had an earnest desire to exercise a good influence over those of my own age, and younger, who were my companions, and felt that I would have an opportunity to do so if I continued teaching. I found no difficulty in the government of my school; I loved order and system, and after I gained the affection of my pupils, they yielded a ready and cheerful obedience to all my rules and regulations. I look back to those years as the pleasantest of my life, and regard my labors in teaching and establishing Sabbath-schools with much satisfaction. The attachments then formed between teacher and pupils have never been broken, and though more than fifty years have passed, I still meet, now and then, in different parts of the West, those who were associated with me in school, and they recur with pleasure to the days we spent together.

ANTI-SLAVERY MATTERS.

During the time I was engaged in teaching, I was not idle in anti-slavery matters. The subject of gradual emancipation, or manumission of slaves, was agitated in various parts of the State. A paper, called the Greensboro *Patriot*, was started at Greensboro, edited by William Swaim, a young man of rare talent. He advocated the manumission of slaves, and though he met with a storm of opposition and was assailed by other papers, he continued his course boldly and independently. He received letters from various parts of the State full of threats and warnings. These he published in his

paper, and replied to them in editorials. Many
public speakers and writers engaged in discussion
with him, but they could not cope with him, and
generally retired from the combat much worsted.

Some plan of gradual manumission was the theme
of general discussion at that day, but none of the
advocates spoke or seemed to think of immediate
and unconditional emancipation. Manumission societies were organized in different counties. The
first, I believe, was organized at New Garden, Guilford County. I was a member of it, and can well
remember the proceedings. We also had several
State Conventions, which were largely attended, and
at which addresses were delivered and speeches
made, by prominent men. The various branches
were represented by delegates. The first convention of this kind was held at Jamestown, in Guilford County, and William Swaim, editor of the
Greensboro *Patriot*, took an active part in the proceedings. His cousin Moses, a lawyer of Randolph
County, delivered a lengthy and able address, which
was afterward printed and widely circulated. It was
a strong abolition speech, and would not have been
allowed a few years later. Several lenient slaveholders united with us in those meetings, and advocated plans for gradual manumission. About this
time the same subject was agitated in East Tennessee, and similar societies organized in that part of
the State.

Benjamin Lundy, of that locality, started a paper,
called the *Genius of Universal Emancipation*, which
I subscribed for and read as long as it was published.

At our next convention, which was held at New Garden Meeting-House, Elihu Emory and James Jones, of East Tennessee, attended as delegates from that State. Both were active members of the Society of Friends—able men and good speakers. The last convention that I attended was held at General Gray's, in Randolph County. He was a wealthy man and owned a number of slaves, but was interested in our movement. The meeting was held in his large new barn, which was covered but not weather-boarded, and which afforded ample room for the assembly. Quite a number of slaveholders were present who favored gradual manumission and colonization. They argued that if the slaves were manumitted, they must be sent to Africa; it would not do for them to remain in this country; they must return to Africa, and this must be made a condition of their liberty. A motion was made to amend our constitution, so that the name of our organiizaton would be, "Manumission and Colonization Society." This produced a sharp debate. Many of us were opposed to making colonization a condition of freedom, believing it to be an odious plan of expatriation concocted by slaveholders, to open a drain by which they might get rid of free negroes, and thus remain in more secure possession of their slave property. They considered free negroes a dangerous element among slaves. We had no objection to free negroes going to Africa of their own will, but to compel them to go as a condition of freedom was a movement to which we were conscientiously opposed and against which we strongly contended. When the vote was taken, the motion was carried by a small majority. We felt that the slave power had got the ascendency in our society, and that we could no longer work in it. The convention broke up in confusion, and our New Garden branch withdrew to itself, no longer co-operating with the others. Our little anti-slavery band, composed mostly of Friends, continued to meet at New Garden until the majority of the members emigrated to the West, preferring to live in a free State,

The laws relating to slavery were constantly made more oppressive. A law was finally passed prohibiting slaves who had been set free by their masters from remaining in the State, except in exceptional cases, where they had been manumitted for meritorious conduct.

Slavery and Quakerism could not prosper together, and many of the Friends from New Garden and other settlements moved to the West. In the summer of 1822, my brother-in-law, Benjamin White, sold his farm and prepared to move with his family to Indiana. I was anxious to accompany him and visit the Western States, a strange, new country then, where so many of my relatives and acquaintances had settled. With the consent of my parents I engaged to go with him and drive his team to the Far West, as it was then called, a distance of six hundred miles. The road we proposed to travel crossed the Blue Ridge at Ward's Gap, in Western Virginia, led through East Tennessee and Kentucky, and reached the Ohio River at Cincinnati. This was considered the best route for loaded wagons. I was then engaged in teaching at Dover Meeting-House, about ten miles from my father's, but closed my school in August, and prepared for the journey. My brother-in-law was provided with a tent and all the necessary equipments for camping out, and stored provisions and cooking utensils in his wagon. It was a trial to part from my dear parents, and from my youngest sister Priscilla, the only child left at home.

After taking leave of them, I set out on the journey with my brother-in-law. Every thing seemed bright and pleasant before us. The weather was fine, and the novelty of pitching our tent at night beneath the tall pines or by the roadside, and camping out, was very attractive to me. Our little party, consisting of my brother-in-law and my sister, their four children, his niece, and myself, were all in good spirits, and enjoyed to the utmost the varied and beautiful scenery of mountain, forest and stream. We seemed to breathe new life and vigor with every breath of pure mountain air, and soon accommodated ourselves to the inconveniences of travel. At night we slept soundly near our camp fire, leaving our large watch dog to guard the camp. We traveled alone until we had passed Abingdon, Virginia, when we overtook a six-horse team with two men. They had been to the lead mines, near New River, and were returning to their home in Kentucky, near Crab Orchard. They proved to be pleasant companions, and we agreed to travel together. Although Kentuckians, they were anti-slavery in sentiment, and there was perfect harmony between us on the subject.

One morning, soon after we had left camp, three
or four rough-looking men rode up hastily behind
us and commanded us to stop.   They said they had
lost a valuable little dog, a pet, and that they believed we had it concealed in our wagon.   We told
them we had not seen it, and had no use for another
dog, having one to each wagon.   This did not seem
to satisfy them, and they said they must search our
wagon and see.   My brother-in-law told them they
were welcome to look in the wagon.   They dismounted from their horses, and after my sister and
her children had got out of the wagon, they crawled
in and tumbled the things about.   I said to my
brother-in-law, "We must watch them or they will
steal something," and, stepping up to the wagon,
took out the rifle we used for shooting game, thinking they might take it.   The Kentuckians, meanwhile, were standing by their own team, and when
the ruffians had done searching our wagon, they
went to search the other.   We knew from the first
that the story about the dog was only a pretense.
We were confident that the party of men were
hunting for a negro, a fugitive slave, and thought it
best to let them satisfy themselves that there was
none with us; otherwise they might continue to
harass and molest us.   But the Kentuckians were
not so passive.   Their wagon had nothing in it but
lead and horse feed, but they were not willing to
yield to the ruffians the right of search.   The
younger Kentuckian stood near the wagon with
the lash of his heavy whip wrapped around his
hand, and the butt clasped between his fingers,

prepared to strike a violent blow. He dared them
to approach, and said "I would like to see one of
you put your head inside my wagon. I know what
sort of dogs you are hunting. It is runaway negroes
you are after, and I'll venture that neither of you
are able to own a negro. If I had one in my wagon
you could not get him, for you have shown no authority for searching private property." The elder
Kentuckian added a few sharp words, and the ruffians, not liking to encounter such resolute men,
mounted their horses, and rode away, cursing and
swearing. We did not see them again, and were not
further molested. The next night we camped near
the house of a Methodist minister. Having occasion
to go to the house on an errand, I met the gentleman
and entered into conversation with him. He was
pleasant and sociable in his manner and gave me
much information concerning that locality. I saw no
slaves about the house, and introduced the subject
of slavery. I found that he was opposed to it. I
related our adventure with the party of men, and he
said that we were not the first movers who had been
molested. A gang of ruffians, moved by the prospect of the large reward generally offered in such
cases, frequently stopped emigrant wagons and
searched them for runaway negroes. Not long before, a negro had been found secreted in a mover's
wagon, on his way to a free State, and had been
captured.

We met with no accident or detention on our
journey, yet we were five weeks on the way. Such
a rate of progress seems exceedingly slow and tedi-

ous in this day of railroads. We camped out all the way, with the exception of one or two stormy nights. During our travel through the mountains, I frequently took my rifle and made excursions in the woods in search of game. I succeeded in killing several wild turkeys, which made a pleasant addition to our stock of provisions. In one of these rambles in search of game, I wandered some distance from the road, but not out of hearing of the wagons ahead. I was making my way through the thick underbrush, with my gun on my shoulder, when I discovered something moving in the bushes not far away. I halted to ascertain what it was, and it soon made its way into an open space and stood in full view. It was a large black bear, the largest I had ever seen. It turned its head toward the noise of the wagons, and thus did not discover me. I lowered my gun and took aim, not stopping to think what the consequence would be if I did not kill it, though I knew that a wounded and enraged bear was a dangerous enemy. The ball penetrated its body but did not kill it. It gave a cry of pain, then whirled around on its hind feet and made for me. I turned and ran as fast as I could, calling the dogs. They had heard the noise and came yelping toward me. The bear was close behind when they came in sight, but when it saw them, it turned and plunged into a thicket. The dogs pursued and soon reached it. A short but fierce combat ensued, in which the bear defended itself well. The dogs received so many hard blows and scratches that they soon retired from the conflict and came running back. The teams had stopped on hearing the noise of the affray, and the men came to see what was going on. I reloaded my gun and we attempted to pursue the bear, but the dogs had been demoralized in the fight and we could not induce them to trail it through the thickets. We hunted for it among the bushes for nearly an hour, but were obliged to give it up. This was my first and last experience in bear hunting.

After reaching our destination, in Wayne County, Indiana, I spent several weeks in visiting relatives, then engaged in teaching, near Richmond. My school-house was near the spot where Earlham College now stands. Several pupils, from Richmond, attended during the winter. After the close of the term, in early spring, I went to Terre Haute, on the Wabash River, on business. There was then a small settlement of Friends on White Lick, about twenty miles southwest of Indianapolis, where the town of Mooresville now stands. That part of the country was then a wilderness, covered with heavy timber. My brother-in-law, Benjamin White, and a few other Friends entered tracts of government land in that vicinity, and they are now dotted with thriving towns and villages, and the Western Yearly Meeting of Friends is held in their midst. This was in the spring of 1823. Indianapolis, the metropolis of the State, was then a new town with few houses. The country between it and Richmond was then unsettled. Where the National pike and Indiana Central Railroad now run, there were only a few paths and wagon trails cut through the bushes.

Through this wilderness I traveled alone on horseback, seeing, no inhabitants after leaving the settlement, on the west fork of White Water, until I reached a small settlement on Blue River, about forty miles west of Richmond.   Here I turned a short distance from my route in order to visit William Macy and his wife, who had been my associates and school-mates in North Carolina.   They had emigrated to the West a year or two before, and settled, with a few other families from North Carolina, on Blue River.   They had entered a quarter section of land, most of it rich bottom land, and had built a little cabin in the woods.   When I reached the cabin, I found the door closed and saw no sign of life but some squirrels that were frisking about on the roof.   I alighted and knocked at the door, but gained no response.   Just then I heard the sound of chopping some distance away, and making my way to the spot I saw William at work with his ax, and his wife piling brush, while their babe sat playing on a blanket spread on the ground.

It was a joyful meeting.   My friends stopped their work and we repaired to the little cabin, which was built in the most primitive style.   It had but one door, the floor was made of puncheons, or split timber, and the fireplace was constructed of the same material plastered with mud.   Round poles served as joists, and had clapboards laid on them to form the loft floor.   My friends seemed well contented in this humble habitation, and as a number of other families had entered land near them, they had a fair prospect of being in the midst of a thriving and thickly settled neighborhood in the course of a few years. In the fall of 1826 I visited them again, and found them living in a good frame-house, with a large barn and other buildings, surrounded by a well cleared and valuable farm. They, in common with the other pioneers of that neighborhood, were now enjoying comfort and prosperity, the results of their own industry. They had removed from North Carolina to get away from the influences of slavery, and here breathed a free atmosphere.

After visiting my old acquaintances in this locality, I went to the settlement on White Lick, passing through Indianapolis on the way. The Court-House was then in process of erection at that place; the State-House was not built for some time afterward. The Legislature had not then met there. A newspaper had just been started, and the editor gave me a copy. The next day, as I was riding alone through the thick woods on my way to White Lick, I took out the paper and opened it. The first thing that struck my attention was a story of a boy who was a witness in court, and was severely questioned by the opposing lawyer who wished to show that his testimony was not reliable. At last the lawyer said to the judge: "I don't think the evidence of this witness can be taken. He does not seem to be very bright or intelligent. I will ask him some questions and you can judge for yourself."

He then said: "Boy, who made you."

The boy scratched his head and replied: "I don't know. I guess Moses did."

The lawyer said, triumphantly, "Now, gentlemen

of the court, you can see that what I said was true. Boy, you may stand aside."

"Stop," said the boy; "I want to ask you some questions. Can I, judge?" He was permitted to, and said to the lawyer: "Who made you?"

The lawyer scratched his head in imitation of the boy and said: "I don't know. I guess Aaron did."

"Well," said the boy; "I have heard that Aaron made a calf, but I didn't know that the thing had got in here."

The whole audience broke out into a laugh at the expense of the lawyer. When I came to the end of the story I laughed aloud, startling the echoes of the silent woods around me. I stopped my horse and looked about, to see if anybody had heard me, but saw no one but a bright-eyed squirrel peering down at me from a tree.

I reached White Lick settlement and spent several days there looking at the land I was to enter, and selecting an eighty-acre lot for myself. I then started for Terre Haute, sixty miles distant, having no road to guide me but an Indian trail, and there being no settlement on the way, except a small one, where Greencastle now stands. I reached this place the first night and stopped at a small log cabin. It had but one room, and this was the sleeping apartment of parents, children and chance visitors. A tramper had stopped there a few days before, professing to be a hatter by trade, and proposing to put up a shop at the place. I did not like his appearance, and having considerable gold and silver in my saddle-bags, which I was carrying to the land office,

I did not wish to be in close quarters with him. He was very inquisitive in regard to my business in that part of the country, but I evaded his questions as best I could. We had to occupy the same bed, and though I was fatigued with my long journey I could not sleep. Anxiety, and a feeling of heavy responsibility for the money of others intrusted to my care, kept me wakeful and uneasy. I put my saddle-bags containing the specie under the head of the bed, and lay in such a position that my companion could not reach it without passing over me.

No attempt at robbery was made that night, but I subsequently learned that a few days afterward, the sheriff of Dayton, Ohio, arrived there and captured this man and put him in irons; he had committed a heavy robbery in Ohio. The day after I left the cabin, I was riding through a dense forest when I encountered a terrific storm. Black clouds drifted rapidly across the sky, and heavy peals of thunder mingled with the noise of the wind in the timber. I dismounted from my frightened horse and stood holding him by the bridle, seeing no way to seek safety. It became very dark, tall trees fell crashing in every direction, and the lightning ran in streams along the prostrate timber. It was an impressive and solemn time with me, for I expected every moment to be crushed by the falling trees or struck by the lightning.

The storm soon passed, and I was left unhurt in the midst of the ruined forest. My heart was filled with thankfulness to God for his great mercy in preserving my life. I at first thought I could not make my way with my horse out of the forest; for the fallen trees completely obstructed the road, but I soon found that the track of the hurricane was narrow, and when I was beyond that the way was clear.

This hindrance prevented me from reaching the settlement near Terre Haute that night, but about dark I came to a house on the edge of Otter Creek prairie, where I spent the night. Next day I arrived safely in Terre Haute, where I accomplished my business at the land office, and got rid of my gold and silver. I then went on seven miles farther, to a little settlement of Friends on Honey Creek, and stopped at Moses Hockett's for the night. I intended to go on the next morning, to another settlement, fifteen miles further down the Wabash, where a number of my acquaintances from New Garden, North Carolina, lived. But Moses Hockett informed me that next day was their monthly meeting, and persuaded me to stay and attend it. At the business meeting, I gave the clerk my certificate of membership, which had been given me by the monthly meeting at New Garden, North Carolina, when I started West. It stated that I was a member in unity with them, and recommended me to the Christian care and kind regard of Friends wherever my lot should be cast. This was a good introduction, and seemed to open my way among strangers. After meeting I had many invitations from those present, and finding that I had been engaged in teaching, they were anxious that I should open a school at their meeting-house. They assured me that I would have a large school. I could not engage to teach, as I expected to return to Richmond after visiting my friends at Termin's Creek, so did not make any agreement. I remained over Sabbath at this place, and next day went on to the lower settlement, where I spent over a week visiting my old associates, and hunting. Deer, wild turkeys, and other game were abundant and afforded us delightful sport. Several families of the Dixes and Hunts, and my old friend David Grose, had settled here, all from Guilford County. About the time I intended to start from this place, wet weather set in. It rained incessantly for several days, and all the streams were swollen so as to be impassable. The ground was thawed and the roads were very muddy; altogether, it was a dismal prospect to a traveler. My friends dissuaded me from attempting to return to Richmond, and I concluded to wait till the streams that lay in my way could be forded. When the rain ceased, I returned to Honey Creek and agreed to open a school there, with the understanding that as soon as the roads were passable I should adjourn the school, for a week or two, and return to my brother-in-law's, near Richmond, for the purpose of getting a supply of clothing, etc. I spent a day or two riding about the neighborhood with William Durham, an elder, and the head of Honey Creek Meeting, for the purpose of getting subscribers to the school, and having obtained a sufficient number of names, I opened the school. It was soon full, and continued large until the close.

Finding that there was a number of young people in the neighborhood who could not attend school in

the busy season, I determined to organize a Sabbath-
school.   There had never been one in that place,
and I knew that to insure its success I must enlist
the interest of the parents.   To affect this object I
called a meeting at the Meeting-House, one Sabbath
afternoon, requesting the young people and their
parents to be present, both members of Friends'
Society and others.   I felt the responsibility I was
taking on myself, and prayed for Divine guidance
and strength and wisdom.   At the time appointed a
large meeting convened.   I spoke of my concern for
those of my own age and younger, whom I saw in
that beautiful prairie settlement, and my desire to
do something to promote their moral and religious
welfare while among them.   I then proposed that
we organize a Sabbath-school, to meet every Sabbath afternoon at the Meeting-House, for the object
of reading and studying the Scriptures, and for mutual instruction in all that was good and elevating.
I spoke of the Sabbath-schools in my native place,
and their beneficial results, and, after I had aroused
the interest of all, I addressed myself particularly
to the parents, saying that much would depend on
the encouragement they gave this undertaking and
the part they took in it.   If they would attend and
heartily join in the proceedings, and encourage their
children to come, we might be sure of an interesting and successful school.   To my great joy, they
united with me fully in the enterprise, and the matter was all arranged.   The school opened the following Sabbath, and was well attended.   It was
held regularly, and increased in interest as long as I

remained in that part of the country. Members of other denominations took part with us, and all seemed to enjoy, and to be benefited by it. This was the first Sabbath-school started in that part of the country. When the roads were settled and the weather was fair and pleasant, I adjourned my school and went to Richmond, as I had arranged to do, missing but one Sabbath-school by my absence.

About the last of May, my cousin, Allen Hiatt, of Clinton County, Ohio, visited me at Honey Creek. He was on his way to Illinois to visit his sister, the wife of Absalom Dillon, who, with several other Friends, had removed from Ohio and formed a little settlement on the Sangamon River, ten or fifteen miles from the place where Springfield, the State capital, now stands. My cousin was very anxious that I should accompany him, as his route lay across the Grand Prairie, a tract of country then entirely uninhabited, and he would find it very lonely traveling several days without company. I felt inclined to go with him, as part of my business to the West was to see the country, so I applied to the trustees for permission to adjourn my school for an indefinite period. This was granted, and I made preparations for the journey. My horse was in good plight for traveling, and when I had provided myself with a pocket compass, a good rifle, and enough provisions to last a week, I felt ready to start. Each of us took a wallet of shelled corn for our horses, and a good blanket as a preparation for camping out.

We were told that there was an Indian trail from Fort Harrison to the forks of the Sangamon River, where we would find a settlement and be not far from our destination ; so we resolved to take this route. Fully equipped, we bade good-by to our friends one bright morning, and started out on the wide prairie. We crossed the Wabash River, at Fort Harrison, four miles above Terre Haute, and entered Illinois. We found inhabitants for several miles, then struck the Indian trail and left behind us all signs of human habitation.

We followed the trail for two days, winding about from northwest to southwest, through the vast unbounded prairie. It led from one small grove of timber to another, which the Indians had used as camping places, and where they had erected scaffolds on which to dry their venison. On the second day the trail grew dim, and toward night it seemed to fade out entirely.

We directed our course to a small grove of timber ahead, which we reached about dark. We prepared to camp here for the night, and were making a tent of green boughs to protect us from the heavy dew, when we were startled by seeing two men coming toward us through the high grass. They soon told their story. They had been lost on the prairie for several days, and were wandering about in search of the trail when they saw our camp-fire and directed their steps toward us. Their provisions had given out two days before, and they were suffering with hunger. We fed •them sparingly that night, on account of their having fasted so long, and the next morning divided our store of provisions with them. They were trying to reach the settlement on the

Wabash, and we were able to guide them on their way by directing them to the route which we had come.

As for ourselves, we hardly knew how to proceed. We knew not how to steer our course for the Sangamon settlement by our compass, and our Indian trail had led us out of our way and then vanished. After some anxious consultation we concluded to go straight west across the trackless prairie. We continued this course until we reached the Sangamon River, where we were again at a loss. We knew not whether to go up or down, but finally concluded that we were too far south, so we turned north and traveled the rest of the day up the river. We looked eagerly about us for some sign of habitation, but saw none, and at night camped in the edge of the timber that skirted the stream. We felt lonely and discouraged. Our stock of provisions was nearly gone and our horse feed was exhausted. The horses could subsist on grass, but what were we to do for something to eat? We now realized that we were lost, and began to forebode all kinds of disaster. To increase the discomfort of our situation, great clouds of mosquitoes surrounded and began to torment us, and the howl of wolves was heard in the distance. We hampered our horses and turned them out to graze, but the mosquitoes troubled them so much that they sought the smoke of our camp-fire for relief. We built several fires and surrounded ourselves by a cloud of smoke, preferring this discomfort to the torment of the mosquitoes. We slept but little during the night, our minds being full of anxiety. The wolves howled almost continually, those near us seeming to answer those farther off. Sometimes we mocked them, by way of amusement; though it was rather poor amusement under the circumstances.

In the morning we concluded to retrace our steps, feeling satisfied that we should have turned down the river instead of up. We traveled southward all day, seeing no sign of inhabitants, and at night we camped again in the timber, weary and hungry. Our situation was now indeed serious. Our provisions were entirely gone and starvation seemed to stare us in the face. We frequently saw large herds of deer feeding on the prairie, but did not succeed in killing any. We were completely lost, not knowing that our course would bring us to any settlement for hundreds of miles.

In the morning we mounted our horses and continued our journey. This was the sixth day we had traveled without seeing any human being, except the two lost men that came to our camp. We pushed our way onward through the tall grass of the prairie, and about one o'clock in the afternoon we were suddenly cheered by the sound of a bell. We halted to listen, then made our way in the direction whence the sound came. We found a few ponies in the shade of a small grove. One of them wore a bell around its neck, and it was the tinkle of this which we had heard. We supposed they were Indian ponies, and that we were not far from a camp of Indians. We had had very little acquaintance with Indians, and under other circumstances would have avoided meeting with them, but now we were anxious to find them. We took a circle around, looking for some track that might lead us to the camp or village, but found none. The sudden hope that had raised in our hearts died out, and we felt the peril of our situation more forcibly than ever. We traveled on down the bank of the river and had left the group of ponies several miles behind us, when we discovered smoke rising from a point of timber before us, that reached out into the prairie. We supposed this to proceed from the Indian camp we were in search of and hastened toward the place. On nearing it, we saw a small log-cabin, and when we came up to it, we discovered to our great joy that the inhabitants were white people. They were entire strangers to us, but seemed very kind and friendly. Words can not express the thankfulness that filled my heart; I was gladder to see these people than I had ever been to see my nearest friends. No one can realize our feelings who has not had a similar experience. The people welcomed us to their cabin and soon prepared for us an excellent dinner of fresh venison, warm corn-bread, wild honey, milk and butter. They told us that three families, their own and two others, had settled in that locality the year before, and had raised a very good crop in the summer, It was twenty-five miles to their nearest neighbors, near the forks of the river. The settlement they referred to was the one we had been trying to find.

We tarried with these kind people until the next morning; then, with proper directions, we struck

our course, and reached the settlement that evening.
There was no ferry-boat at the river, but we found
a man, living near by, who offered to take us across
in his canoe. We accepted his offer and put our
saddles and saddle-bags in the canoe, compelling our
horses to swim after us. I came near losing my
horse in the river. He got fast in the branches of a
tree that had fallen into the water, and struggled so
hard to get loose that he was completely exhausted,
and when he reached the bank, he was not able to
rise out of the water. We kept his head above
the surface by the bridle, and after a little time he
gathered strength to climb the bank. After waiting
awhile to give our horses rest and let them feed, we
traveled on a few miles to Absalom Dillon's, the
place of our destination. We found a small settlement of Friends and others who had "squatted,"
as it is called, on government land. They had selected their land and were waiting for it to come into
market. We were kindly received by our relatives
and others, at this place, and I spent several days
here very pleasantly.

One day a party of us went out on the prairie,
which was dotted with beautiful flowers, and gathered a plentiful supply of delicious strawberries.
Other days were spent in hunting and in riding
about to look at the country. In one of our excursions we visited the place where the city of Springfield now stands. A little cluster of cabins marked
the site of the present capital. All the people were
"squatters" on government land, as it had not then
come into market. The Dillons were preparing to

visit another place, about forty miles westward, and my cousin Allen Hiatt was inclined to go with them. They asked me to go too, but I told them that ever since I had come to the West I had heard of a better place a little farther on, and now that I had got within forty miles of it, I thought I would turn back. I was anxious to return to my school, and there was a chance of company on the way, which I did not wish to lose.

There was a man in the neighborhood from Hamilton, Ohio, who had come out by way of Vandalia, and who wished to return by Terre Haute. We arranged to travel together, and after preparing provisions for the journey across the Grand Prairie, and bidding our friends good-by, we set out. The first night we lodged at the place twenty-five miles up the river, where Allen Hiatt and I had been so kindly entertained, and the following morning, with nothing but our compass to guide us, we started across the wide prairie. I was satisfied that if we pursued a direct eastward course that we would strike the settlement on the Wabash. We made good progress that day, and camped at night in a small grove of timber.

Next morning Seeley, my companion, declared that our course was leading us too far to the northward, and insisted that we must bear more toward the south. I differed with him on this point. I told him that we were now south of the route that Allen Hiatt and I had traveled when going out, and if we should bear farther south, it would increase the distance, and we should miss the settlement on the Wabash that we wished to reach. If we bore farther north we might strike the trail that I had followed for two days when going out. Seeley, however, still persisted in `his belief. He was much older than I, and a more experienced traveler, but I could not yield to his judgment. I had the advantage of him in several particulars; the compass was mine, the gun was mine, and I had a larger stock of provisions; I could do without him better than he could do without me. Nevertheless, he seemed resolved to part company and pursue his own route, unless I would change my course. It was a serious matter to separate in this vast prairie country where there were no roads or inhabitants, nothing to break the monotony of the level green plain but occasional groves of timber. But I would not change, and my companion would not, so we parted. I steered straight east by my compass, and Seeley bore to the southward. He probably thought I would yield at last and join him, but I held on my way, and the distance between us began to widen. He grew smaller and smaller, and about nine o'clock seemed like a black speck in the distance. At ten o'clock he appeared larger and seemed to be coming toward me. At eleven o'clock he fell into my course, and when I came up to him, he said:

"Are you sure you are right?"

"No," I replied, "I fear I am too far south."

We continued our course directly east until about noon, when we met an Indian on horseback. He halted, and I spoke to him, but he did not seem to understand English, and made signs that he wanted something to eat. We all dismounted from our horses, and I gave him some bread and meat. I then asked him what tribe he belonged to, but he made no reply. I mentioned the names of several tribes, and when I said "Kickapoo," he responded at once. I found that he understood enough English to know the names of places in that part of the country. I inquired the course to Fort Harrison. He pointed straight east, and said "There Terre Haute," then a little farther south, and said "There Vincennes."

Then he marked on the ground to indicate these places and the course, and made us understand by signs that we could not reach Fort Harrison by a straight course, for we could not cross the river. He made motions with his arms to imitate swimming, and showed us that our horses would swim and the water would come over our saddles. He then marked on the ground again, and showed us the course we must take. We must go northeast until the sun reached such a place—pointing to the sun then over our heads — when we would reach the river. We could ford it there, then we must turn southeast and travel in that direction, until the sun reached such a place in the sky. Then we must turn straight east, and would soon reach the settlement.

We followed his directions, forded the river without difficulty, and reached the settlement near Fort Harrison the next day, after a wearisome journey of four days. During the latter part of our journey the weather was very warm, and the last night out was one of the most uncomfortable I ever experienced. During the day we had passed through a wet, swampy district, where the water stood in pools here and there, that were knee deep to our horses. We were pushing forward in hope of reaching a grove of timber which we saw in the distance, when a black cloud rolled up from the west, and the peals of thunder sounded through the sky. It rained heavily and we were soon drenched. Darkness settled around us before we reached the grove, and in trying to make our way to it, in order to camp for the night, we got into one of those morasses I have mentioned. We thought we could pass through it, and pushed on, but the water soon became so deep we were obliged to halt. We turned and tried to make our way out, but did not succeed, and coming to a spot of dry land, in the midst of the water, we concluded to stop. One held the horses while the other looked about.

We found that we were completely surrounded by water, and decided that we had better remain where we were during the night. After hampering our horses and turning them loose to graze, we arranged our saddles and saddle-bags on the ground and lay down. We had blankets to spread over ourselves, but we were yet wet with the rain, and were far from comfortable. The clouds passed away and the stars shone brightly in the clear sky. Being much fatigued, we soon fell asleep, but awoke about midnight chilly and shivering. We got up and exercised by walking and jumping about on our little island, and soon got warm, but we could sleep no more during the night, having to repeat the exercise several times. When daylight came, we saw our horses some two hundred yards from us, grazing on the dry prairie. We found a narrow path by which we could reach them without wading, and gathering up our saddles and blankets, we left our camping place. We made good progress that day, and, as before stated, reached the settlement that afternoon in safety. I left my companion at Terre Haute and arrived at my home at Honey Creek that night. I received a hearty greeting from all my friends, and was very glad to get back. I felt fully satisfied with my adventures in the wild West, and did not care for any more experience of that kind. After one or two days' rest, I reopened my school, and continued it without further intermission until the last of August. Nothwithstanding the exposure I had undergone in my travels, I continued to enjoy the blessing of good health.

Soon after the close of my school I left Honey Creek, and returned to Richmond through the southern part of the State, which had been longer settled than the central part. I went by way of Paoli, Orange County, and Salem, Washington County, where I had numerous relatives living. Two uncles — my father's elder brothers — were among the early settlers of that locality. Large settlements of Friends had grown up in these counties, and a Quarterly Meeting was established near Salem, called Blue River Quarterly Meeting. After spending about a week in visiting my uncles, Libni and Matthew Coffin, and many of my numerous cousins, I went directly to the home of my brother-in-law, Benjamin White, near Richmond. This was my headquarters while I staid in the West, though a part of my leisure time was spent in visiting my other sisters, the wives of Daniel Puckett and Samuel Kellum, who lived about nine miles north of Richmond, in the village of Newport. The time for the Yearly Meeting of Friends was drawing near, and I wished to attend it before starting back to North Carolina. Indiana Yearly Meeting had been established but a short time, and a large house in the suburbs of Richmond had been erected to accommodate the meeting. It was called White Water Meeting-House.

The time for the meeting to open was in the Tenth Mo., October, and this gave me several weeks in which to visit my relatives and prepare for my homeward journey. I had learned that there was a prospect of having pleasant company on my way back. My uncle, Jonathan Hockett, of Highland County, Ohio, and his son Jonathan; Aaron Betts, of the same county, and Benjamin Beeson, of Indiana, were all going on horseback to North Carolina. The time of starting was agreed upon, and after taking leave of my friends in Indiana, and visiting relatives in Clinton and Highland Counties, Ohio, I joined this party and started for North Carolina. We crossed the Ohio River at Gallipolis, then went up the Kanawha River to the Falls. We crossed New River at Pack's Ferry, and our course from that place led across Peter's mountain, across the Blue Ridge at Maberry's Gap, and thence to .Guilford County,

North Carolina. I reached my father's house about the first of November, 1823. I was truly thankful to meet my dear parents and sister again, after a separation of more than a year, and they were greatly rejoiced at my restoration to them in the enjoyment of health and prosperity.

I remained quietly at home several weeks, aiding my father in the work of the farm. Schools generally were taken up, and I saw no opening for employment as teacher that winter. In the early part of winter I was applied to by a friend of mine to go on a collecting tour for him in the mountain regions of Southwestern Virginia. It would occupy me but a few weeks. I undertook the business reluctantly, fearing the inclemency of the weather in that cold mountain region. I crossed the Blue Ridge at Good Spur Gap, and spent about two weeks traveling over portions of Grayson, Wythe, and Montgomery Counties, Virginia. Snow lay on the ground, and the weather was extremely cold. I frequently encountered heavy snow-storms, and this exposure gave me a severe cold. I was gone from home about three weeks, and soon after my return I was taken violently ill with the pleurisy. This distressing disease reduced me very low, but by the aid of a skillful physician, and the tender and careful nursing of my parents and sister, and the blessing of my Heavenly Father, I was so far restored in a few weeks as to be able to walk about a little when the weather was fair. I remained in feeble health the remainder of the winter, and was not able to engage in any heavy physical labor.

One day, late in the winter, I was sitting in a rather dejected frame of mind, meditating on my situation and wondering what I should do, when a boy rode up to the door, and handed me a letter. I opened it and found that it was from Jesse Moore, of Deep River, near Jamestown, requesting me to take a school at that place. He wished me to engage for one year, and assured me that I would have a large school. I gladly accepted the offer, and as soon as my health permitted I opened the school. It was about eight miles from my father's, and by keeping my horse at my boarding place I had the opportunity of riding home at the close of the week. I taught here the whole year, and had a large and interesting school.

CHAPTER IV.

MARRIAGE—REMOVAL TO INDIANA—I LOCATE AT NEW-
PORT AND ENGAGE IN MERCANTILE BUSINESS—
UNDERGROUND RAILROAD WORK — DIFFICULTIES
AND DANGERS OF THE WORK—TRIP TO NORTH
CAROLINA — HEART-RENDING SCENE AT A SLAVE
AUCTION—TEMPERANCE WORK AT NEWPORT.

ON the 28th day of tenth month, 1824, I was
married to Catherine White, daughter of Stanton and Sarah White. We were brought up in the
same neighborhood, and had been acquainted from
childhood. She belonged to the Religious Society
of Friends, and was then a member of Hopewell
Monthly Meeting, to which place her father had removed a few years before, from his former residence
near New Garden. We were married at Hopewell
Meeting-House, after the manner and custom of
Friends.

My wedding-day was my twenty-sixth birthday;
my wife was twenty-one the preceding month. Our
attachment to each other was of long standing. She
was an amiable and attractive young woman of lively,
buoyant spirits. Her heart has ever been quick to
respond to the cry of distress, and she has been an
able and efficient helper to me in all my efforts on

behalf of the fugitive slaves, and a cheerful sharer in all the toils, privations and dangers which we have, in consequence, been called upon to endure.

Soon after marriage I rented a house near my school, and here we first went to housekeeping. My school closed early in the spring, and I concluded to rest awhile from the arduous duties of teaching.

Thinking that my health would be improved by the open-air exercise of farming, and having a very favorable offer made me of a comfortable house, without charge, in that neighborhood, and as much ground as I wished to cultivate, I prepared to engage in farming. This prospect was pleasant to us both, as my wife and I had been brought up on farms. The house was tendered us by our friend and neighbor Shields Moore, who now lives in Indiana. We went to work in good spirits and soon had a garden planted and a crop in. But my plan for farming soon came to an end.

A new school-house had just been completed, about two miles north of Deep River Meeting-House, in a thickly settled neighborhood of Friends. This settlement was called Nazareth, and the school-house received the same name. There was a large number of young people in the neighborhood, for whose benefit the parents were anxious to establish a good school. A committee, consisting of Abel Coffin, Thaddeus Gardner, Zacharias Coffin and Peter Hunt, visited me and asked me to take the school. They added inducements by offering me a good house, free of charge, and agreeing to guarantee my salary, but I declined the offer. I thought they had overestimated my qualifications and reputation as a teacher, and feared that I could not satisfactorily fill the place. They would not accept my answer as final, however, and said they would visit me again, giving me a week to think on the subject. I consulted with my wife and some of our neighbors, and finally agreed to accept the offer. I accordingly sold my crop, and removed to the house near the school.

In my article of agreement, I limited my school to fifty scholars. This number was soon made up, and I employed Susanna Overman, a graduate of Greensboro Academy, as assistant.

This was the largest and most interesting school that I ever taught. During this year I was also engaged in Sabbath-school work. We organized a large Sabbath-school at Deep River Meeting-House, the first ever established in that place. In the early part of 1826 we organized a library association at my school-house, calling it the Nazereth Library Association. We got several of the prominent men of the neighborhood interested in this work, and succeeded in getting a small, yet good collection of books with which to start our library. We then made up a considerable sum of money, and having, by the aid of Jeremiah Hubbard and others, made out a list of valuable books, we sent by Abel Coffin, who was going to Philadelphia, and purchased others. This was the beginning of what grew in time to be a large and interesting library.

When my school closed, I made a donation of my stock and interest in the library to the association.

I was then preparing to move to the State of Indiana. The association afterward obtained a charter and became a corporate body. A year or two after my removal to the West, I received an official notification of a resolution passed by this body, thanking me for the active part I had taken in organizing the association, and for my donation to the library.

In the early part of the ninth month, 1826, we took a final leave of North Carolina. My parents had emigrated to Indiana the previous year, and I was the last one of our family to go. My family at this time consisted of myself, my wife, and our son Jesse, about a year old. My wife's parents were not then prepared to move, but followed the next year. On our way to Indiana we had the company of my wife's cousin, Elias Jessup, and his little family.

We made the journey in light wagons, with good teams, and had a pleasant trip. We took the shortest route, called the Kanawha road, and arrived at our destination in four weeks from the time of starting. We located at Newport, Wayne County, Indiana, where we lived for more than twenty years. This village was in the midst of a large settlement of Friends, and a Quarterly Meeting was then established at New Garden Meeting-House, about a half mile from the village. I bought property in Newport, and finding that there was a good opening there for a mercantile business, I concluded to engage in it. I went to Cincinnati and purchased a small stock of goods and opened a store. This venture was successful, and I increased my stock and varied my assortment of goods until a large retail business was established.

The next year I commenced cutting pork in a small way, besides carrying on my other business. This I continued to do, enlarging my operations every year, and kept it up as long as I remained in Newport,

In the year 1836, I built an oil mill and manufactured linseed oil. Notwithstanding all this multiplicity of business, I was never too busy to engage in Underground Railroad affairs. Soon after we located at Newport, I found that we were on a line of the U. G. R. R. Fugitives often passed through that place, and generally stopped among the colored people. There was in that neighborhood a number of families of free colored people, mostly from North Carolina, who were the descendants of slaves who had been liberated by Friends many years before, and sent to free States at the expense of North Carolina Yearly Meeting. I learned that the fugitive slaves who took refuge with these people were often pursued and captured, the colored people not being very skillful in concealing them, or shrewd in making arrangements to forward them to Canada. I was pained to hear of the capture of these fugitives, and inquired of some of the Friends in our village why they did not take them in and secrete them, when they were pursued, and then aid them on their way to Canada? I found that they were afraid of the penalty of the law. I told them that I read in the Bible when I was a boy that it was right to take in the stranger and administer to those in distress, and that

I thought it was always safe to do right. The Bible, in bidding us to feed the hungry and clothe the naked, said nothing about color, and I should try to follow out the teachings of that good book. I was willing to receive and aid as many fugitives as were disposed to come to my house. I knew that my wife's feelings and sympathies regarding this matter were the same as mine, and that she was willing to do her part. It soon became known to the colored people in our neighborhood and others, that our house was a depot where the hunted and harassed fugitive journeying northward, on the Underground Railroad, could find succor and sympathy. It also became known at other depots on the various lines that converged at Newport.

In the winter of 1826–27, fugitives began to come to our house, and as it became more widely known on different routes that the slaves fleeing from bondage would find a welcome and shelter at our house, and be forwarded safely on their journey, the number increased. Friends in the neighborhood, who had formerly stood aloof from the work, fearful of the penalty of the law, were encouraged to engage in it when they saw the fearless manner in which I acted, and the success that attended my efforts. They would contribute to clothe the fugitives, and would aid in forwarding them on their way, but were timid about sheltering them under their roof; so that part of the work devolved on us. Some seemed really glad to see the work go on, if somebody else would do it. Others doubted the propriety of it, and tried to discourage me, and dissuade

me from running such risks. They manifested great
concern for my safety and pecuniary interests, telling me that such a course of action would injure my
business and perhaps ruin me; that I ought to consider the welfare of my family; and warning me that
my life was in danger, as there were many threats
made against me by the slave-hunters and those who
sympathized with them.

After listening quietly to these counselors, I told
them that I felt no condemnation for anything that
I had ever done for the fugitive slaves. If by doing
my duty and endeavoring to fulfill the injunctions
of the Bible, I injured my business, then let my
business go. As to my safety, my life was in the
hands of my Divine Master, and I felt that I had his
approval. I had no fear of the danger that seemed
to threaten my life or my business. If I was faithful to duty, and honest and industrious, I felt that
I would be preserved, and that I could make
enough to support my family. At one time there
came to see me a good old Friend, who was apparently very deeply concerned for my welfare. He
said he was as much opposed to slavery as I was,
but thought it very wrong to harbor fugitive slaves.
No one there knew of what crimes they were guilty;
they might have killed their masters, or committed
some other atrocious deed, then those who sheltered
them, and aided them in their escape from justice
would indirectly be accomplices. He mentioned
other objections which he wished me to consider,
and then talked for some time, trying to convince
me of the errors of my ways. I heard him pa-

tiently until he had relieved his mind of the burden upon it, and then asked if he thought the Good Samaritan stopped to inquire whether the man who fell among thieves was guilty of any crime before he attempted to help him? I asked him if he were to see a stranger who had fallen into the ditch would he not help him out until satisfied that he had committed no atrocious deed? These, and many other questions which I put to him, he did not seem able to answer satisfactorily. He was so perplexed and confused that I really pitied the good old man, and advised him to go home and read his Bible thoroughly, and pray over it, and I thought his concern about my aiding fugitive slaves would be removed from his mind, and that he would feel like helping me in the work. We parted in good feeling, and he always manifested warm friendship toward me until the end of his days.

Many of my pro-slavery customers left me for a time, my sales were diminished, and for a while my business prospects were discouraging, yet my faith was not shaken, nor my efforts for the slaves lessened. New customers soon came in to fill the places of those who had left me. New settlements were rapidly forming to the north of us, and our own was filling up with emigrants from North Carolina, and other States. My trade increased, and I enlarged my business. I was blessed in all my efforts and succeeded beyond my expectations. The Underground Railroad business increased as time advanced, and it was attended with heavy expenses, which I could not have borne had not my affairs been prosperous. I found it necessary to keep a team and a wagon always at command, to convey the fugitive slaves on their journey. Sometimes, when we had large companies, one or two other teams and wagons were required. These journeys had to be made at night, often through deep mud and bad roads, and along by-ways that were seldom traveled. Every precaution to evade pursuit had to be used, as the hunters were often on the track, and sometimes ahead of the slaves. We had different routes for sending the fugitives to depots, ten, fifteen, or twenty miles distant, and when we heard of slave-hunters having passed on one road, we forwarded our passengers by another.

In some instances where we learned that the pursuers were ahead of them, we sent a messenger and had the fugitives brought back to my house to remain in concealment until the bloodhounds in human shape had lost the trail and given up the pursuit.

I soon became extensively known to the friends of the slaves, at different points on the Ohio River, where fugitives generally crossed, and to those northward of us on the various routes leading to Canada. Depots were established on the different lines of the Underground Railroad, south and north of Newport, and a perfect understanding was maintained between those who kept them. Three principal lines from the South converged at my house; one from Cincinnati, one from Madison, and one from Jeffersonville, Indiana. The roads were always in running order, the connections were good, the conductors active and zealous, and there was no lack of passengers. Seldom a week passed without our receiving passengers by this mysterious road. We found it necessary to be always prepared to receive such company and properly care for them. We knew not what night or what hour of the night we would be roused from slumber by a gentle rap at the door. That was the signal announcing the arrival of a train of the Underground Railroad, for the locomotive did not whistle, nor make any unnecessary noise. I have often been awakened by this signal, and sprang out of bed in the dark and opened the door. Outside in the cold or rain, there would be a two-horse wagon loaded with fugitives, perhaps the greater part of them women and children. I would invite them, in a low tone, to come in, and they would follow me into the darkened house without a word, for we knew not who might be watching and listening. When they were all safely inside and the door fastened, I would cover the windows, strike a light and build a good fire. By this time my wife would be up and preparing victuals for them, and in a short time the cold and hungry fugitives would be made comfortable. I would accompany the conductor of the train to the stable, and care for the horses, that had, perhaps, been driven twenty-five or thirty miles that night, through the cold and rain. The fugitives would rest on pallets before the fire the rest of the night. Frequently, wagon-loads of passengers from the different lines have met at our house, having no previous knowledge of each other. The companies varied in number, from two or three fugitives to seventeen.

The care of so many necessitated much work and anxiety on our part, but we assumed the burden of our own will and bore it cheerfully. It was never too cold or stormy, or the hour of night too late, for my wife to rise from sleep, and provide food and comfortable lodging for the fugitives. Her sympathy for those in distress never tired, and her efforts in their behalf never abated. This work was kept up during the time we lived at Newport, a period of more than twenty years. The number of fugitives varied considerably in different years, but the annual average was more than one hundred. They generally came to us destitute of clothing, and were often barefooted. Clothing must be collected and kept on hand, if possible, and money must be raised to buy shoes, and purchase goods to make garments for women and children. The young ladies in the neighborhood organized a sewing society, and met at our house frequently, to make clothes for the fugitives.

Sometimes when the fugitives came to us destitute, we kept them several days, until they could be provided with comfortable clothes. This depended on the circumstances of danger. If they had come a long distance and had been out several weeks or months—as was sometimes the case—and it was not probable that hunters were on their track, we thought it safe for them to remain with us until fitted for traveling through the thinly settled country to the North. Sometimes fugitives have come to our house in rags, foot-sore and toil-worn, and almost wild, having been out for several months

10

traveling at night, hiding in canebrakes or thickets during the day, often being lost and making little headway at night, particularly in cloudy weather, when the north star could not be seen, sometimes almost perishing for want of food, and afraid of every white person they saw, even after they came into a free State, knowing that slaves were often captured and taken back after crossing the Ohio River.

Such as these we have kept until they were recruited in strength, provided with clothes, and able to travel. When they first came to us they were generally unwilling to tell their stories, or let us know what part of the South they came from. They would not give their names, or the names of their masters, correctly, fearing that they would be betrayed. In several instances fugitives came to our house sick from exhaustion and exposure, and lay several weeks. One case was that of a woman and her two children—little girls. Hearing that her children were to be sold away from her, she determined to take them with her and attempt to reach Canada. She had heard that Canada was a place where all were free, and that by traveling toward the north star she could reach it. She managed to get over the Ohio River with her two little girls, and then commenced her long and toilsome journey northward. Fearing to travel on the road, even at night, lest she should meet somebody, she made her way through the woods and across fields, living on fruits and green corn, when she could procure them, and sometimes suffering severely for lack of food. Thus she wandered on, and at last reached our neighborhood. Seeing a cabin where some colored people lived she made her way to it. The people received her kindly, and at once conducted her to our house. She was so exhausted by the hardships of her long journey, and so weakened by hunger, having denied herself to feed her children, that she soon became quite sick. Her children were very tired, but soon recovered their strength, and were in good health. They had no shoes nor clothing except what they had on, and that was in tatters. Dr. Henry H. Way was called in, and faithfully attended the sick woman, until her health was restored. Then the little party were provided with good clothing and other comforts, and were sent on their way to Canada.

Dr. Way was a warm friend to the fugitive slaves, and a hearty co-worker with me in anti-slavery matters. The number of those who were friendly to the fugitives increased in our neighborhood as time passed on. Many were willing to aid in clothing them and helping them on their way, and a few were willing to aid in secreting them, but the depot seemed to be established at my house.

Notwithstanding the many threats of slave-hunters and the strong prejudices of pro-slavery men, I continued to prosper and gained a business influence in the community. Some of my customers, who had left me several years before on account of my anti-slavery sentiments, began to deal with me again. I had been elected a director in the Richmond branch of the State Bank, and was re-elected annually for six or seven years, by the stockholders, to represent our district. When any one wished accommodation from the bank, much depended on the director from the district where the applicant lived. His word or influence would generally decide the matter. The remembrance of this seemed to hold a check on some of the pro-slavery men of our neighborhood. They wished to retain my friendship, and did not openly oppose my U. G. R. R. work as they might otherwise have done. My business influence no doubt operated in some degree to shield me from the attacks of the slave-hunters. These men often threatened to kill me, and at various times offered a reward for my head. I often received anonymous letters warning me that my store, pork-house, and dwelling would be burned to the ground, and one letter, mailed in Kentucky, informed me that a body of armed men were then on their way to Newport to destroy the town. The letter named the night in which the work would be accomplished, and warned me to flee from the place, for if I should be taken my life would pay for my crimes against Southern slaveholders. I had become so accustomed to threats and warnings, that this made no impression on me—struck no terror to my heart. The most of the inhabitants of our village were Friends, and their principles were those of peace and non-resistance. They were not alarmed at the threat to destroy the town, and on the night appointed retired to their beds as usual and slept peacefully. We placed no sentinels to give warning of danger, and had no extra company at our house to guard our lives. We retired to rest at the usual hour, and were not disturbed during the night. In the morning the buildings were all there —there was no smell of fire, no sign of the terrible destruction threatened. I heard of only one person who was alarmed, and he did not live in town.

The fright of this man created considerable amusement at the time and was not soon forgotten. He was a poor laborer, who lived a mile and a half from Newport, in a cabin which he had built in the woods. About half a mile east of his place, two roads crossed each other, one of them leading to Newport, and near the cross-roads was a large pond of water. This incident occurred in the spring of the year. Having heard that on a certain night the town of Newport was to be destroyed by an army from Kentucky, this man was listening, at the time appointed, for the sound of the approaching army. Soon after dark he was sure he heard martial music near the cross-roads. He hastened to town with all speed, and came into my store, almost out of breath, to give the alarm. We laughed at him, and told him that he heard the noise of frogs in that pond of water, but he would not be convinced. To satisfy him, a young man present said he would mount his horse and go with him to hear the music. He went, and soon returned and informed us that the frogs were making a lively noise in the pond in honor of the return of spring; that was all the music to be heard. The laborer was so chagrined at his ludicrous mistake, that he did not show himself in town for some time.

Slave-hunters often passed through our town, and sometimes had hired ruffians with them from Richmond, and other neighboring places. They knew me well, and knew that I harbored slaves and aided them to escape, but they never ventured· to search my premises, or molest me in any way.

I had many employes about my place of business, and much company about my house, and it seemed too public a place for fugitives to hide. These slave-hunters knew that if they committed any trespass, or went beyond the letter of the law, I would have them arrested, and they knew also that I had many friends who would stand at my back and aid me in prosecuting them. Thus, my business influence and large acquaintance afforded me protection in my labors for the oppressed fugitives. I expressed my anti-slavery sentiments with boldness on every occasion. I told the sympathizers with slave-hunters that I intended to shelter as many runaway slaves as came to my house, and aid them on their way ; and advised them to be careful how they interfered with my work. They might get themselves into difficulty if they undertook to capture slaves from my premises, and become involved in a legal prosecution, for most of the arrests of slaves were unlawful. The law required that a writ should be obtained, and a proof that the slave was their property before they could take him away, and if they proceeded contrary to these requirements, and attempted to enter my house, I would have them arrested as kidnappers. These expressions, uttered frequently, had, I thought, a tendency to intimidate the slave-hunters and their friends, and to prevent them from entering my house to search for slaves.

The pursuit was often very close, and we had to resort to various stratagems in order to elude the pursuers. Sometimes a company of fugitives were scattered, and secreted in the neighborhood until the hunters had given up the chase. At other times their route was changed and they were hurried forward with all speed. It was a continual excitement and anxiety to us, but the work was its own reward.

As I have said before, when we knew of no pursuit, and the fugitives needed to rest or to be clothed, or were sick from exposure and fatigue, we have kept them with us for weeks or months. A case of this kind was that of two young men who were brought to our house during a severe cold spell in the early part of winter. They had been out in the snow and ice, and their feet were so badly frozen that their boots had to be cut off, and they were compelled to lie by for three months, being unable to travel. Dr. Henry H. Way, who was always ready to minister to the fugitives, attended them, and by his skillful treatment their feet were saved, though for some time it was thought that a surgical operation would have to be performed. The two men left us in the spring, and went on to Canada. They seemed loth to part from us, and manifested much gratitude for our kindness and care. The next autumn one of them returned to our house to see us, saying that he felt so much in-

debted to us that he had come back to work for us
to try to repay us, in some measure, for what we had
done for him.   I told him that we had no charge
against him, and could not receive anything for our
attention to him while he was sick and helpless; but
if he thought he would be safe, I would hire him
during the winter at good wages.   He accepted this
offer and proved to be a faithful servant.   He attended night-school and made some progress in
learning.   He returned to Canada in the spring.

Many of the fugitives came long distances, from
Alabama, Mississippi, Louisiana, in fact from all
parts of the South.   Sometimes the poor hunted
creatures had been out so long, living in woods and
thickets, that they were almost wild when they came
in, and so fearful of being betrayed, that it was
some time before their confidence could be gained
and the true state of their case learned.   Although
the number of fugitives that I aided on their way
was so large, not one, so far as I ever knew, was
captured and taken back to slavery.   Providence
seemed to favor our efforts for the poor slaves, and
to crown them with success.

INCIDENTS OF A TRIP TO NORTH CAROLINA.

Early in the spring of 1828 I started to North
Carolina on business for myself and others, taking
with me a small drove of horses to sell.

I was accompanied by Ellis Mitchell, a light mu
latto man, free born.   He was from our neighborhood in North Carolina, where by his industry as a
blacksmith he had become possessed of a comfort-

able little property adjoining the farm of my wife's father, Stanton White. In the fall of 1827 my father-in-law moved from North Carolina and settled in Spiceland, Henry County, Indiana. Ellis had long wished to pay a visit to the western country, but was deterred from making the attempt by a knowledge of the difficulties that beset a colored man, who traveled alone from a slave State to the free States. Therefore, when my father-in-law prepared to start, Ellis saw his opportunity. He offered his services to drive my father-in-law's team, and was gladly accepted.

He made the journey in safety and spent the winter in Indiana, visiting his numerous friends and acquaintances, who had emigrated from North Carolina. When he wished to return home in the spring, he offered to go with me and aid me in driving the horses, and I gladly availed myself of his services. Dr. Henry H. Way, who was then my partner in business, accompanied us on the first day's journey. We stopped at night at a tavern near Eaton, Ohio, had our horses put up and called for supper for three. When we were called to the supper table, however, we found plates and seats for only two. The doctor observed to the landlady that we had ordered supper for three, but that she had prepared for only two, and remarked: "Perhaps you did not understand that there were three in our company."

"Yes, sir," she replied; "I did understand, but we don't admit niggers to our table to eat with white folks. I will give your servant his supper in the kitchen."

11

"He is not our servant," rejoined the doctor; "but a respectable gentleman, fully as worthy as we are, and nearly as white; he owns good property, and is really worth more money than either of us."

"I don't care," she replied; "he can't eat at my table with white folks."

In his quaint, peculiar style of speaking the doctor asked: "Do you ever expect to go to heaven?"

"I hope so," she replied, wondering how such a question could refer to the subject of their conversation.

The doctor said: "If this man should go there, as I trust he will, do you think he will be put in the kitchen?" and then went on to quote several passages of Scripture, with which the woman was apparently not familiar, concluding by saying: "I had much rather eat with this man than with a person who would not eat with him."

But the landlady did not yield, and Ellis had to eat in the kitchen. We traveled through the State of Ohio, but had no further difficulty in regard to Ellis' accommodations until we crossed the river at Gallipolis and entered the State of Virginia. Then, Ellis was a "nigger" and had to go into the kitchen the most of the way. While traveling up the Kanawha River, there was a sudden change of temperature, and the weather, which had been mild and pleasant, became cold and blustering, and snow fell.

Ellis Mitchell became quite sick from exposure, and was hardly able to travel. We wished to stop early, but could find no house of entertainment.

Some time after sunset we arrived at a good tavern and called for quarters. The landlord came out to meet us and appeared very accommodating. He called several negro servants to take our horses, and said to me: "Send your servant with mine to take care of the horses." I told him that I would go to the stable myself to look after the horses, as my companion was sick and I wished him to go in to the fire. I requested the landlord to give him a comfortable room where he could lie down, for he had had a hard ague chill in the afternoon and the fever was now coming on.

The landlord replied: "Oh yes, sir, he shall be properly attended to;" and I told Ellis to go in.

I went with the servants to see that our drove of horses was properly stabled and fed, then went back to the house and inquired about Ellis.

The landlord said: "My niggers will take care of him; don't be uneasy."

But I was determined to see where he was, and how he fared, and walking out of the back door, I proceeded to a negro cabin which I saw a few rods off. Entering it, I saw Ellis sitting on a rough bench in one corner, near a large fireplace in which burned a few sticks of wood. In the opposite corner sat several negro children on the dirt floor, for only half of the cabin, the back part, had a rough board floor. On these boards lay a few old blankets and quilts which afforded all the bed that Ellis could expect for the night.

I went back to the house with my feelings much disturbed, and said to the landlord: "I called for a comfortable room for the sick man, so that he might lie down, but I find him sitting on a rough bench, with no chance to lie down. I want him taken out of that dirty cabin and given a comfortable place to rest and sleep; he is able to pay for it. He is a free man, owning a good property, and at home has nice feather beds to sleep on."

The landlord replied: "I will see that he is made comfortable."

After supper, I went again to the cabin to see how Ellis was faring. I found him lying on the bench, with his overcoat over him. An old straw bed, with some ragged and dirty blankets, had been spread down in one corner for him, but he had refused to lie on it. For his supper he had been given some poor coffee and corn bread, of which he had tasted but little. The floor of the cabin was occupied by the negro servants, men, women, and children. Ellis spent the night on the bench by the fire, sleeping but little.

In the morning the breakfast offered him was the same as his supper, yet when we came to settle our accounts, his bill was the same as mine. Ellis had never been a slave, had always lived in a neighborhood of Friends, where he was respected and kindly treated, and this was the first time he had experienced the effects of slavery. The rest of the way home he fared more comfortably. After crossing the mountains into Patrick County, where taverns were few and far between, we made an early start one morning, and traveled till ten o'clock to reach an inn. We stopped and called for breakfast for two, and, after waiting some time, I was informed that the meal was ready. I stepped into the dining-room, but seeing only one plate on the table, I called to the landlady, and said: "I ordered breakfast for two, and I wish this gentleman to eat with me."

She replied: "After you have done, sir, he may come to the table."

I told her that we had no time to spare to eat, one after the other, for we had a long journey before us that day, and wished to be off as soon as possible."

"I don't care," she said, "niggers can't eat with white folks at my table."

I answered: "That gentleman is nearly as white as I am, and is a worthy man; I have no objections to eat with him."

She still persisted in her refusal; then I said: "I have no time to parley. That man is older than I am; I will give him the preference if either of us have to wait."

She at once set a plate on another table in the room, and set the same fare before Ellis. So we were permitted to eat in the same room.

Ellis concluded that Virginia was a hard place for free negroes, even if they happened to be nearly white, and was glad to get out of the State, and reach his own comfortable home.

After spending a week in the neighborhood of my old home, and disposing of part of my horses, I went farther south, into the edge of South Carolina, on the Pedee River, thence turned my course to-

ward Fayetteville. Fifty miles south of that place
lies the town of Lamberton, where I arrived one
day at noon, and stopped for dinner. I saw a large
crowd of people in the Court-House yard, and
thought that it would be a good opportunity to
dispose of the few horses which I had left. The
landlord informed me that an auction was about to
take place—that a large number of slaves were to
be sold that afternoon to the highest bidders. As
soon as dinner was over, I walked out to the large
lot in front of the Court-House, and looked about
me. The slaves who were to be sold stood in a
group near the auctioneer's stand, which was a high
platform with steps. They appeared intelligent,
but their countenances betrayed deep dejection and
anxiety. The men who intended to purchase,
passed from one to another of the group, examining them just as I would examine a horse which
I wished to buy. These men seemed devoid of
any feeling of humanity, and treated the negroes
as if they were brutes. They examined their limbs
and teeth to see if they were sound and healthy,
and looked at their backs and heads, to see if they
were scarred by whips, or other instruments of punishment. It was disgusting to witness their actions,
and to hear their vulgar and profane language.
Now and then one of them would make some ob-
scene remark, and the rest would greet it with peals
of laughter, but not a smile passed over the sad
countenances of the slaves. There were men, women
and children to be sold, the adults appearing to
be in the prime of life. When the examination

was over, the auctioneer mounted the platform, taking one of the slave men with him. He described the good qualities of that valuable piece of property,—then the bidding commenced. The slave looked anxiously and eagerly from one bidder to another, as if trying to read in their countenances their qualities as masters, and his fate. The crier's hammer soon came down, then another slave was placed upon the stand, and bid off. After several men had been sold in this way, a woman was placed upon the stand, with a child in her arms apparently a year old. She was a fine looking woman, in the prime of life, with an intelligent countenance, clouded with the deepest sadness. The auctioneer recommended her as a good cook, house servant, and field hand—indeed, according to his representation, she could turn her hand to anything, and was an unusually valuable piece of property. She was industrious, honest and trustworthy, and, above all, she was a Christian, a member of the church—as if the grace of God would add to her price! The bidding was quite lively, and she sold for a high price. I supposed that the child was included in the sale, of course, but soon saw that it was to be sold separately. The mother begged her new master to buy her child, but he did not want it, and would not listen to her pleading.

The child was sold to another man, but when he came to take it from her, she clasped her arms around it tighter than ever and clung to it. Her master came up and tore it from her arms amid her piercing shrieks and cries, and dragged her away, cursing and abusing her as he went. The scene moved my heart to its depths; I could endure it no longer. I left the ground, returned to my tavern, called for my horses, and left the town without attempting to do any business. As I mounted my horse, I heard the voice of the slave mother as she screamed: "My child, my child!" I rode away as fast as I could, to get beyond the sound of her cries. But that night I could not sleep; her screams rang in my ears, and haunted me for weeks afterward.

This incident increased my abhorrence of slavery and strengthened my determination to labor for the cruelly oppressed slaves. I resolved to labor in this cause until the end of my days, not expecting that I would live to see the fetters broken and the bondmen free, yet hoping that the time of redemption was not far distant. I returned home with feelings of renewed energy and zeal for the cause of liberty.

I devoted much time and labor to aiding the poor fugitives, but found opportunity to engage in other benevolent work. The Society of Friends had a standing committee, called the "Committee on the Concerns of the People of Color," whose business it was to look after the educational interest of the free colored people among us. I was a member of that committee. A fund was raised every year by our society to sustain schools, and to aid the poor and destitute among the colored people. I was appointed treasurer of this fund. We had several large settlements of free colored people in the limits of our Quarterly Meeting, which were under our care, and we sustained schools among them. With others of the committee, I often visited these neighborhoods to look after the interests of these poor, ignorant people.

I also engaged in the cause of temperance, which was as unpopular then as the anti-slavery cause.

TEMPERANCE.

I will here give a brief sketch of our struggle at Newport in the cause of temperance, and state how we succeeded in firmly planting those principles which afterward made that village noted for its sobriety and good moral influence.

Our war with King Alcohol began in 1830, and continued for several years, resulting finally in a complete victory on our part. Newport was a small village of about twenty families, when I located there in the fall of 1826. A few mechanics, such as blacksmiths, wagon-makers, carpenters, shoe-makers, etc., had opened shops, and there were one or two dram shops where liquor was sold in small quantities. There was no dry-goods store in the village until I commenced business there. I first opened my store with a small assortment of dry-goods, groceries and hardware, such as was needed by the farmers, and gradually enlarged my stock as the demand for the articles increased.

The country was new and thinly settled, but emigrants from North Carolina and other places came in and the population grew in number year by year.

The liquor business increased as the village and neighborhood became more thickly settled, and other dram shops were added. It was no uncommon thing to see a drinking, swearing gang of rowdies about these places of dissipation, or to hear them quarreling and fighting among themselves. Frequently, on the last day of the week a company of roughs from the surrounding neighborhoods would meet at Newport and have a drunken spree.

The only religious denominations in the neighborhood were Friends and Methodists; the former were the most numerous, but the latter had a church organization. Friends in the village became much annoyed by the liquor shops and the noisy disturbances which resulted from them, and a few of us often labored with the liquor sellers, but to no effect. One evening Daniel Puckett, Dr. Henry H. Way and I met, according to agreement, to consult together in regard to this growing evil in our village. We felt that something must be done, if possible, to put a stop to it, but knew that before anything could be effectually accomplished, the public sentiment must be aroused, and that the people must recognize the enormity of this growing evil. How shall we proceed to do this? was the question that we considered. It was suggested and agreed upon that we should try to organize a temperance society, but the next question was, how will this take with the public? We knew of no such organization west of the mountains, and realized that if we engaged in the work it must be as pioneers. We knew that Friends professed to be a temperance society; that our discipline prohibited our members from distilling, importing or vending spirituous liquors, and from the unnecessary use of the same, but we might differ as to what the necessary use of liquor was.

Friends were not, as a general thing, total abstainers from liquor, and the question to be considered was, will they sustain us in this move? To succeed, we knew that we must also get the Methodists of the neighborhood interested in the matter and gain their support, so we selected three of the most influential members of that denomination in the place, and invited them to meet us in council.

They came at the appointed time: Edward Starbuck, James Driggins, and another whose name I do not recollect. The result of the council was that we united in calling a meeting at our school-house in the town for the purpose of organizing a temperance society.

Several advertisements were written and signed by the six persons present: three Friends and three Methodists. These were posted in different parts of the village, and the result was that a public excitement was created and that a large number of people—both men and women—assembled at the school-house on the appointed evening. A chairman was chosen and the meeting called to order; then a committee to prepare a constitution and by-laws was nominated. This committee retired, but as the writings had been previously prepared, they soon returned and reported. Then, on the motion to adopt, the battle commenced. We expected to meet with opposition, but were not prepared for such formidable opposition from many of the prominent religionists of the neighborhood. King Al-

cohol and his votaries opened fire on our little band
of cold-water adherents, but we were well prepared
for defense, having enlisted for the war, and expected a long hard struggle. Our number was
small, but we felt that one, rightly armed, could
chase a thousand, and two could put ten thousand to
flight.

The battle continued for several hours. The
enemy evidently weakened and lost ground; a few
were captured. The society was organized under
the name of the "Newport Temperance Society,"
and twelve signers to the constitution and pledge
were obtained. The meeting then adjourned, to
assemble again the next week at the same place.
We knew that no church could be obtained for the
purpose of holding such an incendiary meeting, as it
was termed. At the next meeting the opposition
was still formidable. All sorts of accusations were
brought against us, and many flimsy arguments
were adduced to prove that our work should not
go on and could not end in success. Among other
things we were accused of wanting to take away
their liberty as independent citizens, of wishing to
connect Church and State, etc. The result of the
second meeting was the addition of forty names to
the temperance society. The women were now
wide awake, and rallied to our side; this gave us
strength and encouragement.

As the news of our organization spread over the
neighboring country, the excitement became greater.
The frequent expressions were: "Our liberties are
endangered by these fanatics at Newport; they are

turning the world upside down in their fanatical
zeal," etc. Our work was now the absorbing topic
of conversation. The liquor sellers became alarmed;
not only those in Newport, but those in neighboring
villages. Their business was in danger; something
must be done to check the movement that had begun at Newport. They held a council at Williamsburg, a village four miles west of our place, and the
result was that they sent us a challenge for a debate
on the subject, between three men of their choosing
and three men of our choosing. We called a meeting and accepted their challenge, appointing a committee to make all preliminary arrangements, and
to select our three men. Our opponents selected
John Hough and E. Lee, of Williamsburg; and Joseph Lomax, of that vicinity, as their champions;
all of them were Democrats. Lee was a merchant
in Williamsburg, interested in the liquor business
there, and was considered a strong debater. Our
committee chose Dr. Henry H. Way, Willis Davis,
our school teacher, of Newport; and Abel Lomax,
from the neighborhood of Williamsburg. Abel
Lomax had been a member of the State Legislature for several years, having been elected on the
Whig ticket, and was a thorough temperance man.

It was agreed that the meeting should be held at
our school-house, commencing at two o'clock in the
afternoon. A large company gathered, and strict
attention was given to the proceedings. Esquire
Curtis presided over the meeting, which lasted till
twelve o'clock at night. The debate was long and
hot on the side of the opposition, but their argu-

ments were calmly and forcibly met by our valiant men, and a complete victory was gained for temperance.

Notwithstanding the opposition we had to contend with, and the flouts and jeers directed against us, even by professors of religion, we persevered in the work, holding frequent meetings, appointing committees to labor in the cause, visiting the liquor dealers and those who patronized them, and in every way we could forwarding a cause which seemed to us a righteous one.

Our number increased, many who had first opposed us falling into rank, and in less than one year we had between three and four hundred signers to our pledge. Public sentiment had so changed in our village and neighborhood, that a man who had any regard for his reputation would not be seen going into a liquor shop to purchase liquor for any purpose. Several of our liquor dealers were starved out for want of custom. They closed their shops and moved away when their licenses expired, not being able to renew them for want of the requisite number of freehold signers to their petitions. Many of the drinking, rowdy class in our neighborhood moved away into a more congenial atmosphere, so that quite a change was wrought in our quiet little village and the surrounding neighborhood. All the dram shops were now gone except one; that was kept on a small scale. We had labored much with the proprietor of this shop; he often promised to close his establishment but failed to do so, and finally bade us defiance. His license had not yet expired, and he thought that we could not move him. We called a meeting at the school-house to consider his case. We invited him to it, but he refused to come, and still defied us. We passed a resolution, proscribing him as an enemy to the peace and harmony of our town, and declaring that we would have no dealings with him and no social intercourse, except in case of sickness or death, while he persisted in his nefarious business. I volunteered to carry the resolution to him, and labor with him, having been well acquainted with him for many years. I did so, and in my conversation told him that it was impossible for him to stem the current of public sentiment; that he had been kindly entreated by both men and women, and fair offers had been made to him by those who felt a deep interest in his welfare, but he had turned a deaf ear to all our pleadings, and bade us defiance. Now, I told him, we were determined to stop the liquor business in Newport, and we should watch him, day and night, and prosecute him for every unlawful act, but I pleaded with him to stop at once, then no prosecution would be brought against him. I told him that we were his friends, not his enemies, and sought only his good. He finally yielded and gave up the business, and moved away. Not a drop of liquor was now sold in our town; we had succeeded beyond our most sanguine expectations. But we did not rest in this quietness.

A stranger to the most of us, by the name of Mann, came to Newport, and rented a house, under the pretense of keeping a grocery. He moved into the dwelling attached to the store, but we soon found that his groceries were to consist of a general assortment of liquors. He had managed to get the requisite number of signers to a petition for license to sell liquor; he had obtained them slyly in our township. As soon as it was known in Newport, we got up a remonstrance and obtained over four hundred signers to it. The next week was Commissioner's Court at Centerville. Eli Osborne and I were appointed to attend court, and present the remonstrance when the license was applied for. We did this, and the license was not granted. We returned home rejoicing at our success, but next day Mann employed a lawyer, who succeeded in making the court believe that they were obliged to grant the license, as the requisite number of freeholders had signed the petition. Mann now rejoiced over us, and bade us defiance. He opened his liquor shop, and drinking companies soon gathered from surrounding neighborhoods, and drunken men were again seen in our streets. We labored with him, to no effect. But this reign of terror was of short duration. The Temperance Society held frequent meetings; we had many able temperance lecturers; our committees were at work; we were vigilant in all our efforts, and endeavored· to watch over and guard the reformed drunkards. One of these reformed drunkards lived on the opposite side of the street from this shop; but he was faithful to his pledge, and did not yield to the temptation which was kept prominently before him.

At a late hour, one night, a few weeks after this

liquor shop had been opened, a pistol was fired from it, and the shot passed through a pane of glass in the house across the street, entered the bedroom where this reformed man and his wife were sleeping, and lodged in the wall a few inches above their heads, waking them immediately.

Early next morning this man went to Centerville and got out a writ for the liquor seller, and the sheriff came and arrested him and lodged him in jail to await his trial before the next court. While he was in jail his property was attached for debt. It was difficult for him to find bail, but at last he succeeded in getting bailed out of prison, as it was some time till court convened, and he left for parts unknown. He never returned to Newport, for he knew that other writs awaited him. This closed the liquor traffic in Newport.

We elected Esquire Curtis, one of our strong temperance men, to the Legislature from our district, and while he was our representative, we sent up a petition for a special act of the Legislature for the protection of our village against the liquor traffic. Special acts could sometimes be obtained under the old Constitution of the State, and through the influence of Esquire Curtis and others an act was passed, so that no liquor could be sold in the corporate limits of Newport, for any purpose, without a permit from the trustees of the town. Now, we had gained a complete victory over King Alcohol in Newport, and public sentiment had been so changed that there was no dram shop in New Garden Township.

Some of our citizens thought that it was neces-

12

sary to have some spirits kept in Newport for medical and mechanical purposes, and the temperance society appointed me liquor seller, as there was no drug store in the place at that time, and no stock of medicines except the small assortment which I kept.

I reluctantly submitted to become liquor seller and obtained a permit from the trustees. I procured at Cincinnati, from Allen & Co., druggists, three two-gallon jugs, one filled with French brandy, one with wine, the other with alcohol. Thus, my stock of liquor consisted of six gallons, which lasted for several months. I was the only liquor dealer in Newport for about a year, then Dr. Way opened a drug store, and I gladly turned the business over to him. Newport still remains a temperance town, having been guarded and protected for more than forty years, as no other town in the State has been, so far as I have any knowledge. After our work at Newport seemed to be accomplished, we extended our labors to other towns and villages near, but met with little encouragement. Public sentiment was opposed to us; the people did not seem prepared to receive temperance doctrine at that early day.

CHAPTER V.

NEWPORT STORIES—THE CUNNING SLAVE—ROBERT BUR-
REL—ELIZA HARRIS—SAM, THE ELOQUENT SLAVE
—PREJUDICE AGAINST COLOR—AUNT RACHEL—A
SLAVE-HUNTER OUTWITTED — SEVENTEEN FUGI-
TIVES.

OF the many hundred cases that came under our
personal notice during the twenty years that
we lived at Newport, Indiana, a few will be given. I
shall not attempt to give dates, nor the names of the
runaway slaves. When the fugitives came to our
house, they seldom gave the name by which they
had been known in slavery, or if they did, we gave
them another name, by which they were afterward
known both at our house and in Canada. The
stories that follow are gathered from the slaves' own
narratives.

THE CUNNING SLAVE.

Jim was a shrewd, intelligent chattel, the property
of a man living in Kentucky. Having in some un-
accountable manner got the idea that freedom was
better than bondage, he resolved to make an effort
to gain his liberty. He did not make his intention
known to his wife or any of his fellow-bondmen,
choosing to make the attempt alone. He watched

for an opportunity to escape, and when it came he started for the Ohio River. He knew that he was a valuable piece of property, and that his master would pursue him and make strong efforts to capture him, so he let no grass grow under his feet till he reached the bank of the river. He wandered along this in the dark for some time, looking for a way to cross, and finally came to the hut of a colored man. He told his story to the negro living in the hut, and offered him part of the small sum of money he had if he would take him across in a skiff to the Indiana shore. The negro knew where a skiff lay drawn up on the shore, and consented to row him across. Jim reached the other side safely, and landed a short distance above Madison. It was now near daylight, and he must hasten to seek a place of concealment. He was directed how to find George De Baptist, a free colored man, who often aided fugitive slaves. George then lived in Madison, but soon after removed to Detroit, Michigan, for his own safety. Jim made his way to the house of this friendly colored man, and remained secreted during the day. Some time in the day, George De Baptist learned that Jim's master had arrived in town with a posse of men, and that they were rudely entering the houses of colored people, searching for the missing slave. By shrewd management on the part of George, the hunters were baffled, and the next night Jim was conducted through corn-fields and by-ways to a depot of the Underground Railroad. He was forwarded from station to station, at late hours in the night, until he reached William Beard's, in Union County, Indiana. Here he rested a few days, under the roof of that noted and worthy abolitionist, whose house was known for many years as a safe retreat for the oppressed fugitive. From that place he was conducted to our house, a distance of about twenty-five miles, and, after remaining with us one day, he was forwarded on from station to station, till he reached Canada. Here he remained a few months. In telling his story, he said:

"Oh, how sweet it was to breathe free air, to feel that I had no massa who could whip me or sell me. But I was not happy long. I could not enjoy liberty when the thoughts of my poor wife and children in slavery would rise up before me. I thought to myself, I have learned the way and found friends all along the road; now I will go back and fetch my wife and children. I'll go to old massa's plantation, and I'll make believe I am tired of freedom. I'll tell old massa a story that will please him; then I will go to work hard and watch for a chance to slip away my wife and children."

So Jim left Canada and wended his way back to the old plantation in Kentucky. His master was greatly surprised, one morning, to see his missing property come walking up from the negro quarters as if nothing had happened. Jim came up to him and made a low bow, and stood before him as humble as a whipped dog. In answer to the volley of questions and hard names that greeted him, Jim said:

"I thought I wanted to be free, massa, so I run away and went to Canada. But I had a hard time there, and soon got tired of taking care of myself. I thought I would rather live with massa again and be a good servant. I found that Canada was no place for niggers; it's too cold, and we can't make any money there. Mean white folks cheat poor niggers out of their wages when they hire them. I soon got sick of being free, and wished I was back on the old plantation. And those people called abolitionists, that I met with on the way, are a mean set of rascals. They pretend to help the niggers, but they cheat them all they can. They get all the work out of a nigger. they can, and never pay him for it. I tell you, massa, they are mean folks."

In narrating his story, Jim said: "Well, old massa seemed mightily pleased with my lies. He spoke pleasant to me, and said: 'Jim, I hope you will make a good missionary among our people and the neighbors.' I got massa's confidence, and worked well and obeyed him well, and I talked to the niggers before him, in a way to please him. But they could understand me, for I had been doing missionary work among them, and the neighbors' niggers too, but not such missionary work as massa thought I was doing."

Jim worked on faithfully through the fall and winter months, all the time arranging matters for a second flight.

In the spring, when the weather was warm, he succeeded in getting his wife and children and a few of his slave friends across the Ohio River into Indiana. He got safely to the first station of the Underground Railroad, with his party, numbering fourteen, and hurried on with them rapidly from station to station, until they reached our house. They were hotly pursued and had several narrow escapes, but the wise management of their friends on the route prevented them from being captured. They remained at our house several days to rest, as they were much exhausted with night travel, and suffering from exposure, and while they were concealed in our garret, their pursuers passed through the town.

The hunters went northward by way of Winchester and Cabin Creek, where there was a large settlement of free colored people. While they were searching in these neighborhoods, we forwarded the fugitives on another route, by way of Spartansburg, Greenville and Mercer County, Ohio, to Sandusky. From this place they were shipped across the lake to Fort Malden, Canada. Jim's opinions, as he had expressed them to his master, now underwent a sudden change. He liked the country and the people, and thought that he could make a living not only for himself, but for his family. As to the abolitionists along the route, he thought they were the best people in the world. Instead of cheating the poor fugitives by getting their services without pay, they fed and clothed them without charge, and would help them on their journey; often using their own horses and wagons, and traveling all night with the fugitives. A few years after I had the pleasure of seeing Jim and his family in their comfortable home in Canada. Jim said he hoped God would forgive him for telling his master so many lies. He said he felt no feelings of homesickness, no longings for massa and the old plantation in Kentucky.

ROBERT BURREL.

A colored man, who gave his name as Robert Burrel, came to my house, seeking employment. He said he had been working several months at Flat Rock, in Henry County, but that his employer there had no work for him during the winter, and had recommended him to call on me. He said he had been brought up in Tennessee, but, thinking he had rather live in a free State, had come to Indiana a few months before. I liked his sober and intelligent appearance, and gave him employment in my porkhouse. I found him to be a deeply religious man and a most faithful and trustworthy servant. He was pleasant in his manner and speech, but was never heard to indulge in loud laughter. He seemed to have some serious subject on his mind, over which he was constantly brooding. If any one inquired particularly concerning his past life, he evaded the questions, and it was not until he had been in my employment for several months that he ventured to tell me the true state of his case. He was a runaway slave, and belonged to a man living in East Tennessee. He had married a free colored woman living there, and was as happy as it was possible for a slave to be, until he learned that his master was about to sell him to a trader who would take him to the far South. Then he ran away, leaving his wife and two children, and made his way to Indiana. His object was to gain enough money to buy his freedom and send for his family. He had been working with this end in view, but had kept his fears, hopes and anxieties in his own heart, lest he should be betrayed and lose the liberty that was so sweet. His story gained my sympathy, and I promised to aid him in any way I could. We often consulted together concerning his wife and two little boys. He represented his wife as being a Christian woman, and said that she was a member of the Methodist Church; to which he also belonged. She had promised to remain faithful to him, and to await patiently the result of his effort. I discouraged his attempt to buy himself, as it would take several years of hard work, and might then be a failure. I advised him to save all the money he could, and perhaps some way would open by which his wife and children could get to him, and go with him to Canada. But he felt very timid about sending for his wife and children before securing his own freedom, for he feared they would be tracked and his whereabouts discovered.

I continued him in my employ, putting him in my linseed oil mill, and paying him extra wages for his care and good management. In conversation with him, one day, I found that he knew something about John Rankin, a noted abolitionist and Presbyterian clergyman, formerly of East Tennessee, but then living at Ripley, Ohio.

I wrote to friend Rankin, giving the outlines of Robert's story, and asking him if he thought the wife and two children could be brought to Ohio without arousing the suspicions of Robert's mas-

13

ter and leading to his detection. He wrote me, in reply, that some of his family were going to East Tennessee soon, on a visit to their relatives there, and he thought they could have an interview with Robert's wife, and arrange to have her and the children removed to Ohio. I kept up a correspondence with him on the subject, and ascertaining that it would cost about forty dollars to move the woman and children to Ohio, I sent him that amount, to be applied for that purpose. I sent a message to be delivered to Robert's wife, telling her that if she would come to Ripley, Ohio, she could gain information of her husband. The message was delivered to her by the friends of John Rankin, but they did not succeed in gaining her confidence, and she would not come to Ohio, fearing that it was a scheme to betray her husband. So the project failed at that time, and John Rankin returned the money I had sent him ; but two years later we renewed our efforts, and succeeded in bringing the woman and her children to Ripley. From this place, lest somebody should have traced them from Tennessee, hoping to learn the whereabouts of Robert, they were taken to Cincinnati. Soon afterward they were brought to my house in Newport, and there was a joyful meeting between husband and wife, after a separation of four years.

I purchased for them a little home in Newport, which Robert paid for by his work, and here they lived happily several years, with none to molest or make them afraid. When the fugitive slave law of

1850 was passed, they left and went to Canada for greater security.

THE STORY OF ELIZA HARRIS.

Eliza Harris, of "Uncle Tom's Cabin" notoriety, the slave woman who crossed the Ohio River, near Ripley, on the drifting ice with her, child in her arms, was sheltered under our roof and fed at our table for several days. This was while we lived at Newport, Indiana, which is six miles west of the State line of Ohio. To elude the pursuers who were following closely on her track, she was sent across to our line of the Underground Railroad.

The story of this slave woman, so graphically told by Harriet Beecher Stowe in "Uncle Tom's Cabin," will, no doubt, be remembered by every reader of that deeply interesting book. The cruelties of slavery depicted in that remarkable work are not overdrawn. The stories are founded on facts that really occurred, real names being wisely withheld, and fictitious names and imaginary conversations often inserted. From the fact that Eliza Harris was sheltered at our house several days, it was generally believed among those acquainted with the circumstances that I and my wife were the veritable Simeon and Rachel Halliday, the Quaker couple alluded to in "Uncle Tom's Cabin." I will give a short sketch of the fugitive's story, as she related it.

She said she was a slave from Kentucky, the property of a man who lived a few miles back from the Ohio River, below Ripley, Ohio. Her master and mistress were kind to her, and she had a com-

fortable home, but her master got into some pecuniary difficulty, and she found that she and her only
child were to be separated. She had buried two
children, and was doubly attached to the one she
had left, a bright, promising child, over two years
old. When she found that it was to be taken from
her, she was filled with grief and dismay, and resolved to make her escape that night if possible.
She watched her opportunity, and when darkness
had settled down and all the family had retired to
sleep, she started with her child in her arms and
walked straight toward the Ohio River. She knew
that it was frozen over, at that season of the year,
and hoped to cross without difficulty on the ice, but
when she reached its banks at daylight, she found
that the ice had broken up and was slowly drifting
in large cakes. She ventured to go to a house near
by, where she was kindly received and permitted to
remain through the day. She hoped to find some
way to cross the river the next night, but there
seemed little prospect of any one being able to
cross in safety, for during the day the ice became
more broken and dangerous to cross. In the evening she discovered pursuers nearing the house, and
with desperate courage she determined to cross the
river, or perish in the attempt. Clasping her child
in her arms she darted out of the back door and ran
toward the river, followed by her pursuers, who had
just dismounted from their horses when they caught
sight of her. No fear or thought of personal danger entered Eliza's mind, for she felt that she had
rather be drowned than to be captured and sepa-

rated from her child. Clasping her babe to her bosom with her left arm, she sprang on to the first cake of ice, then from that to another and another. Some times the cake she was on would sink beneath her weight, then she would slide her child on to the next cake, pull herself on with her hands, and so continue her hazardous journey. She became wet to the waist with ice water and her hands were benumbed with cold, but as she made her way from one cake of ice to another, she felt that surely the Lord was preserving and upholding her, and that nothing could harm her.

When she reached the Ohio side, near Ripley, she was completely exhausted and almost breathless. A man, who had been standing on the bank watching her progress with amazement and expecting every moment to see her go down, assisted her up the bank. After she had recovered her strength a little he directed her to a house on the hill, in the outskirts of town. She made her way to the place, and was kindly received and cared for. It was not considered safe for her to remain there during the night, so, after resting a while and being provided with food and dry clothing, she was conducted to a station on the Underground Railroad, a few miles farther from the river. The next night she was forwarded on from station to station to our house in Newport, where she arrived safely and remained several days.

Other fugitives arrived in the meantime, and Eliza and her child were sent with them, by the Greenville branch of the Underground Railroad, to Sandusky, Ohio. They reached that place in safety, and crossed the lake to Canada, locating finally at Chatham, Canada West.

In the summer of 1854 I was on a visit to Canada, accompanied by my wife and daughter, and Laura S. Haviland, of Michigan. At the close of a meeting which we attended, at one of the colored churches, a woman came up to my wife, seized her hand, and exclaimed: "How are you, Aunt Katie? God bless you!" etc. My wife did not recognize her, but she soon called herself to our remembrance by referring to the time she was at our house in the days of her distress, when my wife gave her the name of Eliza Harris, and by relating other particulars. We visited her at her house while at Chatham, and found her comfortable and contented.

Many other fugitives came and spoke to us, whom we did not recognize or remember until they related some incident that recalled them to mind. Such circumstances occurred in nearly every neighborhood we visited in Canada. Hundreds who had been sheltered under our roof and fed at our table, when fleeing from the land of whips and chains, introduced themselves to us and referred to the time, often fifteen or twenty years before, when we had aided them.

On the first day of August, 1854, we went, with a large company from Windsor, to attend a celebration of the West India emancipation. The meeting was held in a dense settlement of fugitives, about eight miles south of Windsor. Several public speakers from Detroit were in our party. A plat-

SAM, THE ELOQUENT SLAVE. 151

form had been erected in a grove near the school-house, where Laura S. Haviland had established a school for fugitives. The day was fine, and there was a large crowd of colored people, who had come from various settlements to hear the speaking. Here we met quite a number of those whom we had helped on their way to freedom, and the gratitude they expressed was quite affecting. One old white-headed man came to my wife, and said he wanted to get hold of her hand. She reached her hand to him, and while he held it, he said: "Don't you 'member me, Misses?"

She looked at him closely, and said: "No, I believe I do not remember thee."

Then the old negro said: "La me! Misses, don't you 'member when dey was close after me to take me an' you hid me in de feather bed and saved me? Why, bress your heart! if it hadn't been for you I should nebber been here. It's more dan twenty years ago, and my head is white, but I hasn't forgot dat time."

She shook his hand heartily, and said: "Now I remember thee."

At Amherstburg, generally called Fort Malden, and many other places, we met with many, both men and women, whom we had assisted on their way to liberty, and their expressions of thankfulness and regard were very gratifying to us.

SAM, THE ELOQUENT SLAVE.

The subject of this sketch was the property of a man living near Lexington, Kentucky. He had a wife and several children whom he was permitted to visit frequently, was well treated by his master, and had no fear of being sold away from his family; so his condition was a very favorable one, compared with that of many other slaves. But this state of security came suddenly to an end. The master died and the heirs decided to sell Sam, but as he was very powerful, and a dangerous man to deal with when his spirit was roused, no one dared to take possession of him and tell him that he was sold away from his family. What could not be done by force was accomplished by stratagem. Sam was sent into the jail to take a box of candles, and, all unsuspecting, walked into the trap. Several men were hidden behind the door, and leaping out suddenly, they knocked him down, overpowered and bound him. He then learned that he was bought by a negro trader, who intended taking him to the South. Just before the coffle started, Sam's wife was permitted to come to the jail to bid him goodby, but her distress was so great and she wept so loudly that she was hurried out and taken away without having been able to say a word. Sam was taken to Mississippi and sold, but after several months managed to escape, and after much difficulty and many hardships found his way back to Lexington, Kentucky, where he hoped to find some one who would purchase him and allow him to remain near his family, but in this effort he did not succeed.

Hearing that pursuers were on his track, he left that neighborhood, and succeeded in making his way to Newport, Indiana, where he arrived in the dead of winter, in a destitute and suffering condition. I persuaded him to remain till better weather, when the roads would be open and traveling easier, and he remained till spring, I in the meantime furnishing him with employment at good wages. It may be in place here to mention that the abolitionists were frequently accused, by pro-slavery people, of availing themselves of the labor of the fugitive slaves by employing them several months on the promise of good wages, then raising the alarm that the masters were in pursuit, and hustling them off on the road to Canada without paying the wages due them. It is almost needless to say that this accusation was false. During that winter there was a monthly prayer-meeting, held in the Wesleyan Chapel at Newport, on behalf of the slaves, and I asked Sam to attend one of these meetings with me. He at first hesitated, so fearful was he of being betrayed, but on being assured that there was no danger, he consented to go.

It seemed strange to him that white people should pray for slaves ; he had never heard of such a thing before. As others were telling stories of the sufferings of slaves, I suggested to Sam that he should give his experience. To this he consented, with reluctance, and I rose and informed the meeting that a fugitive slave was sitting by my side, whose story I was sure would be interesting to all present. Sam then rose from his seat and gave a short history of his suffering, together with a vivid description of the horrors of slavery, and so interested his hearers that they expressed a desire to hear him again.

He was prevailed upon to speak another time, when a larger number would have an opportunity to hear him, and a meeting was appointed for this purpose. When the evening came the church was crowded. Sam was conducted to the pulpit by the minister and myself. We made short introductory speeches, then Sam spoke for more than an hour to the attentive and deeply interested audience. They had not expected to hear good language from a slave who had had no educational advantages, and were surprised to find his speech resembling that of a practiced orator. Sam had, during the life of his indulgent master, had frequent opportunities of hearing public speeches in Lexington, and this experience, which had been a sort of education to him, added to his native eloquence, enabled him to hold his audience spellbound, while he depicted in glowing words the cruelty of slavery and the manifold sufferings of the slaves. He then gave an account of his own trials, and pictured in a touching manner the scene of his wife's separation from him when he was bound in jail, and finished with an appeal to the audience so full of pathos that the heart of every one was touched, and nearly all his hearers were melted to tears.

Some of them declared afterward that they thought Henry Clay could not surpass him in eloquence. Shortly after this the United Brethren held a Conference in Newport, and wishing to have Sam address them, a deputation called at my house, to speak with him on the subject. They were shown into the parlor, where a fire was burning, and as I sat talking with them, Sam came in with an armful of wood to replenish the fire.

One of the deputation said: "Is this the man?" and I answered, "Yes;" then remarked to Sam that these men wished to see him. Sam went out quickly and did not return. When I went to look for him, I found him outside the kitchen door, with a large butcher knife in his hand, ready to defend himself. He thought that the men had come to take him, and was determined to sell his life or liberty as dearly as possible. When the matter was explained, he went in to see the men, and afterward spoke for them. In the spring he was sent on to Canada, where he was out of the slave-dealer's power forever.

PREJUDICE AGAINST COLOR.

A white man from Massachusetts moved with his family to Missouri, bought a farm and settled there. One of his neighbors had a slave, a young man nearly white, who was willed free at a certain age. The time of his bondage had nearly expired when the gentleman from Massachusetts hired him of his master, and after he became free, he continued in the same service. He proved to be a very intelligent, industrious and trusty man, and his employer soon gave him the entire control of the farm and all affairs of out-door business. The family did not have good health in their new home, and becoming dissatisfied with the locality resolved to return to Massachusetts.

The farm was sold and the other property disposed of, and they were about to start eastward, when the husband and father sickened and died. A short time before he breathed his last, he called his servant to his bedside and requested him to take charge of his wife and two daughters and see them safely back to their home in the East.

The man promised faithfully that he would fulfill this request, and soon after the funeral was over the little party started. It was before the time of railroads or turnpikes in the West, and they went in a wagon, drawn by four horses, the colored man driving the team, and attending to all matters connected with the journey. Passing over the prairies of Illi-. nois and Indiana, they found the mud very deep and the roads almost impassable, it being late in the fall, and when they reached Indianapolis they concluded to remain there during the winter. The young man found employment with his team, and supported the family by his work.

The two daughters were well educated and accomplished young ladies, and when they became known were greeted as acquisitions to the society of the place. They were members of the Presbyterian Church and taught in the Sabbath-schools of that denomination, and being good singers were invited to join the choir.

The mulatto man in their family, who was really almost white and possessed none of the negro features, was very gentlemanly in his appearance and manners, and so kind and attentive to them and thoughtful for their welfare, that one of the daughters became very much attached to him. He had long loved her in secret, without daring to speak, but now, finding that his love was reciprocated, saw no reason why they should not be married.

The mother gave her consent, and accompanied her prospective son-in-law to obtain the marriage license.

On the evening of the wedding, the news spread through the city that a negro had married a white woman, and an infuriated mob filled the street in front of the house, and with hoots and yells proceeded to search for the man—several shades lighter than some of themselves—who dared to marry a white woman. The bridgroom escaped by a back way and fled to the woods for safety, as if he were a fugitive slave. Not finding him, the mob dragged the bride out of the house and rode her on a rail through the streets, as a demonstration of the popular indignation. The bridgroom remained concealed in the woods for awhile, finding no way to communicate with his wife, and not daring to venture back to get his clothes or to say good-by. He was in deep distress and knew not what to do.

The city was in an uproar of excitement, and the indignant citizens were searching the houses of the colored people for this terrible criminal who had committed so great a sin as to marry a woman a shade lighter than himself, and that with the full approbation of her mother and sister. It was evident that he could not show himself in Indianapolis again with safety. He moved eastward and got into a colored settlement at Flat Rock, Henry County, from which place he was directed to my house at Newport.

The news of the marriage flew all over the State. The newspapers were full of it, and the public sentiment was aroused. The dreadful prospect of amalgamation loomed before the people like an impending curse. It must be put a stop to at once. The Legislature was in session at Indianapolis at the time this occurred, and they took immediate action concerning it. They passed a law placing a heavy penalty on any clergyman or magistrate who should marry a white person to one in whose veins there was a drop of colored blood. Several members of the Legislature, and a number of prominent citizens visited the offending family and urged them to apply for a divorce.

The poor girl was almost crazy with trouble, having been disgraced by being ridden on a rail, and alarmed by the threats of the outrageous mob, and her mother and sister were also alarmed, and finally, through fear, they yielded to the threats and persuasions of their visitors, and signed a petition for a divorce. The Legislature at once divorced the couple, and the young lady was declared free from the disgraceful alliance. It was found to be a very nice point in carrying out the new law, to detect the drop of colored blood. No minister or magistrate was safe in marrying any couple. The law would not work, and was repealed the following year.

Many people blamed me for taking in Charley, the young colored man, and harboring one whom they regarded as a great criminal. I gave him employment, and he remained with me for several months. He proved to be quiet, orderly and industrious, and very gentlemanly in all his ways, yet many of the women in our town and neighborhood were as much afraid of him as if he were a murderer. My wife and a few other women had no such foolish fear of poor Charley, but sympathized with him in his troubles. Soon after he came to my house, I called a council of a few of my particular friends, those who stood by me and sustained me in all my anti-slavery efforts. We were not in favor of amalgamation and did not encourage the intermarriage or mixing of the races, but we were in favor of justice and right-dealing with all colors. This seemed to be the united feeling of those in council. We looked upon such marriages as a matter of choice with the contracting parties, and not as a crime or a sin. Many reasons might be given why we did not encourage such a choice, but we did not criminate those who had made the choice.

The object of this council was to take into consideration the propriety of sending a deputation to Indianapolis to learn the true state of things there, to ascertain the feelings of Charley's wife and her mother toward him; and to obtain his clothing, which he had been compelled to leave behind in his hasty flight.

Charley was in deep mental distress, and needed the counsel and sympathy of his friends. He was not sensible of having committed any crime in marrying the woman he loved, and who professed to love him in return, but all his hopes of happiness were destroyed, and he was regarded as a criminal. He was likewise deeply concerned for the welfare of the family that had been placed in his care by the dying husband and father.

George Shugart volunteered to go to Indianapolis, and get Charley's clothes and learn the feelings and wishes of the family. It was just at the time that the Legislature had taken action in the case, and the family were so confused and alarmed that they could make no definite plans for the future. They thought it best to remain where they were until spring. The horses and wagon had been sold, at a heavy sacrifice, and they had no means of continuing their journey then. So the messenger brought little comfort to Charley. He remained in my employ until late in the spring, when he learned that the mother and her two daughters had left Indianapolis and gone to Cincinnati. As soon as he received this information he went to Cincinnati, where he joined them. Soon after the whole party disappeared from Cincinnati. No one knew where they went, but it was supposed that they returned to Massachusetts, and that the husband and wife lived together unmolested.

AUNT RACHEL.

The subject of this sketch, one of those good old darkey aunties whom we have all known or heard of, was brought up in Lexington, Kentucky. She was a slave, a house servant, and had a kind and indulgent master and mistress, to whom she was much attached. She had the principal charge

of household affairs. Her husband belonged to
another person in the neighborhood, but was often
permitted to visit her. They had a family of several children, and were as happily situated as it was
possible for slaves to be. They knew that they
were liable to be separated and sold away from each
other, and this disturbed their happiness. At last
the dreaded misfortune came to them. The husband
was sold, and taken to the far South, and the wife
never saw him nor heard from him afterward. This
was a terrible shock to Aunt Rachel, and had it not
been for her children, she said she would have
prayed to die. But for their sake she bore her
grief, not thinking that she would ever be called
upon to part from them, or to experience deeper
pangs of sorrow than those she had already known.
She knew not what was in store for her. Two years
afterward her old master and mistress died, and she
and her children were sold at public sale. The
children were bid off by citizens of Lexington, but
Aunt Rachel was sold to a Southern slave-trader.
Now, indeed, came trouble. No one but a mother
who has been separated from the children she loves
can understand the depth of her distress, or sympathize with the anguish of her heart. Aunt Rachel
was torn away from her children and taken South in
a gang of slaves, which the trader had bought for
the Southern market. In Mississippi she was sold
to a cotton planter, and immediately set to work in
the cotton field. She had never been accustomed
to out-door work, and could not keep up with the
other cotton pickers. For this she was cruelly pun-

14

ished, and her allowance of food reduced. Finding
that her strength was failing her under this hard
treatment, she resolved to run away, and try ·to
make her way back to her old Kentucky home.
She hoped, if she lived to get there, to prevail on
some of her white friends. at Lexington to buy her,
and thus enable her to stay near her children. She
thought of the great distance she must traverse, and
of the dangers and hardships of such an undertaking,
but she said to herself: "It is death to stay here,
and I had rather die in the attempt to get away."

It was now the beginning of summer, and she
thought she could live on berries and fruits the
most of the time. She slipped off one night and
made good headway during the hours of darkness,
hiding in the cane-brakes when daylight appeared.
The next night she ventured to the negro quarters
of a plantation, and got some provisions. Her long
and toilsome journey was attended with much
danger and suffering, and occupied the most of the
summer. She finally reached her old home in Lex-
ingion, Kentucky, and secreted herself with a friend.
She did not dare yet to make herself known to
her children, lest it should lead to her detection,
but sometimes could hardly control herself when
she saw her youngest child, a little girl three years
old, playing in the adjoining yard. She remained
in concealment for some time, while· her colored
friends tried to find some one in Lexington who
would purchase her. They were unsuccessful in
their attempts, and it was deemed unsafe for her to
remain longer in the place, as it had by this time

become known to a number of the citizens of Lexington that she had escaped from her master and was there. She thought she would start northward and try to reach Canada, but while her colored friends were making arrangements for her journey to the North on the Underground Railroad, she received the alarming intelligence that her master from Mississippi had arrived in Lexington in pursuit of her. He had had no clue to her whereabouts, but judged that in her flight she would be guided by that instinct which leads one across rivers and mountains to the spot endeared by associations of home and kindred.

Soon after reaching Lexington he learned that she was secreted somewhere in the town. He offered a reward for her capture, and a diligent search commenced. The police were on the alert, and poor Aunt Rachel was soon captured and dragged to jail for safe keeping. Her master was greatly incensed because she had run away, and put him to so much trouble and expense in pursuing her, and was very abusive and threatening in his language to her. He gave her a few keen cuts with his whip, as tokens of what was in store for her, and told her he would have his pay out of her when he got home ; he would double her task, and if she did not perform it he would cut the hide off of her with his whip.

Aunt Rachel trembled but made no reply; she knew that she was in his power. Handcuffs were put on her wrists, and a chain with a heavy ball fastened around her ankle. Thus ironed, she lay in the jail for more than a week, while her master was engaged in buying a small company of slaves for his plantation in Mississippi. When ready to start South, he hired a wagon in which to transport his slaves to Louisville, at which point he intended to put them aboard a down-river boat. Aunt Rachel was placed in the wagon, with her heavy irons on. After a wearisome day's travel, they stopped in front of a tavern, where they intended to spend the night. It was quite dark, for they had been compelled to travel some time after night-fall in order to reach a place where they could find quarters. While her master went into the house to see about getting entertainment, Aunt Rachel gathered up the ball and chain in her manacled hands, slipped out of the hind end of the wagon, and slid down into a deep ravine near the road. She crouched under the side of the bank and lay as still as death. She was soon missed, and the search for her began. Her master, and those he called to his assistance, ran in every direction, with lighted lanterns, looking for her, but they overlooked her hiding-place. She was so near, almost under the wagon, that they did not think of searching where she lay. She remained perfectly still, except the tumultuous throbbing of her heart; and this she thought would surely betray her when those in search passed near her hiding-place.

Finally, all became quiet, and the search seemed given up for the night. Then Aunt Rachel gathered up her chain and crawled off into the woods, making her way through the darkness as fast as her fetters would allow. She did not venture to follow any road or beaten path, but wandered on through the woods, as best she could, for two or three miles. Being quite weary under the weight of her irons, she stopped to rest. It was cool weather, late in the fall, and she soon felt chilly. Looking about, she discovered some hogs lying snugly in a leafy bed under the side of a large log, and frightening them away, she crept into their warm bed. She now felt comfortable, and soon fell into a refreshing sleep that lasted an hour or two. When she awoke she felt quite refreshed, and ready to pursue her journey. Her situation was indeed forlorn. She had eluded the grasp of her master, but manacled as she was, how could she ever make her way to freedom and safety? Must she not perish of hunger in the lonely woods? How could she free herself from her hand fetters, and from the heavy chain that was chafing her ankle and making it sore? As she reflected on these questions, distress filled her mind, and she wept. She knew of no friend but God, and she prayed to him in this. hour of need; she asked him to guide and help her. She seemed to feel his presence with her, in answer to her petitions, and a glow of comfort warmed her heart. She moved on, to look for a safe place where she might hide during the day, and came to a small stream of water, on whose banks were a number of large stones. She placed two stones close together and laid her chain across them, then lifting another stone in her fettered hands, she managed by repeated blows and by frequently turning it, to break the chain; thus freeing herself of the greater part of it, and of the heavy ball. Several links, however, were left hanging to the band riveted around her ankle; from this she could not free herself. She lay in the woods during the day, and at night ventured to a house where she saw some colored people. She was kindly received, and furnished with food. The man succeeded in getting her handcuffs off, which was a great relief to her, but having no file, he was unable to relieve her of the iron band on her leg. This colored brother gave her directions for her journey, and put her on a route that would reach the Ohio River, opposite Madison, Indiana. He even ventured to take two of his master's horses out of the field, and help her on her way several miles.

The next night her progress was slow on account of her manacled ankle, which by this time was swollen and very painful. Some time before daylight she ventured to approach a hut, which was situated near the road she was traveling. She discovered a negro man kindling a fire, and made herself known to him. He received her kindly, and his wife ministered to her needs. She remained secreted during the day at this hut, and at night felt strengthened and ready to pursue her journey. The man had a file, and succeeded in filing off the rivet, and loosening the band from her leg. He then applied what simple remedies he had at hand, and succeeded in some measure in assuaging the pain and swelling of the ankle. At night this kind friend helped her on her way, and conducted her to the house of a colored man, who lived near the Ohio River, below Madison. This man was a slave, but had a kind and indulgent master, who allowed him the use of a skiff, and permitted him to go over the river to trade. Aunt Rachel prevailed upon him to take her across the river that night, and he landed her near Madison, directing her how to find a settlement of free colored people near that place. At this settlement she fell into the hands of a trusty colored man, who lived about ten miles out in the country, where he owned a good farm, and was comfortably situated. Aunt Rachel found a quiet home at his house, which was fortunate for her, as she was now almost unable to travel. The chafing of the iron band around her ankle had caused inflammation, and made a very painful sore. She was able, however, to move about enough to do housework. She remained at this place all winter, unmolested. In the spring a fugitive was captured in the neighborhood, and Aunt Rachel and her friends became alarmed for her safety. She was put on the Underground Railroad, and brought to our house at Newport. She was anxious to remain with us for awhile, hoping that by some means she might hear from her children, concerning whom she was very anxious. She thought she would be safe from pursuit, for her master in Mississippi would not be likely to spend much more time and money looking after her. My wife needed help at that time, and agreed to hire her for a few weeks. We soon found her to be one of the best housekeepers and cooks we had ever employed. She was careful and trustworthy, and exemplary in all her ways. We became much attached to her; indeed, the neighbors and all who knew her had a great deal of respect and liking for Aunt Rachel. Every one who heard her story, as she related it in simple yet thrilling language, felt a deep interest in her case. She staid with us more than six months, and would have remained longer had it not been considered unsafe. Some Kentuckians were scouting about through our neighborhood looking for fugitives. They made their headquarters at Richmond, at a hotel which was a well-known resort for negro hunters. Aunt Rachel became alarmed, and we thought it best for her to go on to Canada, where she would be safe. A good opportunity in the way of company for the greater part the way offered just then, very fortunately.

A committee of men and women Friends, appointed by New Garden Quarterly Meeting to attend the opening of a meeting at Young's Prairie, Michigan, were just about starting on this mission. Aunt Rachel was acquainted with most of them, and wished to accompany them, and they were very willing to engage in Underground Railroad work, though the Quarterly Meeting had not appointed them to that service.

We provided Aunt Rachel with warm and comfortable clothing for her journey to the North. A well-filled trunk was placed in one of the carriages, and Aunt Rachel took her seat by one of the women Friends. She presented the appearance of a sedate and comely Quaker woman, quite as suitable to be appointed on the committee as any of the company. Aunt Rachel traveled very agreeably with this committee to Young's Prairie, Cass County, Michigan.

She remained at the Friends' settlement there for several days, and was then sent on the mail coach to Detroit. At that city she called on some people to whom we had directed her, and they sent her across to Canada. She found employment in the homes of white families in Windsor and Norwich, where she remained for several months. Then she married a respectable colored man by the name of Keys, who owned a comfortable little home. Here I met with her eight years afterward, when on a visit to the fugitives in Canada, in company with William Beard. The meeting was very unexpected to Aunt Rachel, as she had no previous knowledge of our arrival in the country. We rode up to her little home, and hitched our horses at the gate, some distance from the house. Aunt Rachel was in the yard at the time, picking up kindling wood. She stood still a moment until she recognized me, then dropped her wood and rushed to meet me, shouting and praising God. She exclaimed: "Is it possible the good Lord has sent you here?" then, with tears running down her black cheeks, she threw her arms around me, and asked many blessings on my head. Her emotions and manifestations of joy at meeting me quite unmanned me for a time. She led us into the house, which was snug and comfortable, and introduced us to her husband. He appeared to be a very friendly, kindhearted man. Aunt Rachel informed me that she had suffered a great deal with her leg, where she had worn that cruel chain. At one time she lay for several months under treatment of some of the

15

best doctors in Detroit. They decided that to save her life the limb must be amputated. She consented that the operation should be performed, and the doctors came with their surgical instruments, but her husband would not give his consent. He believed that she could get well without losing her limb. The doctors yielded, the limb was spared, and she did get well.

A SLAVE-HUNTER OUTWITTED.

The story that I am about to relate may, in some of its particulars, seem improbable or even impossible, to any reader not acquainted with the workings of the southern division of the Underground Railroad. That two young slave girls could successfully make their escape from a Southern State and travel hundreds of miles, hiding in the day, in thickets and other secluded places, and traveling at night, crossing rivers and swamps, and passing undiscovered through settlements, appears more like a story of romance than one of sober reality. But I will not test the reader's credulity by leaving this story unexplained; I will give a few items regarding the manner of the escape of many slaves from the South. I have always contended that the Underground Railroad, so called, was a Southern institution; that it had its origin in the slave States. It was, however, conducted on quite a different principle south of Mason and Dixon's line, from what it was on this side. South of the line money, in most cases, was the motive; north, we generally worked on principle. For the sake of money, people in the South would help slaves to escape and convey them across the line, and by this means, women with their children, and young girls, like the subjects of this story, were enabled to reach the North. They were hidden in wagons, or stowed away in secret places on steamboats, or conducted on foot through the country, by shrewd managers who traveled at night and knew what places to avoid.

Free colored people who had relatives in slavery were willing to contribute to the utmost of their means, to aid in getting their loved ones out of bondage; just as we would do if any of our loved ones were held in thralldom. It was by some line of the Southern Underground Railroad that two slave girls, living in Tennessee, managed to escape and reach Cabin Creek, Randolph County, Indiana, where lived their grandparents and most of their near relatives, who were free.

This neighborhood was settled principally by free colored people who had purchased government land in forty or eighty acre lots; in some instances a quarter section—one hundred and sixty acres—had been entered. A dense settlement of free colored people had formed at Cabin Creek, and a good school had been established there, under the auspices of New Garden Quarterly Meeting of Friends.

Near the center of the colony lived the grandparents of the two girls mentioned, and there the girls staid, after their long and perilous journey, enjoying their newly gained liberty, and hoping that their master would never learn of their whereabouts. But they were not destined to dwell here in safety.

Their master had come to Richmond; ostensibly to look about the neighborhood and buy cattle, but really to gain some trace of his slave property. He hired spies and sent them into different neighborhoods, Cabin Creek among the rest, and thus the girls were discovered. When the master learned that his two slave girls were so near, he felt as if they were already in his power, but when he heard more concerning Cabin Creek neighborhood and the character of the colored people there, he began to think it might not be so easy to effect a capture. When a slave-hunter came to Cabin Creek, the people banded together to protect the fugitive he was after, and as they were very determined in their defense it was a difficult matter to capture the slave. They had prearranged signals for such occasions, and the alarm soon called the people together.

The master of the two girls obtained a writ and placed it in the hands of an officer, then gathered a company of roughs from Richmond, Winchester and other neighborhoods, and rode out to Cabin Creek at the head of a large company of armed men. They marched to the cabin where the two girls were, and surrounded it.

The alarm was given as soon as the company were seen approaching, and a boy mounted a horse and rode off at full speed to spread the alarm. He was fired at by some of the company, and a rifle ball grazed his arm, making a slight flesh wound. This only hastened his speed and increased the excitement. The grandfather of the two girls was away from home, but the brave old grandmother seized a corn-cutter and placed herself in the only door of the cabin, defying the crowd and declaring that she would cut the first man in two who undertook to cross the threshold. Thus she kept the slave-hunter and his posse at bay, while a large crowd of colored people collected. Quite a number of white people came also, some out of curiosity or sympathy with the master, and others who sympathized with the fugitives. It is said that there were more than two hundred people gathered around the cabin. The sound of the horn, and the message of the boy, had brought together most of the colored people in the settlement. An uncle of the slave girls, who lived near by, seeing the crowd as they rode up, placed himself near his mother, on the outside of the door, and several other sturdy negroes stood by his side.

He was a shrewd sharp fellow, with a fair education, and kept his presence of mind under the exciting circumstances. He demanded to see the writ, and it was handed to him by the officer. He read it over carefully, and tried to pick flaws in it. He denied that it gave them any authority to enter that house to search for property. The laws of Indiana did not recognize human beings as property until they had been proven to be such, and that was a difficult thing to do. He said that he doubted very much whether the man who had obtained this writ to arrest two slave girls could prove them to be his property. Furthermore, he did not believe the girls were in that house. He extended the debate with the master as long as possible, and in the meantime several colored people had been permitted to pass in and out under the sharp edge of the old woman's corn-cutter, but no white person had been admitted.

While the debate was going on, arrangements were being made, both outdoors and indoors, for the escape of the girls. The uncle understood all this perfectly, and he was doing his part toward success, by prolonging the palaver. The girls dressed in boys' clothes, and put on slouch hats; then, while the debate outside grew warm and excitement began to run high, and the slave-hunters to declare that they would enter the house, in spite of the corn-cutter and other obstructions, the girls passed out of the door with other negroes, and made their way through the crowd. Two fleet horses, with light but very capable riders, stood near the side of a large log, screened from the sight of the crowd by some tall bushes. The girls stepped quickly on the log and sprang, one on each horse, behind the riders, and were soon out of sight. When the uncle knew that the girls were at a safe distance, he began to moderate and proposed a compromise. Speaking in a whisper to his mother, he appeared to be consulting with her on the subject, and finally said, that if the master of the girls would agree to give them a fair trial at Winchester, he and his posse would be allowed to enter the house peaceably. This was agreed to, and the grandmother laid aside her weapon of defense, and appeared calm and subdued. The master and his posse rushed in to seize the girls, and those outside, who could not see into the house, listened to hear the girls' screams of terror and pleadings for mercy while their master bound them. But they heard nothing of the kind, only oaths and exclamations from the men as they searched about the cabin and up in the loft. The hunters were baffled; the girls were not to be found. The darkies seemed in a good humor, and there was a general display of white teeth in broad grins. Some of the white folks also seemed amused, and inclined to make sport of the misfortune of the master. It was no laughable matter to him—to be duped by negroes and to lose such valuable property as these girls were, either of whom would soon be worth one thousand dollars. Some in the crowd were unfeeling enough to jest at his loss, and to advise him to look around and see if there was not a hole in the ground where the girls had been let down to the Underground Railroad.

When the master fully realized how he had been outwitted, his wrath knew no bounds, but his hired assistants tried to comfort him with the thought that they could soon ferret out the fugitives, and promised to make a thorough search through all the abolition neighborhoods.

The girls were taken a short distance on the Winchester road; then through by-ways and cross-roads they were brought through the Cherry Grove settlement of Friends to Newport, a distance of about twenty miles. The girls were much exhausted when they arrived at our house, having had a hard ride, part of the way in the night. After taking some nourishment, they were placed in a private room to rest during the remainder of the night, and were soon sound asleep. We did not apprehend any danger that night, as we supposed a vigorous search would be made at Cabin Creek and neighboring settlements, and that our town would not be searched till the hunt in the other localities had been prosecuted and proved fruitless.

Some time the next day, a messenger arrived at my house from Cabin Creek, and told us that after failing to find the girls at their grandfather's, the posse of pursuers had divided into several squads to search the different neighborhoods, and that one company were on their way to Newport. That afternoon several strangers were seen rambling about our village, inquiring for stray horses, and going abruptly into the houses of colored people living in the suburbs. It was not difficult to guess what was their real business. I was busy in my store when I learned of the conduct of these strangers, but went at once to the house and told my wife that negro hunters were in town, and that she must secrete the two girls. She was used to such business, and was not long in devising a plan. Taking the two girls, who had by this time been dressed in female apparel, into a bedroom, she hid them between the straw tick and feather tick, allowing them room for breathing, then made up the bed as usual, smoothed the counterpane and put on the pillows. But the girls were so excited and amused at the remembrance of how they outwitted massa, and of their ride, dressed in boys' clothes, and at their novel position, that they laughed and giggled until my wife had to separate them, and put one in another bed. I went back to my store and left Aunt Katy, as every one called my wife, to manage affairs at the house. If the searchers attempted to enter our house, she was to rattle the large dinner bell violently, and at this signal the neighbors would rush in, and I would get the proper officers and have the negro hunters arrested for attempting to enter my house without legal authority.

But these proceedings were not necessary. The hunters did not have courage enough to enter my house, though they knew it was a depot of the Underground Railroad. Hearing that threats were made against them in the village, they left without giving us any trouble.

We kept the girls very secluded for several weeks until the master had given up the search, and gone home. Then having other fugitives to forward to the North, we sent them altogether *via* the Greenville and Sandusky route to Canada, where they arrived in safety.

CHAPTER VI.

NEWPORT STORIES CONTINUED—SEVENTEEN FUGITIVES
—TWO SLAVE GIRLS FROM MARYLAND—ANECDOTE
OF A VISIT TO CINCINNATI—STORY OF LOUIS TAL-
BERT—JOHN WHITE.

THE largest company of slaves ever seated at
our table, at one time, numbered seventeen,
though we often had parties of from ten to fifteen.
The party referred to, arrived at our house about
dawn one morning, having been brought in two
covered wagons from Salem, a settlement of Friends
in Union County. The distance was about thirty
miles, and the journey occupied the most of the
night.

It was an interesting company, consisting of men
and women, all apparently able-bodied and in the
prime of life. They were of different complexions,
varying from light mulatto to coal black, and had
bright and intelligent expressions. They were all
from the same neighborhood, a locality in Kentucky,
some fifteen or twenty miles from the Ohio River,
but belonged to different masters.

For some time they had been planning to escape,
but had kept their own counsels, not venturing to
divulge their secrets to other slaves. A place of

rendezvous was agreed upon, and at the appointed time they repaired.to it, carrying small bundles of their best clothes which they had found opportunity to carry out previously and hide. One young man, who was engaged to be married, succeeded in getting his intended wife, a beautiful mulatto, from her master's place, and took her with him. Most of them had managed to save some money, and they found this of great service in helping them on their way. The leader of the party had made arrangements with a poor white man, living on the bank of the Ohio River, whom he knew to be trustworthy. This man owned a wood boat and a skiff, and promised for the consideration of a liberal sum of money to have his boat in waiting, on a certain night, at a secluded point, and to take the party across the river to a point on the Indiana shore, some miles above Madison.

At the time appointed, the party succeeded in getting together, and hastened to the river. Their white friend was in readiness for them, and landed them safely on the Indiana shore before daylight. They hurried into the woods, to find hiding-places among the hills and in ravines during the day, for they knew that they would be pursued, and that their masters would make great efforts to capture such valuable property.

The next night they left their hiding-places and moved cautiously northward, not daring to travel in the road, but making their way through corn-fields and across plantations. At one time, when they had just crossed a road and entered a corn-field in the river bottom, they heard the sound of horses' feet, in the road near by. Two or three men, who were riding ahead of the main party, saw the fugitives and gave the alarm. The pursuers instantly dismounted and rushed into the corn-field, but having to climb a high rail fence they did not gain on the runaways. The party of fugitives scattered, and fled rapidly through the wilderness of tall, full-bladed corn. The field they were in was large, and other corn-fields joined it, lying in the rich river bottom, so that they had the advantage of shelter all the way. The pursuers, fifteen or twenty in number, divided and rushed after them with guns in hand, calling on them to stop or they would be shot down. Some of the fugitives recognized the voices of their masters, but they heeded them not. They ran on with all their might, each one looking out for himself or herself. Several shots were fired at them as they ran, and they heard the bullets whistle through the corn around them. They outstripped their pursuers, and ran from one corn-field to another in the bottom land until they had gone two or three miles. Hearing no sound of their pursuers, they stopped to take breath and see if all their party were safe.

A few of them had kept in hearing of each other, and by a low whistle were soon brought together. More than half the company were still missing. They moved on, a short distance, very cautiously, and gave another whistle, which was responded to, and in a few minutes the young man and his intended wife and two other women joined. They repeated their whistle, but heard no response.

About half the company were now together, including all the women. It was near morning, and as they did not feel safe in the corn-fields, they resolved to make their way, if possible, to the woods among the hills, and hide there during the day.

They succeeded in this attempt, but just as they were entering the woods they were greatly alarmed by hearing, a little distance behind them, the report of several guns, fired in quick succession. They feared that their missing comrades had fallen into the hands of the enemy. They hastened forward in the woods, and concealed themselves in a thicket of young trees and bushes. Soon after daylight they were alarmed by hearing the sound of some one chopping with an ax near them. They cautiously reconnoitered, and found that it was a colored man chopping wood. One of the party ventured to approach him, and found him to be friendly. His house was not far off, but he did not think it safe to take them to it, as the hunters might come there to look for them. He conducted them to a safe hiding-place, and furnished them with food, of which they were greatly in need. They had lost their bundles in their flight through the corn-fields, and were thus deprived of their little stock of provision and spare clothing.

The next night their colored friend conducted them to a depot of the Underground Railroad, the Hicklin settlement, where fugitives were always kindly received and cared for, and helped on their way to other stations. Here they remained in concealment during the day, feeling great anxiety about their missing comrades—fearing that they had been captured and taken back to slavery. During the day, however, Hicklin, at whose house they were, learned that there were other fugitives in the vicinity, among his neighbors who were abolitionists, and when he went to ascertain the facts concerning them he found them to be the comrades of the party at his house. They had met with a free colored man who had conducted them to this neighborhood. Two of them had received gunshot wounds, which were very painful but not dangerous. Several hours after they had evaded the hunters in the corn-field, and while trying to make their way to the woods, they had come upon a party of the hunters who were lying in ambush, having dismounted from their horses and tied them in the bushes. The fugitives saw the horses, and instantly comprehending the situation, they started off at full speed and ran for life. The pursuers fired at them, but they did not stop, though one received a number of small shot in his back and shoulder, and the other was wounded by a rifle ball that passed through his clothes and made a gash several inches long in his side. They reached the woods and soon distanced their pursuers, and saw them no more.

The two companies were glad to meet again, and soon prepared to renew their journey to the North. Their friends at Hicklin settlement provided two wagons and transported them to the next station, and they were hurried on from station to station, traveling at night and hiding during the day, until they reached my house, as I have mentioned. On that morning my wife had risen first, and when she heard the two wagons drive up and stop, she opened the door. She knew the drivers, who were from Union County, and who had been at our house on similar errands before. She spoke to these conductors, and asked: "What have you got there?"

One of them replied: "All Kentucky."

"Well, bring all Kentucky in," she answered, then stepped back to our room and told me to get up, for all Kentucky had come. I sprang up and dressed quickly, and when I went out, I found the fugitives all seated in the room, my wife having welcomed them and invited them to take chairs and sit down. I said to one of the conductors:

"The train has brought some valuable looking passengers this time. How many have you?"

"Only seventeen this load," he replied.

"Well," I said, "seventeen full-grown darkies and two able-bodied Hoosiers are about as many as the cars can bear at one time. Now you may switch off and put your locomotives in my stable and let them blow off steam, and we will water and feed them."

My wife and our hired girl soon had breakfast prepared for the party, and the seventeen fugitives were all seated together around a long table in the dining-room. We assured them that they could partake of their food without fear of molestation, for they were now among friends, in a neighborhood of abolitionists, and a fugitive had never been captured in our town. Their countenances brightened at this assurance, and they seemed more at ease.

Several of our near neighbors came in to see this valuable property seated around our table, and estimated that, according to the owners' valuation, they were worth $17,000. Two of the company were still suffering from the wounds they had received. After breakfast, Dr. Way and Dr. Stanton were invited in to see the wounded fugitives. They took the two men to their office near by and examined them. They extracted a number of small shot from the back and shoulders of one, then dressed his wounds and the wound of the other, who had been struck by a rifle ball. The men then seemed comfortable, and were very thankful for this kind treatment.

This interesting company of fugitives remained two days at my house to rest and prepare for their journey northward. Having lost their bundles of clothing, as mentioned, many of them were in need of garments and shoes. These were furnished to them, and when all were made comfortable, I arranged for teams and suitable conductors to take them on to the next station. It was decided, for greater safety, to forward them *via* the Mississineway route, though that was not the most direct line to Canada. When all necessary arrangements were made, the fugitives left my house shortly after dark in two wagons drawn by good teams, and accompanied by suitable conductors. The station they were directed to reach that night was the house of John Bond, a well-known friend to the slave, who lived in a Friends' settlement on Cabin Creek. The distance was something over twenty miles, and as the road was new and rough, it would take them the most of the night to reach the station. The conductors returned the next day with the teams, saying they had arrived safely with the fugitives at the station and left them there. Early the next morning, after the fugitives had left my house, a messenger, who had been sent by Aquilla Jones, of Richmond, arrived at my house, and informed me that fifteen Kentuckians, in search of fugitive slaves, had come to Richmond the night before, and were stopping at the hotel of one L—— B——, who was a well-known friend to the slave-hunter. Aquilla Jones did not know of any fugitives passing recently, but supposed that if there were any in the neighborhood I would be likely to know it. I immediately started a messenger on horseback to overtake the party of fugitives, and to have them scattered and secreted among their friends, thus to remain until further orders. Expecting that the fugitives were still at John Bond's, I wrote a note to him apprising him of their danger, but they had been forwarded that morning to a Friends' settlement in Grant County, some twenty-five or thirty miles further on. The intervening country being thinly settled, it had been thought safe to let them travel in the daytime.

On receipt of my message, John Bond mounted his horse and pursued the party. He overtook them that night, and had them scattered and concealed among friends. They remained in their hiding-places for several weeks, until the hunters had given up the chase and returned home; then

16

they came together again, and were forwarded on from station to station, by way of Adrian and Detroit, Michigan, until they reached Canada in safety. On their way they rested a few days in a settlement of abolitionists not far from Adrian, and here the young man and his intended wife, whom I have previously mentioned, were legally married. A few years afterward I had the pleasure of visiting them in Canada, and dining with them in their own comfortable little home. They had a beautiful son, about a year old, and proudly said: "We can call him our own; old master can not take him from us and sell him."

We will now turn back and notice the proceedings of the bloodhounds in human shape who were on the trail of the fugitives. The morning after the fifteen Kentuckians arrived at Richmond, they employed several roughs of that place to accompany them as guides. These roughs were always ready to help capture fugitives, for the sake of money, and professed to know all the abolitionist neighborhoods toward the North.

The Kentuckians divided into three companies, each having a guide. One company was to go by the way of Hillsboro and Spartansburg, another by way of Williamsburg and Economy, and the third through Newport and Cherry Grove. They hoped in this way to strike the trail of the fugitives, and arranged to meet at Winchester, the county seat of Randolph County, and give an account of their search. The party that was to come by way of Newport, came through town one or two at a time, some distance apart, so as to avoid exciting suspicion in regard to their business. When they met children in the street, they inquired if any stray horses or cattle had been seen, and then asked if any fugitive slaves had been in town lately. In this way they learned that a large company of fugitives had been at my house a few days before, but that they had gone on to Canada.

The three companies met at Winchester according to agreement, but no discoveries had been made except by the company that passed through Newport. It was now decided that two of the companies should follow up the supposed line of the Underground Railroad to the lake, and watch for the fugitives at the points where they would be most likely to pass over to. Canada. The guides professed to understand the route and to know the places where the fugitives would most likely be harbored. The third company, with some additional guides from Winchester, were to canvass the different settlements of Friends in that neighborhood and around Newport, in the hope of gaining some clue. to the fugitives, if they were still sheltered among the abolitionists there. They were told by some who were favorable to their cause, that it was quite probable that Levi Coffin, the notorious nigger thief of Newport, had got intelligence of their movements, and had hid their slaves among some of his friends in the neighborhood, for he had many friends there no better than himself, and there were many in Richmond who would give him warning of pursuers. This part of the company, after an unsuccessful search through the various neighborhoods, returned to Richmond, stopping on the way at a tavern three miles north of Newport. Here they uttered many threats against me, declaring they would hang me or shoot me, and burn my houses. The tavern-keeper was friendly toward me, though he did not believe in aiding runaway slaves, and he felt alarmed for my safety. After the hunters were gone, he mounted his horse and came to see me and warn me of my danger. He advised me to keep closely at home, not to venture out alone lest my enemies should take my life. I thanked him for his kindness, but told him that I felt no fear of danger. I had obeyed the commands of the Bible, and the dictates of humanity, in feeding the hungry, clothing the naked, and aiding the oppressed, and I felt no condemnation for it. I should go about my business as usual, and if duty called me from home, I should pay no attention to the threats of slave-hunters, but attend to my duty.

The hunters made their headquarters at L—— B——'s tavern in Richmond, while awaiting the return of their companions from the lakes. They were not idle in the meantime, but made frequent night raids through our neighborhood and other settlements of abolitionists, supposing that their slaves might still be harbored among us.

One evening, in company with several roughs of Richmond, they started toward Newport, making terrible threats against me. They would burn me out, if it cost them ten thousand dollars; they would shoot me down at sight or drag me into the woods and hang me to a limb, etc., etc. These threats were made publicly, and one of my friends who heard them became much alarmed for my safety. He mounted his horse and rode to Newport to give me warning. He arrived at my house about midnight, when all of us were asleep. He knocked loudly at the door, and when I arose and let him in, he repeated in an excited manner the threats he had heard, and seemed much alarmed. I thanked him for the interest he manifested in my welfare, and told him to make himself entirely easy, for I anticipated not the slightest disturbance. According to the old proverb, I said barking dogs never bite, and if these men intended to do such terrible things to me, they would not have told of it publicly. I discovered that he had a couple of loaded revolvers with him, and told him to put them away, for I did not want such weapons; I did not depend on fire-arms for protection. He said he thought he might come in contact with the slave-hunters on the way, and would need these to defend himself with. I had his horse put up, and persuaded him to go to rest. When morning came, my buildings were all standing, there was no smell of fire about the premises, I was not hanging to a tree, and my friend had found no use for his revolvers.

The hunters, who had gone northward toward the lakes, returned without having obtained any clue to their valuable missing property. They remained at Richmond a few days, then the whole party returned South. But before going, they conferred upon me a high honor. They said that they could never get the slightest intelligence of their slaves after they reached my house, and declared that there must be an Underground Railroad, of which I was president. They repeated this several times in Richmond, and I heard of it when next I went to attend the board of bank directors at that place.

Some of my friends asked me if I had heard of my promotion to office, and when I said I had not, they told me what the Kentuckians had said. I replied that I would accept that position or any other they were disposed to give me on that road— conductor, engineer, fireman or brakeman. This was the first time I ever heard of the Underground Railroad.

The saying of the Kentuckians soon became widely circulated, and I frequently received letters addressed to "Levi Coffin, President of the Underground Railroad." I had the honor of wearing that title for more than thirty years, and it was not until the great celebration of the Fifteenth Amendment to the Constitution, by the colored people at Cincinnati, that I resigned the office, and laid aside the name conferred on me by Southern slave-hunters. On that occasion I said that our underground work was done, and that as we had no more use for the road, I would suggest that the rails be taken up and disposed of, and the proceeds appropriated for the education of the freed slaves.

A few weeks after the Kentucky slave-hunters had left Richmond, I was summoned, with several of my neighbors, to appear before the grand jury

at Centerville, the county seat of our county, where
court was then in session. I at once guessed the
cause of the summons. Knowing that L—— B——,
of Richmond, was one of the grand jurors, I supposed that he was acting in the interests of the
slave-hunters who had recently made their headquarters at his house, and that I was to be indicted
for harboring fugitive slaves, while my neighbors
were summoned as witnesses. Though almost sure
that this was the case, I felt no alarm. I thought
that if the grand jury should find a bill against me,
and I should be compelled to stand a trial in court,
and be convicted of a violation of the fugitive slave
law, and have to suffer the penalty, it might be the
means of advancing the anti-slavery cause, and of
raising up other friends for the slave. Some of the
ablest lawyers of that district were my friends, and I
knew that I would have plenty of defenders. These
were some of my reflections as I rode to Centerville,
a distance of eleven miles, in company with Daniel
Puckett, Dr. Henry H. Way, Samuel Nixon, and
Robert Green, who had been summoned to appear
with me before the grand jury. When I entered
the court-room I discovered that I was personally
acquainted with a majority of the jurors, and knew
some of them to be strongly anti-slavery in their
sentiments. Bloomfield, of Centerville, was foreman of the jury. He asked me whether I knew of
any violations of the law in our neighborhood within
a certain time, any cases of assault and battery, or
other outbreaks. I told him that I knew of nothing
of the kind, adding that we were nearly all aboli-

tionists, and were a peaceable people. The foreman then turned to L—— B——, and said:

"Mr. B——, I believe that it is you who are interested in the negro question. If you wish to ask Mr. Coffin any questions, you can proceed."

L—— B—— then asked me if I understood the statute in regard to harboring fugitive slaves. I told him that I had read it, but did not know whether I understood it or not. I suggested that he turn to it and read it, which he did. I told him that I knew of no violation of that statute in our neighborhood. Persons often traveled our way and stopped at our house who *said* they were slaves, but I knew nothing about it from their statements, for our law did not presume that such people could tell the truth. This made a laugh among the jury, with the exception of L—— B——. I went on to say that a few weeks before a company of seventeen fugitives had stopped at my house, hungry and destitute, two of them suffering from wounds inflicted by pursuers who claimed them as slaves, but I had no legal evidence that they were slaves; nothing but their own statements, and the law of our State did not admit colored evidence. I had read in the Bible when I was a boy that it was right to feed the hungry and clothe the naked, and to minister to those who had fallen among thieves and were wounded, but that no distinction in regard to color was mentioned in the good Book, so in accordance with its teachings I had received these fugitives and cared for them. I then asked:

"Was I right, Friend B——, in doing so?"

He hesitated and seemed at a loss how to reply. I continued: "How does thy Bible read? Was it not as I have said?"

"Yes," he answered, "it reads somehow so."

He evidently wished to change the subject. He next asked me if I understood the statute in regard to hiring free colored people who had not given bond and security, as the law required, that they would not come upon the county for support. I told him that I had read it, but, perhaps, did not understand it, and requested him to turn to it and read it. He did so, and I then said: "I presume I am guilty of violating that statute, for I am in the habit of hiring service whenever I need it, without distinction of color, and without asking any questions in regard to that law."

One of the jury asked me if I knew of any case in the county where the requirements of that statute had been fulfilled.

I replied: "No, not one. It appears to be a dead letter in this part of the State, and many of our best lawyers believe it to be an unconstitutional act of the Legislature."

The foreman then said: "Mr. B——, I believe Mr. Coffin understands the negro law about as well as you do. If you are through asking questions, he need not be detained."

"I have no further questions to ask him."

As I was retiring I said: "I do not know whether I understand the law as well as Friend B—— does; but I know that I have more to do with aiding the

17

fugitives and less to do with aiding their pursuers, than he has."

Dr. Henry H. Way was then called in. L—— B—— questioned him in regard to the party of seventeen fugitives, and asked him at whose house they had stopped in Newport.

"At Levi Coffin's," the doctor replied, and in answer to questions gave a full description of them; adding that he and Dr. Stanton had dressed the wounds of the two men who had been shot.

B—— asked: "Did you know that they were slaves, escaping from their masters?"

The doctor replied: "We had no evidence except their own statements. They *said* they were slaves from Kentucky, but their evidence is worthless in law in this State."

Here they got into an argument in regard to law, in which the doctor completely confounded B——. The foreman finally interfered, told B—— that he was wrong, and dismissed the doctor. The other witnesses were called in and questioned, but their testimony all amounted to the same thing, showing that the fugitives had been sheltered at my house for several days, and that anybody who wished to see them had access to them. Notwithstanding B——'s attempt to implicate me, the jury found no bill against me.

Anti-slavery sentiment had largely increased in our county, and this effort of B——'s to indict me for harboring fugitive slaves soon became widely known and had a tendency to kill him politically.

TWO SLAVE GIRLS PROM MARYLAND.

The laws of Indiana, Illinois and Ohio allowed persons from a slave State to pass through with their slaves if they did not stop to locate. If they made any purchases amounting to location, the slaves were to be considered free.

The following case came under this law: Two brothers from Maryland, by the name of Dawes, each accompanied by his family and one slave girl, were traveling through Indiana on their way to the State of Missouri, when the illness of the wife of Elisha Dawes, the elder brother, compelled them to stop for a time near Winchester, Randolph County, Indiana. During their stay at that place, they decided to locate there and to buy a tan-yard which was for sale at Winchester, at a great bargain; they being tanners by trade. The terms were agreed upon and were satisfactory to both paties, but before the writings were drawn or the bargain closed, the thought occurred to the Dawes brothers that if they located in Indiana they would lose their slaves; they could not hold them in a free State. This would be a heavy loss to them, as the girls were valuable property, the one belonging to the elder brother being nearly grown, and the other about fourteen years old. They knew not what to do, and consulted with the man with whom they were stopping, who was pro-slavery in his sentiments. He advised them not to close the contract for the property until they had disposed of the slave girls, then the money thus obtained would give them a good start in business. In accordance with his advice, they concluded to take the girls to Kentucky by way of Cincinnati, sell them there, and with the money obtained from their sale, buy a quantity of hides in Cincinnati, then return to Winchester and close the contract for the property. Their friend and adviser agreed to go with them and aid them in disposing of their slaves and purchasing stock. But notwithstanding all their wise precautions they made one serious mistake. They contracted for a lot of tan-bark and for some household furniture, which in the sight of the law amounted to location, and the moment they did so the slaves were free. When ready to go to Cincinnati, they fitted up a light covered wagon, drawn by two horses, and taking the two slave girls and their friend, they started from Winchester in the middle of the day, and passed through Newport between sunset and dark. The slaves were out of sight behind the hay in the back part of the wagon, and were not noticed by any one as the party passed hastily through our village. They were hardly out of sight when Dr. Hiatt, an abolitionist from the neighborhood of Winchester, arrived at my house. He understood the whole matter, and knew that the men violated the law of the State in taking the two girls out of it to sell them as slaves. When he learned that they had started to Kentucky, he had mounted his horse and followed them, hoping to reach Newport before they did, and have them arrested as kidnappers. He had not supposed that they would reach Newport that night, but they had driven rapidly, and he had not succeeded in getting ahead of them. We at once called a meeting in our school-house, and by ringing the bell and sending out runners, we soon had most of the citizens convened. Esquire Curtis presided at the meeting. Dr. Hiatt gave the outlines of the story, and as he had in writing all the particulars of the purchases which the men had made near Winchester, he was able to prove that they had violated the law of the State and should be arrested as kidnappers. But there was no time to delay; if anything was to be done to save the girls, it must be done at once. The masters had only eleven miles to travel until they would be out of the State. The questions to be immediately considered were: Who will file an affidavit and procure a writ? Who will pursue the men to-night, arrest them as kidnappers, and bring them before Esquire Curtis for trial?

There were no volunteers in the meeting, so I suggested the names of two or three persons who would be suitable to go; but they declined. My name was then suggested. I said: "Yes, I expected to have it to do from the first, but I wanted to see if any others were willing." I at once filed an affidavit before Esquire Curtis, and he issued a writ and placed it in the hands of John Hunt, who was the constable.

It was now after night and quite dark, and rain was beginning to fall. The constable summoned his posse before leaving the school-house—ten able-bodied, resolute men, making, with himself and me, twelve men in the company. We had to go home and get our suppers, saddle our horses and prepare for traveling in the rain; and it was ten o'clock when we were all mounted and ready to start. The constable and I led the way. It was quite dark, the rain was falling heavily and the mud in the road was deep; so our progress was necessarily slow.

After riding about two hours, we discovered the white cover of the travelers' wagon which was standing in the yard of a farm-house, about a hundred yards from the road. We rode up the short lane that led to the house, and calling out the man of the house explained our business to him; then leaving the others outside, the constable and I went inside and arrested the two slaveholders, who were in bed. They were naturally much surprised at being thus disturbed in the middle of the night, and when they learned the reason, they were very angry and used oaths and hard names quite freely.

The two slave girls were lying on a pallet on the floor, in the same room. They knew not what to think of being thus aroused, but I spoke to them reassuringly, and told them not to be alarmed. Elisha Dawes seeing me speak to them, ordered them not to say a word. I paid no attention to him, but told them they were in a free State, and were now free according to the law of the State, and that they need not be afraid to speak. I assured them that we would protect them and see that they were not sold into slavery.

The constable told the men that they were his prisoners, and must go back with us to Newport for trial. They reluctantly obeyed his orders, leaving

their friend from Winchester and two of our men to
bring the wagon and the two girls next morning.
It had now ceased raining, and the moon had risen
and gave a dim light. As we rode back to Newport
with the two slaveholders, one of them said:

"I would like to see the man who filed that affidavit; I would put daylight through him."

I rode up by his side, and said: "If it will afford
thee any satisfaction to see that person, look at me ;
I am the man. But it is not I that you have to contend with; it is the State of Indiana. You have
violated the law of the State by attempting to take
your slaves out of the State after making purchases
that amounted to location. We are able to prove
this. The. moment you made the contract at Winchester, the girls were free, and now, in the sight
of the law, you are kidnappers carrying off free
persons to sell them into slavery. The lightest penalty for this is five hundred dollars' fine and two
years' imprisonment in the penitentiary. You shall
have a fair trial ; nothing will be done unfairly. The
case will come up before court, where you will have
the benefit of counsel and jury. There will be a
preliminary hearing before Esquire Curtis at Newport, and he will no doubt bind you over to appear
in court."

After hearing these statements, the slaveholders
ceased their abusive language. They appeared to
be alarmed at the serious aspect of the case, and
were more subdued and friendly in their manners.
When we reached Newport, I took them to my
house and had their horses put in my stable. Next

morning, when the two slave girls were brought to
town I gave them quarters at my house, and entertained the whole company two days free of charge.
I treated the men as kindly as I could, and sought
to make their position as prisoners as pleasant
as possible. They desired to send to Winchester
for witnesses, having a brother-in-law and some
others in their company whom they wished to
be present at the trial, and I sent a messenger to
bring these persons. I also sent to Centerville for
a lawyer, Abner Haines, now Judge Haines, of
Eaton, Ohio. It was on account of sending for
these persons that the trial was postponed until the
second day. Just before the hour set for trial, Lawyer Haines read to the two prisoners the law bearing
on their case, and cited several instances of a similar kind that had been tried in court, resulting in the
conviction of the defendants. He told them that
the very moment they had made purchases preparatory to location their slaves were free, and that
their attempt to take the two girls out of the State
and sell them amounted to kidnapping ; and assured
them that if prosecuted they could not escape conviction and the penalty for that offense.

They were much alarmed at this and wished to
compromise with me, in some way, that I might not
appear against them, or carry the case into court.
They offered to give up the slave girls to me if I
would not appear against them. I told them that I
would consent to this on one condition, and that
was that they should make out papers of emancipation for the girls. This they agreed to do, and Law-

yer Haines wrote out the papers at once, and they were signed and acknowledged before Esquire Curtis. The slave girls were then given into my care, and the prisoners discharged.

Before starting back to Winchester, Elisha Dawes asked me to let him take his girl—the oldest one—home with him as a nurse for his child. He promised to treat her well, and said he did not know how his wife, who had a young child, could do without her. I asked him why he did not think of that before he started to sell the girl, and said that now I could not trust her with him. So the two girls were left at our house, and the men returned to Winchester. I sent the girls to school, and had the care and oversight of them for several years. The older of the two married a respectable colored man, and is still living. The younger went to Canada of her own choice, and died there a few years afterward.

The Dawes brothers located at Winchester, and being told by some of their pro-slavery friends that I had scared them out of their slaves, and being assured that the whole proceedings were illegal and could be upset in law, they became very much dissatisfied. They were much enraged at me, and made so many threats against me, that some of my friends advised me not to go to Winchester for some time, lest I should meet with harm. I replied that I often had business at Winchester, and that when it called me there I should not stay away on account of the threats of the Dawes brothers. They finally resolved to prosecute me, and went to Centerville to employ some of our best lawyers, but did not succeed in getting any one to undertake the case. A few weeks after their return to Winchester, my business called me to that place, and the first person I saw after dismounting from my horse was Elisha Dawes, who happened to be on the street. I walked straight up to him and shook hands with him, and inquired after the health of his family. He appeared quite cordial in his manner. I often met him and his brother afterward, and kept up a friendly acquaintance with them for several years. At one time when I met with Elisha Dawes, he told me that his father, who lived in Maryland, and who was anti-slavery in sentiment, was quite rejoiced that the slave girls had been taken away from them.

ANECDOTE OF A VISIT TO CINCINNATI.

While living at Newport I often went to Cincinnati on business, and on one occasion when my wife and little daughter were with me, a free mulatto woman and her fugitive slave daughter — nearly white—were put in my charge. I took them back to Newport in my carriage, stopping on the way at a tavern near Hamilton. At supper the landlord seated us all at the table, except the mulatto woman, who, he intended, should eat with the colored servants. After the meal was over, I told him that he was quite partial, to admit a slave to the public table and exclude a free woman. He was much astonished and could not believe that the girl was a slave.

"Why," he said; "she is white, perfectly white."

"That may be," I replied; "but she is nevertheless a slave. Color is no protection in the South."

The landlord then acknowledged the inconsistency of his conduct, and we enjoyed the joke very much.

At another time when I was in the city accompanied by my wife and daughter, Hiram S. Gillmore, a noted abolitionist and one of my particular friends, asked me if I knew of any person in from the country with a wagon who would take a fugitive slave girl out to a place of safety. He then gave me the outlines of her story. She had come from Boone County, Kentucky, having run away because she learned that she was to be sold to the far South. Knowing that she would be pursued and probably retaken if she started northward immediately, she conceived a plan like that adopted by Cassie and Emmeline when they ran away from Legree, in "Uncle Tom's Cabin." She hid herself in the interior of a large straw pile near her master's barn, having previously arranged apertures for air, and a winding passage with concealed entrance, by which her fellow-servants who brought her food could enter. Here she remained six weeks, while her master with a posse of men scoured the country in search of her. Like Cassie who looked from her hiding-place in the garret, and heard the discomfited Legree swearing at his ill luck as he returned from the unsuccessful pursuit, this young woman could hear in her hiding-place, in the straw pile, the noise of horses' feet and the sound of talking, as her master and his men returned from their fruitless search for her. When the hunt was over, she stole out and made her way safely to the Ohio River, crossed in a skiff and reached the house of a family of abolitionists in Cincinnati, where she was kindly received, and furnished with comfortable clothing.

In answer to the inquiry of Hiram S. Gillmore, I replied that I was there in a carriage, and would take her out, if she would be ready when I called for her at nine o'clock next morning. At the appointed time we started. The young slave woman was nearly white, was well dressed, and presented quite a lady-like appearance.

At the end of the first day's travel, we stopped about four miles above Hamilton, at a private house, the residence of one of my friends—a democrat, by the way—who had often invited me to call at his house, with my wife, and pay his family a visit. The gentleman's daughter ran out to meet us, and I said to her: "Well, Ellen, I have brought my wife with me this time; now guess which of these ladies she is."

She looked from one to the other, hardly able to decide, but, finally, judging perhaps from the Quaker bonnet my wife wore, decided on the right one. The gentleman and his wife now came out to meet us, and when I introduced the young lady with us as a fugitive slave, they were full of surprise and curiosity, having never seen a fugitive slave before.

I told them her story, and then said to my friend: "Will she be safe here to-night, Thomas?"

"I reckon so," was the reply.

"I don't want any *reckon* about it," I rejoined;

"I shall put her in thy care, and I don't want thee to let anybody capture her." She was kindly treated.

Next morning—it being the Sabbath day—we went on about eight miles to West Elkton, a Friends' settlement, to attend meeting and spend the day. Meeting had just commenced when we arrived. My wife took the fugitive into meeting with her and seated her by her side. This was the first time the girl had ever attended a Quaker meeting. At its close I introduced her to a number of our friends, as a run away slave from Kentucky. She was the first that had been seen at that place, and a mysterious influence seemed to invest her at once. Men lowered their voices as if in awe, when they inquired about her, and some of them seemed alarmed, as if there was danger in the very air that a fugitive slave breathed. I spoke in a loud, cheerful tone and asked: "Why do you lower your voices? Are you afraid of anything? Have you bloodhounds among you? If so, you ought to drive them out of your village." We stopped at the house of Widow Stubbs, a thorough abolitionist, and soon afterward one of her near neighbors, a man with whom I was well acquainted, came in to inquire concerning the girl.

He asked if she was safe, whether she had not better be secreted, etc., all the time speaking in a low tone. I said: "What is the matter, Henry? What makes thee speak so cautiously? Is there any one in your village who would capture a fugitive slave? If there is, hunt him up and bring him here.

I would like to see him and to introduce this young lady to him. I think we could make an abolitionist of him. For my part, I have no fears of any one in this village, and think thou may make thyself quite easy."

In the course of the afternoon quite a number of people came in who seemed concerned in a similar manner for the safety of the girl, but seeing me so entirely at ease, their fear and anxiety passed away.

This public exposition of a fugitive slave, at Friends' meeting and in the village seemed to have a good effect in the place, for West Elkton afterward became one of our best Underground Railroad depots, and the timid man first alluded to became one of the most zealous workers on the road.

A STRUGGLE FOR LIBERTY.

Louis Talbert was an intelligent colored man, who belonged to a slaveholder living in Kentucky, a few miles back of the Ohio River, above Madison. Louis was not content with being a chattel that could be bought and sold, but kept planning how he might gain his freedom. For several years he had quietly and shrewdly been gaining all the information he could in regard to that land of liberty he had heard of so often, and at last concluded to make the attempt to reach it. He ventured to divulge his secret to several of his trusty friends and fellow-servants in the neighborhood, and twelve of them agreed to join him in the attempt to gain freedom. They met frequently, late at night, in the woods or some other secluded place in the neigh-

borhood, to consult together and to make their
plans. The chief difficulty that they would have to
encounter in their journey was the Ohio River—
they had no way of crossing it, and knew not what
to do. Finally, Louis Talbert, who was the leading
spirit among them, suggested the construction of a
raft. This at once solved the problem, and the time
to start was agreed upon. On the appointed night
the party made their way to a point on the river
bank, selected by Louis. Having some suitable
tools with them, they soon prepared two logs and
pinned them together. When the little raft was
launched upon the water, it was found that only two
persons could ride on it at a time. Their expectations of all getting across that night were disappointed, for it was late when they reached the river,
and only six had been transported to the Indiana
shore when daylight warned the party to seek concealment. They hid in the thickets, on each side
of the river, during the day, and when night came
the remaining six were safely ferried across. But
this delay operated against them, and came near
proving fatal to their hopes. When so much valuable property was found to be missing in the neighborhood they had left, it created great excitement
among their masters and other slaveholders. A
large company started out to hunt for the runaways,
and crossed the river at various points, in order, if
possible, to intercept them in their flight. The
second night, when all the fugitives were safely over
the river, they started on their way northward
through Indiana. They made but little progress

before day began to dawn, and soon had to seek places in the bushes, where they could remain in safety during the day. By this time, some of the hunters had got ahead of them, and had given the alarm, and offered large rewards for their capture. In the counties of Indiana bordering the Ohio River, fugitive slaves were in as much danger of being captured as on the other side of the river, for there were many persons on the look-out for them who hoped to get the rewards offered by the slaveholders in such cases.

The next night Louis and his companions left their hiding-places, but being pinched with hunger, they sought to obtain some food before starting on their journey northward. They went to a house to buy some provisions, not thinking that they were in great danger. But a large party of hunters were in the neighborhood, and were soon apprised of their presence. The fugitives were closely pursued by a large party of armed men, the party from Kentucky having been joined by a number of ruffians in the neighborhood, who were as eager in the chase as they would have been in a fox or a deer hunt. Louis and his companions ran in different directions, and endeavored to hide in the woods and corn-fields, but most of the party were captured, only Louis and three others succeeding in making their escape. After traveling several nights, during which time they suffered much from hunger and exposure, they reached my house. We received and cared for them, and they remained with us several days, resting from their fatiguing and anxious journey. They were then put on the old reliable road leading to Canada, and reached that country in safety.

Louis remained there about one year, then returned to Indiana, and staid a few days at my house. He said he was on his way back to Kentucky. He had two sisters still in bondage, and was determined to make an effort to bring them away. They belonged to a man living about thirty miles back from the river. Louis felt much anxiety about them, as they were young women grown 'and were regarded as valuable property by their master. He feared that they would be sold to traders and taken to the far South, as such property was in demand and would bring high prices. I tried to dissuade Louis from such a hazardous undertaking. I told him that he would risk his own liberty and might not be able to effect the rescue of his sisters, but he was determined to go. He was well acquainted in that neighborhood with both colored and white people, and, relying on his shrewdness and judgment, he made the bold venture. After crossing the river into Kentucky, he moved cautiously in the night season from one negro quarter to another where he was acquainted. He encouraged several of his particular friends to join him and prepare to make the journey to Canada. He assured them that he was well acquainted with the route and could conduct them safely, and told them of the many good friends they would find on the road who would help them on their way to liberty. The sweet word of liberty, and the hope of all its blessings and privileges, thrilled their hearts, and they at once agreed to make the effort to gain it under the leadership of Louis. The plans were all made, both men and women being in the party who were to attempt to escape.

Louis went several nights to the place where his sisters were, and watched about the house, trying to get an interview with them, but they were house-servants, and were kept in at night so closely that it seemed impossible for him to make himself known to them and talk with them without discovery.

One moonlight night as he was watching the house, trying to attract the attention of his sisters, their master saw and recognized him. The signal for pursuit was at once given and the alarm raised. A neighbor who had several bloodhounds was summoned, and the dogs were put on the trail. By this time, however, Louis had reached the woods, and being well acquainted with the country, he knew how to choose the paths that would be most difficult for the pursuers. Louis knew how to charm the dogs, and he received no harm from them.

He baffled his pursuers and made good his escape, bringing with him four or five of his slave friends, including two women. Thus, though he failed to get his sisters, his mission was not entirely unsuccessful. He made his way to the Ohio River with his company, and finding a skiff they crossed in safety to the Indiana side. They then proceeded as rapidly as possible to a station of the Underground Railroad, and that line soon brought them to my house. They remained with us a short time, and were then forwarded to Canada.

After seeing his friends safe in that country, Louis returned to Indiana and attended school at a manual labor institution, in Randolph County, called the Union Literary Institute. It was chartered by the State of Indiana for the benefit of colored students. Louis remained here nearly two years, making satisfactory progress in his studies and gaining the esteem of all who knew him. During vacation in the first year he made a second attempt to rescue his sisters from slavery, but was again unsuccessful in getting them, though he succeeded in bringing out of bondage another company of his friends. He still did not abandon the hope of rescuing his sisters.

At the school which he attended, Louis became acquainted with M. W., a young white man who lived in Hamilton County, Indiana. To him Louis communicated his resolve to make another effort to get his sisters out of slavery. M. W. became so much interested in the matter that he agreed to accompany Louis on his next trip into Kentucky.

Some months afterward Louis went to Westfield, Hamilton County. He was then on his way to Kentucky to make another attempt, and reminded his friend of his promise, but M. W. had just been married and declined to go. He directed Louis to the house of L. Pennington, who lived in the neighborhood. This Friend tried to discourage Louis from making the attempt; telling him that he would risk his own liberty and might not achieve that of his sisters. But Louis was determined to go, and made a confidant of a young man by the name of

N. W., who was interested in his case and who agreed to accompany him. They made all their plans and appointed the time for starting. They were to take the train at Indianapolis and go to Madison, then cross into Kentucky and proceed secretly on their mission. These arrangements were made a week or two before the time fixed for starting, and might have been successful had not N. W., in the meantime, unwisely made a confidant of one of his acquaintances at Indianapolis, telling him all the particulars of the case. This friend in turn confided the whole matter to another person living in Indianapolis, who knew Louis' master in Kentucky, and who immediately wrote to him, giving all the particulars, and telling him the day and hour that Louis intended to take the train at Indianapolis for Madison.

Louis' master, as soon as he received this information, gathered a posse of men and started to Indianapolis, arriving there the night before Louis was to start South. He obtained a writ for arresting his slave and put it in the hands of an officer, then, with the witnesses who were to prove his property, he waited to capture Louis as soon as he should come into the depot.

The next morning Louis, who was all unconscious of the danger he was going into, walked into the depot to get aboard the train and found himself confronted by his master. He could not save himself, either by resistance or flight, and soon found himself heavily fettered. N. W., who was to accompany him, was a short distance behind, but seeing the excited crowd in the depot and learning that Louis had been captured, he turned back and went immediately home and told the news to Louis' friends.

Louis' master said to him: "I would have paid any price to get hold of you, and now that you are in my power, I will make an example of you. You have carried off thirty-seven thousand dollars' worth of slave property."

Louis had been a very successful missionary among the slaves in Kentucky. Beside bringing a number out of the house of bondage, he had directed others how to get on the Underground Railroad and go right through to Canada where they would be free. They had listened with deep interest to his stories of Canada and liberty, and frequent stampedes of slaves from that part of Kentucky was the result.

Louis' master took him back to Kentucky strongly bound, and exhibited him in fetters in many towns and public places in that section of the country, in order, as he said, to make an example of him, and to intimidate other slaves who might have thoughts of running away. But the master soon found that he had a troublesome piece of property on his hands. He did not dare to turn Louis loose and set him to work, for he might stray off and take a good deal of valuable property with him, of his own kind. He kept him bound for several weeks, waiting for a favorable opportunity to sell him, and finally disposed of him to a Southern slave-dealer for the sum of seven hundred dollars. This was considered a low price, but there was some risk in buying such a shrewd, wily fellow as Louis, who had dared to run away from his master.

Louis was taken on board a steamboat, with other slaves, to go down the river to a Southern slave market. He was kept bound for several days on the journey, but managed to gain the confidence of his master, so that his fetters were taken off and he was allowed the same privileges that the other slaves had. His master knew that he would not be likely to sell so well if he was kept bound, for the purchasers would think he was a dangerous fellow, and undesirable as a piece of property.

As soon as Louis was turned loose he began to look out for a chance to escape. They were now near the mouth of the Ohio River, and Louis was very anxious to make his escape from the boat before they entered the Mississippi River, at Cairo. But he found no opportunity, and they were soon on the broad stream of the Mississippi. The night after they reached this river, Louis determined on a plan of escape. A small boat or yawl was tied to the rear end of the steamboat and floated in the water. It was kept there for the convenience of landing passengers without rounding to the steamer, and for putting the mail ashore at different points along the river. Louis planned to get into this boat under cover of darkness, and arranged with the chamber maid to cut the rope that bound it to the steamer. Two other slave men, to whom Louis had confided his plans, had agreed to go with him, but at the last moment their hearts failed them and they concluded to stay. Louis got into the boat, and the colored chamber-maid, faithful to her promise, cut the rope, and he paddled away in the darkness.

Louis was now in the middle of the Mississippi, with a slave State on each side of the river. He knew how to row well, and soon made his way to the Missouri side. He pulled up stream near the bank for some time, but found that it was hard work, and that he made little headway. When daylight appeared he tied the yawl in a secluded place on the shore, and sought a hiding-place, where he spent the day. When night came, he felt that he must seek some food, for he was now very hungry. He concluded to abandon the yawl and make his way up the river by land. After walking some distance he came to a farm, and discovering several negro huts he ventured to approach one. He was kindly received and furnished with a supply of food. He gained some information about the country between that place and Cairo, and pursued his journey. He lay by during the day, and traveled at night until he reached the Mississippi River, some distance above Cairo. He suffered from hunger and various hardships, but found some true friends among the slaves near the river. Here he rested awhile in safe concealment, then was helped across the river into Southern Illinois. In this section fugitive slaves found few friends, for most of the settlers were from slave States, and were disposed to capture all runaways. Through this country Louis cautiously made his way in the night season, venturing now and then to call at a house and beg for food. In a few places he found friends, and was enabled to rest in safety, and recruit his strength.

Thus he slowly made his way through Illinois into Indiana, and arrived at the house of Levi Pennington, in Hamilton County, just three months from the day he first called there. Friend Pennington was much surprised to see him, having heard of his capture at Indianapolis, and of his being taken back to slavery by his master. After resting awhile here, Louis returned to school and resumed his studies.

We learned afterward that Louis' new master, the slave-trader, was much enraged when he discovered his loss, and blamed the captain of the boat for having his yawl where it was so easy of access. When they arrived at Memphis, he sued the captain for the price of his slave, contending that the captain was responsible for the loss of his property. The trader lost the suit, and had the costs to pay, then the captain sued him for the detention of the boat, and gained the suit, and the trader had to pay seven hundred dollars. Then the captain sued him for the value of the yawl which his slave had carried off, and got judgment against him, which it is said cost him seven hundred dollars more. According to this statement, Louis Talbert was a dear piece of property to the negro-trader.

JOHN WHITE.

John White was the slave of a man who lived in Kentucky, just opposite Rising Sun, Indiana, on the Ohio River. He married a slave woman, the daughter of her master, who lived in the neighborhood, and they had several children. He was very much attached to his family, and visited them as often as he was permitted by his master. Hearing one day that his master intended to sell him to the far South, and knowing that he would thus be separated from his family, he determined to run away. Carrying his plan into execution he crossed the river into Indiana, where he had some friends—free colored people—and by them was directed to my house at Newport. Here he remained some weeks, and my deepest sympathies were aroused in his behalf. He was naturally very bright and intelligent, but his mind seemed overclouded with gloom at the prospect of leaving his family in slavery. He finally started toward Canada, stopping on the way at Raisin Institute, near Adrian, Michigan, a school open to all, irrespective of color, where he met that noted abolitionist and noble-hearted woman, Laura S. Haviland, having been directed to her by me. He remained in Canada several months, but being anxious and concerned about his family, resolved to return to his abolition friends in the States, to see if something could not be done, and accordingly came back to Raisin Institute, in Michigan. It was then winter and not a suitable season to make an attempt to rescue his wife and children, so he remained at the institute during the winter and spring, and attended school. He was very eager to learn, and made rapid progress in his studies.

In the summer he returned to my house, at Newport, and consulted with me regarding the project

19

he had so much at heart.   A messenger was sent to
his colored friends, at Rising Sun, to see if arrangements could be made with them to aid his family
in escaping, but nothing definite could be determined upon.   Not willing to give it up, John White
remained several months at Newport—working and
attending school, and in the winter ventured to
go to Cincinnati, hoping to make arrangements with
the colored stewards of the Louisville and Cincinnati packets, with whom he was acquainted, but
failed in this.   He then returned to Michigan, where
he remained a year or two, continuing his education
at the Raisin Institute, but never forgetting his
anxiety about his wife and children, and his hope to
see them free.

His story finally so enlisted the sympathies of
Laura S. Haviland that she resolved to aid him in
his desire, and, with that purpose in view, went
down to Rising Sun and introduced herself to John's
colored friends, who were, by the way, almost white.

Disguising herself, she went with one of the
women across the river into Kentucky, ostensibly to
pick blackberries.   Going to the house where John's
wife lived, the colored woman introduced Laura
Haviland as her aunt, and the mistress gave John's
wife permission to accompany them in their search
for blackberries.   This afforded the opportunity
which had been so long desired, and the wife soon
heard the message from her long lost husband, and
was made acquainted with the plans for the escape
of herself and her children.

During this interview the arrangements were all

made and the time fixed, and on the appointed night John crossed the river from Rising Sun, and brought away his wife and six children from their place of bondage. This was the opportunity for which he had worked and prayed so long, and success seemed at last to have crowned his efforts. But alas! it was only a gleam of light before a darker night.

Reaching the river they entered a skiff, and attempted to row across to a point above Rising Sun, where a wagon was to meet them, but the water was high and the current swift and strong, and in spite of their efforts, they floated down the river some distance below Rising Sun, and were unable to reach the landing where the wagon was waiting.

Daylight coming on, they hid in the thickets and remained there all day, and at night unwisely ventured out into the high road. There had been ample opportunity for the master to gather a posse of men and start in pursuit, and the fugitives had not proceeded far when they found themselves hemmed in between two companies of pursuers. The wife and children were recaptured, but John sprang into the thickets and managed to elude the pursuers. He could not protect his family by staying with them; he would only be caught himself, and he sought safety in flight, but the cries of his wife and children rang in his ears, and the thought of their anguish lacerated his heart.

He lay out in the woods several days, and then made his way to the hut of a free colored man, where he obtained food, of which he was sadly in need, being almost famished. Here he was found and captured by Wright Ray, a noted negro-hunter, of Madison, Indiana, who was in search of other fugitives at that time. He took John to Madison, then across into Kentucky, and lodged him in jail. When questioned, John had the shrewdness to give —not his own name—but that of a fugitive with whom he became acquainted in Canada. He said that his name was James Armstrong, that he was the property of the widow Armstrong, of Augusta, Kentucky, but had lived several years in Michigan. Wright Ray pretended to go to the widow Armstrong, and buy her slave James at a low price "as he ran," and then told John that if he had any friends in Michigan who would raise the money in a certain time, that he would sell him for three hundred and fifty dollars. At John's request the sheriff wrote to an address in Michigan, giving this information, and the letter came into the hands of Laura S. Haviland. Though all the names were fictitious, she concluded that the person referred to was John White, and immediately took measures to obtain his liberty. She came to our house—we were then living at Cincinnati—and told her story, intending to go on to Madison, Indiana, cross over into Kentucky, and see if the slave in jail was really John White. I persuaded her to remain, and sent instead, my nephew, M. C. White, giving him letters to Judge Stevens, of Madison, and other noted abolitionists, who might be of service to him in his mission. He went to Kentucky, found that the slave in question was John White, and then entered into negotiations to obtain his freedom. In presence of Judge Stevens, of Madison, he made a contract with Wright Ray to pay the three hundred and fifty dollars on the following conditions: Wright Ray was to bring John White to Madison, and place him on board the packet bound for Cincinnati; the money was to be deposited with the clerk of the boat, and be paid over when John was safely delivered to his friends in this city.

M. C. White then returned to Cincinnati, and made known the success of his mission. I borrowed the money—as Laura S. Haviland had not time to obtain it before she started—and sent him back to Madison. The terms of the contract were carried out, and John White arrived at Cincinnati. The boat came in before daylight, when the clerk who had the money in charge was asleep, but M. C. White informed Wright Ray that he would take John up town and return at eight o'clock to pay over the money.

As soon as John reached my house he was concealed, as it was not thought safe for him to be seen in the streets, lest he might be recognized by some one who had seen him in Kentucky.

Then, following my instructions, M. C. White returned to the boat and told Wright Ray that he was ready to pay over the money, but informed him that the slave was not the person he (W. R.) thought he was, that he was a free man (taking the ground that all men are free until they forfeit their liberty by crime), and that if he received the money, he would be guilty of kidnapping, and must risk the consequences. Ray, however, decided to take

the money and it was paid over to him. Lawyer
Joliff, and I obtained a writ as soon as possible—
which was at nine o'clock—and placed it in the
hands of an officer with instructions to arrest
Wright Ray, but when the officer went to the boat
Ray was not to be found. We immediately forwarded the writ to Judge Stevens, at Madison,
and Ray was soon afterward arrested at that place
and lodged in jail, where he remained several
months, awaiting the opening of court. The case
would, without doubt, have gone against him had it
been tried, but the presence of John White as prosecuting witness would have been necessary, and his
friends feared to risk his freedom, so the case was
allowed to go by default.

John returned to Michigan, almost broken-hearted.
All his endeavors to gain the freedom of his wife
and children had been in vain, and he never saw
them again. They were shortly afterward sold and
separated, the master taking a price for his own
daughter. Laura S. Haviland wrote to him several
times, portraying in the strongest terms the sin of
selling his own child. Her letters made a deep impression on his mind, and he was so much distressed
that he became almost insane; he would walk the
floor of nights, hour after hour, striving to make
terms with his guilty conscience. He made great
efforts to buy back his daughter and her children,
but without success, and it was thought that this
trouble shortened his days.

CHAPTER VII.

DISCUSSION OF THE ANTI-SLAVERY SUBJECT — ANTI-
SLAVERY SOCIETIES AND LECTURERS — OPPOSITION
TO THE MOVEMENT — SEPARATION OF FRIENDS OF
INDIANA YEARLY MEETING — ACTION WHICH CAUSED
THE SEPARATION — REUNION — THE COMMITTEE
FROM LONDON YEARLY MEETING — INTERVIEWS
WITH THE COMMITTEE — LAST INTERVIEW WITH
WILLIAM FORSTER — VISIT TO CANADA IN 1844 —
MEETINGS WITH FUGITIVES — THEIR STORIES — A
SPECIAL PROVIDENCE — AUNT SUSIE'S DREAM — THE
STORY OF JACKSON — A MOTHER RESCUES HER
CHILDREN.

THE subject of slavery had been talked about
and discussed at Newport and in other neighborhoods of Friends in our part of the State, by
Friends and others who felt for those in bonds as
bound with them, for several years previous to the
agitation of the Free Labor question. Abolitionism
at that time was very unpopular. Some Friends
advocated colonization, or gradual emancipation,
and many joined the popular current of opposition to abolitionism. Some of us felt that there
was need of more earnest labor and renewed exertions on behalf of suffering humanity, even among

Friends who professed to bear a testimony against slavery—that an effort should be made to enlighten the minds of the people, and to advance the cause of immediate and unconditional emancipation on Christian principles. We felt that this movement could be forwarded by giving circulation to such publications as were calculated to create an interest in the cause of the oppressed and suffering slave. To promote this object, a few of us, of Newport and vicinity, held, in the year 1838, a conference to consult in regard to our duty in this matter. Daniel Puckett, and other prominent Friends, took an interest in the conference. The result was that we decided to establish an anti-slavery library at Newport, and to collect all the books, tracts, and other publications on the subject that we could, and circulate them among the people. There was then a depository of anti-slavery publications open at Cincinnati. The sum of twenty-five dollars was subscribed, and I was authorized to obtain the publications that we needed. I afterward bought others with my own means, and kept up the supply. We gave away these publications, or loaned them until they were worn out. The effect of this effort was manifested in a deep and increasing interest on the subject of slavery, in our neighborhood. We often held library meetings, as we called them. In that day of mobs and the ridicule of abolitionism, it would not do to call them abolition meetings, even though the anti-slavery sentiment was on the increase in Indiana. About that time a number of Friends, who were in favor of immediate and unconditional emancipation, joined with others in the formation of the State Anti-Slavery Society of Indiana, which was organized at Milton, in Wayne County.

In the year 1840, Arnold Buffum, a member of the Society of Friends, and one of the noble band of twelve that organized the American Anti-Slavery Society, in 1833, on the ground of immediate and unconditional emancipation, came to the West for the purpose of holding meetings among the people; to talk about the wrongs and sufferings of the slave, and to excite an interest in his behalf. It was a work that lay near his heart and one to which he believed himself called by his Heavenly Father. He believed that he was required to plead the cause of the oppressed; to speak for the dumb, and to show forth the cruelty of slavery. He had labored extensively in the Eastern States, and had encountered much opposition in the path of his duty. Some of those who had opposed his labors in the East, endeavored to block up his way and spoil his influence in the West, by writing defamatory letters to their friends here. In these letters they made statements concerning him in which there was not a particle of truth. These stories were circulated wherever he went, with a view to prejudice the people against him; but his enemies were foiled in their designs. One of the wicked and foolish stories told concerning him was, that he was an amalgamationist, and had a colored woman for his wife. But the people among whom he traveled could soon see for themselves that this was a falsehood. His amiable and excellent wife, who accompanied him in all his travels for the purpose of sustaining and comforting him, and who was in full sympathy with him, was a highly esteemed member of the religious Society of Friends, and had no connection with the colored race.

After laboring for some time in Ohio, Arnold Buffum made his way to our neighborhood and came directly to my house. I had never seen him before, but had heard much of him and his work, and the cold reception that he had met with in many places. I gave him a hearty welcome to my house and our State, and told him that when I heard he was pleading the cause of the poor slave in Ohio, I had earnestly desired that the Lord would send him to Indiana. We appointed a meeting for him at our meeting-house in Newport, and there was a good audience of Friends and others, to hear him on the subject of slavery. He made a good impression, and a number of meetings were held in our place; appointments also were made in other neighborhoods.

Daniel Puckett, a noted minister among Friends, accompanied him to some of these neighboring meetings, and Jonathan Hough, another well-known Friend, was his companion when he went to Winchester, and other places in Randolph County. After he returned to Newport, I went to Center ville, our county seat, and obtained the privilege of holding a meeting in the Court-House. At the appointed time, I accompanied him to the place. We had a large meeting, but there was some disorder. The mob spirit plainly manifested itself, but was

finally quelled without any serious disturbance.
Buffum was used to such demonstrations, and was
not embarrassed by them in the least. He was the
first anti-slavery lecturer who had spoken in that
part of the State, and he had ignorance as well as
prejudice to contend with. From Centerville we
went to Spiceland, in Henry County, where we had
an appointment, and held two meetings. We also
held two meetings at Greensboro, then went to
Raysville. These meetings were well attended, but,
strange as it may seem now, many Friends seemed
shy of them, appearing to be afraid to risk their
reputation by attending an abolition meeting. They
professed to be as much opposed to slavery as any
one, but seemed to be more opposed to abolitionism. Different religious denominations partook of
this same prejudice, and we found ourselves opposed
by the cultured as well as the ignorant. It tried a
man's soul to be an abolitionist in those days, when
brickbats, stones and rotten eggs were some of the
arguments we had to meet.

Arnold Buffum did not attempt to organize anti-
slavery societies. His mission did not seem to be
that work, but the endeavor to rouse an interest in
the minds of Friends and others on behalf of the
slave, and to prepare the way for more efficient
action.

He labored for several months in Wayne and adjoining counties, making my house his headquarters
His anti-slavery lectures in the different neighborhoods created an excitement among the people, and
set them to thinking and talking on the subject,

and debating it among themselves. The arguments that Buffum used made deep impressions on many minds, and caused them to reflect on a subject to which they had previously given little attention.

Soon after Buffum's first tour in Indiana, Louis Hicklin, a Methodist preacher, from near Madison, Indiana, traveled over the same ground, delivering anti-slavery lectures, and organizing anti-slavery societies. The agitation of this subject was now fairly under way. Anti-slavery lecturers began to canvass the State, strong anti-slavery societies were organized in various places, and the subject received more thoughtful attention than had before been bestowed upon it. A State Anti-Slavery Convention was held at Newport, and was largely attended by delegates from various parts of the State. Newport was called by the pro-slavery party, "the hot-bed of abolitionism." My house was generally the home of the lecturers and speakers who were traveling through our neighborhood, pleading the cause of the slave. I was always glad to entertain them, and to do all I could in forwarding the cause we had so much at heart. Charles Burley, Frederick Douglass and other speakers from the East were among those who stopped at my house.

But as the anti-slavery movement gained strength, the opposition to it became more powerful. Politicians and other prominent men opposed it, and their influence gave encouragement to the lower classes who possessed the mob spirit and who often interrupted the anti-slavery meetings. When Fred. Douglass made his first lecturing tour through the

West, accompanied by other prominent speakers from Massachusetts, he had to contend with prejudice expressed in the most insulting manner.

At their meeting at Richmond, while they were on the stand speaking, rotten eggs were thrown at them, and at Pendleton they were pelted with brickbats, stones and eggs, until they were driven from the platform. M. C. White, my wife's nephew, who was on the platform, had two of his front teeth knocked out by a brickbat, thrown by one of the mob. Such disgraceful disturbances were of frequent occurrence in various parts of the State, when meetings were held to plead the cause of the slave. This, however, only served to forward the anti-slavery cause among quiet, well disposed citizens. Daniel Worth, a prominent Wesleyan minister, was made President of the State Anti-Slavery Society, and several State Conventions were held at Newport, Wayne County, and Greensboro, Henry County. The work commenced by Arnold Buffum, in 1840, went on with increasing interest, being sustained by Dr. Bennett and other prominent speakers who devoted much time and labor in pleading the cause of the oppressed, until the eastern, middle and northern counties of the State became so strongly abolitionist in sentiment, that the number of the people were very small who would risk their reputation in giving aid to the slave-hunters. Public opinion became so strongly anti-slavery in our neighborhood, that I often kept fugitives at my house openly, while preparing them for their journey to the North, without any fear of being molested.

But, notwithstanding this large increase of anti-slavery sentiment, the pro-slavery party still held the reins of government, in both Church and State, and there was a strong opposition to the abolition movement. The doctrine of immediate and unconditional emancipation was unpopular. Some prominent members of the Society of Friends opposed it, and favored colonization or gradual emancipation.

This difference of opinion subsequently led to a separation in Indiana Yearly Meeting of Friends, which occurred in 1843, and was a sore trial to many of us. The causes of this painful separation are fully set forth in the history of the separation of Friends of Indiana Yearly Meeting, compiled by Walter Edgerton. The two Yearly Meetings continued their separate organizations for thirteen years, but a reunion was finally effected, to the rejoicing of many hearts on both sides.

We were proscribed for simply adhering to what we believed to be our Christian duty, as consistent members of the Society of Friends, in regard to the anti-slavery movement; in uniting with others in anti-slavery societies, opening our meeting-houses for anti-slavery meetings, to plead the cause of the oppressed, and laboring for the spread of anti-slavery truth in every way we could, consistent with our profession as Christians. We asked only liberty of conscience—freedom to act according to one's conscientious convictions. We did not wish to interfere with the conscience or liberty of others, but strictly to live up to that part of our Discipline which bore a testimony against slavery. We had no new doctrine to preach; we advocated immediate and unconditional emancipation as we had done all our lives. This we understood to be the doctrine and testimony of the Society of Friends for generations past. But abolitionism was unpopular; an odium was attached to the very name of abolitionist. It tried men's souls in those days to meet the current of opposition.

Strange as it may seem to the rising generation who read the part of Friend's Discipline relating to slavery, and who would naturally suppose that they would give their support to every movement opposing slavery, there was a spirit of opposition to abolitionism attributable to various causes, which had almost imperceptibly crept in among Friends, and which manifested itself in the Yearly Meeting. A few leading members were colonizationists, some were gradualists, and many were led to believe that there was some disgrace about abolitionism—they could hardly tell what—and they fell in with the current of opposition. Charles Osborne, that faithful servant of the Lord, who preached no new doctrine, had experienced no change, but followed the same course and advocated the same anti-slavery doctrine that he had for forty years. He, with many others of our prominent and faithful ministers, Daniel Puckett, Thomas Frazier, Abel Roberts, Isam Puckett, Martha Wooton, etc., were proscribed and considered disqualified for service in the church, because they could not conscientiously adhere to the advice of the Yearly Meeting. We were advised not to unite in abolition societies, nor to open our meeting-houses for abolition meetings.

This took place at the Yearly Meeting in the fall of 1842. These advices were sent down to Quarterly and Monthly Meetings, with a committee to see that they were carried out. Thus we had no alternative; we must separate, or be disowned for opposing the advice of the body, as they called it. In the winter of 1843 we called a convention at Newport, Indiana, which was largely attended by members of the various Quarterly Meetings who felt aggrieved with the action of the Yearly Meeting.

We spent some time in prayerful deliberation and the result was the reorganization of Indiana Yearly Meeting and the establishment of the Yearly Meeting of Anti-Slavery Friends. No change in the Discipline was thought necessary. Five Quarterly Meetings and twelve Monthly Meetings were organized and established; these constituted the New Yearly Meeting. As soon as these meetings were organized the opposite party seemed to take alarm, and ceased to prosecute the proscriptive measures which had caused the separation.

By this loosening of the cord they no doubt saved many of their members, who sympathized with us, but who on account of the change in policy were not driven to the necessity of separating from the body. Thus a large number of Friends in the limits of Indiana Yearly Meeting retained unity with us and brotherly feeling toward us, and many of the members of other Yearly Meetings sympathized

with us. We had many able ministers, both men
and women, with us, and we experienced many
precious meetings, where the overshadowing wing
of Divine Goodness was sensibly felt to hover over
us and bless our assembly. The trials and sufferings through which we had passed together made
us near and dear to each other. This feeling
remains with those still living, to the present day,
and is renewed whenever we meet. Several of our
most prominent ministers of the present day were
connected with anti-slavery Friends; many of the
older ones have gone to their reward.

As time rolled on, and the anti-slavery sentiment
increased, and the odium attached to abolitionism
lessened, many of the younger members of the old
Yearly Meeting came forward nobly and joined us
on the anti-slavery platform, and many of the older
ones acknowledged that the Yearly Meeting did
wrong in pursuing the course that brought the separation, and manifested the most friendly feeling
toward us. The Yearly Meeting made a change in
the Discipline in regard to acknowledgments from
those who had once been members; thus leaving the
door open for a reunion. Many of the older ones
on both sides had passed away. There seemed
now to be nothing to keep us longer apart, so we
dissolved our separate organizations, and in most
or all of the Monthy Meetings, where anti-slavery
Friends lived, a proposition was made to the
Monthly Meeting in writing, to unite in a body
without making any acknowledgment. This proposition was accepted in most cases, at that meeting,

without making an appointment. Thus a happy reunion was effected.

In the year 1845, London Yearly Meeting issued an address to the anti-slavery Friends who had separated from Indiana Yearly Meeting, and appointed a committee to accompany it and to endeavor to heal the breach. This commmittee was composed of four prominent and influential Friends— William Forster, George Stacy, Josiah Forster and John Allen. They arrived in this country in time to attend the Yearly Meeting at Richmond in the tenth month of that year.

The Yearly Meeting of Anti-Slavery Friends was in session at the same time at Newport, ten miles distant. We supposed that the committee would attend our meeting also, but in this we were mistaken. The old Yearly Meeting appointed a committee to give such information as they desired. The day after that Yearly Meeting closed, the English Friends paid a short social visit to Charles Osborne, who was stopping at my house. Several other Friends were present. During this short interview some intimation of their intended course was given, influenced perhaps by the counsel of the advisory committee of the old Yearly Meeting. They returned the same evening to Richmond, which was their headquarters. They concluded to visit the distant meetings or outposts of anti-slavery Friends, before visiting the larger body at Newport, and other meetings in that vicinity. After they left Newport several of the leading anti-slavery Friends thought it necessary to confer together a little on the circumstances of their conclusions, believing that the course of action the committee had decided upon would not heal the breach or effect the object of their mission to this country. This conference resulted in our addressing a letter to the committee, in brotherly love, suggesting a different course. This letter was signed by fourteen prominent Friends — Charles Osborne, Daniel Puckett and others—and Benjamin Stanton, Henry H. Way and I were nominated to carry it to them at Richmond before they started West, and to have an interview with them. We were kindly received by the committee, and had a free and open conversation with these noble Christian men on the subject of their mission. We fully believed that the course they were about to pursue would not bring the differing parties together as they desired, and as we also greatly desired.

We thought that if the leading influential members of both parties could be brought together, and the causes of the differences that produced the separation investigated, and clearly set forth to the committee, they might be able to judge clearly and intelligently, and to advise in the matter. But they thought that their minute of appointment from London Yearly Meeting would not justify them in taking that course, as the address of that meeting was to anti-slavery Friends, advising them to cease holding their separate meetings and to return to the body from which they had separated. London Yearly Meeting did not understand all the causes of the separation, but took it for granted that the

Society of Friends was everywhere an anti-slavery body, and bore a testimony against slavery both in Europe and America. They did not understand the different sentiments among us in this country in regard to anti-slavery action—that the spirit of colonization and gradual emancipation was deeply seated in the minds of many Friends here, notwithstanding that, in their General Epistle, London Yearly Meeting had denounced colonization as an odions plan of expatriation. They were not aware that the great body of the Society of Friends in America had, with nearly all other religious societies, thrown the weight of their influence against the few true abolitionists who advocated immediate and unconditional emancipation.

Friends in America, as a body, had fallen into the popular current and denounced abolitionism, though there were in all the Yearly Meetings noble exceptions, persons who had to suffer on account of their testimonies, and who stood firm in the face of opposition and battled for the right.

These members of the minority sympathized with us who had dared to stand firm in the cause of the oppressed and suffering slave, and to the testimony of the Society of Friends against slavery. We often received letters of cheer and encouragement from members of other Yearly Meetings. Charles Osborne, who was widely known and loved as a faithful minister of the gospel, and who had traveled and labored much in the ministry, was among the number proscribed and pronounced disqualified for labor in the church.

Friends in England had no such trials to pass through; abolitionism was popular there, and they were united in their sentiments on the anti-slavery subject. They united with others in anti-slavery societies, and opened their meeting-houses for anti-slavery meetings. In this country our meeting-houses were refused for such purposes, when we wished to assemble to plead the cause of the slave and to try to enlighten and awaken public sentiment on the subject of slavery. We apprehended that the English Committee were not fully apprised of all these circumstances, which led to our separation, hence our letter to them and our interview with them. All these matters were carefully laid before them, and received a kind and respectful hearing, but they could not feel it right to change their programme.

They had decided to visit all the different neighborhoods of anti-slavery Friends belonging to our Yearly Meeting, call the Friends together at their meeting-places, and after reading to them the address of London Yearly Meeting, advise them to discontinue their separate organizations, and return to the body. This was as far as they thought they were justified by their appointment to go; they felt that they could not act as umpires or mediators between the two parties. We assured them that such a course of action could not effect a reunion. We said that anti-slavery Friends had counted the cost and suffered much before they separated; that our meetings had been much blessed, and that we had abundant evidence that our assemblies had been

owned by the great Head of the Church. We had
been forced to take the step we did by the act of
Indiana Yearly Meeting, and if we enjoyed religious
society at all there was no alternative for us but to
continue our meetings. Until a different spirit was
manifested by the body we had separated from, we
could not relinquish or discontinue our organizations; we believed that the cause we had so much
at heart would suffer by such a course. We were
fully convinced that their labors in the direction
they had decided upon would not effect the object
desired. This seemed to make a deep impression
on the mind of dear old William Forster; indeed,
all of them seemed full of love and kind feeling toward us. They talked freely with us on the matter,
expressing their earnest desire that the unity of the
body might be restored. We desired the same
thing, but we were not disposed to cry Peace,
peace, when there was no peace. Those days
were trying and proving seasons to many of us.
We parted from the committee in love and kind
feeling, leaving them to ponder over our suggestions. But they pursued the course planned out,
visiting the various neighborhoods of anti-slavery
Friends on the outskirts of our Yearly Meeting,
calling the people together at their different meeting-places, reading the address to them, and advising them to discontinue their separate organizations.

The result was what we had anticipated; anti-
slavery Friends were not prepared to accept their
advice or to adhere to their counsels. I wish to
speak of these dear Friends from England with

much love, and to hold in kind remembrance their many good works, and their devotedness to the cause of. Christ. But I think they erred in judgment—as it is possible for good and wise men to do —and I believe they were fully sensible of it before they left this country. Our separate organization was kept up, and it was nearly eleven years after their visit that a satisfactory reunion was effected.

Their meeting with anti-slavery Friends at Newport was held about three days before they started home. When they arrived in town in the morning, a short time before the appointed hour of their meeting, they took quarters at the house of William Hobbs, a prominent member of the old Yearly Meeting. At the close of the meeting, I invited them to our house to dine, but they declined, having promised to return to William Hobbs'. I told them I wanted them to pay me a visit before they left town, having learned that they had to return to Richmond that evening. I said I had something to show them, which I thought would interest them, and which they would be.likely to remember after they returned to their own country.

William Forster said: "We will go home with thee now," as it was on their way to their stopping place. He took me by one arm, George Stacy by the other, and the other two Friends followed us. When we arrived at our house, I seated them in the parlor, excused myself for a moment, and went into a back room where there were fourteen fugitive slaves, who had arrived the night before. An old white-haired grandmother was there, with several of

her children and grandchildren; one of her daughters had a child three months old. I invited them
all to follow me into the parlor to see the four English Friends, telling them the gentlemen lived
on the other side of the ocean where there was no
slavery, and were true friends to the slave. This
seemed to remove all fear from them, and they followed me into the parlor. I had them to stand in a
semicircle, and introduced them to the English
Friends as fugitive slaves fleeing from the land of
whips and chains, and seeking safety in the Queen's
dominions. The Friends all rose and shook hands
with them. Taking the child in my arms, I said:
"See this innocent babe, which was born a slave,"
and handed it to George Stacy, who stood near me.
He took it in his arms and fondled it, for it was a
pleasant looking child. All the Friends seemed
deeply interested, and asked the fugitives many
questions. The old woman seemed to be quite intelligent, and answered their questions readily.

William Forster said: "It is a long road to Canada; do you think you will ever reach that country?" He did not know the facilities of the Underground Railroad.

The old negress replied: "De Lord has been with
us dis far, an' I trust He will go with us to de end
of de journey."

William Forster said: "Thou art old and feeble."

"Yes, massa," she replied, "but I'se been prayin' de good Lord a great while to let me breathe
one mouthful of free air before I died, and bress his
great name, He opened de way so dat we got off

safe and He has guided us to dis good man's house, and he and his good wife has give us clothes to make us warm, and when we rest a little so we can stand more night travel, he says he will send us on. May de Lord bress him! You see, gent'men, dat de Lord is good to us and helps us."

Many more questions were asked by the Friends, and answered by the old woman and others of the party. The Friends seemed so interested that they hardly knew how to close the interview. When the fugitives retired, I turned to George Stacy, and said:

"For pleading the cause of innocent babes like the one thou held in thy arms, and sheltering the fugitives, such as you have seen, we have been proscribed. Now, my dear friends, if you fully understood the difference of sentiment that exists, and the course pursued by some of the leading members of Indiana Yearly Meeting, which led to our separation, you could not advise the discontinuance of our organization, while they persist in their course toward us. Your efforts have strengthened the opposition to our labors."

I then alluded to the course pursued by the committee of the old Yearly Meeting, when they visited the Quarterly and Monthly Meetings to enforce the epistle of advice issued by the Yearly Meeting. My remarks seemed to make a deep impression on their minds. William Forster said: "It must have been very trying, indeed," to which the others assented. Their time had now expired and we must

separate, but, before starting, William Forster said
to his companions:

"We must not leave this country without having
a more deliberate opportunity with Levi Coffin; I
do not feel satisfied." After consulting together a
few moments, they asked me if I would be willing
to meet them at Richmond. I said that I would,
and told them to appoint the time and place most
convenient to themselves, and I would endeavor to
meet them promptly. They had an appointment
for the next day at Dover, which would close their
labors in that part of the country, and suggested
that I meet them the day following, at nine
o'clock in the morning. The place appointed was
the house of my cousin, Elijah Coffin, in Richmond, where they made their headquarters. I
suggested having another Friend to accompany me,
but they seemed to prefer an interview with me
alone. I met them at the hour appointed, having
a deep sense of my incompetency to engage in
debate with four well-educated and well-informed
English gentlemen. William Forster was a prominent and widely known minister, George Stacy was
clerk of London Yearly Meeting, and Josiah Forster and John Allen were highly esteemed elders.
How could I, a lay-member of a proscribed body
of abolitionists, venture to differ from or call into
question the acts of these wise Christian fathers
in the church? These feelings and thoughts passed
through my mind as I proceeded to Richmond, and
I prayed earnestly that I might be guided and
rightly directed in everything I uttered—that self

might be entirely subdued and nothing but the cause of Christ and his poor have any place in my mind. I was cordially greeted by the committee and conducted to a room which had been prepared for the meeting, where we would not be interrupted.

All diffidence or embarrassment had passed away; I felt calm and quiet in my mind, and much openness and freedom seemed to be felt by us all. William Forster opened the conversation by saying that when they were at my house their time was so limited that I did not have the opportunity of expressing all that I wished to say on the subject of our trials and in regard to their labors among us, and that he felt it was right to give me a further opportunity, and hoped that we might be brought nearer together in sympathy. I then commenced where our conversation at my house had ended, and gave them, in detail, the beginning and continuance of our difficulties on the anti-slavery subject, showing how the opposition spirit gained the ascendency and proscribed Charles Osborne and other prominent Friends.

I spoke more fully of the measures adopted by the Yearly Meeting, which caused many of us to pass through deep trials and sufferings, and finally brought about the separation, and said that I believed the matter was not fully understood by London Yearly Meeting, that if it had been, they would not have issued that address advising us to discontinue our separate organization. Yearly Meetings are not infallible, I continued, and individuals are not infallible, and you, my dear friends, may have erred in judgment from lack of a full understanding of this difficulty, for you are only men.

George Stacy, who sat near me, patted me affectionately on the knee, and said: "We know that, Levi; we are very poor creatures of ourselves."

William Forster said: "I hope thou wilt award honesty to our purpose."

I said: "Certainly I will. I love you as Christian brothers and have no doubt of the honesty of your purpose, but your labors will not have the desired effect. Our organization will not be discontinued until a different spirit is manifested by the opposing party, and Indiana Yearly Meeting opens the way for a reunion." The committee asked many questions, which I endeavored to answer carefully. They seemed to be deeply impressed and often said in the course of my statements, "How painful and trying that must have been." They appeared very humble and manifested much love and kindness in their manner toward me. I felt perfect freedom during the interview, notwithstanding the misgivings I had felt beforehand. After spending two hours together we parted, with many expressions of love and kind feeling. After their return home, I received several communications from them which expressed the same brotherly feelings. Eight years afterward London Yearly Meeting issued an address to the President of the United States and the governors of the various States in America, on the subject of slavery.

William Forster, that noble anti-slavery Christian minister, volunteered to carry the address and visit all the governors and heads of departments in our Government. Josiah Forster, his brother, and two other Friends, John Candler and William Holmes, were appointed to accompany him in this undertaking. I was then living in Cincinnati. I heard of their arrival in America, but had no knowledge of their having reached this city until I went to Friend's Meeting one First day, and saw William Forster sitting at the head of the meeting, with his brother Josiah by his side. I was rejoiced to see these dear friends again.

William Forster was favored to preach the gospel with great power and unction that day. As soon as the meeting closed he made his way to me and grasped my hand, having previously recognized me. He told me that they had arrived in the city the evening before and had taken quarters at Abraham Taylor's, and invited me to go with them and dine. I excused myself, as we had company to dine with us that day, and invited them to visit us, which they promised to do. We then had charge of the Colored Orphan Asylum. In the afternoon they made us a visit and spent a few hours very pleasantly. They had the orphan children collected together, and spoke in an interesting manner, imparting much wholesome counsel to them. Learning that the asylum was a benevolent institution, dependent on contributions for support, they gave some money to be applied as we saw fit. We had taken charge of the asylum a short time, to try to build it up and get it in a good condition. When the English Friends were ready to start away, Will-

iam Forster declined to get into the carriage, saying that he would walk with me a short distance, as
he wished to have some conversation with me before
we parted. We walked together slowly for several
squares. He said he had often thought of me since
we parted at Richmond, eight years before, and
expressed the kind feelings he still had for me.

I expressed the same for him, and went on to
say that the breach was not yet healed in Indiana
Yearly Meeting, but a very different feeling was
now manifested toward us. Many of our opposers
showed a kind and loving spirit; several of the
prominent members of the old Yearly Meeting
had acknowledged to me that the Yearly Meeting
did wrong in taking the course that brought about
the separation. I believed the way was opening
for a reunion; many of the younger members
of the old Yearly Meeting were now boldly advocating the cause we had espoused; the proscriptive
measures were no longer prosecuted; and a change
had been made in their Discipline, which opened a
door for us to reunite with them. William Forster
seemed much rejoiced on hearing these statements.
I told him that a change of public sentiment was
rapidly taking place in the North, both in Church
and State, and that abolitionism had lost much of
the odium formerly attached to it. This also seemed
to rejoice his heart, and he said he earnestly hoped
that a happy reunion would soon be effected in Indiana Yearly Meeting. He expressed much satisfaction and comfort in our interview, and said that
it was probably the last time we would meet in this

world, but that he hoped we would meet in the realms of never-ending peace and joy. We parted with much love for each other.

The next day the party visited the governor of Kentucky, then went by way of Indianapolis to Illinois, Wisconsin, and Missouri, and continued their tour through the Southern States, visiting the governor of each State. They had a kind reception and respectful hearing in every instance. This arduous work and extensive travel proved too much for the strength of William Forster. He was taken sick, and died in East Tennessee, before their mission was completed. A full account of his peaceful and happy close is given in the "Memoirs of William Forster," edited by Benjamin Seebohm. He was buried in Friends' burying-ground, at Friendsville, Blount County, East Tennessee.

The remaining members of the delegation finished the work of their mission, and returned to England in the spring of 1854. When I heard of the death of this dear old Friend and faithful servant of the Lord, it was a great comfort and satisfaction to me to remember our last interview in Cincinnati.

FIRST VISIT TO CANADA.

In the fall of 1844, William Beard, of Union County, Indiana, a minister of the religious Society of Friends, felt a concern to visit, in gospel love, the fugitive slaves who had escaped from Southern bondage and settled in Canada. A number of them had stopped at his house in their flight, and had been forwarded by him to my house, a distance of thirty miles. He felt that I was the person who should accompany him on this mission, and came to see me to present the subject. I heartily united with him, having felt a similar desire. We then laid the concern before our different Monthly Meetings, where it was cordially united with, and a certificate of unity and concurrence was given us. Thus provided with the proper credentials, and with the love of God in our hearts, we set out on our mission to the poor fugitives, intending also to visit the missionary stations among the Indians in Canada.

We started on horseback on the sixteenth day of the ninth month—September. On our way we visited several colored settlements in Ohio and Michigan, and held meetings with the people.

We reached Detroit on the twenty-fifth of the ninth month, about noon, and in company with Dr. Porter, a noted abolitionist of that city, spent the afternoon visiting the colored schools and various families of fugitives, many of whom remembered us, having stopped at our houses on their way from slavery to freedom. In the evening we attended a good meeting among the colored people, and visited Aunt Rachel, whose story of escape and suffering is given elsewhere. She had come over from Canada and settled in Detroit. She was married, and had a kind husband. I had not seen her since she left my house, eight years before.

On the twenty-sixth we passed over to Windsor, on the Canada side. Here, and at Sandwich, we visited a number of colored families, many of whom recognized me at once, having been at my house in the days of their distress when fleeing. from a land of whips and chains.

The Queen's Court was in session at Sandwich while we were there, and a white man was on trial for having, under the inducement of a bribe, decoyed a fugitive across the river into the hands of his master. We went into court and listened for a time with much interest to the lawyers pleading. We heard Colonel Prince reaffirm the proud boast of England, that the moment a fugitive set his foot on British soil his shackles fell off and he was free. We afterward learned that a heavy penalty of fine and imprisonment was placed on the culprit.

From Sandwich we made our way down the Canada side of the Detroit River to Amherstburg, generally called Fort Malden, near the head of Lake Erie. In this old military town, and in the vicinity, a great many fugitives had located. The best tavern, or house of public entertainment, in the town, was kept by William Hamilton, a colored man. While at this place we made our headquarters at Isaac J. Rice's missionary buildings, where he had a large school for colored children. He had labored here among the colored people, mostly fugitives, for six years. He was a devoted self-denying worker, had received very little pecuniary help, and had suffered many privations. He was well situated in Ohio, as pastor of a Presbyterian church, and had fine prospects before him, but believed that the Lord called him to this field of missionary labor among the fugitive slaves who came here by hundreds and by thousands, poor, destitute and ignorant, suffering from all the evil influences of slavery. We entered into deep sympathy with him in his labors, realizing the great need there was here for just such an institution as he had established. He had sheltered at this missionary home many hundreds of fugitives till other homes for them could be found. This was the great landing point, the principal terminus of the Underground Railroad of the West.

We held meetings among the fugitives here and in the various settlements in the neighborhood. Isaac J. Rice accompanied us on these visits, and down the lake to Colchester and Gosfield. Here we had several meetings and visited many families, hearing thrilling stories of their narrow escapes, their great sufferings and the remarkable providences that attended their efforts to gain freedom. They told how they had prayed to the Lord, asking him to be with them and protect them in their flight from their tyrannical masters, and how he had never forsaken them in their time of need, but had fulfilled his promise to go with them. They frequently spoke as if they had held personal conversations with the Lord, and their simple and untutored language was full of expression of praise and thanksgiving. I was often led to believe that these poor ignorant and degraded sons and daughters of Africa, who were not able to read the words of the precious Savior, were blessed with a clearer, plainer manifestation of the Holy Spirit than many of us who have had better opportunites of cultivation. My heart was often touched and my eyes filled with tears on hearing their simple stories, or listening to their fer-

vent earnest prayers in the services of family devotion, which we held from house to house. Holding
meetings in families and in public constituted our
work among them. We visited all the principal settlements of fugitives in Canada West, as well as the
various missionary stations among the tribes of
Indians there, and had an interesting and satisfactory season among them. We spent nearly two
months in this way, traveling from place to place on
horseback, as there were no railroads in that section
then.

Leaving Gosfield County we made our way to
Chatham and Sydenham, visiting the various neighborhoods of colored people. We spent several days
at the settlement near Down's Mills, and visited the
institution under the care of Hiram Wilson, called
the British and American Manual Labor Institute
for Colored Children. Friends in England had furnished the money to purchase the land and aid in
establishing the institution; Friends of New York
Yearly Meeting also contributed to aid this work.
The school was then in a prosperous condition.

From this place we proceeded up the river
Thames to London, visiting the different settlements
of colored people on our way, and then went to the
Wilberforce Colony. This was the only settlement
we visited in our travels where we did not find fugitives who had been sheltered under my roof and fed
at my table during their flight from bondage.

At the close of our religious meetings I generally
addressed the colored people on the subject of education. I urged the parents to send their children

to school, and to attend Sabbath-schools and night-schools themselves whenever opportunity offered ; to learn at least to read the Bible. We had visited most of their schools, and I contrasted their present situation and advantages with their former state of servitude, where they were not allowed to learn to read. I sometimes mentioned that I had had the privilege of aiding some of them in the time of their distress, of sheltering them under my roof and feeding them at my table when they were fleeing from the hardships and cruelties of slavery and seeking safety and freedom in the Queen's dominions. Whenever I touched that subject it brought out shouts of "Bless the Lord! I know you. If it hadn't been for you I wouldn't be here ;" and at the close of the meeting the people would come round us to shake hands in such crowds that it was impossible for all to get hold of our hands. Some would cling to our garments as if they thought they would impart some virtue. I often met fugitives who had been at my house ten or fifteen years before, so long ago that I had forgotten them, and could recall no recollection of them until they mentioned some circumstance that brought them to mind. Some of them were well situated, owned good farms, and were perhaps worth more than their former masters. Land had been easily obtained and many had availed themselves of this advantage to secure comfortable homesteads. Government land had been divided up into fifty-acre lots, which they could buy for two dollars an acre, and have ten years in which to pay for it, and if it was not paid for at the end of that time they did not lose all the labor they had bestowed on it, but received a clear title to the land as soon as they paid for it.

We found many of the fugitives more comfortably situated than we expected, but there was much destitution and suffering among those who had recently come in. Many fugitives arrived weary and foot-sore, with their clothing in rags, having been torn by briers and bitten by dogs on their way, and when the precious boon of freedom was obtained, they found themselves possessed of little else, in a country unknown to them and a climate much colder than that to which they were accustomed.

We noted the cases and localities of destitution, and after our return home took measures to collect and forward several large boxes of clothing and bedding to be distributed by reliable agents to the most needy. Numbers arrived every week on the different lines of the Underground Railroad, destitute of every comfort and almost of clothing ; so we found that end of our road required Christian care and benevolence as well as this. We were gratified to learn that the colored people of Canada had organized benevolent associations among themselves, for the purpose of assisting the newly arrived fugitives as far as they could.

William Beard and I afterward made short tours to Canada at different times to look after the welfare of the fugitives. At the time of our visit, in 1844, there was said to be about forty thousand fugitives in Canada who had escaped from Southern bondage.

While mingling with the fugitives in Canada we heard many interesting stories of individual adventures and trials, a few of which will be given.

The first may be appropriately called :

A SPECIAL PROVIDENCE.

There lived in Mississippi, a black woman who was poor, ignorant, and a slave, but rich in the knowledge of the truth as it is in Jesus, and strong in unwavering faith. Working in the field under the driver's lash, or alone in her little hut, she never ceased praying to God, asking him to help her to escape, and assist and protect her on the long journey to the North. She had heard there was a place called Canada, far to the northward, where all were free, and learned that, in order to reach it, she must go a long way up the Mississippi River, then cross over and steer her course by the north star. Finally, her prayers seemed to be answered, and she had perfect faith that she would be preserved through all the dangers that would menace her if she ran away.

One night, when all around were wrapped in sleep, she put a small supply of food and some clothing together, in a little bundle, and, stealing away from the negro quarters, left the plantation and plunged into the forest, which was there a labyrinth of swamps and cane-brakes. She made her way through this slowly, for several days, often hearing the bloodhounds baying on her track, or perhaps in search of other fugitives. Slaves often fled to these swamps and took refuge among the thickets, preferring the companionship of the deadly moccasin snake and the alligator, and the risk of death from starvation or exposure to the cruel treatment of their masters, and the keen cut of the overseer's lash.

This slave woman managed to evade the dogs by wading in pools and streams of water, where she knew they would lose the scent and be thrown off her trail. One time, however, she heard the deep baying of the bloodhounds coming toward her, when she was some distance from any water. There was no way of escape and she knew they would soon come up with her, and perhaps tear her to pieces before the pursuers could reach them. In this dire extremity, she fell on her knees and asked God to preserve her—to give her some sign of his protecting power; then, with all fear gone, she rose to her feet and calmly watched the dogs approach. As they came near, she took from her pocket a handful of crumbs—the remainder of the food she had brought—and held them out toward the hounds. They came up to her, but instead of seizing and mangling her, they gamboled about her, licked the crumbs from her hands, then ran off through the forest.

This remarkable preservation she felt was the sign she had asked of God, and, falling on her knees once more, she dedicated herself wholly to him, vowing that if she reached Canada, the rest of her life should be devoted solely and entirely to his service. She had a long journey after that, lasting for several months, and encountered many dangers, but was preserved safe through them all. She traveled at night and hid in the thickets during the day, living mostly on fruit and green corn, but venturing now and then to call at negro huts and beg for a little of the scanty food which they afforded. When she came to rivers and streams of water too deep for wading, she made rafts of logs or poles, tied together with grape-vines or hickory withs, and poled or paddled herself across as best she could. Reaching Illinois, she met with kind people who aided her on to Detroit, Michigan. Here also she found friends and was ferried across to Canada. A colored minister who witnessed her arrival says that, on landing, she fell on her knees and kissed the shore, and thanked the Lord for his wonderful mercy in preserving her through so many dangers and bringing her at last to the land of freedom. She then arose and jumped up and down for half an hour, shouting praises to God and seeming almost delirious in her great joy. We were informed that she was a devoted Christian worker, and was earnestly endeavoring to fulfill her vows and promises to the Lord.

AUNT SUSY'S DREAM.

The following story was related to us at Amherstburg, by a negro woman. She had been a slave in South Carolina, and though she had longed all her life to be free, no opportunity for escape had presented itself. At last, when she was approaching middle age and was the mother of several children, she was taken to one of the Northern-States, by her master and mistress, who went there on a visit.

She ran away from them, and by the aid of kind
people on the way reached Canada in safety. She
rejoiced to think she was free, and would have been
perfectly content in her new home had not the
thought of her two children in bondage troubled her.
Their images were constantly before her during her
waking hours, and in dreams she sought them in
their Southern home.

One night she dreamed that she was gifted with
the power of flight, and soared over the long distance that separated her from the objects of her
love. She alighted near her children and was en-
tranced in the joy of a happy meeting, when their
master approached and tried to take them from her.
She placed one on each of her wings, and, rising
high in the air, flew back to Canada. Her heart
was so full of joy at this fulfillment of her dearest
hopes that she shouted aloud. With the shouting
she awoke, and realized that she was still bereaved,
but gathered comfort from her dream, regarding it as
an omen that her children would be restored to her.
The following lines were written by an English lady,
to whom I related this incident, in the year 1864,
when on a mission to England in behalf of the
Freedmen:

<blockquote>
A mother was sleeping,
Yet silently weeping,
And sorrow stole over her heart like a wave;
For while liberty blest her
The feeling oppressed her
That her children were still in the land of the slave.
</blockquote>

22

A mysterious power,
Had seized her that hour,
And her once timid heart had grown fearless and brave;
And regardless of dangers,
Of bloodhounds and rangers,
Undaunted she flies to the land of the slave.

Far, far to the southward,
Her flight is still onward,
From Canada's shore, by Ontario's wave;
To the warm plains outspreading,
Where the planter is treading,
That land which is known as the land of the slave.

How her pulses are swelling!
In her old cottage dwelling,
She beholds the two girls she has come there to save;
And, embracing, doth tell them,
That no one shall sell them,
She'll bear them away from the land of the slave.

The children caress her,
And smiling address her—
"Dear mother! you come to snatch us from the grave!
For our master has told us
This day he has sold us,
To the lonesome rice swamps of the land of the slave."

Then gently that mother
Lifted one and the other
Upon those soft pinions, so mighty to save;
Her children upraising,
While the master stood gazing,
She bears far away from the land of the slave!

The mother was sleeping,
At an end was her weeping,
And loud was the shout of rejoicing she gave;
But alas! on awaking,
The vision forsaking,
Her children were still in the land of the slave.

Oh! ye English mothers,
Ye sisters and brothers,
Who love the free children whom Providence gave;
Now, without stint or measure,
Give for those, from your treasure,
Whose children are still in the land of the slave.

THE STORY OF JACKSON

We heard from his own lips, while visiting at his house in Canada. He had formerly been the property of a man living in Kentucky, who found him to be a trusty servant, and frequently sent him on business errands some distance away. Jackson was married to a woman who was the property of another man, but his master hired her time, and the husband and wife were permitted to live together. They had one child at the time the story begins.

One day Jackson was sent away to a distant market with his master's team, and while he was gone his wife and child were sold by their master to a Southern trader, who removed them to a place about thirty miles distant, where the gang of slaves was gathered, preparatory to starting South the next day. The wife, torn so suddenly from her home, was frantic with distress, and prayed to God to trouble her husband's heart that he might know something was wrong, and come to her rescue. Her prayer was answered, for her husband had a strong presentiment on the day mentioned that all was not well at home, and not being able to account for it, hastened his return and learned the facts. Taking two of his master's horses that night, he started in pursuit; rode all night and just before daybreak reached the place where his wife was. She had slept none, but had prayed through all the hours of darkness, and so confident was she that her prayer would be answered that as she lay in the cabin with the rest of the gang of slaves, she kept her head turned in the direction whence her husband would come, and listened intently for the sound of his horses' feet. When she did hear him, she took her child in her arms, slipped out quietly in the dark, and joined him. There was no time for explanation or rejoicing then ; they were still in the midst of danger and must fly to a place of safety before they uttered the feelings of their full hearts. Mounting the horses, and riding at full speed, they made some distance before the growing light of coming day warned them to seek a hiding-place. They concealed themselves in the woods all that day, and pursued their journey northward during the night. Finally, they reached the banks of the Ohio River, and leaving the horses, they crossed to the other side, where they found friends who directed them on their way. In the northern part of Ohio, they stopped in a quiet settlement, where the people were abolitionists. Here they had a good situation offered them, and thinking they would be safe from pursuit in this secluded neighborhood, they accepted the offer and went to work.

Here they remained several years, very happy in their humble home, and here two more children were born to them. By their industrious habits and good conduct they gained the esteem of those around them, and seemed secure in the protection

of so many friends. The law, however, still regarded them as slaves, and they learned in time
that they were not safe, even on the soil of free
Ohio.

An agent, sent out from Kentucky in search of
other fugitives, came into this neighborhood, and
recognizing Jackson, lost no time in conveying the
news to his master. As soon as he received the
intelligence, the master gathered a posse of men
and came in pursuit. They pounced upon the unsuspecting family and were dragging them back to
bondage, when Jackson's friends learned what had
happened and came to the rescue. Hastening to
the county seat, they obtained a writ, and pursuing
the party arrested the master for kidnapping, and
brought them all back to the Court-House for trial.
Shrewd lawyers were employed, who picked a flaw
in the writ which the master had obtained, and the
slaves were released. The master hastened to renew his writ, intending now to gain full legal possession of his property. But Jackson's friends were
wide awake, and did not risk another arrest. They
hurried the fugitives from the Court-House by a back
way, through an alley, to a place where a wagon
and two swift horses—procured for the occasion—
were in waiting. They were quickly stowed in the
wagon, then the driver took the reins, and off they
went at full speed. The master and his posse pursued them, but in vain. Jackson and his family
were conveyed to the lake that night, and put on
board a steamer. They crossed safely to Canada,
and made their home in Gosfield County.

At the time he related this story, Jackson was living on land of his own, in a house erected by the industry of himself and family, and surrounded by peace and prosperity. He and his wife often related to their children the story of their early hardship and suffering, and when they contrasted their present with their former lot their hearts overflowed with gratitude to God for his protecting and guiding care.

A MOTHER RESCUES HER CHILDREN.

While at Fort Malden, on Lake Erie, we heard of a brave woman named Armstrong, who had recently gone back to Kentucky and rescued five of her children from slavery. We were anxious to see her and hear the story from her own lips, and accordingly visited her at her home in Colchester, about ten miles below Malden. She was a portly, fine-looking woman, and we were much impressed with the noble expression of her countenance. She told us that about two years before she and her husband, with their youngest child, a babe a few months old, made their escape from Kentucky. Their home in that State was about ten miles from the Ohio River, at a point opposite Ripley, the home of that worthy divine and noted abolitionist, John Rankin. After crossing the river, they found friends who helped them on their way to Canada.

They gained freedom for themselves, but they were not happy; they had left seven children in slavery. The mother wept and prayed over their fate, and planned continually how they might be rescued. She felt that she must make some attempt to bring them away, but her husband thought of the risk and danger attending such an effort on her part, and tried to dissuade her from going. She said: "I inquired of the Lord concerning the matter. I prayed most all night, and the Lord seemed to say, 'Go.'

"Next morning I told my husband I was going, that the Lord would go with me and help me. I had all my plans laid; I dressed in men's clothes, and started. I went to our friends in Ohio, and had all the arrangements made for a skiff to come over to the Kentucky side. I took by-ways and through fields to old master's farm, and got there in the early part of the night. I hid myself near the spring, and watched for my children, for I knew some of them would come to get water. I had not been there long before my eldest daughter came. I called her name in a low voice, and when she started up and looked round, I told her not to be afraid, that I was her mother. I soon convinced her, and her alarm passed away. I then told her my plans, and she said she could bring the rest of the children to me when master and mistress got to sleep. The night was very dark, and that favored our plans. She brought all the children to me but two; they were sleeping in the room with old master and mistress, who had gone to bed, and she could not get them out without raising the alarm. I started with the five, and hastened back to the river as fast as we could go in the dark. We found the skiff waiting for us, and soon crossed. On the other side, a wagon was ready to take us in, and the man with it drove us a few miles to a depot of the Underground Railroad. Here we were secreted during the following day, and next night were forwarded on to another station, and so on from station to station till we reached Sandusky, where we were put on board the Mayflower—called the Abolition Boat. We landed safely at Fort Malden two weeks ago, and are out of old massa's reach now. The Lord did help me, and blessed be his holy name!"

She said she had made arrangements with her friends in Ohio, living near the river, to try to get her two other children and send them to her, and she had faith that they would succeed.

CHAPTER VIII.

FREE LABOR——TESTIMONY OF JOHN WOOLMAN AND OTHERS——MY CONVICTIONS——FREE-LABOR SOCIETIES OF NEW YORK AND PHILADELPHIA——OUR ORGANIZATION IN THE WEST——REMOVAL TO CINCINNATI—— FREE-LABOR BUSINESS——SOUTHERN COTTON PRODUCED BY FREE LABOR——INCIDENTS OF A SOUTHERN TRIP——INTERVIEWS WITH SLAVEHOLDERS.

FOR several years my mind had been deeply impressed with the inconsistency of abolitionists partaking indiscriminately of the unpaid toil of the slave. I thought that to be consistent in bearing testimony against slavery, we should discourage unpaid labor and encourage paid labor as far as practicable. I knew, however, that it would be very difficult to abstain entirely from the products of slave labor. I was then engaged in mercantile business—retailing dry-goods and groceries, a large portion of which was produced by slave labor, and I knew of no facilities for obtaining free-labor goods. I had heard Charles Osborne, a worthy minister of the Society of Friends, express his sentiments on the subject, and they made a deep impression on my mind. Charles Osborne had long been a consistent and thorough abolitionist, and was

23

the editor of the first anti-slavery paper published in America—so far as I have any knowledge—which advocated immediate and unconditional emancipation. The paper was called the *Philanthropist*, and was published at Mount Pleasant, Ohio, in 1816. The statement that this was the first paper favoring immediate and unconditional emancipation may be called in question by some, as the *Genius of Universal Emancipation*, published by Benjamin Lundy, in East Tennessee, has long had the credit of being the first. But I know that the statement I make is correct. Benjamin Lundy was a journeyman printer under Charles Osborne, in Mount Pleasant, and went from that office to East Tennessee. He was accompanied by Charles Osborne's son Isaiah, who aided him in printing the *Genius of Universal Emancipation*. The *Philanthropist* was also the first paper ever published in the United States, which promulgated the doctrine of the impropriety of using the products of slavery.

In a printed address to the Society of Friends, written many years after his removal to the State of Indiana, Charles Osborne makes the following remarks: "On whom has the mantle of Woolman fallen? We have approved and admired his course on the subject of slavery for more than half a century, but with a few exceptions we have halted and stumbled at the most essential part of his Christian testimony: that of abstaining from the gains of oppression." This subject was discussed by prominent abolitionists of Ohio and Indiana, and a paper called the *Free Labor Advocate* was established at

Newport, Indiana. It was edited by Benjamin Stanton, and the subject of free labor was ably advocated in its columns.

About the year 1844 I became so strongly impressed with the horrors of slavery, and its results, which were ever before me, that I was led to reflect more deeply on the subject than I had done before, and to view it in all its practical bearings. I read the testimony of John Woolman and other writers, and became convinced that it was wrong to use the product of slave labor. I felt that it was inconsistent to condemn slaveholders for withholding from their fellow-men their just, natural and God-given rights, and then, by purchasing the fruits of the labor of their slaves, give them the strongest motive for continuing their wickedness and oppression. Knowing so well the sad realities of life on the Southern plantations, I felt that in purchasing and using cloth made from cotton, grown by slaves, I made use of a product which had been planted by an oppressed laborer, fanned by sighs, watered with tears, and perhaps dressed with the blood of the victim. The words of John Woolman found an echo in my heart: "Seed sown with the tears of a confined, oppressed people—harvests cut down by an overborne, discontented reaper, make bread less sweet to the taste of an honest man, than that which is the produce or just reward of such voluntary action as is a proper part of the business of human creatures."

The free States furnished a good market for the products of the South, and made slave labor valuable to the master. If it had not been so, then

John Randolph's prophecy would have been fulfilled —the slave would not have run away from his master, but the master from his slaves, for they would have been a burden and expense to him. The object of the slaveholder was to make money by selling the cotton, sugar, etc., produced by his slaves, and without a market for these he would have been deprived of the great motive for holding the negroes in bondage. Northern consumers, by their demand for articles thus produced, stimulated the system by which they were produced, and furnished the strongest incentive for its continuance.

I felt by purchasing the products of slave labor, I was lending my individual encouragement to the system by which, in order to get their labor without wages, the slaves were robbed of everything else. In the language of Charles Stuart: ''Their bodies are stolen, their liberty, their right to their wives and children, their right to cultivate their minds and to worship God as they please, their reputation, hope, all virtuous motives, are taken away by a legalized system of most merciless and consummate iniquity. Such is the expense at which articles produced by slave labor are attained. They are always heavy with the groans and often met with the blood of the guiltless and suffering poor.'' ''If our moral sense would revolt at holding a slave ourselves and using his unpaid labor, it should also revolt at using his unpaid toil when held by another.''

With these strong convictions, I determined, as a matter of conscience, to abstain so far as I could from the products of slavery, and in my business to

buy and sell, so far as possible, only the products
of free labor. I had learned that there had been
associations formed at Philadephia and New York,
which were manufacturing goods of free-labor cotton, and that they had obtained free-labor groceries
from the British West Indies, and other countries,
where slavery did not exist. I decided to go to
Philadelphia and New York, and ascertain how the
business of these associations was managed —
whether it was a mere speculation to make money
or was conducted on conscientious principles, and
whether the goods purchased were really the products of free-labor. When I arrived at Philadelphia
and made inquiries, I found that the business was
conducted by such men as Enoch Lewis, Abraham
L. Pennock, Samuel Rhodes, George W. Taylor,
James Mott, James Miller McKim, Charles Wise,
etc. These were all prominent abolitionists, and
well known as conscientious men of high reputa-
tions; many of them were leading members of
the religious Society of Friends. They had erected
a cotton factory, which was conducted by George
W. Taylor. I found that instead of making money
at it, they were carrying on the business at a heavy
sacrifice, being actuated solely by conscientious
principles. The cotton they were manufacturing
was obtained from Friends' settlements in North
Carolina. I was personally acquainted with their
agents in that State who obtained it for them, and
knew them to be reliable men. After becoming
fully satisfied that there was no deception, that from
the field to the factory the cotton could be relied

upon as the product of free labor, I purchased as good an assortment of cotton goods as I could obtain. The assortment was not extensive; in prints particularly it was quite limited. The goods were mostly staple articles that afforded little profit.

I next went to New York, and found the business there conducted by such men as Robert Lindley Murray, Lindley M. Hoag, and other equally reliable and conscientious men. They dealt mostly in free-labor groceries, West-India sugar, molasses, coffee, etc., and had arrangements for obtaining free-labor rice, indigo, and other articles. They also kept Laguira, Mocha, and other coffee, the product of free labor. Here I purchased my groceries, though at a higher price than I had been accustomed to pay for slave products. The assortment of free-labor goods obtainable was so limited and the prices of so many articles higher, that I knew my profits would be curtailed, and I would lose many of my customers. In addition to the heavy pecuniary sacrifice I would sustain, I expected to meet with opposition and ridicule, though I knew that the free-labor subject had taken deep hold of the minds of many abolitionists in my own and other neighborhoods, and that many who desired to bear a faithful testimony against slavery wished to get a supply of the products of free labor.

Cotton yarn was then much used among the farmers in the West in making jeans, linseys, etc., for their own wear. This article I could not obtain from the Philadelphia cotton mills, as they only made warp for their own manufactures. To obviate this difficulty, I purchased a bale of their free-labor cotton and shipped it to Indiana, and prevailed on a Friend, who owned a small cotton mill near Richmond, to clear his machinery of other cotton, and make this bale into warp for me. I obtained, afterward, a larger supply of cotton, and visited the cotton mills at Dayton and Hamilton, hoping to get it manufactured separately. I at first met with difficulties, for the proprietors were not willing to clear out their machinery, but the foreman of one of the mills at Hamilton was an abolitionist, who felt an interest in promoting the cause, and he agreed to do the work for me, though it entailed additional labor.

Beside the many obstacles I had to encounter in obeying the dictates of my conscience on this subject, I had to contend with innumerable discouragements, and to endure much ridicule. I had to meet the arguments of the pro-slavery party, but I also had the support of many warm friends, who harmonized with me and encouraged me in the work, and who were willing, at any sacrifice, to abstain from the use of slave-labor products. In my own neighborhood such prominent men of our society as Daniel Puckett, Benjamin Thomas, Samuel Charles, Jonathan Hough, Dr. Henry H Way, Benjamin Stanton, and many others, were warm advocates of free labor, and in other neighborhoods I had many true friends, such as William Beard, Jacob Grave, Daniel Worth, and others.

My custom was confined measurably to abolitionists, and the supply of free-labor goods that could be obtained was inadequate to meet the demand. Better facilities for supplying the demand were much needed. The free-labor subject had been agitated in various communities of anti-slavery people, and by this time the principles involved in it had become widely known and had been adopted by many in various parts of the Western States. In Ohio and Indiana conventions were held for the purpose of devising some plan whereby free-labor goods could be supplied to all who desired to use them.

In Ohio, such men as Thomas Morris, Samuel Lewis, Dr. William H. Brisbane, Dr. G. Bailey, and John Joliff, had taken an interest in the subject. Several plans were suggested, but as no suitable person could be found to carry them out they were abandoned.

In the autumn of 1846, a union convention of those interested in the subject of free labor was held in Friends' Meeting-House at Salem, Union County, Indiana. It was largely attended by prominent men of Ohio and Indiana. From Cincinnati came Dr. Brisbane, John Joliff, Edward Harwood, Thomas Franklin, and others.

The convention held two days and during that time the subject was ably discussed. A resolution was passed to raise a fund of thee thousand dollars to be loaned for five years, without interest, to some suitable person for the purpose of enabling him to open a wholesale depository of free-labor goods at Cincinnati. A committee was appointed to select the person, and to report his name to the convention the next day. The committee made choice of me and reported my name to the meeting. The resolution appointing me to the position was carried by acclamation, but I could not give my consent to accept the position. I thought it would prove too great a sacrifice to me to "pull up stakes" and move to Cincinnati. I had lived in Newport twenty years, and was much attached to my house and to my friends and acquaintances there. A few years before I had built a dwelling-house, taking much pains to make it comfortable and convenient in all its appointments, with the expectation of occupying it as long as I lived. Neither I nor my wife thought that we would like city life, so notwithstanding the deep interest I felt in the concern, I declined to accept the position.

The committee was continued for the purpose of finding some suitable person who would undertake to carry out the proposed plan, and individuals of different neighborhoods were appointed to raise the fund of three thousand dollars, by soliciting subscriptions from those who were interested in the subject. But the committee did not succeed in finding a suitable person to undertake the business, and again applied to me and urged me strongly to go to Cincinnati and open the desired depository.

During the winter I received many letters from different parts of the country soliciting me to engage in the proposed business. I was thought to be the most suitable person to engage in such an undertaking as I had already had several years' experience in dealing in free-labor goods at Newport. I finally consented to go to Cincinnati for five years, and try the experiment. I sold out my business at Newport, rented my house and moved to Cincinnati the twenty-second day of April, 1847, having previously rented a store and dwelling-house in the city.

We fully expected to return to our home in Newport at the expiration of five years, or sooner, hoping that some suitable person would be found to take the business off my hands and continue it. I went to Philadelphia and New York that spring and purchased as good an assortment of free-labor cotton goods and groceries as could be obtained. The demand for such articles was increasing, and the Philadelphia Association had enlarged their business and were furnishing a better supply of cotton goods. Beside selling their own manufactures, they were obtaining from England a finer quality of cotton goods than their own mills furnished. The English goods were manufactured at Manchester under the auspices of a free-labor association, and could be relied upon as being the product of free labor.

I opened the store in Cincinnati and sent out printed circulars, which were widely circulated by friends of the enterprise. Orders from various parts of the West soon began to come in—far exceeding my meager assortment of cotton goods. I had not been able to obtain a sufficient supply of brown muslins, sheeting, cotton yarn, carpet warp, etc. This difficulty I knew might be remedied if I could obtain a supply of cotton, for there were several cotton mills in this vicinity that manufactured yarn, wicking, twine, batting, etc. Having been reared

in the South and having acquaintances in nearly all
the cotton-growing States, I knew that there were
many settlements there of the poorer class of farmers who owned no slaves and hired none, part of
them doing this from principle, part of them because
they were too poor to do otherwise. These small
farmers generally raised from one to ten bales of
cotton for market ; a few raised larger quantities. I
learned through correspondence that a good supply
of free-labor cotton could be obtained from this class
of people, and resolved to avail myself of the opportunity thus afforded. The previous winter, Nathan
Thomas, a worthy member of the Society of Friends,
who lived near Newport, Indiana, had gone with his
wife to spend the winter with some of her relatives
living near Holly Springs, Mississippi. Pleasant
Diggs, the uncle of Nathan Thomas' wife, with
whom they spent most of the time, had been reared
in a neighborhood of Friends and was opposed to
slavery. He owned no slaves and hired none, and
the cotton which he raised was the product of free
labor. Knowing Nathan Thomas to be interested
in the free-labor cause, I requested him to ascertain
if cotton could be obtained in that part of the State,
which could be relied upon to be clear of slave
labor. He wrote me that a large quantity was
raised by free labor, but that it had all been ginned
and baled by slave labor, as none of the farmers in
that neighborhood owned a cotton gin. He added
that he knew of other neighborhoods, in that
county, where free-labor cotton was raised.

I corresponded with Samuel Rhodes, of Philadelphia,· concerning the information I had received from Nathan Thomas, and informed him that William McCray, who lived near Holly Springs, Mississippi, a son-in-law of Pleasant Diggs, made about thirty bales of cotton annually, cultivated entirely by free labor, and that he was willing to put up a gin and gin his own and his neighbors' cotton by free labor, if we would furnish him the gin and allow him to pay for it in cotton.

I suggested that the Philadelphia Association should join me in this enterprise, for I believed they could obtain a larger supply and a better quality of cotton than they got from North Carolina, and perhaps at less cost. The subject was brought before the board, and an agreement was at once made. I was authorized to purchase a cotton gin and ship it to William McCray, of Mississippi. I at once applied to James Pierce, of Cincinnati, who manufactured cotton gins for the South, and purchased an excellent thirty-saw gin for $300, and shipped it immediately that it might be put up at once, and be ready for use in the fall.

The Philadelphia Association authorized me to employ Nathan Thomas as our agent to go South, next winter, to see that all the arrangements made with the cotton planters were strictly carried out. The second winter that Nathan Thomas spent in the South, he was· authorized by the Philadelphia Free-Labor Association to travel through the different Southwestern States, and hunt out the settlements of small farmers and ascertain what quantity of free-labor cotton could be obtained. He traveled through parts of Mississippi, Tennessee, Louisiana, Texas and Arkansas, and gave the information he obtained in a series of letters, which were afterward published by the managers of the Free-Labor Association of Ohio Yearly Meeting.

The gin I shipped to William McCray proved to be an excellent one, and was known in that part of the country as the "Abolition Gin." Arrangements were made to purchase all the free-labor cotton in reach of that gin, and other arrangements were made by which it could be hauled to Memphis—the nearest shipping point free of slave labor. At Memphis it was to be delivered to a commission merchant, formerly of Philadelphia, who employed no slave labor, and who was recommended by Samuel Rhodes, and others, as a reliable man. This merchant shipped the cotton up the river by boats that employed no slaves. By these means large quantities of free cotton were sent from the South, and we obtained a full supply. The Philadelphia Association was enabled to ship cotton to the Manchester mills in England in exchange for a finer class of goods than they were making, and I was supplied with all the cotton I could purchase, for manufacturing at Cincinnati. I had made arrangements with Gould, Pearce & Co., of Cincinnati, to spin cotton yarn, carpet warp, twine and candle wicking, and with Stearns & Foster to make batting and wadding from the cotton which I furnished. Afterward, I induced Gould, Pearce & Co. to put up looms and make brown muslin for me, in addition to the other articles.

When these arrangements were completed and the work in operation, I furnished the Philadelphia and New York Associations with heavy brown muslins, cotton yarn, carpet warp, twine, wicking, batting and wadding in exchange for their goods, for several years. I was authorized by the Philadelphia Association to employ Nathan Thomas to spend the third winter in the South to superintend the cotton business—to see that all the arrangements were carried out, and to engage the next year's crop of cotton in various localities. In engaging cotton, Nathan Thomas always promised to give the market price and no more, thus affording no advantage to the producer which would prove a motive for deception. Suitable persons were appointed agents in the different neighborhoods to receive the cotton and pay for it, and the producers were thus saved the trouble and expense of hauling it to a distant market. We also had arrangements for shipping from Hamburg and Eastport, on the Tennessee River.

The next year I traveled over part of the same ground, visiting free-labor neighborhoods in Hardin and McNairy Counties, Tennessee, and Tishomingo County, Mississippi. I found quite a number of settlers from Guilford County, North Carolina, and being acquainted with some of their relatives in that locality, I was kindly received and made welcome among them. I talked freely on the subject of slavery, explaining Friends' principles and testimony in regard to slavery and war, and dealing in or unnecessarily using intoxicating liquors. Strong

drink seemed to be much in use in that part of the
country. I also explained the feelings and views
of many Friends and other conscientious people in
the North in regard to the use of the unpaid toil of
the slave. I talked freely with many slaveholders
on these subjects, and was kindly treated by them.
Many of them understood something of the principles of Quakers regarding slavery, and discovering
from my dress and language that I was a Quaker,
they seemed disposed to talk freely and asked many
questions.

I explained our principles to them as well as I
could, and said that we bore a testimony against
slavery in our Discipline, and that no person could
be a member of our society who owned a slave. I
told them that I was a Southern man, having been
born and brought up in North Carolina, in the midst
of slavery, and was well acquainted with the system.
I was and always had been opposed to slavery, but
it was no part of my business, in the South, to interfere with their laws or their slaves. I was attending
to my own affairs, and did not intend to busy myself with other matters.

I had shipped to Eastport, Mississippi, and Hamburg, Tennessee—the points from which our cotton
was shipped North—a quantity of flour, cheese and
other produce. The boat on board which I had
shipped these articles was one of the best on the
Tennessee River, and as it was a popular boat for
travelers, we took on a number of passengers at different points. They were all Southerners, from various places in Tennessee, Mississippi and Alabama,

and most of them were merchants who had been to Louisville to replenish their stock of goods. The majority of them were slaveholders, but they appeared to be a very civil and gentlemanly set of men. Several of them seemed disposed to make my acquaintance and to find out who and what I was, whence I came and whither I was going. I was aware that Northern men were watched with jealous eyes in the South.

I made myself sociable with the passengers, and when they learned that I was from Cincinnati, and had a large cargo of produce on board which I was shipping to Eastport and other points to sell or exchange for cotton, and that I was brought up in the South, and had many relatives and acquaintances there, their jealous suspicions seemed to be entirely removed and they treated me with much respect. Different ones politely invited me to drink with them, according to the fashion prevalent in the South, but I declined, saying that I was a temperance man and used no liquor, except as medicine.

In the course of our journey I talked freely on the subject of slavery, speaking of its evil influences and my conscientious convictions in regard to it. On one occasion I got into a warm debate with one of the passengers by the name of Bell. He was a merchant of Farmington, Mississippi, and a member of the Legislature of that State.

I had given him and several others my business card, which bore my name and the words, "Commission merchant and dealer in free-labor cotton goods and groceries." He asked me what "Free-labor cotton goods" meant. I told him it meant just what it said—goods produced by free labor, and went on to say that I dealt exclusively in such goods, and was then on my way South to collect free-labor cotton.

He became excited and angry, and began to ask questions. I explained to him calmly the whole free-labor subject, speaking of the class of men in the free States who were interested in it, and my own conscientious convictions that induced me to engage in the work. I told him that many of our best citizens, both East and West, who believed that slavery was wrong and who felt for those in bonds as bound with them, had come to the conclusion that they could not consistently partake of the unpaid labor of the slave, and that this feeling was largely on the increase. This brought up the whole subject of slavery. Bell advocated it excitedly, and said that he would not live in a free State, that the blacks were made to serve and the whites to govern, etc., and went on to give the usual pro-slavery arguments.

Most of the passengers had gathered round us by this time to hear the debate. I spoke of the evils of slavery, of its horrors and cruelties, many of which I had witnessed myself while living in the South—the separation of husbands and wives, parents and children, etc. I dwelt largely upon the deleterious effects of slavery on the white population of the South, the disregard of marriage bonds, the license which slavery afforded, etc. I referred to several instances which had come under

24

my notice in North Carolina, where men of high
political and social standing had lived with their
slave women and reared families of mulatto children.
I said that I had always been opposed to amalgamation, which was the direct result of slavery. I referred to the slaves of mixed blood whom we saw
in every part of the South, and spoke of the com-
mòn practice of fathers selling their own children. I
then gave him an instance which came under my
personal observation. A planter of Mississippi,
named William Thompson, had come to Cincinnati
a few years before, bringing with him fourteen of his
slaves, all his own children and grandchildren, and
the slave woman with whom he had lived, the
mother of his children. He had sold one of his
cotton farms, and wished to buy land in a free State
and settle his children where they would be safe
after his death. He was referred to me for advice
regarding a suitable place to locate, and I directed
him to a colored settlement in Darke County, Ohio,
where land could be bought at a reasonable price,
and where his children could have the benefit of a
good school. He went to that locality, bought a
farm and saw his people comfortably settled.

He then returned to Mississippi, and the next
year sold his other farm and brought another company of slaves to Ohio, among whom was a middle-
aged colored woman, with five or six yellow children, whom he acknowledged to be his own. He
bought land for this party, and lived among them.
Thompson claimed to be a member of the Baptist

Church. This, I said, is the state of morals which slavery produces.

I then referred Bell to another instance in his own State. Major William Phillips, a wealthy cotton planter, who lived near Yazoo City, Mississippi, was a gentleman of high social standing, and was for some years a member of the legislature. His white children were grown and settled in homes of their own when he lost his wife. He married a second wife, lived with her a few years, then separated from her, giving her a farm and a few negroes. He then took one of his own slaves, a young mulatto woman, and kept her as his wife. He had several children by her, and concluding that he wanted them to be free, he sold his plantation and one hundred and thirty of his slaves, and brought his slave woman and her children to Cincinnati. He purchased a valuable piece of property on Broadway, where he now lives, professing to keep the mulatto woman as a hired servant. His children attend school, which they would not be allowed to do in your State. I have been told that two of his sons, who live in the South, have followed their father's example and keep slave women for wives.

By this time my friend Bell had become quite calm, and did not attempt to contradict my statements. An old gentleman from Alabama, a slaveholder, who sat near by, spoke several times during the debate, confirming my statements in regard to the evils of slavery. The company that had gathered round seemed to listen to the conversation with interest. I endeavored to speak with moderation, maintaining at the same time my independence and my right as an American citizen to express my conscientious convictions.

The gentleman from Alabama said that he believed slavery was a curse to the South, and that he would be willing to give up his slaves at any time if they could be properly provided for.

After this discussion, Bell became very sociable, and finding that I expected to travel in his county, he invited me to call and see him, offering me the hospitality of his home. I told him that if I should be in his neighborhood I would accept his invitation.

At Hamburg, Tennessee, I stored a part of my produce with William Campbell, a merchant, and went on to Eastport, thirty miles farther, where I discharged the rest of my freight. The next day I returned to Hamburg, and stopped at a tavern in that village. On the Sabbath I inquired if there was any church in the place, and was directed to a Methodist church, in the edge of the town, where there was to be preaching that day. I found the meeting-house to be a log cabin, with nothing to fill the cracks between the logs. The congregation consisted of eight or ten white people, half a dozen negroes, and several dogs. The men all chewed tobacco and spit on the floor, the women dipped snuff, and the dogs quarreled and fought with each other. The sermon was good, but no one seemed impressed by it except an old negro woman, who sobbed aloud and rocked herself to and fro. After meeting, the minister invited me to go home with him and spend the night. He lived four miles on the road I had to travel the next day, so I accepted his kind invitation. I inquired of the landlord where I could procure a horse to use a week or two, and he said I could have one of his. I asked him if he was not afraid to trust a stranger, and he replied: "I am not afraid to trust a Quaker." I thanked him for his kind offer, but thought he might be deceived by wolves in sheep's clothing.

I went home with the preacher, and spent the night at his house very pleasantly. He owned no slaves, and said that he had always been opposed to slavery, although he had been reared in the South. Some of his neighbors were slaveholders, and that night when we were talking on the subject of slavery, he lowered his voice, and spoke in a subdued tone. I asked him why he did so, and he replied:

"You are a stranger here, and we do not know who may be eavesdropping and listening to our conversation." The night was dark and rainy, and a person might have listened under the window without being discovered.

I told my friend that I would not live in a country where I could not talk freely and speak above my breath in my own house. The next day the preacher kindly accompanied me to a neighborhood of non-slaveholders, where Nathan Thomas had engaged free-labor cotton. We went to Lemuel Lancer's, who owned a cotton gin worked by free labor, and who acted as agent for us in purchasing cotton from those of his neighbors who owned no slaves. I spent a few days pleasantly at this place, then visited other neighborhoods of free-labor farmers in Hardin and McNairy counties, Tennessee. I then went into Tishomingo County, Mississippi, and finding myself in Farmington, I called on my friend Bell, at his store. He received me cordially, and invited me to spend some time with him, but as I wished to reach another neighborhood that afternoon I declined his invitation.

He introduced me to several merchants of the place, and as it seemed to be a leisure hour, we seated ourselves in the shade near Bell's store and entered into conversation. One old gentleman named Jones asked me many questions about the Quakers, saying he had read some of their writings and thought he should like to live among them. Bell had introduced me as a merchant from Cincinnati, and the conversation turned on that place and business matters there. He said he thought provisions and goods might be bought on better terms in Cincinnati than in Louisville, where their merchants usually went to buy their stock. One of the merchants said the reason he did not go to Cincinnati to buy goods was because he understood there were so many free negroes there that a gentleman could not walk the street without being insulted by them. I told him that I had lived there several years and had never been insulted by a colored person; as a general thing the colored people were very civil.

Another man said that he understood we were amalgamated in Cincinnati, mixed up with the negroes—that white men had colored wives, etc. I replied that we had a great many people of mixed blood in Cincinnati, but that they all came from the South. This caused a laugh, and I went on to say, I knew of no case of amalgamation occurring in Ohio, but I knew many instances of white men bringing their yellow children from the South to our State to be set free, and I knew of two or three cases of white men having colored wives. About a year ago two good-looking young white men from this State came to Cincinnati, bringing with them mulatto women, whom they claimed as wives. They wished to purchase land and settle in Ohio, and having been referred to me for advice respecting a suitable locality, they called on me. I went with them to the place where they were stopping—the Dumas House, a hotel for colored people, kept by a colored man—to see their families. One of the women had three children; the other was younger and was finely dressed and decked with jewelry. I asked the husband of the latter if this was his wife? He answered in the affirmative. I then turned to the other man and asked him if the elder woman was his wife, and if those three children were his? He answered, "Yes." I then asked the men if they were legally married to these women? They said they were not; that the women were slaves, and according to law in Mississippi the marriage of slaves was not legal. Well, I said, it is not legal for you to live this way in Ohio. The law of our State will not permit it. If you intend to keep these women as your wives, you must be legally married. A few days afterward the men obtained license and were legally married to the colored women. Such cases as these, I continued, are all that I know of in Cincinnati. We of the North are opposed to amalgamation.

One of the merchants present said that he had heard that if fugitive slaves reach Ohio, the abolitionists would harbor them and help them on their way to Canada. Well, I replied, we have all sorts of people in Ohio. I heard a story about a runaway slave a short time before I left home. It was told to me by a Presbyterian minister, who ought to be truthful. He said that the fugitive slave escaped from his master and made his way through Ohio on his way to Canada. He generally traveled at night and lay concealed during the day, but when near the northern boundary of the State, he concluded that it would be safe to travel in the day, not knowing that his master was on his trail and close behind him. That day his master had heard several times that his slave was a short distance ahead, traveling on the main road. The fugitive stopped at a house near the road to beg for something to eat, as he was very hungry. It happened that the people were good folks, who thought it right to feed the hungry, and they invited him in. The lady of the house began to prepare some food, and her husband went out to chop some stove-wood. While he was at the wood-pile, which was near the road, the slave's master rode up and inquired if he had seen a negro pass along the road that day.

The man quit chopping and asked: "What kind

of a looking fellow is the negro you are after? Is he black or brown or of mixed blood, and where was he from?" When the master had given a full description of his slave and answered the other inquiries, the man said: "Yes, I saw just such a negro pass along here to-day."

The master brightened up and said: "That is my slave. What time of day was it when he passed? How long ago did you see him?"

"It has not been more than an hour; he can't be far ahead."

"Did you speak to him?"

"Yes, I talked with him for some time."

"What did he tell you?"

"Well—he told me a good deal about himself."

"Now, sir," said the master, "I wish you would tell me all you know about him. He is my property and I intend to capture him at any cost, I will pay you fifty dollars if you will aid me to get hold of him"

The man deliberated for some time, then said: "I don't know that that would be just right, but I'll tell what I will do. I'll go and counsel with Deacon Jones, who lives at that next house, about a hundred yards off, and if he says it is right I'll tell you all I know about your slave."

He then dropped his ax, and started to see Deacon Jones. The master rode by his side, and stopped at the deacon's gate, while his companion went into the house. The man staid so long counseling with the deacon that the master grew impatient,

25

and when, at last, the man came out he asked him, hurriedly: "What did the deacon say?"

The man, however, was in no haste. He scratched his head and hesitated awhile, then replied:

"He said he did not think it would be any harm to tell you all I know about your slave."

The master asked, more impatiently than before, "Well, what *do* you know about him. Can you tell me where he is now?"

The man replied: "I don't know exactly where he is now, but when you were talking to me at the wood-pile he was in my house."

They returned together to the house, the master in no very good humor. The man asked his wife about the negro, and she replied: "He has been gone more than half an hour. When he saw his master ride up, he slipped out of the back-door, and hid in the bushes, and when you were at Deacon Jones', I saw him running like a turkey right toward Canada. You can't catch that fellow!"

The merchants all laughed at this story, and said it was a Yankee trick. They asked me no more questions about runaway slaves. I had a free and open conversation with them regarding my business in that part of the country. I informed them that I could not deal in slave-labor cotton, on conscientious principles, and gave them a clear understanding of the free-labor business, and of the class of people in the North who were engaged in it.

The old man Jones said he knew that the Quakers were a quiet and peaceable people who were opposed to slavery, and that they had a right to live according to their conscientious convictions. He concluded, by saying: "I think that Mr. Coffin is about right, and that slavery is a curse to our country."

I received several warm invitations to stop over night, but I declined them and continued my journey. I was thankful that I had met with so good an opportunity to advocate anti-slavery principles among the slaveholders.

I visited in various neighborhoods the planters who produced free-labor cotton, and those who owned gins worked by free labor. I found all the arrangements made by Nathan Thomas working well. On account of drought, the cotton produced that year was considered but half a crop, but I found in Tishomingo County, Mississippi, one hundred and twelve bales of free labor cotton, in McNairy County, Tennessee, six hundred and sixty-six bales, and in Hardin County, two hundred and sixty-three bales. All this had been ginned by free labor, and was ready for shipment north on the Tennessee River. From Marshall County, Mississippi, several hundred bales were shipped by way of Memphis to Philadelphia. After spending nearly two weeks traveling and visiting in these neighborhoods, and talking freely everywhere on the subject of slavery, I returned to Hamburg. After finishing my business there and at Eastport, I returned home, feeling thankful that I had found such an open field for spreading anti-slavery principles in the South. I believe that our traveling through the cotton-growing States and buying free-labor cotton, encouraging paid labor and discouraging unpaid labor, were the means of preaching abolitionism in the slave States, and was really pleading the cause of the poor slave.

Notwithstanding the facilities we had for procuring large quantities of free cotton and the arrangements I had made for manufacturing staple articles in Cincinnati, I found it to be a losing business. On account of the additional expense of procuring free-labor cotton and the difficulty of obtaining and keeping an assortment of dry-goods and groceries, it soon became evident after I opened the store in Cincinnati that the enterprise would not sustain itself unless it could be conducted on a much larger scale than my means allowed.

Only about half the sum proposed to be raised to aid me in the work was ever raised. It was much easier to pass resolutions in conventions than to carry them into effect. I invested all my available means in the free-labor business and had to use borrowed capital besides. To help sustain me in the work, I connected with it a commission produce business, which entailed much additional labor.

By this time the demand for free-labor goods in the West had largely increased. I received orders from nearly all the free States west of the mountains, from Canada, and from two of the slave States, Kentucky and West Virginia. My supply was not equal to the demand, and I could not fill the orders for a large assortment. The Philadelphia Association had but one mill for manufacturing cotton, and their prints were coarse in quality. Often, for want of goods, they could fill my orders only in part.

The New York Association often lacked a full supply of groceries so that I was unable to obtain enough to fill all my orders. I sold usually in wholesale quantities, and though I did a large business for several years, it was at a constant pecuniary sacrifice, so far as free-labor goods were concerned.

It required a much larger capital than I was using to make it a self-sustaining business. In order to supply the increasing demand for free-labor goods, it was necessary to enlarge our manufacturing busines; that required a large capital, and men of large capital could not be induced to invest in the business. Few of that class were in sympathy with the free-labor movement.

I felt anxious for some capitalist to take charge of the business, and release me from it—I wanted to return to my comfortable home in Indiana—but many of my friends seemed to think that if I let go of the helm the ship would stop. They encouraged me to hold on, and suggested the organization of a joint-stock company. It was accordingly advertised that a convention would be held at Salem, Union County, Indiana, on the nineteenth of November, 1850, for the purpose of forming a Free-Labor Association. The convention was largely attended, and a deep interest was manifested in the subject under consideration. In conformity with the resolutions passed, a committee was appointed to take steps to form a joint-stock company, with sufficient capital to enlarge our manufacturing business. The company was organized under the act of the General Assembly of the State of Ohio relative to incorporations for manufacturing and other purposes. A charter was obtained, and a board of trustees, consisting of William H. Brisbane, Samuel Lewis, John Joliffe, Thomas Freeman, Richard Gaines, Thomas Franklin and myself, were appointed. William H. Brisbane was elected president, Thomas Franklin was secretary, and I was chosen to be treasurer. The title of the company was, "Western Free Produce Manufacturing Company." Books were opened and an appeal was issued to the friends of the cause to come forward and take stock in the company. In order to get as many as possible interested in the work, the stock was divided into small shares. According to our constitution and charter, the company could not go into operation until a specified sum was subscribed and paid in. A number of the friends of free labor responded to the call, but their subscriptions did not reach the sum required; so the enterprise proved to be a failure, and had to be abandoned. The fugitive slave law was enacted that year, and the anti-slavery cause seemed shrouded in gloom, but in the midst of these discouragements we were encouraged by the intelligence of the spread of the free-labor cause in England. A little periodical entitled "*The Slave —His Wrongs and Their Remedy*," was started there about the first of that year, for the purpose of advocating free-labor principles. From the first number we gained the information that twenty-six free-labor associations had been established, and that notwithstanding the issue from the press, at Newcastle, of more than one hundred thousand tracts and papers on free-labor subjects, within the three months past, it was difficult to meet the demand for information on this important branch of the anti-slavery enterprise. The free-labor warehouse, at Manchester, had more than equaled the expectations of the proprietor, and efforts were being made to supply him with additional capital for extending operations, and also to open a warehouse in London.

The associations in England had depended, to some extent, on cotton furnished by the free-labor associations in America, but the cultivation of free-labor cotton in other countries was becoming more extensive. Great Britian had received more cotton from the East Indies the previous year than ever before—it amounted to two-thirds more than the import of the preceding year—and the cultivation of cotton had been commenced on the west coast of Africa. Experiments on the island of Jamaica the previous year had proved the soil and climate to be admirably adapted for its cultivation, the cotton produced being pronounced clean and of good staple and color.

These accounts from England were encouraging to the friends of the free-labor cause in this country; we hoped to be able soon to procure a better assortment of free-labor goods. I was also encouraged to continue my efforts in this cause by receiving from the East an able and interesting report—printed in pamphlet form—giving an account of what had been done there in the interests of free labor. It was called "The Report of the Board of Managers of the Free-Labor Association of Friends, of New York Yearly Meeting, adopted at the annual meeting of the Association, held Fifth month 27th, 1851," and was signed by direction and on behalf of the board of managers, by Benjamin Tatham, secretary. A list of the names of the members of the association was given. The number was eighty-three, which comprised many of the most prominent members of New York Yearly Meeting, by which it appeared that the Yearly Meeting was alive to the free-labor subject. This contrasted strongly with the apathy manifested by many Friends of Indiana Yearly Meeting. The report showed that the New York Association had been actively at work, and had recently furnished the mill at Manchester, England, with fifty bales of free cotton. Friends of the free-labor cause in the West seemed anxious for me to continue the business at Cincinnati, and some additional means were furnished that enabled me to continue the manufacture of free cotton and to obtain a better supply of free-labor goods. By close financiering and strict economy I kept up the business at Cincinnati for ten years, then sold out, and retired from mercantile life with very limited means.

CHAPTER IX.

UNDERGROUND RAILROAD WORK IN CINCINNATI—A
REMINISCENCE — THE FUGITIVE COOK GIRL — A
COMPANY OF TWENTY-EIGHT FUGITIVES — AUNT
BETSEY—JACK AND LUCY—ASSESSMENTS ON UN-
DERGROUND RAILROAD STOCK — A PRO-SLAVERY
MAN SILENCED—THE STORY OF JANE.

WHEN we moved to Cincinnati in the spring
of 1847, my wife and I thought that perhaps our work in Underground Railroad matters
was done, as we had been in active service more
than twenty years.

We hoped to find in Cincinnati enough active
workers to relieve us from further service, but we
soon found that we would have more to do than
ever. When in the city on business, I had mingled
with the abolitionists and been present at their
meetings, but some of them had died, and others
had moved away, and when I came to the city to
live, I found that the fugitives generally took refuge
among the colored people, and that they were often
captured and taken back to slavery.

Most of the colored people were not shrewd managers in such matters, and many white people, who
were at heart friendly to the fugitives, were too

timid to take hold of the work themselves. They were ready to contribute to the expense of getting the fugitives away to places of safety, but were not willing to risk the penalty of the law or the stigma on their reputation, which would be incurred if they harbored fugitives and were known to aid them.

Abolitionists were very unpopular characters at that time, both in religious and political associations, and many who favored the principles of abolitionism lacked the moral courage to face public opinion, when to do so would be to sustain an injury in their business and to lower their reputation in public esteem.. But there were a few noble exceptions—brave and conscientious workers—who risked every thing in the cause they believed to be right. I had already risked every thing in the work—life, property and reputation—and did not feel bound to respect human laws that came in direct contact with the law of God.

I was personally acquainted with all the active and reliable workers on the Underground Railroad in the city, both colored and white. There were a few wise and careful managers among the colored people, but it was not safe to trust all of them with the affairs of our work. Most of them were too careless, and a few were unworthy—they could be bribed by the slave-hunters to betray the hiding-places of the fugitives. We soon found it to be the best policy to confine our affairs to a few persons, and to let the whereabouts of the slaves be known to as few people as possible.

When slave-hunters were prowling around the

city we found it necessary to use every precaution. We were soon fully initiated into the management of Underground Railroad matters in Cincinnati, and did not lack for work. Our willingness to aid the slaves was soon known, and hardly a fugitive came to the city without applying to us for assistance. There seemed to be a continual increase of runaways, and such was the vigilance of the pursuers that I was obliged to devote a large share of time from my business to making arrangements for their concealment and safe conveyance of the fugitives. They sometimes came to our door frightened and panting and in a destitute condition, having fled in such haste and fear that they had no time to bring any clothing except what they had on, and that was often very scant. The expense of providing suitable clothing for them when it was necessary for them to go on immediately, or of feeding them when they were obliged to be concealed for days or weeks, was very heavy. Added to this was the cost of hiring teams when a party of fugitives had to be conveyed out of the city by night to some Underground Railroad depot, from twenty to thirty miles distant. The price for a two-horse team on such occasions was generally ten dollars, and sometimes two or three teams were required. We generally hired these teams from a certain German livery stable, sending some irresponsible though honest colored man to procure them, and always sending the money to pay for them in advance. The people of the livery stable seemed to understand what the teams were wanted for, and asked no questions.

It was necessary to use every precaution, and I thought it wise to act, as the monkey did, take the cat's paw to draw the chestnut from the fire, and not burn my own fingers. I generally gave the money to a second person to hand to the colored man. We had several trusty colored men—who owned no property and who could lose nothing in a prosecution—who understood Underground Railroad matters, and we generally got them to act as drivers, but in some instances white men volunteered to drive, generally young and able-bodied. Sometimes the depot to which the fugitives were consigned was not reached until several hours after daylight, and it required a person of pluck and nerve to conduct them to their stopping-place. If the party of fugitives were large they were soon scattered among the abolitionists in the neighborhood, and remained in safe concealment until the next night.

While the fugitives were resting and sleeping, their friends provided suitable wagons and drivers for the next night's travel to another depot, perhaps twenty-five or thirty miles distant. After our drivers had breakfasted, fed their horses and rested a few hours, they would return home.

Learning that the runaway slaves often arrived almost destitute of clothing, a number of the benevolent ladies of the city—Mrs. Sarah H. Ernst, Miss Sarah O. Ernst, Mrs. Henry Miller, Mrs. Dr. Aydelott, Mrs. Julia Harwood, Mrs. Amanda E. Foster, Mrs. Elizabeth Coleman, Mrs. Mary Mann, Mrs. Mary M. Guild, Miss K. Emery, and others, organized an Anti-Slavery Sewing Society, to provide suitable clothing for the fugitives. After we came to the city, they met at our house every week for a number of years, and wrought much practical good by their labors.

Our house was large and well adapted for secreting fugitives. Very often slaves would lie concealed in upper chambers for weeks without the boarders or frequent visitors at the house knowing anything about it. My wife had a quiet unconcerned way of going about her work as if nothing unusual was on hand, which was calculated to lull every suspicion of those who might be watching, and who would have been at once aroused by any sign of secrecy or mystery. Even the intimate friends of the family did not know when there were slaves hidden in the house, unless they were directly informed. When my wife took food to the fugitives she generally concealed it in a basket, and put some freshly ironed garment on the top to make it look like a basketful of clean clothes. Fugitives were not often allowed to eat in the kitchen, from fear of detection; notwithstanding the following little reminiscence which appeared in print about a year ago. It was given as a typical circumstance of our experience.

"SCENE.—Before the war; a house in Cincinnati. Two negroes newly arrived, and evidently plantation hands, eating heartily in the kitchen. Two planters and the marshal of Cincinnati, coming hastily up the street. A lady (Aunt Katy) enters the parlor hurriedly and addressing a broad brimmed Quaker, speaks: 'Levi, make thee haste. I see strange men coming with that pestilent marshal.' Levi goes out and meets them at the gate.

"Marshal—'Good-morning, Friend Coffin. We are seeking for two runaways.'

"Coffin—'Two escaped slaves thee would recapture?'

"Marshal and both owners—'Yes, yes. Can you tell us where they are?'

"Coffin—'Was one boy very black and rather heavy set; the other yellow and but slightly built?'

"Both owners—'Yes, yes! You describe them exactly.'

"Coffin—'I saw two such boys, not half an hour since, pass this gate; they inquired where the Cincinnati, Hamilton and Dayton depot was, and if you haste you may reach the depot before the train leaves.'

"Away go the marshal and the slave-owners, while Coffin re-enters the house and addressing his wife, says:

"'Mark, Katie, I did but say the boys passed the gate, but said not whether they went in or out. Go, hurry them with their meal, while I hitch up the old bay horse to drive the poor souls a station or two beyond the city, where they can embark with safety.'"

THE FUGITIVE COOK GIRL.

At one time, a slave girl who ran away from Covington, came to our house, and my wife let her assist the cook in the kitchen, until a suitable opportunity for her escape to Canada should arrive. She did not ask what her name was or make any inquiries about the master or mistress she had left, for it was the policy in our family to make no inquiries of slaves, in some intances, that we might be burdened with no information if the slave-hunters should ask questions of them.   One morning when the girl mentioned was eating her breakfast in the kitchen, a man came into the parlor and inquired of a young man, one of the boarders who was sitting there, reading, if he knew of a runaway slave in that family.   The young man said that we often hired colored servants, and called "Aunt Katy" in to speak to the man.

He made known his errand to her by saying: "One of my neighbors has lost his cook girl, and we think she is here or in this neighborhood."

My wife replied: "I do not know anything about your cook girl, but will inquire of my servant; perhaps she will know."

She then called in our cook and made the inquiry in hearing of the man, receiving an answer in the negative.   Our daughter was in the kitchen, and heard the inquiry, and hastened the slave girl up a back stairway, leading out of the kitchen.

If the man had stepped into the kitchen, at first, he might have seen the object of his search sitting at the table eating.   He withdrew from the house, and walked up and down the sidewalk in front of it, till noon.   Henrietta, the cook, resolved to aid her fugitive fellow-servant to escape from quarters so closely guarded, and taking her up stairs, dressed her in a new black silk which she had just bought and made up, and put on her head a fashionable bonnet, which was provided with a vail. Then attiring herself for the street, the two went boldly out of the front door, just as the man had turned his back and was walking toward the next square. They followed behind him, at the distance of half a square, until they reached a side street, then, turning off, they made their way across the canal to a settlement of colored people, where the fugitive remained for two weeks. At the end of that time she returned to our house, and we took her and several other fugitives with us when we went to Canada on a visit a short time afterward.

My wife said: "I did not know whether she was a cook girl, chambermaid, nurse girl or field hand, for I had never inquired, and I did not think it necessary to ask her when her pursuer was standing in the next room, ready to take her back to slavery."

A COMPANY OF TWENTY-EIGHT FUGITIVES.

The fugitives generally arrived in the night, and were secreted among the friendly colored people or hidden in the upper room of our house. They came alone or in companies, and in a few instances had a white guide to direct them.

One company of twenty-eight that crossed the Ohio River at Lawrenceburg, Indiana—twenty miles below Cincinnati—had for conductor a white man whom they had employed to assist them. The character of this man was full of contradictions. He was a Virginian by birth and spent much of his time in the South, yet he hated slavery. He was devoid of moral principle, but was a true friend to the poor slave.

Sometimes slaves would manage to accumulate a little money by working at making baskets at night or on the Sabbath, and when they had saved a few dollars they were very willing to give it all to some white man in whom they had confidence, if he would help them across the river and direct them how to reach the Underground Railroad.

Thus I have always contended that this road was a Southern institution, being conducted however on a different principle from what it was on this side Mason and Dixon's line. The company of twenty-eight slaves referred to, all lived in the same neighborhood in Kentucky, and had been planning for some time how they could make their escape from slavery. This white man—John Fairfield—had been in the neighborhood for some weeks buying poultry, etc., for market, and though among the whites he assumed to be very pro-slavery, the negroes soon found that he was their friend.

He was engaged by the slaves to help them across the Ohio River and conduct them to Cincinnati. They paid him some money which they had managed to accumulate. The amount was small, considering the risk the conductor assumed, but it was all they had. Several of the men had their wives with them, and one woman a little child with her, a few months old. John Fairfield conducted the party to the Ohio River opposite the mouth of the Big Miami, where he knew there were several skiffs tied to the bank, near a wood-yard. When I asked him

26

afterward if he did not feel compunctions of conscience for breaking these skiffs loose and using them, he replied: "No; slaves are stolen property, and it is no harm to steal boats or anything else that will help them gain their liberty." The entire party crowded into three large skiffs or yawls, and made their way. slowly across the river. The boats were overloaded and sank so deep that the passage was made in much peril. The boat John Fairfield was in was leaky, and began to sink when a few rods from the Ohio bank, and he sprang out on the sandbar, where the water was two or three feet deep, and tried to drag the boat to the shore. He sank to his waist in mud and quicksands, and had to be pulled out by some of the negroes. The entire party waded out through mud and water and reached the shore safely, though all were wet and several lost their shoes. They hastened along the bank toward Cincinnati, but it was now late in the night and daylight appeared before they reached the city. Their plight was a most pitiable one. They were cold, hungry and exhausted; those who had lost their shoes in the mud suffered from bruised and lacerated feet, while to add to their discomfort a drizzling rain fell during the latter part of the night. They could not enter the city for their appearance would at once proclaim them to be fugitives. When they reached the outskirts of the city, below Mill Creek, John Fairfield hid them as well as he could, in ravines that had been washed in the sides of the steep hills, and told them not to move until he .returned. He then went directly to John Hatfield, a worthy colored man, a deacon in the Zion Baptist Church, and told his story. He had applied to Hatfield before and knew him to be a great friend to the fugitives—one who had often sheltered them under his roof and aided them in every way he could

John Fairfield also knew me and knew that I was a friend to the slave. I had met him several times, and was acquainted with the plan of his operations in the South, but I was opposed to the principles on which he worked. I will have occasion to refer to him at another time and will explain more fully his plans, and the reason why I opposed his operations in the South. When he arrived, wet and muddy, at John Hatfield's house, he was scarcely recognized. He soon made himself and his errand known, and Hatfield at once sent a messenger to me, requesting me to come to his house without delay, as there were fugitives in danger. I went at once and met several prominent colored men who had also been summoned. While dry clothes and a warm breakfast were furnished to John Fairfield, we anxiously discussed the situation of the twenty-eight fugitives who were lying, hungry and shivering, in the hills in sight of the city.

Several plans were suggested, but none seemed practicable. At last I suggested that some one should go immediately to a certain German livery stable in the city and hire two coaches, and that several colored men should go out in buggies and take the women and children from their hiding-places, then that the coaches and buggies should form a procession as if going to a funeral, and march solemnly along the road leading to Cumminsville, on the west side of Mill Creek. In the western part of Cumminsville was the Methodist Episcopal burying ground, where a certain lot of ground had been set apart for the use of the colored people. They should pass this and continue on the Colerain pike till they reached a right-hand road leading to College Hill. At the latter place they would find a few colored families, living in the outskirts of the village, and could take refuge among them. Jonathan Cable, a Presbyterian minister, who lived near Farmer's College, on the west side of the village, was a prominent abolitionist, and I knew that he would give prompt assistance to the fugitives.

I advised that one of the buggies should leave the procession at Cumminsville, after passing the burying-ground, and hasten to College Hill to apprise friend Cable of the coming of the fugitives, that he might make arrangements for their reception in suitable places. My suggestions and advice were agreed to, and acted upon as quickly as possible, John Hatfield agreeing to apprise friend Cable of the coming of the fugitives. We knew that we must act quickly and with discretion, for the fugitives were in a very unsafe position, and in great danger of being discovered and captured by the police, who were always on the alert for runaway slaves.

While the carriages and buggies were being procured, John Hatfield's wife and daughter, and other colored women of the neighborhood, busied themselves in preparing provisions to be sent to the fugitives. A large stone jug was filled with hot coffee, and this, together with a supply of bread and other provisions, was placed in a buggy and sent on ahead of the carriages, that the hungry fugitives might receive some nourishment before starting. The conductor of the party, accompanied by John Hatfield, went in the buggy, in order to apprise the fugitives of the arrangements that had been made, and have them in readiness to approach the road as soon as the carriages arrived. Several blankets were provided to wrap around the women and children, whom we knew must be chilled by their exposure to the rain and cold. The fugitives were very glad to get the supply of food, the hot coffee especially being a great treat to them, and felt much revived. About the time they finished their breakfast the carriages and buggies drove up and halted in the road, and the fugitives were quickly conducted to them and placed inside. The women in the tight carriages wrapped themselves in the blankets, and the woman who had a young babe muffled it closely to keep it warm, and to prevent its cries from being heard. The little thing seemed to be suffering much pain, having been exposed so long to the rain and cold.

All the arrangements were carried out, and the party reached College Hill in safety, and were kindly received and cared for. But, sad to relate, it was a funeral procession not only in appearance but in reality, for when they arrived at College Hill, and the mother unwrapped her sick child, she found to her surprise and grief that its stillness, which she supposed to be that of sleep, was that of death. All necessary preparations were made by the kind people of the village, and the child was decently and quietly interred the next day in the burying-ground on the Hill.

When it was known by some of the prominent ladies of the village that a large company of fugitives were in the neighborhood, they met together to prepare some clothing for them. Jonathan Cable ascertained the number and size of the shoes needed, and the clothes required to fit the fugitives for traveling, and came down in his carriage to my house, knowing that the Anti-Slavery Sewing Society had their depository there. I went with him to purchase the shoes that were needed, and my wife selected all the clothing we had that was suitable for the occasion; the rest was furnished by the noble women of College Hill.

I requested friend Cable to keep the fugitives as secluded as possible until a way could be provided for safely forwarding them on their way to Canada. Friend Cable was a stockholder in the Underground Railroad, and we consulted together about the best route, finally deciding on the line by way of Hamilton, West Elkton, Eaton, Paris and Newport, Indiana. West Elkton, twenty-five or thirty miles from College Hill, was the first Underground Railroad depot. That line always had plenty of locomotives and cars in readiness. I agreed to send information to that point, and accordingly wrote to one of my particular friends at West Elkton, informing him that I had some valuable stock on hand

which I wished to forward to Newport, and requested him to send three two-horse wagons—covered—to College Hill, where the stock was resting,
in charge of Jonathan Cable. I said: "Please put
straw in the wagons so that they may rest easy on
the journey, for many of them have sore feet, having traveled hastily over rough ground. I wish you
to get to College Hill to-morrow evening; come
without fail."

The three wagons arrived promptly at the time
mentioned, and a little after dark took in the party,
together with another fugitive, who had arrived the
night before, and whom we added to the company.
They went through to West Elkton safely that
night, and the next night reached Newport, Indiana.
With little delay they were forwarded on from station to station through Indiana and Michigan to
Detroit, having fresh teams and conductors each
night, and resting during the day. I had letters
from different stations, as they progressed, giving
accounts of the arrival and departure of the train,
and I also heard of their safe arrival on the Canada
shore.

I often received intelligence of the arrival in Canada of fugitives whom I had helped on the way
to liberty, and it was always very gratifying to me.
I was well known on the different routes of the
Underground Railroad, and people wrote to me of
the success of my shipments. From the stories of
hundreds of slaves who arrived at our house, having made their escape on foot through cane-brakes
and forests, across rivers and mountains, or hidden

in wagons, or concealed amid cotton bales on steamboats, the following have been selected:

A BRAVE WOMAN.

A slave family of ten, consisting of a man and his
wife, and their eight children, some of them grown,
lived in Kentucky, about fifteen miles from Covington. Their master, in order no doubt to prevent
their attempting to cross into Ohio and escape,
often told them that he intended to set them free,
and assured them that they should never have to
serve any one but him. Aunt Betsey, the mother
of the family, was a trusty old servant, and he
reposed considerable confidence in her, giving her a
standing pass, and sending her frequently to Cincinnati with a wagon and two horses, to take vegetables to market. She faithfully fulfilled all her
duties, and though often urged by her colored
friends in Cincinnati to escape while such good
opportunities were allowed her, she refused to do
so, trusting that her master would do as he had
promised, and that all her family would be free.
But she learned, after awhile, that he intended to sell
some of her children, and became fully convinced
that there was no hope of the fulfillment of his
promise. She had not been allowed to go to the
city for some time, and she feared her pass would be
taken from her, and that she would not be permitted
to go to the city any more. But undismayed at
these discouragements, she began to plan for the
escape of the whole family. Her husband, more
timid than herself, and much less energetic, was

afraid to make the attempt, for he thought they certainly would be captured and brought back, and their condition would then be worse than ever. She urged it so much, however, that he finally yielded and consented to go, leaving all the arrangements to her. One night when her master and mistress had retired, and there was no one about who would act as a spy on her movements, she got out the horses and wagon, and prepared a load, as if she were going to market; first putting their clothing and bedding in the bottom of the wagon, then piling vegetables on top.

In the evening she had asked a little white boy who lived in the neighborhood, if he did not wish to go to the city with her, and he, pleased at the prospect of seeing so large a place as Cincinnati, eagerly accepted her invitation. She told him she would take him that night, but he must not mention it to his parents, lest they should not let him go. He was on hand at the hour of starting, and the whole party got into the wagon and started on their journey. Aunt Betsy drove the horses over the road which she had usually traveled on her way to the city, and just before daylight came to the town of Covington. Before entering it she stopped the team, unloaded the vegetables, secreted her husband and children among the clothing and bedding, and then scattered the vegetables smoothly over the top. Her husband's fear and indecision had increased during the journey, and his courage entirely failed him when they neared Covington.

27

He wanted to go back, and only the firmness and decision of his wife compelled him to go on.

Aunt Betsey, having seen her family stowed away out of sight, mounted the seat again, with the white boy by her side. When they reached the ferry, she handed the reins to him, and took them again when they were across the river. The ferrymen asked her no questions, for they had often seen her going to market, and supposed that she had the pass she usually carried. After reaching the city, she drove to the house of a colored friend on North Street, where there was a dense colored population, and the wagon was unloaded as soon as possible. The bedding, etc., were stored in the basement of a colored Wesleyan church, and the family scattered among several friends, where they could find places of safety and concealment. Aunt Betsy then drove into Broadway, and after going several squares stopped the team, and told the white boy that she must go to the market and that he must remain and watch the horses.

I had been duly notified of the arrival of the party, had already received some of them into my house, and was now applied to for further assistance. I soon planned an arrangement by which the team could be returned and no clue gained to the whereabouts of the fugitives. A colored man went to a German who could speak but little English, and hired him to drive the team across the ferry to Covington, telling him some one would take charge of it there. When they reached the wagon, they found the little boy crying; he said he was tired of waiting for Aunt Betsey, she was gone so long to market.

The master next morning, finding his slaves gone, started in pursuit, and when he reached Covington he found the team, the little boy and the German driver. The child could tell nothing, except that he had gone to market with Aunt Betsey, and that she left him to mind the horses and did not come back. The master had the German arrested, but as he knew nothing about the affair, except that he had been hired by a colored man whom he did not know, to drive the team across to Covington, he was soon discharged. The master continued his search in Cincinnati; he informed the police, and had them on the alert; offered a large reward for the fugitives, and did all in his power to find them, but could gain no clue to their retreat.

A close watch was kept on every road leading out of the city, and the friends of the fugitives dared not move them in any direction for more than a week. At last we hit upon a plan to get them out in disguise, in open daylight. The males were disguised as females, and the females as males, and thus attired they were seated in elegant carriages, and driven out of the city at different points, exactly at noon, when most of the people were at dinner. Those who were on the look-out for a company of frightened, poorly dressed fugitives, did not recognize the objects of their search, for it was quite common for the colored gentry to go out riding in that style. They were taken about thirty miles from the city, and thence proceeded by night travel to Canada. Their bedding and clothing were boxed, and shipped to a trusty friend in Detroit.

In connection with my efforts for this party of fugitives, an incident occurred which has often been related with much gusto by those whom it amused. The Ladies' Anti-Slavery Sewing Society fitted out the family with necessary clothing, and it devolved on me, as usual, to collect money to defray expenses. I started out to call on some of the stockholders of the Underground Railroad, and stopped first at the pork-house of Henry Lewis, whom I knew to be a true friend to fugitives, and always ready to contribute when there was need. Walking into the office, I found Henry, his brother Albert, and M. B. Hagans, now Judge Hagans, who was then Henry Lewis' book-keeper. There were also three strangers sitting in the office, slaveholders from Kentucky, who had come on business connected with pork—Henry Lewis generally bought their hogs and the hogs of others in their neighborhood. I said: "Henry, I want to raise a little money for a family of poor people; they are in need, and I am called on for help." I knew that Henry would understand me.

He asked: "Are they very poor?"

"Yes," I replied, "among the poorest of the poor, and must suffer if they are not helped; thou knows I am often called on in such cases."

Henry remarked to the company in the office: "I never care to ask Mr. Coffin many questions when he calls for money to help the poor, for I know that he is often applied to in such instances, and will not take hold of a case without he is satified that it is a case of real need. I am always willing to contribute when he calls." He then handed me a dollar, and said: "Now, gentlemen, show your liberality."

His brother Albert and M. B. Hagans each handed me a dollar, and the three Kentuckians, not wishing to be behind the others in generosity, handed me a dollar apiece. I thanked them and retired, with six dollars in my pocket for the poor family.

About a week afterward three or four other Kentuckians, from the same neighborhood, were in Henry Lewis' pork-house on similar business, and in the course of their conversation they made use of threats and curses against the abolitionists, accusing them of harboring their slaves and helping them on to Canada. Henry Lewis interrupted them, and said: "Gentlemen, you needn't say a word about the abolitionists helping your slaves to get away. There were three of your neighbors here the other day—all slaveholders—and an old gentleman came into this office to beg some money to help a family of fugitives to get to Canada, and they every one contributed. Now, what have you got to say, seeing that your own folks have turned abolitionists?" They uttered a few more oaths, and dropped the subject.

It was the custom of myself and other abolitionists in the city to try the roads before starting out a company of Underground Railroad passengers. If we suspected there were watchers lying in wait at the outlets, we sent out a carriage or wagon, containing some noted abolitionist and a number of free colored people, and much merriment was excited when they were pounced upon by the watchers, who shortly learned their mistake and retired discomfited.

A large proportion of the fugitives who came to my house in Cincinnati were from Kentucky. The Ohio River, after they ran away from their masters, was the principal barrier between them and freedom but they generally found some means to cross it. They could not cross on the ferry-boats from Kentucky without producing a pass, indorsed by some responsible person known to the ferryman.

Another story of Kentucky fugitives is that of a couple whom we will call

JACK AND LUCY.

They were husband and wife, and belonged to a man who lived ten or twelve miles from Cincinnati. They were very valuable property, and the master, through reverses of fortune or for some other reason, was obliged to dispose of them. He sold them to a Southern slave-trader, and promised to deliver them at Louisville, at a certain time, in season for a down-river boat. The night after the bargain was made, they were locked in a back-room up stairs, for greater safety. In spite of this precaution, they managed to escape. Tying their bed-clothing together, and fastening one end securely to the bedpost near the window, they let themselves down to the ground in the back-yard, and ran away, barefooted, bareheaded, and very thinly clad. When they reached the bank of the Ohio, they found a little skiff tied to the shore, and breaking it loose, they got in and rowed across to the other side. Reaching Cincinnati, they went to the house of a colored friend, who brought them immediately to my house, where they arrived about daylight.

They were placed in a garret chamber and locked up, none but myself and wife knowing of their presence in the house.

Their escape was discovered in the night, and the master with a posse of men started immediately in pursuit. They crossed the river between Covington and Cincinnati, about the same time that the fugitives were crossing below the city. Supposing that they had not had time to cross yet, the pursuers watched the river for some time, in hope of capturing them, not knowing that they were safely ensconced in our garret. Finding himself foiled, the master then went to Covington, and had handbills printed, offering four hundred dollars' reward for his property. Jack and Lucy were worth a thousand apiece, and their owner felt that he had rather pay a large reward for them than to lose them entirely. These handbills were distributed among the policemen of Cincinnati, and scattered about the city, and one of them soon came into my hands.

A vigilant search was made for several weeks, but no less vigilant were we who secreted the fugitives. From a small window in their room, Jack and Lucy saw their master passing up and down the street in front of the house, and often some of his company passed by, late at night, as if reconnoitering, but no attempt was made to search the premises. After

keeping Jack and Lucy secreted in our garret for
two weeks, during which time the ladies of the
Anti-Slavery Sewing Society provided them with
clothing, the hunt seemed to be over and it was
decided to send them on to Canada.

Money was to be raised to hire a carriage to take
them away, and I considered myself appointed to
collect it. Starting out one morning, I went into a
store where I was slightly acquainted. I did not
know whether the proprietor was friendly to the
cause or not, but asked him if he had any stock
in the Underground Railroad. He inquired what
road that was, and when I told him it was the one
on which fugitives slaves were sent to Canada, he
replied:

"If that is the road I believe I have a little stock
in it."

I then told him that there was an assessment on
the stock, and that I was authorized to collect it.

"How much will mine be?" asked the merchant.

"Mine is a dollar," I replied, "I suppose thine
will be the same."

I received a dollar, and went on to another store
whose keeper was a Jew. I did not know his sentiments, but as soon as I informed him that money
was wanted for Underground Railroad purposes, he
handed me two dollars. I went next to a wholesale
drug store, and explaining my errand, received one
dollar from each of the proprietors, who were abolitionists; then to a queensware store and received
a similar amount from each proprietor. I next
called at a wholesale grocery on Pearl Street, where

I had business to transact. I knew that the principal member of the firm was not in sympathy with my anti-slavery work, but resolved to speak to him on the matter. Meeting him at the door, I introduced the subject, and the following conversation took place:

"Hast thou any stock in the Underground Railroad, Friend A——?"

"No!"

"It pays well; thou ought to take stock; it makes one feel good every time he is called on for an assessment."

"I want nothing to do with it. I don't believe in helping fugitives."

"Stop, my good friend, I don't believe thou knowest what thou art talking about. Suppose thy wife had been captured and carried off by Indians or Algerines, had suffered all the cruelties and hardships of slavery, and had escaped barefooted, bareheaded and with but little clothing, and must perish without aid, or be recaptured and taken back into slavery; suppose some one was to interest himself in her behalf and call on me to aid in restoring her to freedom, and I should refuse to do it and say, 'I want nothing to do with helping fugitives'—what wouldst thou think of me?"

"I do not expect my wife ever to be in such a condition."

"I hope she will not be, but I know of somebody's wife who is in just such a condition now, and I have been called on for help. It always does me good to have the opportunity to help in such cases, and as I am never permitted to enjoy any good thing without wishing others to partake with me, I thought I would give thee the opportunity to enjoy this with me." Then I told him of the man and wife who were sold to a negro-trader to be taken to the far South, and related how they made their escape, bareheaded, barefooted and thinly clad, and hastened to the Ohio River in the dark, over ten miles or more of rough road, while their hearts were full of fear and dread lest they should be recaptured. At the river they found a skiff which they succeeded in breaking loose, and crossed safely to the city, where they found good quarters. I said: "Great exertions have been made to find them and drag them back to slavery, but the efforts have not succeeded; the fugitives have been kept in close quarters. We think now that it may be safe to forward them on the Underground Railroad to Canada, but they must be suitably provided for the journey, and money must be raised to help them on their way. Now I want thee to take stock to help us clothe and forward these people; I know thou wouldst feel better to contribute for their relief. Now I have done my duty; I have given thee the opportunity to contribute, and if thou art not disposed to do so, it is thy look-out, not mine." I then left him and went into the counting-room to transact some business with the book-keeper. When this was done, I turned to go, but as I was passing out of the store the merchant, who was waiting on a customer, called to me. I stopped, and he came to me and said in a low tone:

"I will give you a trifle if you want something."

I replied: "I want nothing; but if it is thy desire to contribute something to help those poor fugitives I told thee about, I will see that it is rightly applied."

The merchant then handed me a silver half-dollar. I took it, and said: "Now I know thou wilt feel better," then left the store. About a week afterward I was passing down Walnut Street, below Fourth, when I saw this merchant coming up on the opposite side. When he saw me, he crossed over and coming up to me, smiling, he shook hands, and asked, in a whisper: "Did they get off safely?"

I laughed outright, and exclaimed "Ah, thou hast taken stock in the Underground Railroad, and feels an interest in it; if thou hadst not taken stock thou wouldst have cared nothing about it. Yes, they got off safely, and by this time are probably in Canada."

A PRO-SLAVERY MAN SILENCED.

Beside dealing in free-labor goods, I carried on a large commission business, receiving and selling all kinds of country produce. One of the merchants with whom I had frequent dealings was M. C——, who was pro-slavery in his sentiments, profane in his speech, and who often threw out slurs about abolitionism and negro-stealing. He came into my store one morning to inquire about some produce he wished to purchase, and greeted me with, "Good-morning, Friend Levi, how are you?"

"Only tolerably well," I replied, "I do not feel very bright this morning; how art thou?"

"Oh, first rate; but what is the matter with you that you don't feel bright this morning—have you been out stealing niggers?"

"There's no need of stealing them," I replied; "they come about as fast as we can take care of them. There is one here now; he arrived in the city last night and met with a colored man, who took him to the house of Preacher Green, pastor of Allen Chapel, whom he knew to be a friend to fugitives. Green brought him to my house this morning."

"Where do you keep them?" M. C—— inquired; "in your cellar?"

"No," I answered, "we don't put people in the cellar; we take them into the parlor or sitting-room. This poor man has suffered nearly everything but death; he has traveled a long distance, and been on the way several months, suffering from cold, hunger and exposure. He formerly lived in Kentucky, but was separated from his family some years ago and sold to a negro-trader, who took him to the South, and sold him to a cotton planter in Mississippi. He was set to work in the field, but not being used to picking cotton he could not keep up with the others who were accustomed to the work. When he fell behind or failed to perform his task, he received such severe cuts from the whip carried by the cruel overseer that the blood ran down his back, and the wounds left scars and painful sores. At night the cotton was weighed by the overseer, and if this man's share lacked the required weight he was stripped, tied up, and cruelly whipped. At night the slaves had to prepare their scanty store of food for next day, or go without and suffer hunger. This man concluded that he would endure such a life no longer; he had rather die in the woods in endeavoring to escape, than to live in such cruel bondage. He had heard that there was a country far to the north where all people were free, and he started for Canada. He was trailed by dogs and torn by them, and captured and put in jail, but he would not tell where he was from, and finally he broke jail and made his escape. After enduring much suffering and passing through many dangers, he reached this city last night, barefooted and clothed in rags. Preacher Green, a colored man, brought him to our house early this morning, and we have already provided him with food and clothing. Preacher Green collected a little money among the colored people, and has gone out to buy a pair of shoes for the fugitive."

M. C—— listened to my story with strict attention. When it was finished, I stepped from behind the counter, and said: "Come with me to my house, near by, and see the poor fellow. He seems quite intelligent, and tells a straight story."

"Where is he?" M. C—— repeated; "in your cellar?"

I spoke with emphasis, and said: "No! I told thee we did not put people in the cellar; he is in the sitting-room."

We walked out together, and had reached the

door of my house when I stopped suddenly, and said: "There is one thing which I forgot. If thou sees him thou must pay a dollar to help him on his way; wilt thou do it?"

M. C—— shook his head, but I looked him in the face, and said: "I guess thou wilt; come in."

We entered the house, and I introduced the fugitive, calling him Sam—his real name I did not know. "Now, Sam," I said, "tell this gentleman the story thou told me this morning. Tell him the reason thou ran away, and what thou suffered in thy long journey. Don't be afraid, there is no danger."

Sam told his story in simple and touching language, and M. C—— listened with interest, asking questions now and then. Sam showed his scars and wounds in confirmation of his story.

I then told M. C—— that it was not safe for Sam to remain longer in the city, and we had decided to send him on that morning. We intended to put him aboard the train for Detroit, and we had but a short time in which to raise the money to purchase his ticket. I said: "Preacher Green will be here in a short time to take Sam to the depot. He has raised some money among the colored people, and I told him I would try to raise the rest that was needed. I want thee to help us."

M. C—— pulled out his purse, and handed the fugitive a dollar. We then returned to the store, and I said to my companion: "Now, my good fellow, go and tell it! Thou hast laid thyself liable not only to a heavy fine, but to imprisonment, under the fugitive slave law. Thou gave a fugitive slave a dollar to help him to Canada; I saw thee do it."

He turned toward me with a peculiar look, and said: "D—n it, you've got me!"

I told the story on him frequently when I met him in suitable company, sometimes asking those present if they had heard of friend C——'s conversion; he had been converted to abolitionism, and had taken stock in the Underground Railroad. This always created surprise and merriment. M. C—— declared that he dreaded to meet me, and never again troubled me with slurs or insinuations about abolitionism and negro-stealing.

THE STORY OF JANE.

Jane was a handsome slave girl, who lived in Covington, Kentucky, her old master and mistress having moved from Virginia, and settled in that place some years before the time our story opens. She was kindly treated by her owners, and her old mistress, who was very fond of her, taught her to sew and do housework, and took such pains in teaching her that she became quite skillful in needlework and everything pertaining to housekeeping. Jane's lot was a pleasant one, and until she reached the age of sixteen none of the evils of slavery shadowed her life. Then her old master died and she became the property of his son, who took possession of the premises and assumed the care of Jane's old mistress. This son was a wicked, thoughtless man, and poor Jane was completely under his control. After living with him some time, she became the mother of a beautiful little girl, who was almost as white as her father, Jane's master.

Those who have seen quadroons and octoroons will remember their peculiar style of beauty, the rich olive tint of the complexion, the large bright eyes, the perfect features, and the long wavy black hair. A hundred romantic associations and mysterious fancies clustered around that class in the South, owned, as they often were, often by their own fathers and sold by them.

Jane was a house-servant, and did not have to work under the lash or toil in the fields, as many slave-women were compelled to do, but she felt keenly the degradation of her position and longed to be free, that she might live a purer life. She had experienced a change of heart and become a Christian, and this offended her master. He decided to sell her, when her little girl was about three years old. The old mistress was opposed to it, but her words had no effect; the master declared that he would sell Jane to the first trader that came along. Jane's mistress informed her of the fate in store for her, and said that she longed to save her from it, but was powerless. Jane was greatly alarmed, and in her distress went to tell her grief to an English family, who lived near by, kind-hearted people, who were opposed to slavery. They were much attached to Jenny, as they called her, and felt great sympathy with her in her distress. The old gentleman went to see her master, and tried to dissuade him from his purpose of selling Jane, but he could not be moved. Nothing was said about the child. The old gentleman told me afterward that he had no thought that the brute would sell his own child. Next day the old Englishman and his son-in-law concluded that by their united efforts they could raise a sum sufficient to purchase Jane, supposing that her master would sell her at a fair price. They went to him and offered him five hundred dollars for her, intending to secure her freedom and to allow her reasonable wages until she paid back the amount. But the master refused to take it. He said Jane was a handsome girl and would bring a high price down South; he would not take less than eight hundred dollars for her, and thought perhaps he might get a thousand. This was more money than Jane's friends were able to give; they thought it was an unreasonable price, and gave up the idea of buying her. A few days afterward the master sold Jane and her beautiful child to a Southern negro-trader, receiving eleven hundred dollars for them both—nine hundred for the mother and two hundred for the child.

When Jane learned that she was sold, to be taken to the far South, her distress was indescribable. She and her little girl were to go together, but she knew not how soon they would be separated. She slipped into the house of her English friends, almost overwhelmed with grief, and begged them to help her in some way, to save her from being sent away. They felt deeply for her distress, but what could they do? Jane was to have one day, in which to wash and iron her clothes, then she must start away with her new master, the slave-trader.

28

The old Englishman concluded to go over to Cincinnati that day and see William Casey, a worthy colored man of his acquaintance, and counsel with him about Jane. Casey soon suggested a plan to get her over the river and put her on the Underground Railroad for Canada. The old man knew very little about the Underground Railroad, but he had full confidence in William Casey, knowing him to be a true and reliable man, and agreed to carry out his suggestions if possible. Casey said he would get a skiff and go across the river in the early part of the night to a wood-boat that lay at the bank in the lower part of Covington. The nights were then dark, and he thought he could carry out his plan unmolested. The old Englishman was to apprise Jane of the plan, and tell her to watch for an opportunity to slip out into a certain dark alley, where he would be in waiting. He would then conduct her to the wood-boat where Casey agreed to be, and she could be rowed across to the city under cover of darkness, and secreted in some safe place.

Her English friend managed to communicate the plan to Jane, and she watched diligently for an opportunity to escape, but she was kept busy, till late, washing and fixing her clothes preparatory to starting on her journey next day, and her mistress or some one else staid in the room to watch her.

Jane's heart throbbed with anxious excitement as the time drew near for the door to be closed, and no opportunity offered for her to get away. She did not want to leave her little girl, but knew not how she could take her out of the house without exciting suspicion. She went into the yard several times in the evening, and finally the child who had remained awake—something altogether unusual—followed her out. This was the very opportunity for which Jane had been watching and hoping, and she did not let it pass. Taking her little daughter in her arms, she made her way into the back alley, and walked rapidly toward the place where she was to meet her friend, the Englishman. The child, as if knowing that something was at stake, kept perfectly quiet.

Jane's friend was waiting at the rendezvous, though he had almost given her up, and concluded that it was impossible for her to get away. Together they proceeded to the river, Jane trembling so much with excitement that she was obliged to give her child to her conductor to carry. Walking across the wood-boat, the Englishman perceived a man waiting in a skiff, and though it was too dark to distinguish faces, he felt confident that it was the faithful Casey, and handed him the child. Then assisting Jane into the skiff, he bade her good-by, with a fervent "God bless you!"

Casey brought the fugitives to our house, where they arrived about midnight. We knew nothing of the circumstances beforehand, but were accustomed to receive fugitives at all hours. They were soon secreted in an up-stairs room, where they remained in safety for several weeks. About a week after Jane's escape, the old Englishman, who had been afraid to make any inquiry before, came over to Cincinnati to learn what had become of her. He was not acquainted with the Underground Railroad and its workings, and inquired of Casey whether its agents or managers were reliable persons. Casey told him there was a man in the city who could tell him all about it, and also give him information regarding Jane. He then conducted him to our house, introduced him, and told what his errand was.

I informed him that instead of the Underground Railroad being an institution organized for the purpose of making money, it was attended with great expense, and explained the principles by which the managers were actuated, and the motives which prompted us to spend our time and money in aiding the poor fugitives; which so affected the old man that he shed tears. Having answered his questions satisfactorily, I invited him to walk up-stairs with me. I gave a light tap at Jane's door, which was locked, and when it was opened, I introduced to Jane the friend and benefactor, to whom she owed her escape from slavery. Jane threw herself into the Englishman's arms, and they both wept like children. Then he took up her lovely and interesting child and kissed it, after which he had a long conversation with her, giving her much good advice. When he bade her good-by and started away, he gave her five dollars.

Jane's master made great efforts to find her and the child, and after a general and thorough search in the city, men were sent to the lake shore to watch at different points where fugitives were wont to take passage for Canada. He was heard to say that he intended to find her, if he had to put one

foot in hell. When I heard of this expression I remarked that I feared he would get both feet there,
but thought that he would not find Jane.

All this time she was safe and comfortable in her
quarters at our house. She became much attached
to "Uncle Levy and Aunt Katy," as she called us,
and when the time came for her to leave she wept
bitterly. She was put into the care of William
Beard, that active agent for the Underground Railroad, who lived in Union County, Indiana, and he
took her to a colored school in Randolph County,
called the Union Literary Institute, and there left
her to attend school.

About this time, a young slave girl from the far
South, who had made her way to the Mississippi
River, and there secreted herself on an up-river boat,
by aid of a friend, arrived at Cincinnati, and came
to our house. After remaining here a short time,
she was sent to the same school which Jane attended. They studied during the summer term, and
made fine progress, but in the autumn some of the
colored people of Cincinnati visited the school, and
I, fearing that the girls might be discovered—that
the news of their whereabouts might reach their
pursuers—went to the school and bade them prepare for traveling, explaining to them the exigen-
cies of the occasion. They had become attached
to the place and were reluctant to leave, but I told
them that they would incur a great risk by remaining, and they finally consented to go to Canada if I
would accompany them across the lake. I agreed
to do so and we started together, but on the way I

stopped at Oberlin, Ohio, and had a meeting with the friends of fugitives there, and as I could not well spare the time for the journey, a reliable and trust-worthy gentleman offered to go in my stead. The girls being convinced that they could put entire con-fidence in this escort, excused me from the task, and soon were on their way.

Some years afterward I accompanied a party of fugitives to Amherstburg, Canada West, and there had the pleasure of dining with Jane in her own home. She had married an industrious man of nearly her own color, and was comfortably situated and very happy. If it had not been for the interven-tion of the friends of humanity she would doubtless have been toiling, broken-hearted, beneath the burning sun in Southern fields, and ofttimes fallen under the cruel sting of the lash instead of living in peace and happiness in her northern home.

CHAPTER X.

CINCINNATI STORIES CONTINUED—THE RAG BABY—THE
VICE-PRESIDENT'S SLAVE—THE DISGUISED SLAVE—
WOLVES IN SHEEP'S CLOTHING—SALLY, THE SLAVE
MOTHER—LOUIS AND ELLEN—THE MICHIGAN RAID.

A GENTLEMAN from the South, accompanied
by his wife, came to Cincinnati to spend a
short time, and brought with him, as waiting-maid
and general servant, one of his slave girls. He had
not been long in this city before he experienced one
of the annoyances incident to slavery—his slave girl
ran away. She had a longing to taste the sweets
of freedom, and being assisted by some friendly
colored people to whom she made known her desire,
she succeeded in getting safely away from her master and mistress and reaching the house of Thomas
and Jane Dorum, worthy colored people, well known
for their efforts in befriending slaves, who then lived
on Elm Street. The girl remained here a short
time, but as the house was liable to be searched by
the officers whom the master would employ to look
for his missing property, it was not prudent for her
to stay. Jane Dorum or "Aunt Jane," as she was
generally known, sent a message to my wife, asking
her to bring some suitable clothing, and come pre-

pared to take the girl to our house. My wife at once prepared a bundle of clothes and went to Aunt Jane's. Having dressed the slave girl in suitable apparel, she conducted her to our house, where she remained two days. At the end of that time it seemed advisable to take her to another place, for the search for her was being prosecuted with much zeal and energy, and our house was in a public situation; we lived then on the corner of Sixth and Elm Streets.

My wife planned how she could get her away without attracting attention, or rousing the suspicions of persons who might be watching for her, and at last hit upon a plan which seemed good. She dressed herself in fashionable clothes, a plaid shawl, a gayly trimmed straw bonnet, and other articles at variance with her usual garb, and put upon the fugitive garments suitable to the occasion. Then she rolled up some clothes and made a rag baby, being careful to provide it with a vail for its head and face. This she put into the arms of the slave girl, and thus equipped they sallied forth into the street. As they passed along they presented the appearance of a fashionable lady and her nurse-girl—the servant bearing the infant in her arms. They made their way across the canal to the house of William Fuller, an English abolitionist, where my wife left the fugitive, knowing that she would be cared for.

William Beard, of Indiana, that true friend to the slave, was in the city at the time with his market-wagon, a large covered vehicle which often did duty as a car of the Underground Railroad. The case of this slave girl was made known to him, and when he was ready to start for home, he called at William Fuller's house and took in a passenger. The girl reached his house in safety, and was soon afterward forwarded by the old reliable road to Canada.

THE VICE-PRESIDENT'S SLAVE.

Jackson, the subject of this story, was the property of Vice-President Dallas, of Alabama, who was in office during the administration of James K. Polk.

While the master was at Washington, the slave ran away from him and came to Cincinnati. He was a barber by trade, and after remaining here unmolested for some time, he opened a shop, in which he served several years, having a number of patrons and being liked by all who knew him. By some means his master learned of his whereabouts, and sent an agent to secure him. The man arrived in Cincinnati, and without procuring a writ, as the law required, resolved to take forcible possession of Jackson. He gathered a posse of men with pistols and bowie-knives, had the ferry-boat in waiting at the wharf at the foot of Walnut Street, in readiness to take them across to Kentucky as soon as they came on board, and about noon, one day, pounced upon Jackson at the corner of Fifth and Walnut Streets, as he was going to his dinner, and dragged him down Walnut Street to the wharf. Jackson struggled with all his might and calling for help, but most of the men of the stores had gone to their dinner at that hour, and the policemen, who

29

were generally on the side of the slaveholders,
remained out of sight.   Thomas Franklin, a Friend,
who was passing, attempted to interfere and rescue
Jackson, but the men threatened him with their
weapons, and he was obliged to desist.   Jackson
was hurried aboard the ferry-boat and taken across
to Kentucky, where his captors had no fear of his
rescue.

He was bound and carried back to Alabama,
where he remained in slavery two or three years,
and where he married a free woman, a Creole of
Mobile, who possessed some property.   She was
portly in form and had handsome features, with
straight hair and olive complexion.   When dressed
up, she presented the appearance of an elegant
Southern lady.   A plan was soon formed to gain
Jackson's liberty.   His wife was to act the part of a
lady traveling to Baltimore on business, and Jackson, who was small in stature, was to be disguised as
a woman and accompany her as her servant.   When
all the preparations were made, they sent their
trunks on board the regular vessel for New Orleans,
and took passage for that city, in their newly
assumed characters.

At New Orleans they took an up-river boat for
Cincinnati.   On the way the lady stated that she
was going to Baltimore on business, but that she
intended to stop a short time at Cincinnati, and
ordered her servant about in a haughty manner,
keeping her in her room when not engaged in some
service for her comfort.   Some of the Southern
ladies on board advised her not to land at Cincinnati,

as Ohio was a free State, and the laws of that State declared all slaves free as soon as they touched its borders, when taken there by their owners, but to stop at Covington, on the opposite side of the river, and leave her slave there while she transacted her business. She informed those kind ladies that she had no fears regarding her servant's running away, or being enticed off by the abolitionists, for she was much attached to her mistress, and would not leave her under any circumstances.

On the other hand, several Northern ladies, who were on board, took private opportunity to speak to the servant when her mistress was not near, and inform her that she would be in a free State when she reached Ohio, and that she had better seize the opportunity to escape.

Her answer was, that she would not leave her mistress, and the abolition ladies desisted from their attempts to advise and counsel, pitying the infatuation of one who had rather be a slave than be free. When the boat reached the wharf at Cincinnati, the lady took a carriage, and, with her servant, drove to the Dumas House, a public hotel kept by a colored man. Jackson was well acquainted in the city and knew where to find friends. A few hours afterward I received a message requesting me to call at the Dumas House, as a lady there wished to see me on business. I went, accompanied by John Hatfield, a colored man who was a prominent worker in the cause of freedom, and who had received a similar message. The landlord conducted us up-stairs to the ladies' parlor, and introduced us to the lady from Alabama. She was a fine-looking, well-dressed Creole, with straight black hair and olive complexion, presenting the appearance of the ladies one sees in New Orleans and other Southern cities. She was polite and ladylike in her manner, and informed us that she had sent for us, though she was a stranger to us both, that she might consult us on a matter of business. She went on to say that she had a servant with her whose liberty she wished to secure, and she had been referred to us for advice. She was not very well acquainted with the laws of Ohio, and felt at a loss how to proceed. We advised her to have a deed of emancipation made out. I inquired if it was a male or female servant that she wished to emancipate, and she called "Sal" to come from the adjoining room.

The servant came, and made a graceful courtesy to us and stood looking at us It was Jackson, dressed in woman's clothes, but we did not recognize him, though both of us had been acquainted with him before he was taken away.

The lady then ordered her servant to go into their bedroom and open her trunk and get out that bundle. We supposed that she referred to some papers that she wished to show us. While the servant was gone I asked the lady what part of Alabama they were from. She answered, "Mobile." I then inquired what route they came, and she told me of their journey. At this juncture her servant returned, but the bundle seemed to be on the person, who had turned to a man. We recognized Jackson, the barber, at once, and greeted him with a hearty hand-shake. Then followed an introduction to his wife, a full explanation and a hearty laugh over the whole affair. It was decided that it would be unsafe for Jackson to remain in Cincinnati; he was too well known here. He concluded that he would go to Cleveland, where he was not known, and where he could be on the lake shore, so that, if danger appeared, he could step on board a steamer and cross to Canada. It was decided that his wife should remain at Cincinnati until he had made preparations for housekeeping, and established himself in business, if a suitable opening presented itself. His wife had means on which she could depend for support in the interval,

We approved of Jackson's plan, and the next night he took the train to Cleveland. He soon secured a comfortable house and shop, and wrote for his wife. She joined him immediately, and when we last heard from them they were living comfortably and happily at Cleveland. Jackson had a good business in his barber shop, and was troubled with no fear of molestation.

THE DISGUISED SLAVE.

There are numerous other incidents of slaves who escaped in disguise, and in many instances there is humor as well as pathos connected with them. A slave man living in the State of Arkansas resolved to make his escape, and fixed upon a plan, at once daring and safe. He was past middle age, spare in form and below the medium height, so his personal appearance favored his plan.

Procuring the free papers of a colored woman living in the neighborhood, he disguised himself in woman's apparel, put on a cap and a pair of green spectacles, and provided himself with knitting work. Thus equipped, he went aboard of a boat bound for Cincinnati, having made up a suitable story to tell if he should be questioned. The captain examined his free papers, and finding everything satisfactory, he was permitted to take passage, and the journey was accomplished without his disguise being suspected by any one.

In talking he could imitate a woman's voice, but spoke only when spoken to; he devoted himself industriously to his knitting, and affected to be in poor health. Some ladies noticing him said: "It is too bad for that sick old auntie to sleep on deck; let her sleep on the floor in the ladies' cabin," and the chamber-maid accordingly put a mattress there for him. Arriving safely at Cincinnati, he went to a colored boarding house, having enough money left to pay his expenses there, but not enough to take him on to Canada. I was sent for, and after hearing his story raised sufficient means to purchase for him a ticket to Detroit. Before starting on his journey toward the North, I advised him to throw off his female apparel and resume his proper dress, but he said that his disguise had done him such good service so far, that he would wear it till he reached Canada.

WOLVES IN SHEEP'S CLOTHING.

Disgraceful as it is to those whom it concerns, it is nevertheless true, that colored persons sometimes turned traitors to their own race, and, Judas-like, betrayed their brethren for a little money. A man of this character, who had been sent as a spy from Kentucky, applied to me, asking my help and protection, and seeming to be much alarmed lest he should be captured. As other attemps of similar character had often been made, I was on the look-out, and was wary and guarded in what I said. I took the man to the house of one of my colored friends, whom I privately informed of my suspicions, and told him to be on his guard till it should be discovered whether the man was a fugitive or a spy. It was soon ascertained that he was the latter, and the colored people, among whom he had been staying, arose in their indignation, took him out of the city, and administered punishment in the shape of a severe whipping. After this he returned to Kentucky, and was never known to play such a part again.

At another time, a man who had been employed, to act as spy, by some slave-hunters of Kentucky, came across the river in female apparel, and presented himself at the basement of a colored church, in Cincinnati, where fugitives were in the habit of stopping. The sexton's wife was suspicious that all was not right, and sent for me. When I went, I questioned and cross-questioned the suspected fugitive, and feeling almost certain that it was a man in disguise, I turned him over to the colored people, who stripped off the female apparel, and inflicted such a severe punishment upon him that he was glad to escape with his life, and return to the other side of the river.

Such schemes of deception were not uncommon, but they never succeeded in accomplishing their designs. A white man once called at my house, and when he was ushered into the parlor, he introduced himself as a friend of the oppressed slaves, who had often heard of my efforts in their behalf, and wished to enter into an arrangement with me by which a number in Kentucky could be liberated. He made many professions of interest in, and sympathy with, my work for the fugitive, but I did not like his appearance and manner, and after questioning him closely came to the conclusion that he was a spy. I informed him that he was "barking up the wrong tree," and that his little plan of engaging me in an attempt to liberate some Kentucky slaves would not work. I said that I had nothing to do. with slavery on the other side of the river, and did not believe in interfering with the laws of slave States, except by moral suasion. If persons came to my house hungry and destitute, I received and aided them, irrespective of color, but I had no intention of engaging in a plan such as that proposed. The man left discomfited, and I afterward learned that he was a slaveholder, who had designed to entrap me.

At another time a man was introduced to me as a friend of the slaves, and proceeded to inform me that he traveled up and down the river a great deal, being engaged in some capacity on board a boat, and suggested to me that arrangements might be made to help away a number of slaves. I had good reasons for believing that he was an impostor who hoped to entangle me in some scheme that would cause trouble, and answered him in the same manner that I had the slaveholder. Several similar attempts to entrap me were made by agents and spies from Kentucky, but they were unsuccessful.

SALLY, THE SLAVE MOTHER.

Sally, an intelligent woman of brown complexion, belonged to a couple of maiden ladies who lived in Covington, Kentucky, having become their property by inheritance. She had been well trained in household work, and was an excellent cook and housekeeper, besides being skillful with the needle. Her husband, who belonged to another family, had been sold from her when her youngest child was a few months old, leaving her with five children, all girls. He was taken to the far South, and she never heard of him afterward. Sally's eldest two daughters were hired out, but the three younger ones, being too young to be put out to service, were left with her at home.

Sally was a good and faithful servant, and had never suffered the sting of the lash, or other abuse. Her mistresses, probably to dissuade her from taking advantage of her proximity to a free State and running away, often told her that they intended to set her and her children free, but the time was deferred from year to year. Sally often reminded them of their promise without getting any satisfactory reply, and she began to feel that its fulfillment was "mighty onsartain," as she expressed it, but she had no thought of being sold until her mistresses called her into the house, one morning, from the kitchen and told her that she and her youngest three children were sold, and would be taken away that day. She said this announcement was like a thunderbolt; it struck her dumb. She almost fell to the floor before her mistresses, but they did not seem to pity her, or to pay any attention to her. When she found speech she begged to be permitted to go and see her two girls who were hired out, but her mistresses refused her request, and ordered her to go up-stairs to the room where she slept, and pack up her own and her children's clothes, in readiness to start away with her new master. When Sally reached her room up-stairs she set her wits to work to find a way to escape. She managed to get out of the window on to the kitchen-roof, then on to an adjoining shed-roof, from which she slid down to the ground in the back yard. She then slipped out the back way and ran to the house of a widow lady living near by, whom she knew to be friendly, and hastily told her sad story. The lady deeply sympathized with her, and being a mother she could understand the distress she felt on her children's account. She concealed Sally in a safe place, thinking that the children would not be taken away unless the mother was found.

Sally was soon missed, and a diligent search was made for her. The news spread through the neighborhood that Sally had deserted, and a company of men started in pursuit, anxious to capture the runaway slave. They searched among the colored people, thinking she had taken refuge there. They did not think of her being so near her home, and thus overlooked her place of concealment. In the afternoon, when the ardor of the search seemed to have abated a little, the widow lady came over to Cincinnati to consult with some of her friends, whom she knew to be abolitionists, in regard to Sally.

William Casey, a worthy colored man who was a good manager in such matters, was consulted and a plan was soon agreed upon. Sally was to be dressed in men's apparel and taken about midnight to a point in the upper part of Covington, near the Licking River, where William Casey would be to receive her, and bring her across the river. Sally being a small woman, it was somewhat difficult to find men's apparel to fit her, but with her friends' assistance the widow obtained a suit of black summer cloth belonging to a youth, which she took home with her. Sally donned the suit and made a presentable appearance in it, but it was rather thin for the season, it being cool weather in early spring. The undertaking was a hazardous one, both for Sally and for William Casey, for the bank might be watched, but Sally's liberty was at stake, and Casey, who was ever ready to aid his people when in distress, felt it his duty to risk his own safety in order to rescue her from slavery. Sally's lady friend sent a trusty companion with her to the place appointed, and as the night was dark they escaped detection, and the whole arrangement was completed without discovery.

William Casey brought Sally directly to our house on the corner of Franklin and Broadway, near Woodward College. Between twelve and one o'clock in the night I was awakened by the ringing of the door-bell. It was no alarm, for we were used to hearing it at late hours of the night and knew what it meant. I sprang up, dressed hastily, and went to the front door. When I opened it I saw William Casey and another colored person, apparently a boy, standing on the steps. Casey told me he had brought a fugitive whom he wished me to keep in safety for awhile, and I at once invited them in. When we reached the sitting-room, I addressed a few questions to Casey's companion, but received replies that denoted embarrassment. When Casey informed me that it was a woman in disguise I was much surprised, so completely did she make the appearance of a boy, or young man. Seeing that her countenance denoted trouble and that she seemed to wish to avoid conversation, I asked no more questions. Casey said that she would tell her story to us in the morning, and assured her that I and my wife were true friends; that she could confide in us with safety. Casey then left us and went to his home. I went up to our room and told my wife that Casey had brought a fugitive woman in men's clothing, and asked where I should put her to sleep. She told me to take her to the fourth story, and let her sleep with Jane Clark, our colored hired girl, directing me first to go into another room where we had some clothes for fugitives, and get a bundle of women's clothes, and tell Jane to dress the fugitive in proper apparel. I acted according to my wife's directions, and conducted the fugitive to the fourth story. When we reached Jane's door I knocked on it and called her by name, requesting her to open the door, as I had a bed-fellow for her. She rose and unlocked the door, then slipped back to bed. I opened the door and took in Sally who looked like a man. Jane glanced at us wildly, then covered up her head.

I felt a little mischievous and spoke commandingly: "Jane, thou must take this person in bed with thee."

"I sha'n't!" she exclaimed from beneath the bed-clothes.

"Now, Jane," I said; "don't act so ugly; he is a good-looking fellow. But if thou dost not like the idea of sleeping with a man, get up and make a woman of him; here is a bundle of clothes with which Aunt Katy said he could be dressed." Jane now began to understand. She uncovered her head, opened her big eyes, stared at Sally and exclaimed:

"That's no man; you can't fool this chile."

Sally smiled for the first time, and said: "Dear child, I am a woman."

I retired to our room and left them to arrange matters to their own liking. Next morning Sally was neatly dressed and made the appearance of a good-looking, middle-aged colored woman, below medium stature. Her expression was intelligent, but sad, and her countenance denoted anguish of heart. After breakfast she was brought into our room and related to me and my wife her touching story. Her heart seemed ready to break with trouble for her children. She felt that she could not go to Canada and leave them to suffer and die in slavery. She was sold, with her youngest three children, to a man of whom she knew nothing, and did not know where her children would be taken, or whether they would be separated. Her eldest two daughters might soon be sold and taken to the cotton-fields or rice swamps of the far South. Why her mistresses sold her she could not tell; she had had no warning of their intention. It might be that they were pecuniarily embarrassed and needed money. Her heart yearned especially for her youngest child, about three years old, who had weak eyes and was almost blind. She would cry, "Oh, my precious child, what will it do without mother?" then tears would stream down her cheeks.

We advised her to compose herself and remain quietly at our house and await the result. Perhaps now that she was gone, her children would not be taken away. That day the Anti-Slavery Sewing Society held its weekly meeting at our house, and my wife introduced Sally to the ladies and left her to tell her story, which she did with so much pathos and simple eloquence, that when it was finished, there was not a dry eye in the room.

Most of the ladies present were mothers and could sympathize with her feelings as a mother. Her friends took measures to ascertain the fate of her children, and learned that they had been sold to a man living near Lexington, Kentucky. Sally was much grieved at this news, but still hoped to gain possession of the ,two who were hired out. She staid with us several weeks; then, fearing for her to remain longer in the city, I took her to the house of a trustworthy friend in the country, a few miles away, where she stopped several weeks, hoping to hear some news of her children. A vigorous search for her was kept up, and feeling uneasy about her, I brought her back to our house. Efforts were made by some of her colored friends to secure the liberty of her two children who were hired out, and we endeavored to purchase her youngest child from her master in Lexington, but all these efforts failed, and Sally was finally sent on to Canada alone. I heard from her frequently afterward. She married again in about two years, but the consuming grief for her lost children never left her. One daughter finally escaped and went to Canada, but her mother died just before she reached her. There was never a reunion of the family on earth, but let us hope there will be a reunion in heaven, without the loss of one. There all their wrongs will be righted, and their benighted souls will expand in the light and freedom of eternity.

LOUIS AND ELLEN.

A merchant who lived in Newport, Kentucky, and did business in Cincinnati, on the opposite side of the river, owned several slaves, among whom were a man and his wife, named Louis and Ellen. They were favorites with their master and mistress, and enjoyed many privileges not usually allowed to slaves. They had no children, and Ellen's time was fully engaged in fulfilling the duties of the place she occupied in the household. She was intrusted with the keys and the management of household affairs in general, and attended to her duties with as much dignity as if she were a lady, instead of a servant. She was an intelligent woman, of fine personal appearance, tall, and of light complexion, with straight black hair. She had learned to read, used good language, was attractive in her manners, and was liked and respected by every one who knew her. She was a member of a white Baptist church in Cincinnati, and being consistent in her religious professions had the esteem of her white brethren and sisters. She often had the privilege of attending the church to which she belonged. Louis was a confidential servant, of genteel manners and appearances. He was of browner complexion than his wife, and was not her equal in general intelligence. He was often intrusted to make deposits in bank for his master, and to collect checks, and generally did the family marketing in the city. Both Louis and Ellen had standing passes to cross by the ferry-boat to and from Cincinnati, and occasionally the opportunity was given them to make a little money for themselves. Their master and mistress often gave them presents as rewards for their good management, or as incentives to good conduct, and succeeded in rendering them contented with their lot. Their master often promised them that they should never serve any one else. Louis and his wife saved their money, and in the course of ten or twelve years accumulated about three hundred dollars, which they deposited in a bank in Covington, Kentucky. The cashier of the bank knew that the laws of Kentucky did not allow him to deal with slaves, without a permit from their master, but being well acquainted with Louis and Ellen, he ventured to take their money on his own responsibility, and gave them his individual note, to be cashed on demand.

These were palmy days for Louis and Ellen, but they could not last always. Slaves were never secure; their situation was liable to be changed at any time, by the death or bankruptcy of their master. Louis and Ellen experienced a sudden change after their years of content and prosperity.

Their master became embarrassed in his business, and was involved in debt so deeply that he decided to make an assignment of all his property to his creditors. This intention was concealed from his slaves; but Ellen happened to find it out, and felt greatly alarmed—fearing that she and her husband would fall into other hands, and possibly be separated. She came over to Cincinnati and consulted with a prominent member of her church—a bookseller and publisher in the city. She told him her troubles and fears, and asked him about the Underground Railroad, thinking that she and Louis might find it necessary to resort to that means to secure their liberty.

Her friend said that he would help them all that he could; he knew very little about the Underground Railroad, but was acquainted with a gentleman in the city who knew all about it, and would

30

consult with him. Soon after his interview with Ellen, he came to see me, and very cautiously told me the story. He had never taken stock in the road and was ignorant of its operations; and feared that he might involve himself in difficulty or danger. I was much amused at his extreme caution. I told him that the road was in good working order, and if his friends could get across the river safely, I would see that they were started safely on the Underground Railroad. Ellen was over again in a day or two, and her friend gave her the information he had obtained, and encouraged her to put their plan of escape in execution at once, lest the way should be closed. Ellen replied that it would be some time before she could be ready; she had a number of valuable things she did not wish to leave, and she and Louis wanted to get their money from the bank in Covington before they went away. Her friend reminded her of the danger of delay. She replied that her greatest anxiety was in regard to her husband—if she could prevail on him to come over without her, and get away safely, her mind would be easy, and she would stay awhile and get better prepared before joining him. She did not think they would sell her, for her mistress could not do without her, and she thought she could manage to get away; but Louis was not willing to leave her. She believed her master intended to sell Louis, for he had been trying to create a difficulty between them; he had tried to make her jealous by accusing Louis of intimacy with one of the slave girls, and had advised her to turn him off and have nothing more to do with him.   But she knew that Louis was innocent, and she indignantly resented the accusation.   She told her master that she had lived with her husband fourteen years, and he had always been faithful and kind to her, and she would not believe any such thing against him.   (Some time after Louis was gone, the sin of which he was accused was proven on a young white man, connected with the family.)

The day following Ellen's interview with her friend in the city, she was arranging the dinner about noon, when in passing the open door of the sitting-room where her master and mistress were talking, she heard Louis' name mentioned.   She stepped behind the door and listened, and though the conversation was carried on in a low tone, she heard that Louis was sold and was to be taken away the next day.   She was so shocked that it was with difficulty she finished her work and arranged the dinner table.   Louis was in the kitchen, but she did not venture to tell him the news until the family were seated at the table; then suppressing her agitation as well as she could, she communicated to him what she had heard.   The announcement of the trouble in store for him was so sudden and stunning that Louis was almost overwhelmed.   He could not collect his thoughts enough to decide what to do, but Ellen had already rallied from the shock and at once suggested a plan for his escape.   She told him he must act at once, or his pass would be taken from him, then handing him the market basket she told him to go across to the city as if to get some eggs.

She often sent him on such errands, for she had the management of the kitchen and provided articles for cooking; so his movements in this instance would excite no suspicion. Louis was loth to leave her thus, not knowing that he would ever see her again, but she encouraged him by saying that she would join him in Canada at no distant day, and urged him to start immediately, while the family were at dinner. She gave him the address of her friend, the bookseller, in the city, and told him to go directly to him, and consult him in regard to what was best to do next. Louis followed her directions and told his story to the merchant. I was sent for immediately, and when I arrived Louis was weeping bitterly, being much dejected at the prospect of leaving Ellen. I tried to console him by telling him that she would soon follow him, and they would be reunited in a land of liberty; for the present he must remain in concealment and await results. Louis' friend, the merchant, now suggested a plan by which his master would be misled as to his whereabouts. The market basket was to be filled with eggs, and placed, together with Louis' hat and coat, on the wharf where the Newport ferryboat landed. The supposition was that they would be recognized by the ferryman, who knew that Louis had crossed on the boat a few hours before, and that he would communicate the news to Louis' master, who would naturally conclude that Louis, in his despair, had thrown himself into the river and been drowned. I was afraid that if the plan were carried out it would alarm Ellen, but the merchant urged it, and I told him to manage that part according to his liking ; I would take care of Louis, and see that he was safely concealed.

When another hat and coat had been furnished Louis, instead of his, which he left at the merchant's, I told him to follow me on the opposite side of the street, walking a short distance behind and keeping his eye on me ; to notice where I stopped, and to follow me into the house a few minutes after I entered ; I would meet him at the door inside. He did as I directed, and I conducted him several squares to the house of J. B—— and wife, well known friends to the slave. They belonged to the colored race, but were generally taken for white people, so light were their complexions. J. B—— was quite a business man, and a shrewd manager in Underground Railroad affairs. The house this worthy couple occupied was their own property. Here I left Louis for awhile, knowing that he would be in safe hands.

The merchant carried out his proposed plan that evening. At dusk, a sharp, trusty colored man took the basket of eggs, and Louis' hat and coat, to the river, and watching his opportunity when the ferry-boat was on the other side, placed the things on the wharf, where the boat landed. He then passed on a short distance, and concealed himself where he could watch the basket, and had the satisfaction when the boat returned of seeing the ferryman take them up. The ferryman at once recognized the articles, knowing that Louis had been sent to the city for eggs and had not yet returned. He took them to the other side, and gave them to Louis' master, who had been at the wharf there to inquire for Louis, and was waiting the return of the boat, thinking he might be on it. He was much surprised when the basket, hat and coat were handed to him, and exclaimed at once "Louis must have jumped into the river; poor fellow!" He seemed to feel regret, aside from the loss of his property, for Louis had been his confidential servant. He took the things home and showed them to Ellen. It was a terrible shock to her, for at first thought she supposed that in his deep distress Louis might have drowned himself. She said little, however, and hope soon sprang up in her mind; she concluded that it might be a trick arranged by Louis' friends to deceive his master. Her uneasiness was so great that she could not sleep that night, and next morning she wished to go across the river and see if she could hear anything of Louis. Her mistress said she would go with her, so they crossed over and made inquiries about the river and along East Pearl Street, where Louis generally bought eggs, but gained no information. Ellen wished to get rid of her mistress, and requested her to remain at the house of one of her friends, on East Pearl Street, while she went up town, among some of her colored friends, to see if she could hear anything of Louis. The mistress consented, and Ellen hastened to the house of her friend, the merchant. He was absent, but his wife heard Ellen's story, and sent immediately for me.

When I arrived I found Ellen weeping, and in

great distress.   She told me how the basket and hat
and coat had been found, and said that she feared
her husband was drowned. .I told her to dry her
tears, for her husband was alive and safe.

"Oh! where is he?   I must see him!" she cried,
transported in one moment from the deepest sorrow
to the liveliest joy.

I told her that it was not best for her to see
Louis, that such a meeting might open a way for
his discovery, and endanger his liberty, but she
begged so much.that I finally yielded, and promised
to conduct her to him.   She followed me along the
street as Louis had done, walking some distance
behind and going into the house she saw me enter,
and was soon face to face with her husband.   The
meeting was a most joyful one; they threw themselves into each other's arms, and wept happy tears.

Those who witnessed the meeting shared in their
emotion, fulfilling the injunction, "Rejoice with
them that rejoice, and weep with them that weep."
I informed Ellen that the interview must be brief;
she must return to her mistress, whose suspicions
would be aroused by a long absence.   I told her
that she must suppress all signs of gladness, or her
master and mistress would suspect that she had
heard of Louis' safety.

She replied: "They shall not learn it from me."

We encouraged her to make her escape as soon as
possible, and join her husband in his journey to a
land of freedom.   Louis was very anxious for her
to leave at once, fearing that her situation might be
changed and the chance of escape made more diffi-

cult, but Ellen said she did not wish to leave her good clothes and other valuable property behind, or to come away without getting the three hundred dollars they had in bank at Covington. There was so much excitement about Louis' disappearance that she did not dare to attempt to get the money, lest the movement should create suspicion. I asked if their master knew that they had money in bank. Louis said he knew that they had saved some money, but did not know that it was in the bank. I then inquired if they had a bank book, and they replied that they had not; the cashier had given them his note. I told them that was a different thing; the cashier was individually responsible, and not the bank. Louis said that he had rather lose the money than to have Ellen get into any difficulty about it,

I asked Ellen if she did not think her liberty was worth more than the three hundred dollars, and she said, "Yes!" I then advised her not to attempt to collect the money, but to leave her note with her friend, the merchant; after they were gone he could obtain the money and send it to them.

Louis could be kept safely for several days, and that would give her time to collect her valuables and prepare for her escape. She must now return to her mistress, who was waiting for her on Pearl Street. She took her leave reluctantly and hastened away, saying that she would try to come over again in a few days, on the pretense of marketing.

She betrayed no signs of having received any intelligence of Louis, and went home in apparent great distress, completely deceiving her master and

mistress. She succeeded in sending to her friend,
the merchant, several bundles containing her own
and Louis' best clothing; she bundled it up at night,
and, without discovery, conveyed it out of the house
to some trusty friends, who carried it across to the
city for her. In a few days she got permission to
cross the river again, and completed the arrangement for her final escape. J—— B——, at whose
house Louis was concealed, agreed to go over in a
skiff on the night appointed, land at a certain point
in the upper part of Newport—a private locality—
and wait for Ellen in an alley, not far from her master's. As soon as the family were asleep, she was
to meet him there, with several bundles, containing
the rest of her property, and he was to conduct her
across to his house, in the city.

This plan was carried out, and J—— B—— in
company with Ellen arrived at his house about half
an hour after midnight. Ellen's friend, the merchant, and I were present, and witnessed another
happy meeting of husband and wife. I told them
that they must change quarters at once; there had
been so much passing in and out of the house that
night, that it might have attracted the attention of
policemen or others, and it would not be safe for
them to remain longer. I proposed taking them to
a place on Ninth Street, the house of a white man,
who was a strong abolitionist and who would gladly
shelter fugitives.

Ellen, who was neatly dressed, put on a vail so
that no one would know whether she was white or
colored, took my arm and we passed out of the

31

house. We were then on Third Street, from which we passed to Plum, and made our way to Ninth. Louis and the merchant, shortly after we left, passed out, one at a time, then met and followed us up Plum Street, walking a short distance behind. When we reached A—— S——'s house, I rang the door bell. A—— S—— looked out of his bedroom window, up-stairs, and recognized me at once. He came down and opened the door and received the fugitives.

I told him that we would call the next day and make further arrangements for their safety; then the merchant and I returned to our respective homes, walking a few squares together. This gentleman, D—— A—— by name, was a prominent member of Ninth Street Baptist Church, and a popular bookseller and publisher. I told him I thought he was initiated into Underground Railroad work, and as he had now taken stock and had a little experience, I wanted him to manage the case then on hand, and see that the fugitives got safely to Canada. Perhaps he would be willing to go with them; Ellen was a sister in the church with him, and that gave her a claim on him. I told him I would give him a position as conductor on the Underground Railroad, as I was President of the road. He said he was much obliged for my offer but thought that his experience was not sufficient. Next day D—— A—— and I examined the note for three hundred dollars, given to Louis and Ellen by the cashier, who had received their money. I told them to leave it with their friend, D—— A——

and I would put him in a way to collect it. I asked him if he was acquainted with T—— H——, who was cashier of a bank in this city, and he replied that he was not. I said that I would introduce him to T—— H——, who was an abolitionist, and would feel an interest in the case, and probably be of service to him in collecting the money. Louis and Ellen left the note with their friend, as I advised. The next night they were moved to the northwest part of the city, for greater safety. D—— A—— had proposed a plan to them which they were anxious to have executed. He agreed to write a letter for them to their master, dating it some days ahead and giving Chatham, Canada West, as the place from which it was written. This he would inclose in an envelope and send to Elder Hawkins, of Chatham, Canada West, a colored Baptist minister, formerly of Cincinnati, with whom he was well acquainted, who would mail it to their master at Newport, Kentucky. The letter would inform their master that they were free, yet felt that their liberty was not complete, for if they crossed the Canada line into the United States, their liberty would be endangered. If he would send them deeds of emancipation, they would give him three hundred dollars, which was all the money they had been able to accumulate during the many years they had faithfully served him. He was also reminded of the promise he had made so often, that they should be free. This was the substance of the letter.

D—— A—— sent it to Elder Hawkins, and it was mailed at Chatham, Canada West. It was thought safer for Louis and Ellen to go out of the city, and a few evenings afterward they were conveyed to the house of Joel Haworth, a well-known abolitionist, living in Union County, Indiana. Here they remained several weeks, awaiting results.

Their master answered the letter he received from Canada; he refused to comply with their request, but promised them that if they would come back, he would give them free papers, etc. Elder Hawkins sent this letter to D—— A—— and he forwarded it to Louis and Ellen, in Indiana. They knew too well what their master's promises amounted to, and resolved to go on to Canada.

I introduced D. A—— to T. H——, the cashier of abolition sentiments, and made the latter gentleman acquainted with the circumstances of the case. He said at once that he would collect the money which the note demanded; he was acquainted with the cashier at Covington, and if he refused to pay it he would threaten him with the penalty of the law, for dealing with slaves without their master's permission. This, however, was not necessary, for the cashier paid the money without a word. When T. H—— returned from Covington, he handed the full amount to D. A——, who carried it in person to Louis and Ellen, in Indiana. They were much rejoiced to receive the small sum which they had been so many years in accumulating, and which they had feared was lost. They were immediately forwarded on that old, reliable branch of the Underground Railroad, which extended through Union County, Indiana, and reached Canada in safety.

A year or two afterward I was in Chatham, Canada West, and met Elder Hawkins in the street.
He invited me to dine with him, and I accepted his
invitation, promising to be at his residence in time
for dinner. I had some business to attend to, and
several visits to make among fugitives who had been
at our house. Elder Hawkins pointed out his place
to, me, a large brick house, and when my business
was completed and my visits paid, I started to it.
But it was with difficulty that I made my way along
the street. Many fugitives whom I had helped on
their way to freedom had settled in that place, and
the news had spread among them that I was in
town. They thronged to meet me—to shake hands
with me, and say, "God bless you!" I thought as
I made my way through the crowd that I could not
have attracted more attention if I had been the ele-
phant of a traveling show. Many of the fugitives
I did not recognize, but they remembered me. As
I approached Elder Hawkins' house, Ellen rushed
out to greet me, manifesting much joy and gratitude. She and Louis occupied part of the Elder's
house. Louis was not at home, as he was engaged
in tending a saw-mill, a short distance out of town.
He received good wages, and Ellen worked at dress-
making; their combined income supported them
very comfortably. She took me into their apartments, which were nicely furnished, and looked
neat and comfortable. She said they lived very
happily there and were very thankful for their many
blessings. Louis had been converted and had joined

the church, and was now free, both soul and body, which was a great joy to Ellen.

The Elder's wife had prepared a good dinner, and we all dined together. Soon after dinner I parted from them, feeling much pleased with my visit.

THE MICHIGAN RAID.

The farther north from the land of slavery that a fugitive traveled, the more friends he found, and quite a number of runaway slaves, thinking they would be safe in Michigan, stopped there instead of crossing over to Canada. At a place called Young's Prairie, in Cass County, Michigan, where there was a settlement of Friends, and a number of Eastern people, all stanch abolitionists, there had accumulated quite a little colony of colored fugitives who secured homes in the neighborhood. Some families owned small patches of ground on which they had erected comfortable little log houses, and by industry and thrift managed to live very comfortably.

But they were not secure in these humble, vine-clad homes, for Southern bloodhounds in human shape were on their trail, and had scented out their places of retreat. Spies sent out to hunt for fugitive slaves in various neighborhoods in Ohio, Indiana, and Michigan, discovered the colony at Young's Prairie, and ascertained that most of the fugitives had come from Kentucky. Among these spies was a young Kentuckian who professed to be a Yankee and a stanch abolitionist. He claimed to be an agent for some anti-slavery papers which he carried with him, but his speech betrayed him. A Yankee living in Michigan said: "You are not from New England; you are no Yankee; if you were you would say *keow* and not *cow*. You are here for no good purpose, and the sooner you leave this neighborhood the better it will be for you."

Several of the colored families spoken of were from Boone County, Kentucky, and their masters learned of their whereabouts. In that county there was a company organized for the purpose of capturing fugitives, with funds for hiring pursuers. A plan was formed to seize the negroes at Young's Prairie and bring them back to slavery, and about thirty men, with several two-horse wagons for transporting the negro women and children, started to Michigan. Part of the company on horseback went ahead of the wagons to ascertain the exact location of the fugitives, and to have all things arranged for a simultaneous raid upon the different negro cabins scattered around the edge of the prairie, and in small groves in the neighborhood. They were to make their headquarters at Niles, a few miles distant, in an adjoining county, and scatter out through Young's Prairie in small parties, under pretense of looking for land to purchase, or buying stock. By this means they could obtain all necessary information in regard to the location of the colored people without exciting suspicion as to their real mission. Then some of the company were to meet the teams, and conduct the wagons to different localities in the neighborhood, where they would camp until a late hour at night. This arrangement appeared to contain the elements of success, but it did not succeed. Slaves often have. friends living in slave States— people whose principles are unknown to the slave-holders. One of this class, a man living in the neighborhood of the Kentucky slaveholders, became apprised of all their plans for capturing the fugitives in Michigan, but was misinformed in regard to the time they were to start. He wrote to a confidential friend in Cincinnati, informing him of all the plans of the. raiders, but stated the time of their starting incorrectly—they started several days earlier. His friend came directly to me and gave me all the information he had received. I at once set about to intercept their plans. I was well acquainted at Young's Prairie, Michigan. There was a settlement of Friends there, many of whom had emigrated from Wayne County, Indiana, and were among the early settlers of that neighborhood. Some had formerly been my neighbors in Indiana. I had been at Young's Prairie, and visited several of the families of fugitives in that settlement. Friends, had established a school among them, and they seemed to be prospering. I decided to send a messenger at once to apprise them and their friends of their danger. At that day, letters were often eight or ten days in reaching Young's Prairie, and I knew it would not do to risk sending a message by mail; it would not reach them in time.

A. young man then boarding with us, an active and energetic abolitionist, volunteered to go if his expenses were paid. I agreed to pay his expenses, and started him at once. As there were no railroads or stage lines then, we had to depend on private conveyance for the journey. I gave the young man letters to my friends in the various neighborhoods in Indiana, through which he would pass, requesting them to furnish him with fresh horses on the stages of his journey. This was promptly done on his way through Wayne, Randolph and Grant Counties, Indiana, and greatly facilitated his journey to Michigan. But his laborious and energetic effort proved too late; the raid was over. The Kentuckians had started several days earlier than the time named in our informant's letter, and their plans had been put into execution. On the night of the raid they divided their company, and each party made a simultaneous attack on the negro cabins. They seized the unsuspecting inmates as they slept, bound them, and placed them in the wagons. There were desperate struggles at many of the cabins, and a number of the fugitives were bruised and wounded, before they were overpowered and bound. A certain place on the prairie had been agreed upon as a rendezvous, and thither the different companies made their way. In one party of marauders was a Baptist minister, who claimed to be the owner of a negro man and his wife—valuable property. They had leased a piece of land of Zachariah Shugart, a Friend, and had built a snug cabin in which they had lived two or three years. They had one child, a babe a few months old. Being frugal and industrious they had prospered, and were much respected by their neighbors. The minister and his party approached this cabin and tried to gain entrance at the only door, but it was barred inside and resisted their efforts. They demanded entrance, but the negro man recognized his master's voice and refused to open the door.

The party seized an ax, battered down the door and entered. The negro man made weapons of chairs or anything he could get hold of and fought desperately, keeping them at bay for some time, but was at last wounded and overpowered. During this conflict his wife, leaving her babe in bed, crawled out of a small window at the back of the cabin and ran to Zachariah Shugart's. She gave the alarm and then hid herself. Zachariah Shugart mounted his horse and rode as fast as he could to the house of his nearest neighbor, Stephen Bogue, who had a very fleet saddle-horse. As soon as he heard the news, Stephen Bogue mounted this horse and rode with all possible speed to Cassopolis, the county seat, three miles distant, to give the alarm and to obtain a writ and to have the kidnappers arrested.

It was now daylight. A large company of men soon rallied and hastened toward Young's Prairie, to rescue the fugitives. They were headed by a resolute, brawny-armed blacksmith, called Bill Jones, who assumed command of the party. Their company increased rapidly as they entered the prairie, until it numbered two hundred men. The whole neighborhood was aroused, and hastened to the rescue.

Now to return to the cabin whence the alarm originated. Zachariah Shugart, after carrying the

news to Stephen Bogue, went to see what had
become of his tenants and to watch the movements
of the kidnappers. The negro man, after his brave
struggle, had been knocked down, dragged into the
yard, securely bound and placed in the wagon. The
preacher then rushed into the cabin to secure his
other property, but the wife was not to be found,
having escaped, as mentioned, through a back
window when the fight was in progress. The child
was crying, and the minister took it up from the
bed. Although it had been born in a free State, he
claimed it as his property, on the plea that the child
follows the condition of the mother—the rule in
slave States. He carried it out, supposing that
when the mother heard its screams she would come
out of her hiding-place and run to her child—but
no mother came. Young children were worth two
hundred dollars in Kentucky—too much to lose.

The minister mounted his horse with the child in
his arms, and they moved toward the place of rendezvous in the main road, half a mile distant.
About the time they reached the place Bill Jones
and his company arrived, and the other companies
of raiders soon came up. The Kentuckians were all
well armed with revolvers and bowie-knives, and
thought to intimidate their assailants by threats and
a free display of their weapons. But they were
mistaken. On one side of the road stood a low
stake fence, the kind generally used on prairies.
Bill Jones and his company soon stripped the fence
of its stakes, and with these formidable weapons,
the blacksmith commanded his party to charge,

telling them not to leave a kidnapper alive. But
fortunately for the Kentuckians, there were several
Friend Quakers present, who stepped in between
the parties and prevented a collision. The brave
Kentucky slave catchers were completely cowed,
and agreed to go quietly to Cassopolis, the county
seat, and prove their property before the proper
authorities, as the law required.

The negroes who were bound were soon released,
and Bill Jones seeing the Baptist minister on horseback with the infant in his arms compelled him to
dismount, and let the child's father, who was bleeding ırom his wounds, ride in his stead. The minister he compelled to walk and carry the child in
his arms, and whenever they passed a house, the
people were called out to look at that child-stealer,
a preacher. When they reached Cassoplis, Bill
Jones further compelled him to march up and down
the street, and called the attention of the people to
this divine, who had been stealing a negro babe,
and taunted him so much that he actually cried with
vexation. The raiders were here served with a writ
by the sheriff, arresting them for kidnapping, and
were committed to jail where they were kept for
several days—unt l the negroes were on their way
to Canada. A fair trial was promised to the prisoners, and they were allowed to send to Niles for
lawyers. When the time appointed came, a kind of
sham trial was held, and they were dismissed without further punishment than paying costs. These
amounted to a considerable sum, and but one man
in the company had money to pay the bill. The

main object to be gained was the freedom of the negroes. The kidnappers were glad to return to Kentucky without the fugitives, and there was soon a general move of the latter from Young's Prairie to Canada.

After awhile the owners of some of these slaves brought suit for the amount of their full value against those persons who had befriended them. The fugitive slave law visited a heavy penalty on those who befriended slaves, not only fine and imprisonment, but sometimes the payment of the full value of the slaves. The case was tried in the Supreme Court at Detroit. The trial was put off from one session of the court to another, subjecting those who had been sued to much inconvenience and cost in attending court, paying lawyers' fees, etc. But the slaveholders failed to make out the case against them, and the slaves were out of their reach in Canada.

CHAPTER XI.

CINCINNATI STORIES CONTINUED—JOHN WILSON AND
ELIZA—UNCLE TOM—ROSE, THE WHITE SLAVE—
STORY OF JIM AND HIS FRIEND IN A TIGHT BOX.

JOHN WILSON AND ELIZA.

A WHITE man named John Wilson, a machinist by trade, went from Pittsburg, Pennsylvania, to the South, where he spent several years putting up sugar-mills and other machinery. He resided at Bayou Plaquemine, on the Mississippi River, about one hundred miles above New Orleans, and while there became attached to a young woman nearly white, the slave of a planter named Bissell, who lived at that place. He tried to purchase her from her master that he might give her her freedom and make her his wife, and offered a high price, but Bissell would not sell her. The girl, whose name was Eliza, reciprocated the sincere attachment of Wilson, but no slave could be legally married in that State, and it was useless to expect to be his wife in law. She and Wilson remained faithful to each other through several years, and in that time two children were born to them.

Eliza's master finally became suspicious that Wil-

son would try to take her to the North, and resolved
to separate them and send her away from him. She
was an excellent house servant, but he had her
taken from the house and sent, without her children,
to a cotton plantation which he owned about fourteen miles from Bayou Plaquemine, and there set to
work as a common field hand. She was forbidden,
under heavy penalties, to have any communication
with her husband, as she called Wilson, and he was
warned that if he visited her it would be at the risk
of his life, but notwithstanding these threats they
managed to see each other frequently. Eliza's
master heard of these meetings, and had her severely punished for her disobedience.

Wilson had friends at Bayou Plaquemine and
vicinity, and through the help of these and by
means of an arrangement made with the officers of
a Pittsburg boat running on the Mississippi, with
whom he was acquainted, he managed to get Eliza
to the river and to send her to New Orleans, where
she remained for three months, supported by his
bounty. Finally, he hired a white man to take her
from New Orleans to Cincinnati, paying him two
hundred dollars for her expenses and his own
recompense. The man took Eliza on board a boat
bound for Cincinnati, but on the passage gambled
away the money that Wilson had paid him, and had
not paid her fare. He told the captain of the boat
that she was a slave whom he was taking to join her
master and mistress in Cincinnati, and that her fare
would be paid by them at that place. When the
boat stopped at Cincinnati, he told Eliza that she

was now in a free State, and could go where she
pleased, and, taking leave of her, walked down the
gangway, and was soon lost to sight in the crowd
on the wharf.

Eliza pondered awhile regarding the course she
should pursue, then started to leave the boat, not
knowing that her fare was unpaid. As she stepped
on the plank, the captain stopped her and told her
she could not go ashore until her passage money
was paid. She referred him to the man in whose
charge she had been, and told the captain to look to
him for the money, for he was responsible for it,
and requested him to let her pass, as she was a free
woman. But the captain's suspicions were aroused
and he resolved to detain her. Thinking she was a
runaway slave, he arranged to take her across to
Covington, Kentucky, and lodge her in jail till his
boat was ready to start on the return trip, then take
her back with him and deliver her to her master and
mistress, if they could be found.

The sympathies of the colored steward of the boat
had been aroused in Eliza's behalf, and he resolved
to aid her if possible. He hastened up into the city
to the office of lawyer Joliffe, whom he knew as a
tried friend of the slaves, and told the story. Joliffe
sent for me, and we immediately got out a writ for
the captain of the boat, and placed it in the sheriff's hands, with orders to bring him and the woman
before court. The sheriff reached the boat just as
the captain had got Eliza into a skiff, and was preparing to pull across to the Kentucky shore. In two
minutes more it would have been too late. The

sheriff took Eliza in charge, arrested the captain for an attempt to kidnap, and brought them before the Probate Court, the only one in session. Judge Burgoyne, a stanch abolitionist, who was then on the bench, required the captain to show cause for detaining the woman. The captain replied that he had no claim on her except for the amount of her unpaid fare, which was twenty dollars, but as she could produce no papers or other evidence that she was free, he regarded her as a fugitive slave, and had resolved to detain her till the truth could be ascertained.

The Court decided that he had no right to detain her on suspicion, and could not remove her from the State of Ohio without legally proving that she was his slave, and Eliza was set at liberty. Lawyer Joliffe and I soon made up enough money to pay her boat fare, and she was sent to a respectable colored boarding-house on McAllister Street. She had a large trunk full of clothes on the boat, having been well supplied by her husband and friends before leaving New Orleans, and for this she held a check. I sent the check and the price of her passage by a drayman to the boat, and obtained her trunk and had it taken to her boarding-place. That afternoon I and Preacher Green (colored), pastor of Allen Chapel, went to see Eliza, and after convincing her that we were her true friends, and gaining her confidence, she told us her true story; she had previously claimed to be free. She said it was the arrangement made by her husband that she should remain in Cincinnati until he came to her, which

32

would be about Christmas time, as he could not complete his business engagements in the South before some time in December. She had entire confidence that he would fulfill his promise and come to her; yes, follow her to the ends of the earth, she said, for they were attached to each other as much as it was possible for any husband and wife to be.

It was now early spring, and as she would be exposed to the danger of capture if she remained so long in Cincinnati, it was decided that she should be sent to Canada with a party of free colored people who were going from Cincinnati to that country soon, on a visit. After hearing her story, it was deemed advisable to remove her from the boarding-house where she was, as it was too public a place to afford any concealment, and would be among the first searched if her master heard of her whereabouts and came in pursuit.

It was accordingly decided to remove her to our house, but in order that the inmates of the boarding-house should not know where she was gone, she was taken, with her trunk, first to the house of Pastor Green, and then to our house, where she found a secure retreat. When the party of colored people were ready to start to Canada, Pastor Green came with a carriage to take Eliza to the depot where she could join them, but she was unwilling to go so much farther away from her husband and children, and cried and begged to be allowed to remain where she was till she could hear from her husband. Moved by her entreaties, I finally told

her that if she were willing to incur the risk of
staying, she might remain at our house, where we
would employ her at good wages, having learned
that she was an excellent house servant. She
gladly availed herself of this offer and remained.
She and her husband had arranged to correspond
under fictitious names, and I wrote several letters
for her, in which I was very guarded and careful not
to give information that would enable an uninitiated
person to understand the facts of the case. Eliza
received several letters from Wilson, inclosing
money. Letters from the North were frequently
broken open at Southern post-offices, before reaching the persons to whom they were directed, in
order to intercept abolition documents, etc., and in
this way masters sometimes obtained information
of their runaway slaves. Other persons wrote
letters to Wilson for Eliza, who were not so guarded
in their expressions, and one which purported to be
from Wilson's sister, and stated that she was in Cincinnati, at the house of a Quaker, fell into the
hands of Bissell, at Bayou Plaquemine, who broke it
open and read it. He immediately inferred that the
person who pretended to be Wilson's sister was
Eliza, and after causing Wilson to be arrested on
suspicion of aiding a slave to escape, and lodged in
jail, he started in pursuit of his property.

On arriving at Cincinnati Bissell obtained a writ,
from Commissioner Pendery, and put it into the
hands of the marshal with orders to arrest Eliza, if
she could be found, adding, it was said, a hundred
dollars by way of stimulating the officer's zeal and

quickening his efforts. It was conjectured that our house was the house referred to in the letter, but in order to ascertain this beyond doubt, it was planned that a deputy marshal should gain access to the house under the pretense of peddling books, penetrate into the kitchen, and see if there was a person answering Eliza's description. The plan was well arranged and had it been kept secret might have succeeded, but the marshal made a confidant of a local editor—of all persons in the world! It is well known that a local editor can not retain an item of news two hours, without seriously injuring his constitution, and in a very short time I was made acquainted with the whole affair. The same information, afterward, reached me through other channels. Commissioner Pendery had informed a person of the circumstance of Bissell's obtaining the writ, and that person informed Lawyer Joliffe. As soon as Joliffe heard it, he notified me. I also heard of it through Christian Donaldson, who had been informed of it privately.

The slaveholder before leaving Bayou Plaquemine had written to a nephew of his, who was at school at Ann Arbor, Michigan, giving information of Eliza's escape, and her supposed whereabouts, and requesting him to meet him at Cincinnati to act as witness, if she could be found.

It so happened that this young man arrived in Cincinnati the day that Bissell obtained the writ for Eliza's arrest, but instead of going to see his uncle, who was stopping at the Burnet House, he went first to see James Burney, a lawyer. Presenting

letters of introduction from professors in the college
he attended, and from prominent citizens of Detroit,
he informed Lawyer Burney, that during his stay at
the North, he had been converted by the abolitionists, and that his real errand in Cincinnati at that
time was to prevent his uncle from gaining possession of Eliza and carrying her back to slavery, and
that he would do all in his power to aid her in
securing her freedom.   Burney went with him across
the street to the office of Salmon P. Chase, to whom
also he had letters of introduction, and related all
the circumstances.   Chase sent a student from his
office to accompany the young man to my store,
supposing that if such a fugitive were in the city I
would be likely to know it, and from the young
man's introductory letters inferring that he was
trustworthy, and that his intentions were what he
represented them to be.

Arriving at my store, they found that I was
absent, having gone to the railroad depot on business, and they did not wait my return.   As soon as
I returned, Lawyer Thomas, Burney's partner, came
in and informed me that Bissell's nephew had been
there to see me, and related the other circumstances
of the case.   I was disposed to be cautious, and said
that I had no confidence in the anti-slavery preten-
sions of the young man, that I thought it a shrewd
scheme to gain information regarding Eliza, and
added: "He would have gained nothing from me
had I been here."   Lawyer Thomas was returning
to his office, when on crossing a street he saw Bissell making his way up the street toward my house.

Bissell had been pointed out to him the day before, and he recognized him. Thomas hastily returned to my store, to put me on my guard. My store was then on the northwest corner of Sixth and Elm Streets; our dwelling house adjoined it on the north, fronting on Elm and George Streets. While Thomas and I were standing near the front door of my store, Bissell made his appearance on the southwest corner, and stood for awhile, looking anxiously toward our house, then slowly moved on to Plum Street and around the square.

I went into the house and told Eliza that her master was in search of her, that he had just passed down Sixth Street, and that she must dress herself as quickly as possible in her best clothes, and I would send her to a safe place. The news greatly agitated her, and she began to cry. Her chief trouble seemed to be a fear that her husband had got into difficulty on her account. I told her that she had no time to cry, she must dry her tears and act with promptness, for a great deal depended on immediate action. Just then my wife came in; she had been out shopping with two young ladies who were staying with us, one as a visitor, the other a boarder. I gave Eliza into their charge and she was soon made ready. They attired her in her best clothes, of which she had a good supply which her master had never seen. She and the other two young ladies, all closely vailed, then walked out at the front door, in sight of her master who had passed around the square and was now standing on the northeast corner of Sixth and Elm, looking toward the house. He was apparently deceived by the boldness of the movement, and had no suspicion that one of the ladies was his slave. He did not offer to molest them or follow them, and they, according to directions I had previously given them, made their way to the house of Edward Harwood, that noble friend of the slave, at the head of Elm Street, where Eliza was to remain in seclusion until I called for her. That evening I ordered my carriage brought—not to my door—but to a point two blocks away, and entering it drove to Eliza's hiding-place about dark. Taking her in the carriage, I went to Mt. Auburn and there left her for greater safety, at the house of the pastor of a prominent church in the city.

Supposing that the marshal would endeavor to ascertain if Eliza were at my house, I engaged a young colored woman who answered to her description in regard to age, personal appearance, etc., to come and stay at my house a week, filling the position that Eliza had occupied. This girl was free, and there could be no danger, even if she were arrested. She understood the case, and was eager for the fun.

A druggist, named Kent, whose store was on the opposite side of the street from mine, learned all the particulars of the case, and, being a stanch abolitionist, resolved to have some fun at the expense of the marshal, in case that official should make any demonstration. He planned to have his buggy in waiting, and as soon as the marshal was seen in the street to drive hastily up to my door, take in the colored girl, excitedly and hurriedly, as if fearing pursuers, and then drive away with the speed of Jehu. It was supposed that the marshal would give chase, and in that case Kent would manage to be captured, then end the farce by having the marshal and his posse arrested for kidnapping a free girl. The plan promised well, and Kent kept his buggy waiting till a late hour at night, expecting the arrival of the marshal, but that official did not have the moral courage to carry out his arrangement for entering my house, and it all came to nothing.

In the meantime, Bissell's lawyer informed him that he could not take legal possession of Eliza, as he had no bill of sale or other evidence that she was his property, and that if he entered suit, the abolitionists would be sure to defeat him. Eliza had been a present to Bissell's wife from her father, on the occasion of her marriage, and as no paper of conveyance had been given, she was considered in law still the property of her first owner. It was therefore necessary for Bissell to obtain a power of attorney from his father-in-law, before he could proceed further in the case. He immediately dispatched to Bayou Plaquemine for the necessary papers, and resolved to wait in Cincinnati until they reached him, but his nephew, representing to him that a week or two must elapse before they could arrive, invited him to return with him to Ann Arbor, as he could not remain longer away from college. The uncle accepted the invitation, and spent a week or two at Ann Arbor and Detroit.

When he was ready to return to Cincinnati, the nephew telegraphed to Lawyer Burney that his uncle would reach Cincinnati that evening, and it would be well to have Eliza out of the way—thus proving his anxiety and interest in Eliza's welfare to my entire satisfaction.

Eliza was removed from Mt. Auburn to Walnut Hills, where she remained for several weeks in the families of prominent religionists.

Bissell staid in Cincinnati for two weeks after his return, and made every exertion to find her, but could get no clue to her whereabouts, and finally gave up the search and started South. The boat on which he took passage met another boat coming up the river, on board of which was John Wilson, the husband of Eliza, but the vessels passed without the two enemies recognizing each other. Bissell had left Wilson in prison when he came away from Bayou Plaquemine, and expected to find him there on his return, and prosecute him to the full extent of the law, but when he reached home he learned that Wilson's friends had given bond for his appearance, that he had been released from jail, and had gone North.

We now turn to the fortunes of the husband and wife, who had passed through such trying scenes on account of their devotion to each other. As soon as Wilson arrived in Cincinnati, he came to my house seeking for tidings of Eliza. I took him in my carriage to Walnut Hills, and there was a joyful meeting of the husband and wife, who remained so fondly attached to each other through danger, sepa-

33

ration and misfortune. I gave them letters to friends in Michigan, and they went to the home of that noted worker in the cause of freedom, Laura S. Haviland, who lived near Adrian, and was the proprietress of the Raisin Institute, a school in which students of all colors have equal privileges. Here they remained for several weeks, and here they were legally married.

From this place they went to Canada, and remained there awhile, but soon returned to Michigan and settled near Raisin Institute. Eliza had previously had no advantages of education, and her husband wishing her to attend school placed her in the institute, while he found employment in a machine shop at Adrian. With the proceeds of his industry he bought a lot and a snug brick house, near the institute, and here, after many vicissitudes, he and Eliza found themselves in the enjoyment of peace and plenty. Here, after carrying the hero and heroine through all sorts of adventures and narrow escapes, a well regulated tale of fiction would end with the remark that they lived happily ever afterward, but this is a narrative of facts, and must chronicle new undertakings and fresh scenes of danger and distress. A motive no less strong than that which led John and Eliza to join each other and seek a land of freedom, now prompted them to separate, while one braved again the dangers of the land of slavery. The hearts of the parents yearned for their children, and they determined to make an effort to rescue them from bondage. Eliza, being yet a slave in the sight of the law, could not venture southward without jeopardizing her own liberty, so it was arranged that she should remain behind while John made the hazardous attempt to find and carry off their children.

Proceeding to Pittsburg, his former home, he made arrangements with the officers of a Pittsburg and Mississippi River boat, with whom he was acquainted. According to this plan, they were to land him at a point near Bayou Plaquemine on the downward passage to New Orleans, and on the return trip to stop in the night at a secluded place agreed upon—the night and the hour being appointed—where he and his children would be taken on board, if he succeeded in getting them. He went to the neighborhood of Bayou Plaquemine, and by the aid of friends, with whom he communicated secretly, succeeded in gaining possession of his children. He proceeded with caution, concealing his presence in the neighborhood from the knowledge of Bissell, but by some means he was discovered and pursued as he was taking his children to the appointed rendezvous. He was obliged to leave them and flee through the woods and thickets, reaching the landing barely in time to be taken on board the boat before his pursuers reached him. Thwarted and disappointed in his efforts he now sought to make new plans to gain his children, but found that the journeys he had taken and the expenses he had incurred had exhausted his ready means, and that he must seek employment again in order to recruit his finances. Landing at Louisville, Kentucky, on the homeward trip of the boat, he found employment in a machine shop, and made arrangements with the officers of the boat to bring him his chest of tools—which he had left at Pittsburg—on the next trip. In the mean time his securities, those who had signed his bond while he was in jail at Bayou Plaquemine, learning that he had been seen in that vicinity again, sent an officer to arrest him. It was known that he had taken passage up the river, and as it was thought that he would be in Louisville, Cincinnati or Pittsburg, requisitions for his delivery were obtained from the Governor of Louisiana to the Governors of Kentucky, Ohio and Pennsylvania. The officer in search of him stopped first at Louisville, but did not happen to find him, and went on to Cincinnati and Pittsburg. Not gaining any clue of him in either of these places, the officer returned to Louisville, and after a more extended inquiry succeeded in finding him. The Governor of Kentucky was applied to and gave the necessary permission, and Wilson was immediately arrested.

To prevent his escaping on the way to Bayou Plaquemine the officer had him ironed. The water in the Ohio River was so low at that time—the fall of the year—that large New Orleans packets could not run, and the officer took Wilson by rail to St. Louis, Missouri, and there put him aboard of a steamer which was to start down the river next day. Here one of Wilson's friends, from New Orleans, saw him, and, learning the particulars of his case, resolved if possible to aid him to escape. Through his influence the handcuffs of Wilson were taken off, but he was still closely guarded. When night approached, the officer arranged to take Wilson on shore and place him in jail for greater security.

Wilson's friend learned of this and saw that his time to act had come; if he delayed longer it would be too late. Giving a signal to Wilson, that the latter might embrace the opportunity, he managed to engage the attention of the officer a few moments. Wilson slipped back, sprang on the wheel-house, and from that to the wheel-house of another boat lying at the wharf. From this he jumped on the wharf, and as it was now dark he escaped unseen and made his way into the city. Passing through it, he directed his course to the upper wharf, where he knew the Pittsburg boats lay. There he found an engineer from Pittsburg, with whom he was acquainted, and after hurriedly relating his story asked to be taken on board and secreted. The engineer had an interview with the captain, who favored Wilson's cause, and they hid the fugitive in the boat. Next morning the papers gave full accounts of the affair, announcing, in double-leaded headlines, "ESCAPE OF A NIGGER THIEF," and adding that there was a strict search for him in the city, and that no doubt he would soon be recaptured.

The boat on which Wilson was secreted lay at the wharf several days taking on cargo, but he was not discovered, and in time landed safely at Cincinnati. He came immediately to my house and gave an account of his adventures. I had received hundreds of colored fugitives, but this was the first Anglo-Saxon fugitive that had claimed my protection. I took him in my carriage to the Cincinnati, Hamilton and Dayton depot, bought a ticket for him, and saw him started on the way to Adrian, Michigan. Wilson's box of tools were at Louisville, in the machine shop where he had been arrested, and he arranged to have them sent to him. In a few days an iron-bound chest was unloaded from a dray, on the sidewalk in front of my house. It was addressed "Levi Coffin, Cincinnati," but knowing very well whose it was, I merely changed the direction to "John Wilson, Adrian, Michigan," and reshipped it to its destination.

Wilson afterward made other attempts to rescue his children, but did not succeed, and it was not till President Lincoln issued the proclamation of emancipation that these parents indulged in the certain hope of meeting their son and daughter. Even then they were partially disappointed, for the little boy died before they could gain possession of him. The daughter joined her parents, and is now married and living in Ohio.

I met with John Wilson and Eliza again, after an interval of eight years. After the war had closed, but while the Union army was still at Nashville—in the autumn of 1865—I went to visit the colored schools at that place, accompanied by Dr. Massey, of London, who was much interested in the freedmen. One day, just as we were starting from one school building to another, I met John Wilson, who was at work in the government machine shops at that place. After greetings and mutual inquiries, I asked after Eliza, and learning that she was then in

Nashville arranged to go to see her. After visiting the school to which we had started, John conducted us to his residence, and then stepped back that I might enter first and give Eliza a surprise. They occupied two rooms, with a passage between, on the second floor, which was reached by a flight of stairs on the outside. I went up first, followed by Dr. Massey and John. Just as I reached the door of the hall Eliza was passing from one room to the other, carrying something in her hands. As soon as she saw me, she dropped it, and springing forward, clasped me in her arms, exclaiming with great emotion, "You saved me twice from slavery," while tears sprang to her eyes and rolled down her cheeks. This meeting, and the gratitude manifested by Eliza toward me, seemed to make a deep impression on Dr. Massey, and he often referred to it afterward.

John and Eliza soon after returned to their comfortable little home in Michigan, and since that have visited us in Cincinnati several times.

UNCLE TOM.

While we lived at the corner of Franklin and Broadway a runaway slave came to our house in an extremely cold time in the middle of winter. He had been brought up in the neighborhood of Lexington, Kentucky, and belonged to a well-known politician, T. M———. His master had hired him to a cruel task-master, living about twenty miles from Lexington, who treated him with much harshness, often whipping him unmer-

cifully.   He finally concluded that he would bear
it no longer, and made his way back to his master.   He told his master how cruelly he was treated
and plead for a change of situation, but his master was unmoved and ordered him to go back to
his new home, threatening him with severe punishment if he disobeyed.   He left his master, but not
to return to the cruel man to whom he was hired.
He had a different purpose.   He said he had heard,
through some free colored people in Lexington,
that there was a good man living in Cincinnati, by
the name of Levi Coffin, who was a great friend to
the negroes, and would help runaway slaves on their
way to Canada—that country where all were free.
He thought he would try to get to Cincinnati and
find this man.   He had been told that the railroad
from Lexington led to Cincinnati, and he concluded
to follow it.   After going a short distance as if
intending to return to the man who had hired him,
he hid himself and waited till night, then got on the
railroad and walked rapidly on the ties, facing the
cold north wind.   The distance to Covington was
ninety-six miles ; he thought he walked and ran on
the railroad about fifty miles that night.   When
daylight came he hid himself in some corn shocks in
a field, and here, in consequence of his exposure in
his heated and exhausted condition, he took a severe
cold.   Next night he made slow progress on his
journey, being stiff and sore.   When a train passed
he concealed himself in the thickets, then continued his painful journey along the railroad track.
When daylight appeared he sought a hiding-place

again among some corn fodder, but suffered greatly from the cold. Having little left of the scanty morsel of food he had provided himself with, he began to feel the pangs of hunger. The third night he reached the Ohio River, but could find no way to cross. The river was not frozen over, but ice was forming, and it was dangerous to attempt to cross in a skiff even if he had found one. He almost perished with cold and hunger that night.

In the morning he went to the outskirts of Covington, and ventured into a negro hut, where he was supplied with provisions and allowed to remain through the day. The next night he was assisted by a free colored man to cross the river, in a skiff, below Covington. He was directed to the house of a colored man living near the river, of whom he inquired concerning me, saying that he wished to see me. The colored man knew me, and at once conducted him to our house.

He was a stranger and we took him in, hungry and we fed him, not naked but very destitute and we clothed him, sick and we ministered unto him. He was a noble looking man, in the prime of life, of good muscular development, and a pleasant and intelligent countenance. When he entered, my wife exclaimed, "Here's Uncle Tom!" and he was afterward called that by all the inmates of the house and those who visited him. The deep cold he had taken settled on his lungs, producing a hard cough, and, notwithstanding care and kind treatment, it developed into lung fever. He was soon confined to his bed, and we called in Dr. W. H. Mussey, who was ever ready to give aid or medical attention to fugitives and other poor people without charge. The doctor found poor Tom very ill, and requiring prompt attention and careful nursing. We hired a good nurse to stay with him day and night, and Dr. Mussey was indefatigable in his attentions.

Tom had been a strong healthy man, and his vitality did not yield easily to the disease that was preying upon him. For a slave, one whose lot had been cast in that system which tended to trample out every spark of intellect and reduce men and women to the level of brutes, Tom possessed un- usual intelligence. He was a professor of religion and loved the words of the Bible, though the priv- ilege of reading them had been denied to him. Our boarders manifested great interest in Uncle Tom, and rendered him many kind attentions. Favorable symptoms now and then appeared which encouraged hopes of his recovery, but cold and hunger and exposure had done their work, and the disease was too deeply seated for human skill.

Dr. Mussey called in other prominent physicians to see Tom, and consulted with them regarding his case. This was done several times during his illness, which lasted nine weeks. At first, Tom was quiet and rational, then delirium appeared and his mind wandered. He became alarmed at every noise he heard in the house or street, thinking that it was his master coming after him, and would beg pit- eously to be taken to the house of that good man, Levi Coffin. His attendants could not persuade him that he was already there, and when I would go to his bedside and tell him that he was safe at my house, whence no fugitive had ever been taken by their masters, he would seize hold of me and beg me to save him, adding, "If master catches me, he will stretch me out on the ground with stakes, and cut my back to pieces, and I am too weak to bear it; I will die."

I would talk to him in a soothing manner, assuring him of his safety, and he would grow calm, then again start up in the delirium of fever, and beg to be boxed up and sent to Canada, or to be carried to the house of Levi Coffin. Then he would assume another phase; he was independent, he feared no man, the Lord was with him; he was a missionary sent out to preach the gospel, and would pray and preach in a voice so loud that it could be heard in the street. He sometimes imagined that he was out on the wide ocean, or in a river steamer, or in the cars. At other times he would imagine himself pursued and attacked by bloodhounds, then he would spring out of bed and lay hold on anything he could reach, with which to defend himself. As his ravings became more violent, two men were required to control him. He fancied that we were all his enemies, that his nurses and the doctors were trying to poison him, and he refused to take medicine or nourishment of any kind. What was given him had to be administered by force. At one time he did not close his eyes in sleep for forty-eight hours. The doctors decided to try stimulants, and forced him to take a small quantity of brandy and egg, every hour, during one afternoon. This had the desired effect; he dropped into a quiet doze that evening and awoke in a calmer frame of mind. A few more doses of stimulant were given him, and about ten o'clock he fell into a peaceful sleep, awaking next morning at daylight in his right mind. He took a little nourishment and seemed to revive. It was a lesson of instruction to be in his room and witness his resignation to the will of his Divine Master, and to hear him talk of his religious experience and the goodness of the Lord. Several ministers visited him and had seasons of prayer with him. For several days the doctors had great hopes of his recovery, but an unfavorable change in his disease took place, and he quietly and peacefully passed away at two o'clock on the sixth day of the week, after being confined to his bed at our house for nine weeks, and requiring a great deal of care and expense in nursing, which I can say in truth we willingly rendered.

We had poor Tom neatly dressed, and obtained a nice coffin from the undertaker, also hiring a hearse and two carriages. The funeral was appointed at two o'clock, Sabbath afternoon, in Allen Chapel, on Sixth Street, the largest colored church in the city, and notice of it was given in all the colored churches. Rev. George Rogers, a white Wesleyan minister, volunteered to preach the funeral sermon. A large congregation gathered, of both colored and white people, and the chapel was filled to its utmost capacity. The coffin was placed in front of the pulpit. I took a seat by the side of the minister, and at the close of the sermon, I gave a short his-

tory of Uncle Tom, of his death struggle for freedom, his sufferings and long sickness, his dying
expressions and happy close of life. Then the
large congregation moved quietly up one aisle and
down the other, to view the peaceful face of the
dead fugitive. A number of private carriages joined
the funeral procession and followed the body to its
resting-place in the colored burying ground at
Avondale.

A few days after Uncle Tom's death, an old
lady, a prominent member of Ninth Street Baptist
Church, called to see us, and said: "I have been
thinking that you and your wife will occupy a high
place in heaven for nursing and taking care of Uncle
Tom."

I replied: "Thou hadst better advise us not to
depend on works for salvation. If we have true
faith, we shall do good works. We have done no
more than our duty; works without faith will not
save us."

The day that Uncle Tom died I was tempted to
send a telegram to his master, informing him that
his slave was at my house, and that if he would
come at once he could get him, knowing that he
could reach here by railway before the funeral.
Then, if he came, I would take him into the room
and show him the form of poor Tom, cold in death.
I thought strongly of doing this, and was urged by
others to do it, but, on mature deliberation, I decided that it would not be advisable.

TROUBLES OF A LOUISVILLE ABOLITIONIST.

At the time that I was engaged in the work of the Underground Railroad at Cincinnati, there lived in Louisville, Kentucky, a man whom I will call Jones, who was in sentiment a strong abolitionist, and who aided runaway slaves whenever it was in his power. The colored people of Louisville, learning that he was kindly disposed toward their race, frequently applied to him for counsel and assistance when in perplexity or distress.

Louisville was the headquarters in Kentucky for slave-traders, buying negroes for the Southern market, and coffles were often brought in from the surrounding country, preparatory to being shipped on the packets for New Orleans or other Southern ports. Occasionally husbands or wives, who had been separated from their families, would escape from these coffles and make their way to some safe hiding-place among their colored friends, where Jones would be summoned to hear their sad story, and to devise some plan of aiding them to escape. After waiting till pursuit was over, he would proceed to the Cincinnati and Louisville packet, lying then at the wharf, and in his own or some fictitious name engage a state-room for the passage to Cincinnati, and get the key of the room. A short time before the boat started, and while there was a great bustle on the wharf and along the gangway, he would have the fugitives come on board with their bundles—as if they were servants bringing the baggage of their master or mistress—and would direct them by a prearranged signal to pass into the room which he had engaged. Here they found the key on the inside of the door, and immediately locked themselves in.

After a state-room had been engaged, the fare paid and the key given up, no officer or servant of the boat had a right to go into the room, and the passengers would be unmolested on their way to Cincinnati. Jones was always careful to engage and pay for both berths of a state-room, that no one else might occupy part of it. At different times he came to Cincinnati on the same boat with the fugitives and conducted them to my house. The packet boats left Louisville in the morning and reached Cincinnati before daylight next morning, and when he did not come himself, Jones would telegraph to me to apprise me of the coming of the fugitives, and request me to look out for them. This information and request were conveyed in a manner that could convey no suspicions of the truth to others. Sometimes the message read: "Go to box seventy-two, at the post-office, and take charge of my letters or papers which you will find there;" at other times, "Pay forty-three dollars to Dr. Peck on my account;" different numbers being used at different times.

I understood that the number mentioned designated the number of the state-room in which the fugitives were, and could tell whether it was in the gentlemen's or the ladies' cabin. I arranged for some person to go aboard the boat when it reached the wharf, tap at the door mentioned in a way that the fugitives would understand, wait till the door opened enough for him to be recognized, then walk away ; the fugitives would follow him. A colored person was generally chosen to perform this mission, and passed unnoticed amid the crowd of colored porters, draymen and hackmen, who went up and down the gangway, carrying baggage and assisting passengers. Sometimes the fugitives had a trunk of clothing, and as Jones saw that it was checked before leaving Louisville, there was no trouble in presenting the check at Cincinnati, after the fugitives were safe at our house, and obtaining the trunk.

In this manner, during one spring and summer, twenty-seven slaves safely escaped from Louisville, and reached my house in Cincinnati. Among these were many interesting cases, but a reference to them would make this story too long. They were sent on to Canada, where many of them had friends, or husbands, or wives, who had made their escape previously.

Escaping detection in all the cases where he had been implicated, Jones was finally arrested, in a case where he was innocent, tried in court, and convicted on false evidence. Aiding a fugitive slave was at that time a grave offense, and he was sentenced to three years in the penitentiary. On account of some flaw in the evidence, or illegality in the proceedings, his lawyers petitioned for a second trial, which was granted, but he was again found guilty, by another jury. His sentence this time was lessened to two years.

Some new witnesses having been discovered whose

evidence it was thought would prove his innocence, a petition for a third trial was made and granted. This was the fall term of court, and he was returned to jail to await the next term. His bail bond was fixed at one thousand five hundred dollars, but he not being blessed with an abundance of this world's goods could not raise the amount. He was a weakly man, and his previous imprisonment and present confinement in jail, during cold weather, were a further injury to his health. He became very ill and his physician thought that he could not long survive unless he was released from prison, and restored to his home where he could be nursed and cared for by his family. Through the influence of his lawyer and physician, his bail was reduced to one thousand dollars, and his wife and step-daughter went to work to raise this amount to indemnify a prominent citizen of Louisville, who had agreed to sign his bond. But it could not be expected that a man who was guilty of aiding a slave to escape would have many friends in a slave State, like Kentucky, where a negro-stealer, as an abolitionist was called, was looked upon as worse than a horse-thief, and Jones' wife and daughter found it impossible to raise the amount required. Six hundred dollars was the utmost they could command. Jones' step-daughter, an amiable young lady of about eighteen, wrote to me, giving the particulars of the case, and appealing to me in a very pathetic manner to try to raise the remaining four hundred dollars required. With the exception of Jones himself, the family were strangers to me, but my sympathies were

34

aroused in their behalf, and I wished to aid them I had, however, just finished helping a colore woman to raise a sum of money to purchase he daughter from slavery, and felt that in this instanc I could not render any considerable aid.

I wrote a reply to this effect, inclosing a smal sum of money in the letter as a token of my sym pathy. In a short time I received another letter from the same source, acknowledging the receipt of my favor, and still urging me to make an effort in her father's behalf, saying that he would die if not removed from prison. Thomas Wistar, of Philadelphia, one of my intimate friends, was in Cincinnati at that time on business, and I showed him the young lady's letters and related the circumstances of the case. He was much interested, and his sympathy aroused. He gave me five dollars to send to Jones' family, and I forwarded it at once, again expressing my personal inability to do anything that would materially aid them.

Not long afterward there came a third letter, pleading with me most earnestly to make an attempt in some direction to raise the four hundred dollars still lacking. I sent this letter to Thomas Wistar, who had returned to Philadelphia, and asked him to lay the case before those who might be interested, and if they could feel with "those in bond as bound with them," to solicit them to contribute. He replied that he would show this letter to various friends of his, and report results from time to time. He wrote frequently, saying he had received subcriptions to be applied as desired, and in a few days directed me to draw on him for three hundred and fifty dollars, adding that I must raise the remaining fifty dollars. I called on Abram and James Taylor, and showed them Thomas Wistar's letter. They advanced the fifty dollars at once, and I drew on Thomas Wistar for the amount designated, and thus had the four hundred dollars required. The next question was how to get it to Louisville, and have matters there properly adjusted. I knew that prompt action was necessary if Jones was benefited, for the weather was extremely cold, and he was lying sick in jail. I had already devoted considerable time to the matter, and tried to find some suitable person to go in my stead, but in this I failed and the duty seemed to devolve on me.

The Ohio River was frozen over, and there were no boats running. I started to Jeffersonville on the early train, hoping to reach Louisville that afternoon, but the track was covered with ice and snow, the water-tanks were frozen, and owing to the difficulty of travel the train was behind time. Missing connections at Seymour, I did not reach Jeffersonville till midnight, and here I was told that I could not cross the river, as the ferry-boats had stopped running on account of the ice. Next morning I went to the wharf, and finding two men who had a skiff, I made arrangements with them to take me across. There was a narrow channel free from ice where the water was swift, and by skillful management a boat might pass through this nearly to the opposite side. Walking a hundred yards or so, on the ice, we reached the place where the skiff lay, and getting into it, the men pulled up current through the channel, occasionally meeting floes and cakes of ice coming down the stream. At such times, it was necessary to pull up the skiff on the stationary ice till the floating ice passed.

When nearly to the opposite shore we came to a mass of ice that had been jammed up edgewise. The skiff could go no farther, and I left it and walked the rest of the way. It was a hazardous undertaking to attempt to spring from one sharp edge to another, but I reached the shore in safety, and made my way to Jones' house. When I introduced myself to the wife and daughter, and made known my errand, I felt amply repaid for all that I had done. They burst into tears and thanked me again and again, seeming unable to express the full measure of their gratitude. It was then eleven o'clock A. M., on the last day of the week, and I had but little time to spare, as the train on which I wished to return left Jeffersonville at two P. M., so I sent immediately for the lawyer, and when he arrived paid the money into his hands, taking a receipt for it. The limited time at my command did not admit of my going to the jail to see Jones, but the lawyer agreed to get him out of prison that afternoon.

Learning that a channel had been cut across the river at New Albany, I took the stage to the ferry-wharf, and arrived while the boat was on the opposite side. I had to wait some time, and the delay increased my impatience, but finally the boat returned, and I reached New Albany. I found that

I had a very short time in which to reach Jeffersonville, and looked around for a conveyance, but the
omnibuses had all gone. I started up town to find
a livery stable, but seeing a man in a sleigh drawn
by two good horses, I ran to him and told him if he
would take me to the depot, in time for the train, I
would give him a dollar. The man replied that he
had fast horses and thought he could make the distance—nearly three miles—in time, so off we started
at flying speed. When we came into Jeffersonville,
before quite reaching the depot, the train began to
move off. I tossed a dollar to the man, sprang out
of the sleigh, and running as fast as I could, caught
the last car, being pulled up by a gentleman on the
rear platform. I reached home early in the morning. Jones was released from jail a few hours after
I left Louisville. He had taken a deep cold, and
was reduced quite low with severe illness, but after
several weeks of suffering his health improved, so
that he was able to attend to business, and a few
weeks before the opening of court he came to Cincinnati, in the hope of obtaining another witness in
his case.

He came at once to my house, wishing to consult
with me in regard to risking a third trial. I called
a meeting of several of our prominent anti-slavery
men, to deliberate on the subject. We thought
that there was no probability of his being cleared at
his next trial, and advised him not to return, but to
forfeit his bond. Jones seemed to have some hope
that he would be cleared, but as he had been twice
convicted on false evidence, we thought that there

was little prospect of a jury of slaveholders acquitting him of the crime he was charged with, that of aiding a fugitive.

Some of us knew that he was innocent in that case, but that in many other cases he was guilty, and that if convicted the penitentiary would be his doom. Jones finally agreed to forfeit his bond and not return. He wrote to his wife, informing her of his decision, which was in accordance with her advice. I gave him a room in an upper story, and he staid at our house for some time. His case came up in court, but he did not appear, and his bond was forfeited. When court was over his wife came to see him and spent several days, but it was thought best for her not to leave Louisville any considerable time, for Jones' prosecutors might attempt to trace his whereabouts, through her, and she returned to her home. His enemies seemed determined to hunt him out, and supposing him to be in Cincinnati, they obtained a requisition on the Governor of Ohio, from the Governor of Kentucky, for a permit to arrest him. Jones' wife wrote to him from Louisville, giving him intelligence of this movement—addressing the letter to me that no clue to Jones might be obtained. I at once wrote to Salmon P. Chase, then Governor of Ohio, giving him the particulars of the case, and requesting him to let me know if he was applied to for a permit to arrest Jones.

Chase immediately wrote to his former law partner in this city to inform me that, if occasion required, I would hear from him. Close search was made for

Jones, but his enemies failed to get any clue to his whereabouts, and they never applied to Governor Chase. When matters became quiet and the search seemed to be over, Jones' wife joined him, and they took rooms in another part of the city. But they had been settled in their new home only a few weeks, when Jones was discovered by a Louisville officer, who was about to arrest him without legal authority and hurry him off to Kentucky. Jones narrowly escaped by slipping out a back way, and resolved to leave the city at once and seek a place of security. He and his wife removed to Iowa, where they remained for several years ; then returned to Cincinnati, and are still living here. The daughter married in Louisville and remained there. After his return to this city, Jones entered the Eclectic College, studied medicine, and is now a practicing physician.

ROSE, THE WHITE SLAVE.

Among the fugitives who escaped from Louisville and reached Cincinnati, by the aid of Jones, was a woman whom I will call Rose. She was so nearly white that a stranger would never suspect that there was a drop of African blood in her veins. Her form was tall and graceful, her face beautiful, and her expression one of intelligence. She had long, straight black hair, and her hands were as delicate as those of any lady. Although she was a slave, she had never experienced any of the hardships and cruelties of slavery. She was the property of a man who lived in the central part of Kentucky, and being a favorite house servant, she was kindly treated by her indulgent master and mistress. She had a comfortable home, and her tasks were the lighter work of the household, and the use of the needle. But her lot did not remain unshadowed by the evils of slavery. She was seduced by her master and became the mother of a handsome boy, apparently white. On account of the disturbance which this created in the family, the master took Rose and her child to Louisville, and hired her for a house servant to an acquaintance of his who owned no slaves. According to the terms of their written agreement, made for a specified number of years, the employer was to pay fifty dollars a year for her services, and to clothe her and the child, beside paying doctor's bills in case of their sickness.

To Rose's great comfort, she found her new master and mistress to be kind-hearted Christian people. They treated her and her child with kindness, and her new home proved to be a pleasant one. Her little boy soon became the pet of the family. When he grew large enough to attend school, he was admitted to the white schools, as he showed no trace of colored blood. He was a bright, intelligent child, and made rapid progress in learning. When the term of years for which Rose had been hired had nearly expired, her employer received a letter from her master stating that he had sold his farm and was preparing to move to Mississippi, and wished Rose and her child to be in readiness to join him and his family when they came to Louisville to take a down-river boat. Her employer imparted this intelligence to Rose, and said that he and his wife were sorry to part with her, but that she must obey her master's orders. Rose was filled with dismay at the prospect of leaving her comfortable home and going to the far South. Her little boy, she knew, would then be a slave, for in slavery the child followed the condition of the mother, and for herself she dreaded some hard fate, worse than she had yet known. She might be sold to a cruel master and made to toil in the cotton fields, beneath the driver's lash, or she might become the property of some sensual wretch, and she would choose death rather than such a lot. She began to plan a way to escape. Some colored people who knew that Jones was disposed to aid fugitives directed her to consult with him. She sought an opportunity and had an interview with him, during which the whole matter was arranged.

The family with whom Rose had been living had often given her money for her faithful services, beside paying her master the amount agreed upon, and she had saved a sum more than sufficient to pay her passage to Cincinnati. She also had a supply of good clothing for herself and her little boy, and a large trunk. She began to pack her things and make ready for traveling. Her indulgent mistress seemed to understand that she contemplated making her escape, but placed no obstruction in her way. On the contrary, she seemed disposed to encourage her attempt, but asked her no questions lest she should be, in turn, questioned by Rose's master when he came.

Jones went to the Cincinnati packet, and engaged

35

a state-room for a lady and her little boy, entering fictitious names on the clerk's book. He paid for both berths and obtained the key to the room. Later he managed to send Rose's trunk aboard and have it checked for Cincinnati. Rose dressed herself in her best clothing and put a thick vail over her face, and then, leading her little boy, she went aboard the boat, passing unnoticed in the bustle and crowd. In the cabin she saw Jones, who passed before her into the ladies' cabin, and made a signal, designating the room she was to enter. She went in, and finding the key on the inside, locked the door. She and her little boy were unmolested on the trip, and arrived safely at Cincinnati about four o'clock next morning.

In the meantime Jones had telegraphed to me, requesting me to go to box 72 and take charge of his papers until called for. I knew from the number that the state-room referred to was in the ladies' cabin. Just at daybreak, when people began to leave the boat, and draymen and hackmen were going on board to look for freight and passengers, I sent a man to the boat who went to the room numbered 72, and gave a tap on the door that Rose understood. She opened the door and followed the man ashore, and was soon safe at my house, with her little boy. When her vail was removed it was difficult for us to realize that the handsome, well-dressed lady who sat before us was a fugitive slave. The tinge of African blood in her face was so slight that it was hardly noticeable. Her boy, a handsome little fellow, was as white as any child. When breakfast was over and Rose had recovered from the first excitement of her arrival, we took her into our room, and she related to me and my wife the particulars which I have given. We were deeply interested in her at once, and felt that we wanted to exhibit these white slaves to some of our acquaintances, whose sympathies had never been so strongly enlisted for the slave as ours had been. I invited several prominent citizens, who were not abolitionists, to call at my house, saying that I had recently received a curiosity from the South which I wished to show them. They responded to the invitation, and came at the time appointed. I assured Rose that she need not feel any fear or embarrassment in the presence of the men to whom I was about to introduce her; they were all men of honor and high standing, and would give no information that might lead to her detection. I then conducted her into the parlor where they were seated, and introduced her and her little boy as fugitives, fleeing to a land of liberty. The gentlemen were greatly surprised, and said: "Can it be possible that they are slaves, liable to be bought and sold? It is a shame."

They asked Rose many questions, which she answered with clearness and in a ladylike manner, manifesting a keen sense of her degradation as a slave. The gentlemen seemed deeply interested in her case, and expressed much concern for her welfare, saying that they hoped she would reach a land of liberty in safety. While Rose was at our house I introduced her to a number of other persons, whom I wished to interest in behalf of the poor slaves in bondage, as well as the fugitives who escaped.

After she had been with us several days, John Jolliffe, that noble advocate of liberty, took her to his house, as he wished to invite some of his law brethren to see her and her boy. She remained there several days, and Lawyer Jolliffe introduced her to Judge Storer, and other prominent members of the bar. Much interest was manifested by all who saw and talked with her. Some thought that no effort would be made to capture her, and that she might be safe in Cincinnati, but Rose thought that it would be unsafe to remain here, as her master might empower an agent to hunt her out and capture her. John Jolliffe and I decided that it would be best for her to go farther north, so I bought a ticket for her to Detroit, and saw her and her child safely started on their journey. I afterward heard from her; she was living in Detroit and doing well.

STORY OF JIM AND HIS FRIEND IN A BOX.

Not far from Louisville, Kentucky, there lived a slave whom I will call Jim. He had a wife and one child, who belonged to a different master, a person living in Louisville. Jim's master was more indulgent than some slaveholders, and allowed him the privilege of visiting his wife frequently. Jim's parents having grown old, and become worthless, in the sense of property, had been emancipated by their master, and as they could not, according to the law of Kentucky, remain in that State and be free, they had been sent to Ohio, and had settled at New Richmond, twenty miles above Cincinnati, where some of their relatives, free colored people, were living. After they had lived here a year or two, Jim solicited the privilege of going to see them and carrying some presents to them. The work of the summer was over and he had accumulated a little money, enough to pay the expenses of the trip. After some deliberation, his master consented to give him a pass for a week's absence, and per- mitted his little brother, about twelve years old, to go with him to see their parents. He thought there was no danger of Jim's not returning promptly, for he knew that he was much attached to his wife and child, and thought that he would not leave them.

But Jim had other thoughts in his mind; he had a yearning to be free. Although he had a kind master he knew that his situation was liable to sudden change. His master might die, or become involved in debt and be obliged to sell him, or his wife and child might be sold away from him. These thoughts Jim had revolved in his mind for some time, and he now resolved to make a bold stroke for freedom. He also had a plan for aiding one of his friends, a slave, whom I will call Joe.

Joe was the property of a man living about thirty miles from Louisville, but being cruelly treated by his master he ran away, and secreted himself among some colored friends in that city. Jim's plan for aiding Joe was to nail him up in a goods box, and ship him to New Richmond, pretending that the box contained some things which he was taking to his parents at that place. By the aid of some of his colored friends this was accomplished without attracting suspicion. Joe disposed himself as comfortably as he could in the box, the cover was nailed on, and it was directed to Jim's father at New Richmond, in care of Jim himself. Then it was conveyed to the wharf on a dray, to be placed on board the Cincinnati packet as freight for New Richmond. Jim had gone to the boat before and paid the price of passage for himself and little brother to Cincinnati. He showed his pass to the captain and informed him that he had a box to take with him to his father, on which he wished to pay the freight to Cincinnati in advance. This was satisfactory to the captain, and the weight being marked on the box, which was now on the wharf, Jim paid the freight required. The mate ordered the box to be rolled on board, but Jim took hold and helped the deck hands carry it on deck, and saw that it was placed right side up. The boat arrived at Cincinnati before daylight next morning, and landed at the foot of Main Street. Jim wished to know if his friend was all right, and watching his opportunity when the deck hands were engaged in another part of the boat, he leaned down and whispered through a crack in the box, "Joe, is you dar?"

The answer came back, in muffled tones: "I's hyar, all right."

The wharf of the Maysville packet line, where Jim was to take passage for New Richmond, was at the foot of Broadway, two squares above, but the boat was not yet in. Jim had the box containing his friend conveyed on a dray to the upper wharf, where it had to lay several hours in the hot sun‧ shine. As soon as the boat arrived and her freight was discharged, Jim had the box put on board, watching carefully to see that it was right side up. At four in the afternoon the Maysville boat started. Jim walked the deck impatiently, feeling much anxiety about Joe, and watching eagerly for the sight of his destination. The boat reached New Richmond about sunset, and Jim paid the charges on his box of live freight, and had it rolled off on the wharf. Waiting till the boat had gone on her way, Jim ascertained that Joe was still alive, and then looked around for a dray. Seeing none, he hired a wood wagon to transport the box to the house where his father and mother lived, in the outskirts of the village. Jim was glad to meet his father and mother, but was so anxious to release Joe from his confinement that he hardly waited to speak to them. When the box was unloaded, and the man who drove the wagon was gone, Jim took a hatchet and knocked off the box-lid, and Joe crawled out of the narrow quarters where he had been confined for thirty-six hours, without food or drink, except a crust of corn bread. He appeared to be in good condition, and was thankful to breathe the free air of Ohio, which he said was sweet. Jim was much rejoiced at the success of his plan and his friend's safe arrival.

A few abolitionists—white men—who lived near, were called in to see the fugitive, and to advise in

regard to his safety.   It was decided that he must
go to Canada immediately, *via* the Underground
Railroad, and that the line leading through Cincinnati was the best for him to take.   One of the abolitionists who knew me offered to bring Joe to my
house the next evening in his buggy.   He had a
swift horse, and by starting early in the evening he
reached my house about ten o'clock at night.   The
next day I obtained a ticket to Sandusky for Joe,
and put him aboard the night train.   I learned afterward that he arrived safely in Canada.

Jim remained a few days with his parents at New
Richmond, then came to Cincinnati, and called at
my house to inquire about his friend.   He told me
the particulars, which I have given, of Joe's journey
in the box, and also confided to me his own intentions.   He said that the time for which his pass was
good had not yet expired; he had several days to
spare, and he thought of taking a trip to Canada to
see how his friend Joe was prospering.   If he liked
the country himself, he thought he would not
return.   I asked him about his wife and child;
would he leave them in slavery?

He replied: "I hope to get them to Canada before long.   I have been talking with the steward on
board the Cincinnati and Louisville packet.   He is
a trusty fellow, and well acquainted with my wife.
He will go to see her and tell her that I have gone
to Canada to prepare a home for us, and that she
must try to join me."

I said: "But it may be difficult for her to get
away with her child."

Jim replied: "We have a white friend living in Louisville who will plan for her if she will apply to him."

Jim then went to the Louisville packet, where he had left his little brother. He paid .the fare of his brother to Louisville, and had a private understanding with the colored steward; then a short time before the hour for the boat to start, he told his brother that he had some business up town that he must attend to before starting, and hastily left the boat. His brother supposed that he would soon return, but the boat went off without Jim.

Jim returned to my house and took the train that evening for Sandusky. I told him that according to the laws of Ohio he was already free; that when a slave was brought into this State by his master, or came here with his master's permission, the law would protect him if he chose to remain. But if Jim's wife ran away and came to him here, the law could not protect her; she would be liable to be captured and taken back to slavery.

Jim concluded that he would try the English dominions, and reached Canada in safety. When his wife received the message that he had sent her, she resolved to follow him as soon as she could find an opportunity to make her escape. She consulted with Jones, of Louisville, and a few months afterward he managed to get her safely on board the packet for Cincinnati, and telegraphed to me to go to box 73 and take charge of his papers till called for. I knew by the number that the state-room designated was in the ladies' cabin, and that the fugitive was a woman.

According to arrangements previously explained, she, with her child, was brought to our house, and the next night ·was forwarded to Canada, where she joined her husband in safety.

CHAPTER XII.

LOUISA PICQUET, THE OCTOROON—JOHN FAIRFIELD, THE
SOUTHERN ABOLITIONIST—JOHN AND MARY—NAR-
ROW ESCAPES OF FUGITIVES.

AMONG the many interesting cases that came
under my personal notice while engaged in
efforts to aid the slave, that of Louisa Picquet, the
octoroon, is recalled to memory. Her story as told
by herself has been written by Rev. H. Mattison,
pastor of Union Chapel, New York, and published
in pamphlet form. I refer to it for the particulars
given below.

Louisa was born. in Columbia, South Carolina,
where her mother was a slave in the family of John
Randolph, not the celebrated John Randolph, of
Roanoke, but probably one of the same family. As
little Louisa strongly resembled the Randolph children, Madame R. became much dissatisfied, and
caused her and her mother to be sold. They were
bought by a Mr. Cook, of Georgia, in whose
family they remained for some time—Louisa as nurse
girl, her mother as cook. Their master had a large
cotton plantation, warehouses, stores, etc., but was
not a good manager and became deeply involved in
debt. His creditors came to take possession of his

property, and he ran off to Mobile, taking seven
of his slaves, including Louisa and her mother, and
hired them out. Louisa was in the family of a Mr.
English, where she was well treated. She was at
this time a beautiful girl of fourteen, with dark eyes
and hair, rosy cheeks and brunette complexion, but
with no indication of a drop of African blood in her
veins. She attracted the attention and gained the
affection of a young man of nineteen or twenty,
white in appearance, but the slave of a man in the
city of Mobile. He was a coachman and used to
drive when his master's young sisters went out riding. They frequently called at Mr. English's, and
when the coachman rang the bell, it was answered
by Louisa. In this way the acquaintance was
made. He called to see her on Sundays, and
finally asked her to marry him. She loved him in
return, and would have been his wife, with all the
sanction that the law allowed to slaves, had not
circumstances separated them. Her lover was accused to his master of an offense of which he was
innocent, and when he denied it he received a
severe whipping, which made him resolve to run
away. He was strengthened in this resolve by the
advice of his master's partner, an Englishman, who
abhorred the cruelties of slavery.

This gentleman said: "I would go away if I were
you."

The reply was: "I have no money, and I love a
girl here I don't want to leave."

The gentleman then inquired concerning Louisa,
and learning that she was white, said: "There will

be no difficulty in your going away; neither of you will be taken for slaves. As to the other excuse, here is money enough for your traveling expenses."

The young lover hastened to Louisa and unfolded these plans. But she was afraid to venture. She knew that they could not read or write, and was afraid that they would be questioned and discovered. When she made known her decision, her lover was sorry to part from her, but all his arrangements were made and he had resolved to go. So after a long talk they bade each other good-by—destined to meet again under very different circumstances.

Mr. Cook's creditors traced him to Mobile, took possession of his slaves, and sold them to satisfy his debts. Louisa was taken to the public auction rooms, and her merits discussed by various purchasers. The auctioneer recommended her as a good-looking girl, a good nurse, kind and affectionate to children; she had never been put to hard work, as they could see by her white hands, etc. He even noticed her hair, which had lately been cut off because it was prettier than that of her master's daughter, and said, "You see it is good quality, and in a short time it will grow out fine and long." The bidding commenced at six hundred dollars, and mounted by hundreds and fifties to fourteen hundred. The rival bidders were a Mr. Horton, from Texas, who had bought Louisa's mother, and a Mr. Williams, of New Orleans. The former gentleman said that Louisa should go with her mother, but the latter declared that he would have her at any price, and bidding fifteen hundred she was sold to him.

As Louisa was being led away, she heard some one crying and praying, and saw her mother on her knees in the midst of the crowd, with her hands lifted up and her eyes raised toward heaven, streaming with tears. All the people were looking at her, but she did not think of them, she was asking the Lord to go with her only daughter and protect her.

This scene made a deep impression on Louisa, and she remembered it years afterward in waking hours and in dreams. There was no time allowed for saying good-by. The slaveholders did not recognize the claims of natural affection between mother and daughter, but led them away—one to hard work in Texas, the other to a home in New Orleans, where she was to live in daily violation of God's command. Mr. Williams told Louisa of her destination, and the fate in store for her, as he took her on the boat to New Orleans. He said he was getting old, and when he saw her he thought he would buy her and end his days with her. He told her that if she behaved herself she would be treated well, but if not, he would whip her almost to death. He was about fifty years old, and gray-headed, and was very jealous of Louisa lest she should find a lover of her own race. He never allowed her to go out; when she begged to go to church, he accused her of having some object in view, and said there were too many opportunities for rascality there.

He would sometimes say: "Go on, I guess you've

made your arrangement; go on, I'll catch up with you." But Louisa knew his watchful, suspecting disposition and never ventured out.

She had four children while living with Mr. Williams, two of whom died. She was known as his housekeeper and did all the work. He never brought guests to the house, but if he had company took them to the hotel and entertained them. He finally became so harsh and strict with Louisa, and so disagreeable in his ways, that she begged him to sell her, saying that she would rather die than live in that manner. He became much enraged, and said that nothing but death should separate them, and that if she attempted to escape, he would blow her brains out.

Louisa knew that it was wrong to live as she lived with Mr. Williams, for in early childhood Mrs. Cook had explained to her the meaning of the commandments. She had this trouble in her soul all the time, and said to herself: "There's no chance for me: I'll have to die and be lost." She sometimes spoke to Mr. Williams of these scruples, but he only swore about it, and told her *he* had that to answer for himself, and that if she was only true to him she could get religion. But Louisa felt there was no use trying to be religious when she was living in sin, and not-knowing what else to do, began praying that Mr. Williams might die.

She said in relating her story: "I promised the Lord one night, faithful in prayer, if he would just take him out of the way, I'd get religion and be true to Him as long as I lived. If Mr. Williams only knew *that* and could get up out of his grave, he would beat me half to death. Finally he did get sick, and was sick nearly a year. Then he began to get good and talked kind to me. I could see there was a change in him. He was not all the time accusin' me of other people. Then when I saw that he was sufferin' so, I began to get sorry and to pray that he might get religion before he died. It seems he did get religion, for he was so changed."

A short time before his death, Mr. Williams willed Louisa and her children free, and told her, when he was dead, to go to the North and live a new life. He also willed her the household goods, all that he had in the way of property—the house he lived in was rented. After his death Louisa felt a new peace and happiness, for she was *free*.

On· Sunday she went to church for the first time in six years, and was much impressed with the words of the preacher. Mr. Williams' brother soon afterward told her that she must leave the house, as he could not pay the rent, and a colored woman, who took in washing, kindly received Louisa and her children and cared for them till she could make other arrangements. One day she met her late master's brother and he asked her what she was doing. She replied, " Nothing," and he then said that rightly she belonged to him, because his brother had not paid him the money he had borrowed to buy her. He asked her why she did not go North as her master had told her to do. She told him it was because she had no money, and asked him to give her some. He replied that she had better thank God for her freedom, without asking favors, and that his brother had got enough from him. Louisa related this conversation to the humble friend who had kindly taken her in, and was advised to get away as soon as possible.

The furniture left to Louisa by her master was sent to a second-hand furniture store and sold, and with the money thus realized, Louisa and her children came to Cincinnati, having little money left after paying traveling expenses. On her arrival here, Louisa went to the house of a colored woman named Nelson, once a slave in Georgia, whom she had known in former years. She found friends among the colored and white people, and was respected by all. Two or three years after coming to Cincinnati, Louisa married Henry Picquet, a mulatto, formerly a slave and the son of a Frenchman in Georgia. He had been married once before, but his wife was sold away from him. Louisa had thought of her mother during the long years of separation, and in that time had heard from her once. She now endeavored to learn in what part of Texas her mother was, and to ascertain if she could be purchased. She had letters written to different parts of Texas, making inquiries, and succeeded in learning the address of her mother's master. Negotiations were then opened, relative to her mother's purchase, and the master agreed to dispose of her for one thousand dollars. Louisa's next concern was, "How shall I raise this money?" She thought of selling everything she had, but her entire worldly possessions would amount to but a small sum. She then talked with friends on the matter, and was advised by them to go out and solicit money for the purpose. She was at first reluctant to do this, as she had a family to care for, had never traveled, except from New Orleans to Cincinnati, and feared that her efforts would be vain, as there were so many abroad on similar errands, but she finally resolved to make the attempt.

I gave her a recommendation. Joseph Emery, known for many years as city missionary, did likewise, and she received several encouraging notices from the press. With these pasted in her book she started out, first in Cincinnati, where she obtained subscriptions to the amount of about three hundred dollars, and then made her way to other cities and towns in the State of Ohio, where she received various sums. At Cleveland she was advised to visit Buffalo, where the General Conference of the Methodist Episcopal Church was in session. She received letters of introduction to a minister settled at Buffalo, and to another who was there temporarily, as delegate to the Conference, and went to that city. She presented her claims, but received so little encouragement that she decided to go on to New York, having letters to Henry Ward Beecher and others in that city. She did so, and met with excellent encouragement, her collections amounting to two hundred and twenty-three dollars, in a few days. One day in New York she was passing along a street near the Park, when she saw a man on top of an omnibus who looked at her earnestly and seemed to know her. She recognized him instantly as the young man who, years before in Mobile, had asked her to marry him and run away from slavery. He got down from the omnibus, and came and spoke to her. After some conversation, in which she explained how she happened to be there, he told her that he had been in New York ever since he ran away, that he had married a white woman, and that no one suspected him of having a drop of African blood in his veins. He afterward brought his three children to the Park for Louisa to see, and she says they were very pretty, and prettily dressed —the two little girls, white and fair, the little boy a brunette. "Ah," said she, laughing, "that one has the stain on it." She promised to keep the matter secret—the early history of her friend—lest it might break up a family, or cause a white citizen of New York to be remanded back to slavery.

Louisa returned to Buffalo, where for the first time in her travels she was treated with doubt and suspicion. Calling on a minister, who was a delegate to the Conference, from Baltimore, and stating her business, she was received coldly. After looking over her papers and listening to her story, he expressed his opinion that she was not a colored woman, and that the money collected was not for the specified purpose; consequently, that her claims were false and she was an impostor.

Another gentleman in Buffalo, learning of this incident, kindly undertook to aid Louisa and substantiate her claims, for the benefit of those disposed to doubt her. He telegraphed to the banking firm of Evans and Company, of Cincinnati, to whom Louisa referred him, making inquiries in regard to her, and received by mail a full indorsement of her and her representations.

About this time Louisa received news that the master of her mother had decreased the price he demanded from one thousand dollars to nine hundred, which was, of course, cheering news, as it obviated much labor and anxiety. Louisa returned to Cincinnati, and, after some discouragement, succeeded in completing her collections and making up the sum required. The money was sent to the master in Texas, per Adams Express Company, and Louisa's mother was brought to Cincinnati by the same Company at an expense of eighty dollars. To obtain this sum Louisa had to sell some of her household goods. The old woman, who had toiled all her life in bondage, was free at last—thanks to the efforts of her daughter and the kindness of Northern friends.

There was a joyful reunion of mother and daughter after the long separation of years. They parted in wretchedness, at a slave auction in Mobile, with the hopelessness of a life of bondage before them ; they met on a free soil, rejoicing in the possession of freedom, and full of thanksgiving and joy too great for utterance.

JOHN FAIRFIELD, THE SOUTHERN ABOLITIONIST.

It is seldom that one hears of a person who has been brought up in the midst of slavery, surrounded

by its influences from his earliest recollection, being
a hater of the "peculiar institution," but there are
several such cases on record.   Among them is that
of John Fairfield, who has already figured in these
pages in connection with a party of twenty-eight
fugitives, whom he conducted to Cincinnati from
their homes in Kentucky.

His early home was in Virginia, east of the mountains, where he imbibed anti-slavery sentiments—
from what source it is unknown, certainly not from
his relatives, who were all slaveholders.   When
quite a young man, he decided to make a visit to
the State of Ohio, and seek his fortunes in a free
State.   Thinking that it would be a good opportunity to put his anti-slavery principles into practice,
he planned to take with him one of his uncle's
slaves, a bright, intelligent young man, about his
own age, to whom he was much attached.   John
and this young colored man had played together
when boys, and had been brought up together.
They had often discussed plans by which Bill, the
slave, could make his escape to Canada, but no
attempt had been made to carry them out, until
young Fairfield determined to visit Ohio.   The
arrangement was then made for Bill to take one of
his master's horses, and make his escape the night
before Fairfield started, and wait for him at a rén-
dezvous appointed.   This plan was carried out, and
Bill traveled as Fairfield's servant until they reached
Ohio.   Not feeling safe in that State, he went on to
Canada, accompanied by Fairfield, who spent several weeks there looking at the country.   Bill, in

the meanwhile, found a good situation, and when Fairfield left him he was rejoicing in his newly achieved liberty and prosperity.

When Fairfield told me the story, some years afterward, I asked him if he did not feel guilty of encouraging horse-stealing, as well as negro-stealing. I knew that death was the penalty for each of these crimes, according to the laws of Virginia and North Carolina.

The reply was: "No! I knew that Bill had earned several horses for his master, and he took only one. Bill had been a faithful fellow, and worked hard for many years, and that horse was all the pay he got. As to negro-stealing, I would steal all the slaves in Virginia if I could."

After spending several months in Ohio, John Fairfield returned to Virginia, but did not remain long. His uncle suspected him of having helped his able-bodied and valuable servant to escape, and having obtained evidence from some source—probably from Ohio—he set about procuring a writ and having his nephew arrested.

Fairfield learned of his uncle's intention, and concluded to leave that part of the country. Actuated by a feeling of spite, or some other motive, he resolved to take other slaves, as he had taken Bill, and succeeded in getting away with several, some of whom belonged to his uncle. They traveled during the night and hid themselves during the day. Sometimes when they were safely secreted for the day, Fairfield went forward a few miles and purchased provisions, under the pretense of buying for movers in camp; then returned and supplied the party of fugitives. They finally arrived safely in Canada, and Fairfield, liking the country, concluded to make his home there. Bill was now married and comfortably settled.

Fairfield's success in conducting the slaves from Virginia to Canada was soon known to many of the fugitives settled in that country, and having confidence in him, they importuned him to bring away from slavery the husbands, wives, children, or other relatives which they had left behind them in various parts of the South. Some of them had accumulated small sums of money, and offered to pay him if he would undertake the mission.

Fairfield was a young man without family, and was fond of adventure and excitement. He wanted employment, and agreed to take the money offered by the fugitives and engage in the undertaking. He obtained the names of masters and slaves, and an exact knowledge of the different localities to be visited, together with other information that might be of use to him; then acted as his shrewd judgment dictated, under different circumstances. He would go South, into the neighborhood where the slaves were whom he intended to conduct away, and, under an assumed name and a false pretense of business, engage boarding, perhaps at the house of the master whose stock of valuable property he intended to decrease. He would proclaim himself to be a Virginian, and profess to be strongly proslavery in his sentiments, thus lulling the suspicions of the slaveholders while he established a secret understanding with the slaves—gaining their confidence and making arrangements for their escape. Then he would suddenly disappear from the neighborhood, and several slaves would be missing at the same time.

Fairfield succeeded well in his daring adventures, and in many instances brought members of families together in Canada, who had been separated for several years. Husbands and wives were again united, and there were joyful meetings between parents and children. The fugitives settled in Canada had unbounded confidence in Fairfield, and were constantly begging him to bring away their friends and relatives from slavery. He continued this unique business for more than twelve years, and during that time aided, it is said, several thousand slaves to escape from bondage and reach Canada. He was a wicked man, daring and reckless in his actions, yet faithful to the trust reposed in him, and benevolent to the poor. He seemed to have no fear for his personal safety—was always ready to risk his life and liberty in order to rescue the slaves from bondage.

He was an inveterate hater of slavery, and this feeling supplied a motive for the actions of his whole life. He believed that every slave was justly entitled to freedom, and that if any person came between him and liberty, the slave had a perfect right to shoot him down. He always went heavily armed himself, and did not scruple to use his weapons whenever he thought the occasion required their use. He resorted to many stratagems to effect his object in the South, and brought away numbers of slaves from nearly every slave State in the Union. He often stopped at Cincinnati, on his way South, and generally made his home among the colored people. He frequently called to see me, and told me of his daring exploits and plans of operation, to all of which I objected. I could have no sympathy with his mode of action, and at various times urged him to cease his operations in the South and return to his home in Canada and remain there. I would have nothing to do with aiding him to carry out his plans, for I could not indorse the principles he acted upon.

At the time I did not believe half the stories that he told me ; but afterward, learning from other sources of the many instances of his wonderful success, and knowing several of them from personal observation, and hearing stories from fugitives of their deliverance by his aid, I began to think that most of his stories might be true.

Fairfield was always ready to take money for his services from the slaves if they had it to offer, but if they did not he helped them all the same. Sometimes the slaves in the South had accumulated a little money, which they gave gladly to any one who would conduct them out of the house of bondage; and sometimes the fugitives in the North gave their little hoard to Fairfield, and begged him to rescue their relatives from slavery. Though always willing to take money for his services, he was equally ready to spend it in the same cause, and, if necessary, would part with his last dollar to effect his object. Fairfield had various methods of carrying out his

37

plans. When he had obtained a list of the names
of the slaves he wished to bring away, together with
the names of their masters, and an exact knowledge
of the different localities he was to visit in various
parts of the South, he went to work without any
hesitation, relying on his intimate knowledge of
Southern customs to bear him safely through his
perilous mission, and on his ingenuity and daring
to extricate him from any difficulty he might fall
into. Sometimes he engaged in some trading business and remained in the South six or twelve
months at a time, familiarizing himself with different localities, making the acquaintance of the
slaves and maturing his plans. At other times he
would enter a neighborhood where he was an entire
stranger, represent himself as a slave-dealer, and
gain a knowledge of the slaves he wished to take
away. He would make known his plans to them
secretly, and some night they would leave their
homes, and intrust themselves to his guidance.
Fairfield would conduct them safely across the Ohio
River, and after placing them on some branch of
the Underground Railroad, and seeing them started
toward Canada, he would return to the South,
assume another name, and enter another neighborhood, to enact the same over again.

At one time he took a company of slaves from
the northwestern part of Kentucky, and to elude
pursuit made directly toward Nashville, Tennessee.
The company consisted of able-bodied men, who
were all well armed. They took horses belonging
to their masters, and rode as far as they could the

first night, then turned the horses loose and hid
themselves during the day. The next night they
took other horses, and so on, night after night,
until they reached the Ohio River, near Maysville,
Kentucky. Fairfield managed to get the men over
the river and started safely on their way to Canada,
then he returned to the South to continue his
adventurous business.

At one time when he went South he had a few
horses to sell, and took with him two able-bodied,
free, colored men, whom he treated as his slaves,
ordering them about in a peremptory manner.
These men were shrewd and intelligent, and understood his plans. They ingratiated themselves with
the slaves Fairfield had come to rescue, gained their
confidence and ran off with them one dark night,
steering their course to Canada by the north star.
At other times Fairfield assumed to be returning
from Louisiana, where he had been with a drove of
slaves. He had with him, on such occasions, a body
servant whom he professed to treat with great
harshness, but who was really his confidant and
accomplice. Through this servant he gained access
to the slaves he wished to rescue.

Fairfield was several times betrayed and arrested,
in the South, and put in prison, but being a Free
Mason, high in the Order, he managed to get out
of prison without being tried. He broke jail once
or twice and escaped. He often had to endure
privation and hardship, but was ready to undergo
any suffering, for the sake of effecting his object.
He sometimes divided his clothing with a destitute

fugitive, and was willing to make any sacrifice of personal comfort. We often heard of his arrival in Canada with large companies of fugitives, whom he had conducted thither by some line of the Underground Railroad.

Fairfield was once betrayed and captured in Bracken County, Kentucky, and put in prison, where he remained through a winter of unusual severity. Before the time for his trial came, he escaped from jail by the aid of some of his friends, and crossed the Ohio River to Ripley. At the house of a noted abolitionist of that place, Fairfield lay sick for two weeks, having taken a deep cold while confined in jail. When he became well enough to travel he came to Cincinnati, and stopped at the house of a colored friend. I went to see him and had a long talk with him. I again advised him, to quit his hazardous work, in which he constantly risked his life and liberty. I told him I had no sympathy with his mode of operation, and urged him strongly to go home to Canada, and never cross Mason and Dixon's line again. He did not accept my advice, but swore that he would liberate a slave for every day that he had lain in prison. Although a man of strong constitution he appeared to be much broken in health by the hardships he had undergone. After resting a few weeks and recruiting his strength, he disappeared from the city, and no one knew where he had gone.

The next news we had concerning him was that he had crossed the Ohio River, near Lawrenceburg, with a party of twenty-eight fugitives, from Kentucky. The story of this party I have previously related. After that, we heard nothing more of Fairfield for some time. The following autumn I received a letter from George D. Baptist, of Detroit, stating that Fairfield had just arrived there with a company of thirty fugitives from the State of Missouri.

Free colored people in the Northern States who had relatives in slavery heard of Fairfield's successful efforts, and applied to him to bring their friends out of bondage, sometimes offering him several hundred dollars. At one time I was told of one of Fairfield's adventures up the Kanawha River, near Charleston, Virginia. Several colored people in Ohio, who had relatives in slavery at and near the salt works, importuned Fairfield to bring them away, and he at last yielded to their frequent solicitations, and promised to make the attempt. He knew that it would require some time to accomplish his object, as there were several slaves to be rescued, and he laid his plans accordingly. He chose the early spring for the time of his action, as the water was then flush in the Kanawha. Taking two free colored men with him, whom he claimed as his slaves, he went to the salt works on the Kanawha, and professing to be from Louisville, Kentucky, said that he had come to engage in the salt trade. He contracted for the building of two boats and for salt with which to load them when finished. These arrangements afforded time for his colored men to become acquainted with the slaves he wished to rescue, gain their confidence, and mature the plans for their escape.

Some of the slaves were good boatmen, as also were Fairfield's men, and it was planned that when the first boat was finished, one of the slaves and one of Fairfield's men should get into it on Saturday night, and float down the river a short distance to a point agreed upon, and take in a company of slaves, both men and women. They were then to take advantage of the high water and swift current of the Kanawha, and make all possible speed to the Ohio River. This plan was carried out successfully. Search was made in the neighborhood on Sabbath for some of the missing slaves, but no clue was gained. The loss of the boat was not discovered till Monday morning.

When Fairfield learned that one of his boats and one of his men were gone, he affected to be much enraged, and accused his other man of having some knowledge of the affair, and threatened him with severe punishment. The man denied having any part in the plot, but Fairfield professed to doubt him, and said that he should watch him closely.

When the owners of the missing slaves learned that the boat was gone, they at once surmised that their servants had made their escape by that means, and as there was no steamboat going down the river that day, they sent horsemen in pursuit, hoping that the boat might be intercepted at the mouth of the river. But when the pursuers reached that point, they found the new boat tied on the opposite side of the river; the fugitives were gone, and no clue to their course could be obtained.

Fairfield remained at the salt works to await the completion of his other boat, and to watch his other negro servant, of whom he professed to be very distrustful. In a few days the boat was com- pleted, and the next Saturday night it disappeared, together with Fairfield's negro man and ten or twelve slaves. Fairfield was now ruined! Both his boats and both his slaves were gone; and the loss of his property made him almost frantic. He started in hot pursuit, accompanied by several men, determined to capture the fugitives at any hazard. When they reached the Ohio River they found the boat tied to the bank on the Ohio side, but the fugitives were gone.

The pursuers ferried across the river, and, ac- cording to Fairfield's suggestion, divided company and took different routes, with the understanding that they were all to meet at a point designated. But Fairfield never met them, and was never seen at the salt works afterward. He well knew, how- ever, where to meet the fugitives; all that had been previously arranged. After the search was over, he conducted them safely to Canada, *via* the Un- derground Railroad.

Soon afterward Fairfield performed another dar- ing feat, east of the mountains. There were a number of fugitives in Canada, ·nearly white, who had come from Maryland, the District of Columbia and Virginia, and who had a number of relatives of the same complexion in the localities they had left.

There were also some free people living in Detroit, who had mulatto and quadroon relatives in the localities mentioned. Fairfield had often been solicited by these fugitives and free people to bring their friends out of slavery, and he finally agreed to make the attempt if a sum of money was raised for him, sufficient to justify it. The amount was made up and paid to him, and he went East on his hazardous mission.

He spent some time making the acquaintance of these mulattoes and quadroons in the different neighborhoods, and maturing his plans for their escape. Most of them were bright and intelligent, and some of them had saved enough money to pay their passage to Canada. After gaining their confidence and making them acquainted with his plans, Fairfield went to Philadelphia and bought wigs and powder. These cost him eighty dollars—I afterward saw the bill. His first experiment with these articles of disguise was made at Baltimore. Having secretly collected the mulatto slaves of that city and vicinity, whom he had arranged to conduct to the North, he applied the powder and put on the wigs. The effect was satisfactory; the slaves looked like white people.

Fairfield bought tickets for them and they took the evening train to Harrisburg, where he had made arrangements for another person to meet them, who would accompany them to Cleveland and put them aboard the boat for Detroit.

Fairfield, having seen this party safely on the way, returned immediately to Washington City for another company, who, by the aid of wigs and powder, passed for white people. He put these fugitives on the train, and accompanied them to Pittsburg. I received a letter from a friend in Cleveland, informing me of the arrival of both these parties, through Fairfield's agency, which was the first intelligence I had of his operations in the East. From Pittsburg, Fairfield returned to Philadelphia, and finding that he had not enough money to complete his work, he applied to the abolition society of that city for assistance, but, as he was a stranger to them, they hesitated about granting his request.

He told them that Levi Coffin, of Cincinnati, knew him well. George W. Taylor telegraphed to me at once—"John Fairfield wants money; shall we give it to him?"

I replied: "If John Fairfield needs money, give it to him."

He was then furnished with the amount he called for, and made his way at once into Virginia, near Harper's Ferry, for the third company of slaves. One of this company was too dark to be transformed into a white person by means of a wig and powder, and Fairfield was compelled to leave him behind. He regretted to do so, but feared that his appearance would betray the others. Fairfield got the rest of the party to the railroad and took the express train for Pittsburg, but they were soon missed and the course they had taken was discovered. Their pursuers engaged an engine and one car, and followed the express train at full speed, hoping to overtake it and capture them before they reached Pittsburg. The engine overtook the train just as it was entering Pittsburg, but before the cars were fairly still, Fairfield and the fugitives sprang out and scattered, and ran in various directions through the city. The pursuers spang out and gave chase, but did not succeed in capturing any of them. The fugitives soon found safe quarters among the abolitionists, and lay still for several days. Great efforts were made to find them, but they were unsuccessful, and the pursuers finally gave up the hunt and returned home. I received a letter from a friend in Pittsburg giving me these particulars, and shortly after learned that the fugitives had arrived in Cleveland. I also heard of their safe arrival in Detroit. A friend in that city wrote me that Fairfield had just reached there with the best looking company of fugitives that had ever passed through Detroit.

Thus, in numerous ways, John Fairfield was instrumental in rescuing hundreds of slaves from bondage, and in bringing together, in Canada, husbands and wives, parents and children, who had long been separated. He seemed to glory in the work, much as a military commander would in a victory over his enemies.

Although I could not sympathize with or encourage Fairfield's mode of operation, yet I often took in the fugitives whom he aided to escape. Some he brought himself; others traveled by his special directions, secreting themselves on steamboats or making the journey on foot. They generally reached our house in a state of destitution and distress, and we were always ready to succor them. In one instance John Fairfield came from a great distance, bringing a company of fugitives. They did encounter many dangers and hardships on the way, and had suffered much from hunger and exposure. Fairfield's money had all been expended, and his clothes were ragged and dirty; he looked like a fugitive himself. I took him and his company in, and after the fugitives rested and were fitted for the journey they were forwarded to Canada, *via* the Underground Railroad.

Fairfield remained in the city to recruit his strength and renew his clothing; he had left some money and clothing here when on his way South. The company referred to consisted of eight or ten brave, intelligent-looking slaves, who had determined to reach a land of liberty under the leadership of John Fairfield, or die in the attempt. Fairfield had spent some time in their neighborhood, buying eggs and chickens and shipping them to some point on the river. This was his ostensible business: his real errand was to get acquainted with the slaves. He had private interviews with them at night, in some secluded spot in the woods, and made all the plans and arrangements for the journey. Each one of the party he furnished with a revolver and plenty of ammunition.

One of the most intelligent of the fugitives said to me: "I never saw such a man as Fairfield. He told us he would take us out of slavery or die in the attempt, if we would do our part, which we promised to do. We all agreed to fight till we died, rather than be captured. Fairfield said he wanted no cowards in the company; if we were attacked and one of us showed cowardice or started to run, he would shoot him down."

They were attacked several times by patrolers, and fired upon, but always succeeded in driving the enemy and making their escape, keeping near their leader and obeying his commands. Fairfield said that they had a desperate battle one moonlight night with a company of armed men. They had been discovered by the patrolers, who had gathered a party of men and waylaid them at a bridge.

Fairfield said: "They were lying in ambush at each end of the bridge, and when we got fairly on the bridge they fired at us from each end. They thought, no doubt, that this sudden attack would intimidate us and that we would surrender, but in this they were mistaken. I ordered my men to charge to the front, and they did charge. We fired as we went, and the men in ambush scattered and ran like scared sheep."

"Was anybody hurt?" I asked.

In reply Fairfield showed me several bullet holes in his clothes, a slight flesh wound on one arm, and a slight flesh wound on the leg of one of the fugitives.

"You see," he said, "we were in close quarters, but my men were plucky. We shot to kill, and we made the devils run."

I reproved him for trying to kill any one. I told him it was better to suffer wrong than to do wrong, and that we should love our enemies.

"Love the devil!" he exclaimed. "Slaveholders are all devils, and it is no harm to kill the devil. I do not intend to hurt people if they keep out of the way, but if they step in between me and liberty, they must take the consequences. When I undertake to conduct slaves out of bondage I feel that it is my duty to defend them, even to the last drop of my blood."

I saw that it was useless to preach peace principles to John Fairfield. He would fight for the fugitives as long as his life lasted. When Fairfield left Cincinnati I knew not where he went, and did not hear any news of him until some time the next year. I then learned that in the interval he had rescued slaves from Louisiana, Alabama, Mississippi and Georgia, who had been forwarded to Canada on the lines of the Underground Railroad leading through Illinois and Michigan, and that he had just arrived in Canada himself with a company of fugitives from the State of Missouri. Not long afterward Fairfield arrived in Cincinnati, bringing with him a party of slaves from Kentucky. He forwarded them on to Canada, and remained in the city to have the benefit of medical treatment. He had a hard cough, contracted, no doubt, by exposure and hardship, and his general health seemed shattered. I again urged him to quit the perilous business he had been engaged in, and he seemed inclined to accept my advice. He bought a few goods and opened a small store in Randolph County, Indiana, in the midst of a large settlement of free colored people, where he was well known.

He remained here for a year or two, then closed up his business and disappeared. It was thought in that neighborhood that he had gone to Canada, but we could never learn that he had been seen in Canada afterward. We supposed that when he left Indiana he went South. This was a short time before the Rebellion in 1861, and from that time to the present no news of Fairfield has been received by any of his friends. The conjecture is that he was killed in Tennessee, near the iron-works, on the Cumberland River. It was reported through the papers that there was an insurrectionary movement among the slaves in that locality ; that a number of them had obtained arms ; and an alarm started that the negroes were about to rise. This was sufficient to create great excitement in the whole neighborhood, and to bring out a little army of armed men to hunt the suspected negroes. Several negroes who attempted to defend themselves were shot ; others were captured and hung by the infuriated mob. It was reported that a white man, supposed to be the instigator of the movement and the leader of the negroes, was found among them, and that he was killed. He was a stranger in that neighborhood, and his name was not known. I have always supposed that this man was John Fairfield, and that in this way his strange career was ended by a violent death. With all his faults and misguided impulses, and wicked ways, he was a brave man ; he never betrayed a trust that was reposed in him, and he was a true friend to the oppressed and suffering slave.

JOHN AND MARY.

There lived near Lexington, Kentucky, a slave man of unusual intelligence, whose master was in the habit of buying horses and mules and taking them to Georgia and South Carolina to sell. The slave, whom I will call John, was such a trusty servant that he was always taken on the expeditions to the South to aid his master, and was of great service on such occasions. His master treated him kindly, and allowed him some privileges of which slaves are usually deprived.

John had a wife, an intelligent negro woman, named Mary, who belonged to a man in the vicinity, and hired her time of her master, as was sometimes the custom. By this arrangement John and Mary lived together in a snug little house on his master's premises, which they had comfortably furnished by means of their joint industry. They had everything they could hope for in their station of life, and were so happily situated that it seemed they were not to know the darker side of slavery. But their happiness was rudely disturbed by the intelligence that John's master had become involved in debt and had concluded to sell him on the next trip South. This news reached John shortly before the time fixed to start, and he lost no time in communicating it to Mary, and consulting with her as to what should be done. They decided that they would make the attempt to escape. John had some free colored friends in Cincinnati—one of whom was on a visit to that neighborhood at that time, and to him he communicated his resolve, requesting him when he returned to Cincinnati to send some one who would conduct them out of Kentucky and across the Ohio River. He had saved some money, and authorized his friend to offer fifty dollars to some suitable person who would thus run the risk of aiding slaves to escape. The services of a young white man, who was no stranger to the business, were secured, and in due time he came into the neighborhood and made himself known to them. Mary had been sick; she was just then recovering, and hardly able to travel; but not willing to jeopardize her husband's safety by waiting any longer, she resolved to start with them immediately.

They left their house in order; bed neatly made, and everything arranged that no one might suspect their real intentions in case their place was visited shortly after their departure.

They traveled on foot all that night, and hid themselves during the following day in the thick bushes, subsisting on the scanty food they carried with them. They proceeded thus for nearly a week, traveling at night and hiding as best they could in the daytime. Their progress was slow, on account of Mary, who was hardly able to walk. She became very weak, and the last night she was so exhausted that her husband and the guide had to walk one on each side of her, and support her. They reached the Ohio River before daylight at a point where the guide had arranged for a skiff to be placed, and in this they crossed the river. Reaching Cincinnati, they went to the house of their colored friends. I was sent

for, and when I visited them I found Mary very ill
and weak, and unable to take any food. In the
evening I visited her again, and finding her no better,
I went to the office of Dr. W. H. Mussey, that noble
philanthropist, who was always ready to minister to
the needs of the poor fugitives. The doctor was out,
and I left a note requesting him to call at my residence as soon as he returned, at any hour of the
night, adding, in a postscript, "None of my family
are ill." I knew that the doctor would understand,
for he had been called upon in such instances before.

Dr. Mussey came at midnight, and together we
went to see Mary, who seemed to be sinking fast.
The doctor remained with her some time that night,
and attended on her closely for more than a week,
doing everything in his power to relieve her. For
several days her recovery seemed doubtful, but we
at last had the satisfaction of seeing her improve.
At the end of two weeks she was so far restored as
to be able to be removed, and for greater safety was
brought to our house, where she received every care
and attention, and remained until strong enough to
travel.

I was going to Newport, Indiana, on business,
about that time, and concluded to travel in my
carriage that I might take John and Mary with me.
I said to my wife, "It is fashionable to have a
colored driver, and nobody's business who sits on
the seat with me behind," so when the carriage was
brought around, John took the lines and I occupied
the back seat by the side of Mary, who was well
dressed and heavily vailed.

38

We started about three o'clock in the afternoon, and drove across Mt. Auburn, through Clifton, and along the Winton road to Hamilton. We arrived that night at a Friends' settlement at West Elkton, and stopped at the house of 'Squire Stubbs, a well-known abolitionist.

The next day being Sabbath, I attended Friends' meeting, and remained till about three in the afternoon. At that hour we pursued our journey by way of Camden, taking a country road leading up Paint Creek, and coming into the Darrtown and Richmond pike, some distance below Boston, before dark. The moon afforded us light, and we traveled on very pleasantly until about ten o'clock, when we reached the house of my friend Daniel Clark, who lived on Elkhorn, about five miles below Richmond. We halted in the road opposite the house, which stood a few rods back from the highway, and I hallooed to arouse the inmates. Clark's son-in-law, T. Hill, came out into the yard, and, not recognizing me, asked what was wanted.

I replied: "I want to know if you take Underground Railroad passengers here."

Daniel Clark had opened the window of his room, which fronted the road, and recognizing my voice, he cried out: "Yes! drive in."

T. Hill opened the large gate, and I drove into the yard. By this time Daniel had dressed and came out to meet us; we had a hearty welcome. After some conversation and refreshment, we all retired to rest, but before we got to sleep we heard a knocking at the door. T. Hill rose and opened the door. I looked out of the window and saw a wagon standing in the road, and heard the man at the door ask for quarters for a company of fugitives. As they had just received one company, Hill thought that they could not accommodate more, and accompanied this party to the next house, a few hundred yards ahead, where James Hayworth then lived, in Daniel Clark's former residence. The fugitives were comfortably quartered here for the night.

James Hayworth, having learned that I was at the other house with a company of fugitives, came over early the next morning to see me and inquire what must be done with those at his house. He said there were four in the company, three men and one woman. I told him that I knew all about them. I had forwarded them from my house in Cincinnati, on this route, a night or two before I left home. I supposed that they were ahead of me, but as I had traveled part of the time in daytime, and they only at night, I had got ahead of them. I said: "They left West Elkton night before last and were conveyed to Friend Brown's, on Paint Creek; he accompanied them last night to thy house. They are valuable property, and good care must be taken of them. I want thee to get thy carriage ready, and take them on to Newport with me."

"Not in daytime!" he exclaimed.

"Yes," I said, "in daytime; I expect to start as soon as breakfast is over, and I want thee to be ready with thy carriage to go with us."

"But there are four in the company," he replied,

"and that will make an overload in my carriage."

"I will take one of them in my carriage," I said, "which will make four in each."

After breakfast I drove on to James Hayworth's, and found them all ready. I took one of the company in my carriage and led the way. When we arrived at Richmond, James seemed reluctant to pass through the main part, so we bore to the right and passed through the eastern edge of the town, by way of Moffat's mill, on the east fork of White-water. The mill then belonged to William Ken-worthy and Benjamin Fulghum, of Richmond, and as we drew near it, I discovered them among a company of men who were raising an addition to the building, and noticed that their attention was attracted to us. When we got opposite the company, perhaps fifty yards distant, I sang out at the top of my voice the words of an old anti-slavery song,

> "Ho! the car Emancipation,
> Moves majestic through the nation."

The men suspended work to cheer us in reply. They recognized the President of the Underground Railroad at work, and came out in a body to greet us and wish us God-speed. They were mostly Friends, and well known to me; we felt no fear. Pursuing our journey, we turned into the Newport pike and soon came to a toll-gate, with the keeper of which I was acquainted. I said to him: "I suppose you allow the Underground Railroad cars to pass free on this road."

"Yes," he replied; so we passed on without paying.

Just before reaching Newport we came to another toll-gate, kept by an old man named Hockett, lately from North Carolina. He had lately been placed here as gate-keeper, and I was not acquainted with him. I halted, and said to him: "I suppose you charge nothing for the cars of the Underground Railroad that pass through this gate."

"Underground Railroad cars?" he drawled, sleepily.

"Yes," I said; "didn't they give thee orders when they placed thee here to let such cars pass free?"

"No," he replied; "they said nothing about it."

"Well, that's strange. Most of the stockholders of this road are large stockholders in the Under-ground Railroad, and we never charge anything on that road. I am well acquainted with the president of this road, and I know that he holds stock in our road. I expect to see him to-day, and several of the directors, and I shall report thee for charging Underground Railroad passengers toll."

The gate-keeper seemed much confused, and said that he knew nothing about the Underground Railroad.

"Why!" I exclaimed, with apparent surprise, "what part of the world art thou from?"

"North Carliny," he drawled.

"I thought thee was from some dark corner of the globe," I said, and handed him the money, which I had been holding in my fingers during the conversation, and which was but a trifle. I then started on, but had not gone more than a few rods, when the gate-keeper called to me, and asked: "Is your name Levi Coffin?"

"Yes," I replied, "that is my name," but did not check my team, lest he should follow me and give back the money. I had had my sport with him, which was all I wanted. I think he always knew me afterward. That day, in Newport, I met David Willcuts, who was the president of the road, and reported the gate-keeper. We had a hearty laugh over my interview with him.

I stopped with John and Mary at Daniel Huff's, in Newport, and James Hayworth went on to William Hough's, a short distance further, across the creek. The latter place was a noted depot of the Underground Railroad. The company of four fugitives were considered to be in the greatest danger of pursuit, so they were sent on toward Canada that night by the Greenville route.

John and Mary were kept at Daniel Huff's until next day, to wait for the Richmond and Winchester stage, which generally changed horses at Huff's. I had decided to forward them to Winchester by the stage if there were no suspicious passengers aboard. I made out a regular bill of lading to a mercantile firm in Winchester, with the members of which I was well acquainted, and whom I knew to be stanch abolitionists. The bill read thus:

"Shipped in good order and well conditioned, two baboons,* of fine stock and very valuable.

---

*In reference to the views of some slaveholders, who thought that negroes had no souls but were a species of baboon.

Please receive and forward the same to George D. Baptist, Detroit, Michigan, by way of Camden and Fort Wayne; I consider that to be the safest route. Take special care of them; do not allow them to run at large. They are quite tame, but bloodhounds sometimes get on their track, and might injure them. They are male and female; the female is not very stout at present, having just recovered from a spell of sickness. Please give them a warm dry place in which to lie, while at Winchester, and do not let them be too much exposed to idle spectators, as it might annoy them. They will be of little trouble about feeding, as they eat the same kind of food that human beings do, and seem to thrive on it. Put them in charge of a good conductor, who will take special care of them. Your prompt attention to this matter will much oblige your friend, LEVI COFFIN.''

I sealed this and gave it to John, and told him that when the stage stopped at the tavern at Winchester, he and Mary must go directly across the street to the store on the opposite side, and hand that letter to the person they would see behind the counter: they would be taken care of at once. They followed my directions. Dr. Woody, who had formerly been salesman in my store in Newport, happened to be in the store, and the letter was handed to him. He read it, and at once took charge of the mentioned property. The next day I received a letter from this firm, acknowledging the receipt of the property in good order and well conditioned. The letter further said that the old car

Emancipation, Number One, was standing ready with steam up, and that my consignment was put in charge of a special agent and forwarded according to my directions, without delay; and notified me that similar consignments would always receive prompt attention.

I had inclosed a short note to 'Squire Hopkins, of Camden, Jay County, the next depot, which was delivered to him by the agent who conducted John and Mary to that place from Winchester. In a short time I received a note from him, acknowledging the receipt of my consignment, stating that car Emancipation, Number Two, was standing ready, and that the freight was forwarded at once according to my directions, in charge of a special agent. The writer said he hoped I would favor him with more such consignments.

I received intelligence of the safe arrival of John and Mary in Detroit, and afterward had news of their arrival in Canada. They told their friends there that they had no idea there were such white people in the world as those who had so kindly befriended them in their hour of need.

All they had ever known of humanity was exhibited in the tender mercies of the slaveholder.

In this case and many others I have mentioned, there seems to have been no close pursuit; but in many instances the fugitives narrowly escaped capture after they had reached Cincinnati. I will relate two or three incidents of this kind.

NARROW ESCAPE OF A SLAVE WOMAN.

A slave woman escaped from the vicinity of Maysville, Kentucky, with her two children, made her way to Cincinnati, and went to a long tenement house on East Alley, where several colored families lived. In about a week her master arrived in search of her, and having learned of her whereabouts— through the treachery, it is supposed of a negro man who betrayed her hiding-place—he obtained a writ, placed it in the hands of officers, and, with a posse, went to capture her and her children. A colored woman, occupying a separate apartment of the tenement house, was just starting down street when she saw the officers coming, and, divining their object, ran quickly round a back way, gave the alarm, and succeeded in getting the woman and two children secreted and locked up, in her part of the house, just as the party arrived. They searched the rooms that the fugitive had just left, but found no traces of her, and began to hunt in some of the neighboring buildings. The woman who had given the alarm, in the meantime locked her door, and slipping out a back way, came to our house and related her story with much excitement. While she was yet talking, two more colored women came to tell the same story, and ask advice.

I told them all to go back, one by one, and show no alarm. To the first one I gave a large market basket containing a full suit of men's clothing— including an overcoat, as it was then cool spring weather—directing her to disguise the slave woman

39

and send her out by some by-way to the corner of
Fifth and Central Avenue, where some one would
be waiting whom she would recognize. She was to
follow the person at some distance, and would be
conducted to our house. Then the children were
to be disguised and taken out, one at a time, accompanied by a single person, and brought in a round-
about way to the same place.

These directions were followed, and by 11 A. M.—
the alarm had been given early in the morning—
they were all safe at our house. The next night
they were conveyed on the Underground Railroad,
thirty miles out of the city, in the care of a trusty
conductor, and in a few days were beyond the reach
of pursuers. Her master and the officers watched
around the place she had left for more than a week
after she was safe in Canada.

ANOTHER NARROW ESCAPE.

A man and wife escaped from Louisville and
reached Cincinnati by aid of the chamber-maid on
the regular packet, who secreted them during the
passage and fed them. They were acquainted with
a free colored woman, a washerwoman, who had
formerly lived in Louisville, and on their arrival in
Cincinnati made their way to her room, which was
in the basement of a building on Third Street, near
Walnut. She secreted them, and they remained
with her several days. A colored woman, a friend
of hers—living across the canal—learned of the fugitives' hiding-place, and was very uneasy lest they
should be discovered. One night she became so

troubled concerning them that she could not rest, and about ten o'clock made ner way to our house, and told me the story of the fugitives, and related her premonition of danger. I told her that the place where the slaves were hiding was very unsafe and they must come away immediately ; that time enough had elapsed since their flight for their master to come in pursuit of them, and that their hiding-place would probably be the first place searched, as the master knew of their acquaintance with the free colored woman. I told her to conduct me to the place, directing her to walk ahead, and explaining that I would follow a short distance behind. We reached the place about eleven o'clock. The woman with whom they were stopping knew me, and introduced me to the fugitives. I told them that they must leave immediately, directed them to get ready at once, and to leave the house in a manner which I explained. I then went out and in a short time the slave man followed. Turning to the left he saw me on the corner of Third and Walnut Streets, and walking some distance behind me, he reached my house in safety. The slave woman was disguised in a dress and vail belonging to her friend, and, accompanied by the woman who had conducted me to the place, walked out of the house, turned to the right and went up Main Street. In a short time they reached the corner of Franklin and Broadway—where we then resided—and the fugitives were secreted. Twenty minutes after they had left the house of the washerwoman, a posse of men entered it, some at the front, others at the rear entrance. A short search convinced them that their prey had escaped, and they were much enraged to find themselves foiled. The fugitives remained quiet several days, until the search in the city seemed to be over, and were then forwarded *via* the Underground Railroad to Canada.

A HAIRBREADTH ESCAPE.

A slave man who had made his escape from Kentucky, and reached Cincinnati in safety, took refuge among the colored people living on Sixth Street, near Broadway. He remained here several days, without my knowledge, and it was only at the last moment that I learned of his presence and was able to warn him of his danger. I was informed one evening by a white man that a company of slave-hunters were in the city, in pursuit of a slave man—that they had employed spies who had been prowling around the colored settlements all day, under pretense of business that concealed their real errand. My informer was not known as an abolitionist, but was friendly to fugitives; being a business man, he kept his anti-slavery principles in the dark as a matter of policy. Knowing my principles, he divulged to me the intelligence that had been confided to him, and inquired if I knew of such a fugitive in the city. I told him I did not, but that I would inquire of some of the colored people and put them on their guard.

That night I called at Lloyd Lewis', a colored family, with whom fugitives often stopped, and inquired if they knew of a runaway slave lying in concealment somewhere in the city. Louis' wife said that she knew of a fugitive at ——'s, on Sixth Street, below Broadway. I went immediately to the place, and found the fugitive and the man of the house, sitting out in the yard, enjoying the cool evening breeze, which was quite refreshing after the warm day. They had no suspicion of danger, but I soon alarmed them by telling them that there were slave-hunters in the city looking after such a man. I told the fugitive that he was in great danger, and must change his quarters without a moment's delay. It was then about nine o'clock at night. He was conducted, at once, to a certain point on Mount Auburn, at the head of Sycamore Street, where I sent my horse and carriage to meet him and conduct him to the next depot of the Underground Railroad.

I was informed the next day that in less than ten minutes after the fugitive left, the house was entered by his master and a posse of men, who had previously discovered his whereabouts. They searched the house thoroughly, but they were too late; they soon realized that their prey had escaped. I might relate many similar instances that occurred in the city. Fugitives were often spirited away when all the preparations for their capture had been made, and their foiled and baffled pursuers continued to search for them after they had safely reached Canada by way of the Underground Railroad.

CHAPTER XIII.

A PRO-SLAVERY MAN TURNS ABOLITIONIST—FOURTEEN
    FUGITIVES CROSS ON THE ICE—SLAVE CHILDREN
    PLACED IN OUR CHARGE—THE CASE OF WILLIAM
    THOMPSON.

THE merchant to whom I allude, in the following story, was connected with a large commission house on Walnut Street, below Second. The
principal business of the firm was with the South.
They received large quantities of sugar, molasses,
and cotton from the slaveholders, and filled the
orders of their Southern customers for provisions
of various kinds, and other articles. The planters
and Southern merchants regarded this firm as all
right on the slavery question, otherwise they would
not have patronized them and intrusted them with
their business. One of the customers. of this house
lived in Virginia, but owned a large cotton plantation in Mississippi, where he spent a part of his
time. On one occasion he was taking a company
of slaves, which he had purchased in Virginia, to
his plantation in Mississippi. He shipped them at
Wheeling, and intended to keep a sharp watch on
them as the boat passed down the Ohio River, lest

they should attempt to escape. The boat arrived at Cincinnati in the night, and lay at the wharf till morning, discharging freight. The slaves were kept in the back part of the boat, and closely guarded, but one of them, a strong active man, managed to spring on to another boat that lay alongside the wharf, and slip ashore under cover of darkness without being discovered. He made his way through the city, and concealed himself among the hills on the northern limit.

When the planter discovered that one of his men had escaped, he resolved to remain a few days and endeavor to capture him; expecting that his friends in Cincinnati would, of course, give him all the assistance in their power. He could not think of losing so valuable a piece of property without making every exertion to recover it. But it would not do to detain the boat and run the risk of losing other slaves, so he sent an agent to take charge of his slaves, and the boat went on. He went immediately to the mercantile house, of which I have spoken, to tell his grievances, and get assistance and advice. He described his negro's personal appearance very particularly to the members of the firm; but they were too busy to hunt runaway slaves, and referred him to the police. The master related his story to the police and put them on the alert; he also employed others to make a thorough search among the various colored settlements in the city. But no discovery was made that day, and the master continued to mourn the loss of his valuable slave.

The fugitive, whom I will call Jack, lay concealed all that day and the following night among the hills north of the city. Being unacquainted with the locality he knew not what direction to take, and feared to venture into the city to look for people of his own color. The weather was mild, and his hiding-place among the woods and ravines on Vine Street Hill was not uncomfortable to one who had known the hardships and sufferings of slavery.

Jack supposed that his master would not stay long in the city to hunt for him, and concluded to lie still until the search was over. But he had no food, and the second morning he was suffering with hunger. After debating in his mind regarding the best course of action, he decided to venture out and inquire for work at the few houses he saw not far off, and beg for something to eat. Now, it so happened that his hiding-place was near the residence of the merchant of whom I have spoken, who lived on the top of Vine Street Hill, and Jack made his way to this house, little thinking that the owner was his master's friend.

The merchant had his horse and buggy at the gate and was about to start to his place of business, when Jack walked up and inquired for work, saying that he had been hunting work, but had not found any, and concluded by begging for something to eat. The merchant instantly recognized him, from the description given by his master of his runaway slave, and accused him of being the negro who had made his escape from the boat a short time before. Jack confessed that he was, but plead earnestly

with the gentleman not to betray him, and begged
pitifully not to be taken back to slavery. The merchant professed no anti-slavery or abolition sentiments, but as he saw the hunted, famished fugitive
pleading before him, his humanity gained the
ascendency, and he promised Jack that he would not
betray him. His next thought was, "What shall
I do with him?" He had heard of the Underground Railroad but knew nothing of its practical
workings, and knew not where to apply for advice
and assistance. He stood for some minutes in
thought, while poor Jack eagerly scanned his face,
longing to know if he was to be sent back to
slavery, yet dreading to ask.

The merchant finally decided what he should do
next. He had some victuals put into a tin bucket,
which he gave to Jack, and told him to go down a
steep ravine, about one hundred and fifty yards
north of the house, and hide himself in a cleft or
small cave in the rocks—which he pointed out to
him—and remain there till some arrangement for
securing his freedom could be made.

A great load was lifted from poor Jack's heart.
He said: "Thank you, massa! God bless you,
massa," and did as he had been directed. Then the
merchant stepped into his buggy and proceeded on
his way down town, much perplexed concerning his
charge. He had resolved to secure Jack's freedom
if possible, but knew not how to get him to a safe
place, or how to start him on that mysterious road
leading to Canada. Instead of going directly to his
office, he called at the business house of a wholesale

grocery firm on Columbia Street, east of Main. He wished to see one of the firm whom he knew to be an abolitionist. Finding the gentleman in the office, he took him to one side, and said in a low tone: "I have a secret I would like to divulge to you, but do not know whether or not it will be safe. I have got myself into a predicament, and know not how to get out of it."

The other replied: "You need feel no diffidence or fear about divulging any thing to me; what you say will be kept in confidence."

Thus assured, the merchant related the circumstances that had occurred that morning, and asked for counsel and assistance.

His confidant laughed and replied: "I can help you out of that difficulty easily enough. I can take you to a man who knows all about the Underground Railroad, and who will help you out of that dilemma."

The merchant then went to his office, but soon returned, and his friend stepped into the buggy with him and they drove to my store. The grocery merchant, with whom I was acquainted, came into my counting-room, and told me that there was a gentleman waiting in his buggy outside, who wished to see me on some special business. I walked out with him to the buggy and he introduced me to his friend. I knew the merchant at sight, but had no personal acquaintance with him. He related the whole circumstance to me, and seemed to regard it as a very serious affair. I laughed, for I was used to such cases and was amused to see how he regarded it. I told him there need be no difficulty in the matter, and recommended him to go to John Hatfield, a trusty colored man who was used to such business, and relate the circumstance to him. He would go out and take charge of the fugitive and conduct him to some safe place where he could remain until the train of the Underground Railroad was ready to start for Canada. The merchant said he was not acquainted with Hatfield; he wished I would go myself and tell him about the fugitive. He then undertook to describe the place where the fugitive was hid, but I told him that I was not acquainted in that locality, and could not describe it to Hatfield so that he could find it.

"Well, then," replied the merchant, "just step into my buggy and I will drive out and show you where he is hid."

So I took my seat by him in the buggy, and the other gentleman returned to his store. We drove hastily out to the top of Vine Street Hill, and stopped in front of my companion's residence. Hitching the horse at the gate, we walked through the garden and down the hill to the place where the fugitive was trying to conceal himself among the rocks. I saw his head, as he peeped out at us, while we were yet several rods distant. As we neared his place of concealment I called out, commandingly, "Come out of there, Jack; what are you doing among the rocks?" He crawled out, looking much alarmed; he evidently supposed that the merchant had been to get help and had come to take him. I then spoke kindly to him, telling him not to be alarmed, that we were his friends, and ended by cordially shaking hands with him. His countenance brightened, and he seemed to feel that all was right.

A consultation was then held, and it was decided that he must be removed immediately. The place did not afford secure concealment, for people often passed over the hills hunting birds and other small game. I said: "There are plenty of safe places in the city if we can only get him to them safely."

The merchant replied: "My buggy is at your service; take him where you please."

"Not so fast, my friend," I answered; "that would not do at all. Thy buggy and horse are well known, and so am I. It would not do for me to appear in open daylight with a fugitive slave in thy buggy; we might meet Jack's hunters in the street. It would probably lead to his capture, and bring both thee and me into trouble."

A plan for getting Jack into the city was finally agreed upon. Bordering on the west line of the merchant's premises was a strip of woods which opened near the head of Elm Street. A path led down this ravine, by a stone quarry, where some men were at work, near the road, quarrying out stone. These surroundings suggested and aided our plan. According to our directions, Jack took off his coat, rolled up his sleeves, hung his coat on his arm and took the tin bucket in his hand, thus presenting the appearance of a laborer. It was then gardening time in spring, and several people were at work in sight. We made our way into the merchant's garden and passed slowly through it, looking at the vegetable beds and appearing to direct Jack where to work, then crossing the adjoining garden which belonged to the merchant's mother-in-law, we made our way into the strip of woods. Here I directed the merchant and the fugitive to remain until I reached the road, about a hundred yards ahead, that led down the ravine, then Jack was to follow me keeping his eye on me and stopping when he saw me stop. I remarked to the merchant as I started, "It is nobody's business who travels the same road that I do." Looking back in a few minutes I saw Jack following me, and the merchant standing in the woods, anxiously watching us as we passed the men working in the stone quarry. When he saw us pass them without being molested, he went back to his buggy, feeling much relieved. I walked on leisurely, and Jack followed at a short distance. Reaching the head of Elm Street, I proceeded on my way down that street till I came to the house of Edward Harwood, that ever faithful friend to the slave. His good wife met me on the porch and invited me into the house. To her invitation I replied: "Not yet; I will wait for a friend who is near by." Jack had now arrived at the gate. He halted there and stood irresolutely, as if fearing to enter. I said: "Come in, there is no danger," and Harwood's wife, a meet companion for her husband in all benevolent impulses and actions, also invited him in. It is no wonder that Jack was fearful and distrustful; a fugitive always suspected danger, not knowing but that the plans made to secure his safety were schemes to betray him.

The family were at the table in the dining-room, having just completed their noon repast. We walked into this room, and when Harwood rose to welcome us, I said: "Edward, here is a stranger, a man seeking liberty; I want thee to take care of him till he is called for. He is hungry—feed him, and keep him safely for awhile, for he is sought after."

Harwood extended a hearty welcome to the fugitive, and in his good-humored manner of talking, said: "Sit down right here, and eat your fill, and if any one comes in and attempts to molest you while eating, pick up that chair and knock him down."

"Stop, my friend," I said; "I did not tell thee to fight, but to keep him safe till called for." The family had many similar cases in their experience, and did not need further explanation. The fugitive remained with them several days, when a suitable opportunity occurred for his removal from the city. William Beard, a prominent abolitionist from Union County, Indiana, came to town with market stuff in a two-horse wagon, and arrangements were made with him. When he went out of town, he had a negro driver who was dressed in good clothes and wore a white hat, and who bore little resemblance in personal appearance to the half-starved negro who had hidden in the ravines and hills at the head of Vine Street. William Beard took him to

Union County, Indiana, where he tarried a few days, and then took passage for Canada, *via* the old reliable road.

FOURTEEN FUGITIVES CROSS ON THE ICE.

The Ohio River was a great barrier to fugitive slaves. They often escaped from their masters and made their way to the river, but not being able to find any means of crossing, they were overtaken and captured by their pursuers, sometimes being detected while looking for a skiff or some other craft which they could break loose from its fastening and appropriate to their own use. The slaves who lived some distance from the river generally knew nothing about managing a skiff, and if they could find one, they were afraid to venture into it and attempt the passage of the river alone. Sometimes they made a confidant of some colored person living near the river, who would help them across. In the winter, however, when an unusually cold spell of weather stopped navigation and bridged the river over with ice, the main obstacle in the way of the slaves who wished to reach Ohio was removed. At such times we always expected a stampede of fugitives from Kentucky. Large companies sometimes got together and crossed the same night, so that the Underground Railroad did a lively business while this natural bridge lasted.

During one of these cold spells, when the river was frozen over and the crossing was good, a number of slaves, who lived a short distance back of Newport, Kentucky, concluded that it was a favorable time for them to get out of slavery. They had been contemplating such a movement for some time—consulting together and preparing themselves for the attempt to gain their liberty by flight. Some of them had friends and acquaintances among the colored people in Cincinnati, and one of the company ventured to come over on the ice one night, and inform these colored people of the plan their slave friends had made.

The night for commencing the flight was appointed, and it was arranged that some of their colored friends should meet the fugitives at the river and conduct them to places of safety. The company was to divide and land at three separate points, that they might not attract attention and arouse suspicion, by their numbers. This was the plan I suggested when the friends of the fugitives applied to me for advice, and assistance. I also suggested that teams should be in readiness to meet them at these points in order to convey them that night to the next depot of the Underground Railroad. My team and two others were accordingly put in readiness.

Dr. Blunt, of Darke County, Ohio, who often stopped with me when he came to the city on business, happened to be in the city that day, and came to my house in the evening. After supper, he said: "Mr. Coffin, I wish that some of your Underground Railroad passengers would come along to-night. I have never had the pleasure of seeing a fugitive slave, and I would like to see one. There have been a few in our neighborhood, and I have contributed to help them on their way, but I did not see them."

"Doctor," I replied, "thou hast come just at the right time; I can initiate thee into the work to-night. Fourteen fugitives are to cross on the ice at twelve o'clock, and we have three teams and drivers ready to meet them at separate points, and take them out of the city by different roads to a place beyond Mt. Auburn. I expect to see them stowed into the wagons, if they succeed in crossing the river, and then I must see that they all get together safely on top of the hill. That will probably consume the most of the night; dost thou think thou can stand such a jaunt as that?"

"I think I can endure as much as you," he replied, "and I am ready for the adventure."

About eleven o'clock we went to the house of Thomas Dorum, one of the fugitives' colored friends, and where part of the company were to be brought. About midnight we had the pleasure of seeing the expected fugitives arrive, and soon saw them and the other two companies stowed in the wagons, and started on their separate routes. I directed them where to meet, on the top of the hill beyond Mt. Auburn.

The doctor and I then went up Sycamore Street to the place appointed for them to meet, and had the pleasure of seeing them all together. They were able-bodied, good looking men and women—two or three of the men had their wives with them. The men were armed and provided with plenty of ammunition; they seemed determined never to be

40

captured. Dr. Blunt's deepest interest was aroused, and he became quite enthusiastic.

"That's right," said he to the men when he saw their weapons; "let your watchword be liberty or death. Die in your tracks, boys, rather than be taken back to slavery." He directed them to load their revolvers and keep them in readiness.

I told them that my advice was to throw away their revolvers, and look to a higher power for protection, and gave them my views in regard to carrying weapons in a few words, for we had but little time to talk.

The doctor still encouraged them to fight for their liberty, if necessary, and gave them all the money he had with him to help them on their way, retaining only what he thought he would need for his expenses home. I do not remember the amount he gave them, but it was several dollars.

This was a few years before the rebellion. The doctor moved to Kansas soon after this occurrence, and after the war broke out, and I heard that he was made General, and was at the head of an army, I said, when I read accounts in the papers of his victories: "They have one General who will fight for liberty or die, and if slaves come inside his lines, they will never be given up to their masters, even if they are claimed by men professing to be loyal."

SLAVE CHILDREN PLACED IN OUR CHARGE.

In addition to our labors for the fugitives, we often had the care of slave children who were brought from the South by their white fathers, or

by agents, for the purpose of being educated, and
placed in our charge. Besides the care and responsibility thus placed upon us, the children often
proved troublesome and expensive. I will refer to
a few cases.

A prominent lawyer in Tennessee sent two slave
boys—his own children—to Cincinnati in the care
of an agent. On their arrival in this city the agent
inquired for an abolitionist, saying that the master
of the boys wished him to place them in the charge
of some reliable anti-slavery man who would put
them in a good school and look after their interests.
He was referred to me and came to my store, bringing the boys with him. When he made known his
business to me, I declined, at first, to assume the
responsibility. I told him that I was experienced
in such cases and had often found the charge
a troublesome one; besides, I had much business on
my hands, and my time and attention were fully
occupied. I recommended him to take the boys to
the Union Literary Institute, in Indiana, a chartered
institution, established for the benefit of colored
people. It was a well-managed and cheap board-
ing-school about ninety miles distant; but he plead
several excuses—he was a stranger in the country,
the limited time of his stay in Ohio would not
admit of his going with them, etc., and begged and
insisted that I should take charge of the boys, until
I finally promised to do so. He left money enough
to defray their expenses for the first term at school,
and assured me that more would be sent from time
to time, to meet further expenses, and to pay me

well for my trouble. I placed the boys at school, but when the sum was expended I had to advance money to defray their expenses, and never succeeded in getting it refunded.

Another case was that of a slave girl who was brought from Mississippi to this city by her father. She was a handsome girl of about sixteen, as white in appearance as any of our children. She had no education, and her master wished her to attend a good school. He stopped at a hotel, made known his errand, and was referred to me. He came to see me, but I refused to take charge of the girl and recommended other persons to him. He went to see them, but they also refused to accept the charge, and he returned to my house, bringing the girl with him. He laid the case before my wife, and finally succeeded in getting her consent to receive the girl. He left seventy-five dollars to be used in defraying the school and boarding expenses of his slave daughter, and gave me his address, promising to remit more money soon after his return, to pay her board and buy clothing. We at once sent the girl to the Ninth Street public school, and as she was white in appearance no objection was made to her presence there. She had been brought up under the evil influences of slavery, but had not been harshly treated. She was averse to study and unwilling to go to school, and gave us much trouble on that account. Coming from a milder climate than ours, the clothing that had been provided for her was not suitable for winter, and we had to purchase some at once.

Her expenses soon consumed the seventy-five dollars left by her master. I wrote to him several times, inclosing a bill of her expenses, and at last received a reply from him. The letter contained no money, and was couched in abusive language. He said that if the abolitionists were too mean to school the girl, they could send her back to slavery, where she would be better cared for; he would be at no further expense on her account. We kept the girl at school as long as we could prevail upon her to attend. Our counsels and admonitions could not counteract the influences of her early life. She quit school and fell into bad company among the colored people, but finally married a respectable colored man, and withdrew from all improper associations.

In other instances we were more fortunate, though such a charge always brought heavy responsibility and care. Old Judge Cage, a wealthy planter of Louisiana, living several miles distant from New Orleans, had an interest in mercantile business, conducted by his brother in the city. Both were slaveholders. The brother living in the city purchased a light mulatto woman to whom he was much attached, and kept her as his wife. The law did not recognize such bonds, and the children of such marriages followed the condition of the mother and were slaves. This couple had a family of eight children, nearly white. They were brought up as other wealthy gentlemen's children in the South, and had slaves to wait on them. They had good educational advantages in their childhood, and when they grew up, the three eldest children—two sons and a daughter—were sent East to complete their education. The five younger children were still at home when their parents died, their father leaving no will. According to the law they were part of the estate and were liable to be sold, but in the settlement, Judge Cage managed to get them as a part of his share of his brother's estate, so they became his property. But he did not intend to make slaves of them. One of them, a boy twelve or fourteen years old, the judge wished to send to Ohio to be educated, and he wrote to Judge Matthews, of Cincinnati, concerning the matter. Matthews recommended him to put the boy under my care. The first I knew of the case, the boy was sent to me from New Orleans with a letter from Judge Cage, requesting me to take charge of the bearer, and place him in some good school. The writer informed me that he had sent a draft to Judge Matthews to defray expenses, and that all bills would be promptly paid.

I took charge of the boy and placed him at school at the Union Literary Institute, where I kept him for three or four years. All his bills were promptly settled by Judge Cage. A few years before the war, old Judge Cage died, and the settling of his estate devolved upon his son, Duncan S. Cage. The children of his uncle that still remained in the South—four daughters—came into his possession as part of the estate, but he had no wish to enslave his cousins. Shortly before the rebellion, I received a letter from him, stating that he had shipped the

four girls to my care at Cincinnati, and wished me
to take charge of them on the arrival of the boat, and
place them at a school at Oberlin. He inclosed a
draft for five hundred dollars, and said that all bills
would be promptly paid. He requested me to
address him at Baton Rouge, as he was then a
member of the Louisiana Legislature, which met at
that place. On the arrival of the boat I met the
girls at the river, and conveyed them to our house.
They remained with us several weeks, until I could
correspond with the proper authorities at Oberlin,
and make proper arrangements for boarding, and
until we could provide the girls with clothing suitable for this climate. They were well supplied with
fine clothes adapted for a Southern climate, but had
few articles of dress warm enough for service here.
It was autumn when they arrived, and it was necessary to purchase winter clothing. The oldest girl,
a young woman of twenty-one, who had been kept
by a merchant of New Orleans, according to Southern custom, and well furnished with rich dresses and
jewelry, seemed unwilling to go to school. She
said she did not wish to come away from New
Orleans, but Mr. Cage would have her come with
her sisters. She wanted to go back to the life
she had left. I tried to reason with her, and prevail
upon her to change her course of life entirely. I
endeavored to impress upon her mind a sense of
the sinfulness of living in such a way; I told her
that the merchant who kept her as his wife was not
her husband legally, that he could not be in Louisiana, and probably had no intention of making her

his wife by coming North, where their bond could be legalized. If he was honest and sincere in his profession of love for her, he would come to her in the North; while if she returned to him in the South, she would be liable to be enslaved.

But she received letters and money from him, and turned a deaf ear to my counsel. She was determined to go back, and returned to live the life of a concubine. This case gives us a glimpse into the customs and state of morals that existed in the South, and shows the demoralizing influences of slavery.

When all the necessary arrangements were made, I took the three sisters to Oberlin, and deposited with the treasurer of the college enough money to defray their necessary expenses. All bills incurred on their account were promptly settled by Duncan S. Cage, until the war cut off communication between Cincinnati and New Orleans. This gentleman was an officer in the rebel army, and I learned that during the war he lost not only his slaves but all the rest of his property. No money was received from him after the war commenced, and when the means on hand were exhausted, the girls were left without support. I was obliged to bring them from Oberlin to my house and look for situations for them, for their only alternative now was to support themselves by their own labor. They were not accustomed to housework; they could use the needle pretty well, but had not been used to hard work of any kind, so that I found it difficult to get situations for them. I succeeded finally, however, in getting them placed in good homes, where they were looked after and cared for. They are now all married, and are said to be doing well. They were amiable and beautiful young women, and fair scholars.

At another time, three slave children, from the State of Kentucky, were emancipated by their white father and placed under our care while they were obtaining an education. They attended school for several years, making our house their home during the intervals. They were nearly white, and were unusually bright and handsome children. They obtained a good education, grew up, and married respectably.

Thus it seemed to fall to our lot to have such cares upon us, the most of the time, for nearly twenty years after our removal to Cincinnati. It was perhaps attributable, in part, to the fact that my wife and I had been favored to overcome prejudice against color or caste.

THE CASE OF WILLIAM THOMPSON.

My attention was often called to other cases of emancipated slaves. Families of slaves were frequently brought to Cincinnati by their white fathers who wished to emancipate them and locate them somewhere in Ohio. I was often called upon for advice in regard to suitable localities, where land could be obtained on reasonable terms, etc.

Among the many cases to which my attention was called, was that of William Thompson, a planter from Mississippi, of whom some account has pre-

viously been given. He owned two cotton plantations in that State, and about forty slaves.
Wishing to emancipate some of his human property, he came to Cincinnati, bringing with him
fourteen slaves, whom he designed to settle on a
farm in this· State. They traveled all the way
by land, in a common road wagon, with a team
of four mules, and on their arrival in this city
stopped at the Black Bear tavern, on Ninth Street,
where there was a good wagon yard. Thompson
had sold one of his farms to enable him to settle
this family of fourteen in a free State, and intended
the next year to sell his other farm and bring the
rest of his slaves to Ohio. He was a man over
fifty years old, very ignorant and illiterate, and an
entire stranger in this part of the country. He was
at the mercy of unscrupulous, designing people,
and had fallen into the hands of such persons before
I knew anything about him.

Those to whom he made known his business introduced him to J. F——, a well known pro-slavery
lawyer, who had been Judge of the Criminal Court,
and had won an unenviable notoriety by deciding
several fugitive cases that were brought before him
in favor of slavery—in direct violation of law of the
State of Ohio. He lost his position as judge when
the Criminal Court was abolished by an act of the
legislature. When he learned that Thompson had
money with him to the amount of several thousand
dollars and was informed of his intentions, he began
to plan to get the money into his own hands. He
said to Thompson : " As you are a stranger here,

and have but little knowledge of the quality and value of land in this State, I would advise you to rent a house in the city for your people at present, and employ an agent, some responsible person, to purchase land for you, and settle your people on it. Then you can return at once to Mississippi, and attend to your business there, and make preparations for bringing the rest of your people to the North next year. I am well acquainted in the country, and will act as your agent here, if you will place your money in my hands."

All this looked plausible, and Thompson seemed inclined to accept the offer. J. F—— returned to his office and drew up a contract constituting himself agent for Thompson, with full power to invest Thompson's money and locate his people, at his own discretion. Thompson deferred signing the article until the next day, wishing a little time to consider the matter before signing the contract. Somebody had whispered in his ear that J. F—— was not a responsible man, and that he drank too much whisky. This caused Thompson some uneasiness, and he went out among the merchants to make some inquiry. Several of them advised him to have nothing to do with J. F——, and recommended him to come to me, and to act according to my advice. Next morning, a respectable merchant came to my store, and said: "I wish that you would get that Mississippi man out of J. F——'s hands."

"What Mississippi man?" I asked, for I had heard nothing of Thompson.

The merchant then told me who he was, what constituted his business in Cincinnati, and gave an account of J. F——'s endeavors to get hold of his money.

I replied: "I had not heard of such a man being in the city, but if I were to see him, I would advise him to attend to his own business."

While we were talking, another prominent merchant entered my store in company with Thompson, whom he introduced to me. He said "that he had met with Thompson that morning, and advised him to come to me for advice in regard to setling his slaves in Ohio. He was about to make an agent of J. F——; he has an article of agreement written by J. F——, but I advised him not to sign it, and assured him that he could rely upon your advice. I will now leave him in your hands." He then returned to his place of business.

I asked Thompson some questions, in order to inform myself regarding his intentions, and, after answering them, he handed me J. F——'s document to read.

I advised him not to sign it, or to make an agent of any person, but to attend to the business himself; to go into the country where he could buy land on reasonable terms and make his own purchases. I mentioned several colored settlements that afforded the advantages of schools, and told him that I would give him letters of introduction to men in those neighborhoods, who would assist him in selecting a suitable location for his people, and whose advice and judgment he could rely upon.

Thompson's only knowledge of business related to raising and selling cotton, and buying negroes; in regard to money matters he was quite ignorant. I found that he had several thousand dollars in Southern paper with him, which was at a small discount here, and advised him to deposit it in bank at what it was worth, so that he could draw it out, as he had need, in our currency. I informed him that he could not purchase land in the country with Southern money. He had, besides, several hundred dollars in gold, which I advised him to take with him. He appeared to have no knowledge of banking business, and it seemed difficult for him to understand anything about it. I told him that I would go with him to the bank where I kept my deposits, and assist him in this matter, charging him nothing for my trouble, but he appeared confused and reluctant. I referred him to two or three prominent business men, telling him that he could consult with them and return to my store at one o'clock, when I would give him further directions about locating his people, and furnish him with letters of introduction. He returned at that hour, seeming more cheerful, and settled in his mind. He said that he wanted me to act as his agent, to take charge of his people and locate them; he would place all his money in my hands except enough to take him home. I told him that I could not assume the responsibility—that he ought not to put his money into another person's hands, but to keep it in his own and attend to it himself. He then urged

me to go with him to the country and assist him to
find a suitable location, offering to pay me well for
my time and trouble. I told him that I could not
leave my business, and that it was unnecessary for
him to incur additional expense. I advised him to
settle his people in Darke County, Ohio, near the
Union Literary Institute, which was situated near
the State line, dividing Ohio and Indiana. This
institution, as I have mentioned before, was established for the benefit of colored children; it had a
charter granted by the Indiana Legislature. I told
Thompson that there were large settlements of colored people on both sides of the State line, land
could be purchased on reasonable terms, and I
considered the locality in every way a suitable one.
I said that I would give him a letter to a friend of
mine living near there, who was an abolitionist and
a good man in every sense of the word, and who
would take an interest in his people, and assist him
in finding a good location. I examined his paper
money, and again advised him to deposit it in bank
at its worth, as it was not current in the country,
and would not be taken at par value for land. By
his request I went with him to the bank to deposit
his money, but I could not prevail on him to get a
bank book and deposit the money in his own name;
he insisted on having it deposited in my name. I
finally consented to this arrangement and gave him
my check for the amount. I gave him a letter to
Nathan Thomas, made out a map of the road he was
to travel, and gave him all necessary directious. I
went with him that afternoon to the wagon-yard,

where his slaves were staying, and to my surprise I
found that, with the exception of one old woman,
all had complexions that showed they were related
to the white race. Thompson informed me that the
whole family were children or grandchildren of the
old negro woman, with the exception of one young
woman, who was the wife of her oldest son.

This daughter-in-law, who had several small children, Thompson had bought, that she might accompany her husband. I next inquired about the father
of the family, and Thompson confessed that he was
their father. Two or three of his sons were grown
to manhood.

J—— F——, the lawyer, came while we were
talking, and appeared much disappointed when
Thompson stated his conclusions, and refused to
sign the document which the lawyer had drawn
up, constituting himself Thompson's agent. He
said that his charge for writing the document was
five dollars; Thompson paid it and appeared glad to
get rid of him so easily.

The next morning the party started on their
way to Darke County, according to my directions.
Thompson delivered my letter to Nathan Thomas,
who went with him to look for a farm, as I
requested. They soon found a suitable farm on
the Ohio side of the State line, near Union Literary
Institute. Thompson purchased it and settled his
family on it. In a few weeks he returned to Cincinnati, bringing one of his yellow sons with him.
He purchased a carriage here and harnessing to it

two good mules, which he had brought with him, he started back to Mississippi.

In the autumn of the next year, after selling his remaining farm and his crop of cotton, he fitted out another team and brought to Ohio all the rest of his slaves, with the exception of one man, whose wife and children belonged to another master, and who preferred to remain with them in slavery. Thompson sold this man to his wife's owner.

This latter company of slaves numbered twenty-six, including women and children. Among them was a woman of between twenty-five and thirty years of age, who had several mulatto children. Thompson confessed that these were his own children. Their mother had lived on the farm which he had just sold; so it appeared that he kept a slave wife on each of his plantations. Yet Thompson was a professor of religion, according to his own representations, and a member of the Baptist Church.

Such personal histories as this show the demoralizing and corrupting influences of slavery.

Thompson wished to buy land for each family and for his sons. I advised him to deposit his money— most of which was in Southern paper—in the bank, and to draw it out whenever he found a tract of land that he could purchase at low rates for cash. This plan suited him in regard to buying land, but he wished to leave his money with me, and draw on me instead of on the bank. He said he desired to deposit ten thousand dollars with me, and have me to loan it out for him. I said that I did not wish to take the responsibility, and advised him not to loan the money just then; opportunities might soon offer for purchasing land on good terms for cash, and he had better deposit his money so that he could draw it at any time. He seemed to place much confidence in me, and still insisted that I should take charge of his money. Knowing that he was ignorant of business matters in this part of the country, and might easily be defrauded by such men as J. F——, I at last consented to assume the responsibility and receive his money. He placed ten thousand dollars in my hands, which I deposited in bank, subject to his order at any time, and for which I gave him my individual obligation.

Thompson went to the locality where he had settled his first company of slaves, and soon found opportunities to purchase several tracts of land. He drew his money, bought the land, and located his people on it. He remained in that settlement, making his home with his first family.

CHAPTER XIV.

MAJOR PHILLIPS—A SLAVEHOLDER'S COLORED FAMILY—
   MY TRIP WITH THE MAJOR DOWN THE RIVER—
   INCIDENTS OF THE JOURNEY—DISCUSSIONS WITH
   SLAVEHOLDERS—INSIGHTS INTO SOUTHERN SOCIAL
   LIFE—A WHIPPING ON BOARD A BOAT.

A FEW years after my experience with Thompson, I was called to assume another troublesome and responsible charge. As it involved experiences of varied characters, and gave an insight into some of the internal workings of slavery, I will give it at some length. The principal personage in the case was Major Phillips, an old gentleman nearly eighty years of age, who, when I first knew him, lived on Broadway, in this city, in a fine residence nearly opposite the Presbyterian church. He had moved to this city from a large cotton plantation in Mississippi, near Yazoo City. Having engaged extensively in cotton planting, there he had accumulated a large fortune, part of which was invested in slaves; he owned a hundred and forty at one time. Before coming to Cincinnati he sold the greater part of his real estate and most of his slaves, bringing to this city several of his favorite servants, whom he emancipated. Among these was a mulatto woman, with four or five small children, nearly white, whom he claimed as his own. He also brought with him one of his grandsons, a boy about fifteen years old, the son of his daughter, who was dead. He had two or three white sons whom he had settled in business in New Orleans, some years before he moved to Ohio, giving them a large estate.

They had every advantage, but proved to be reckless and dissipated ; they soon squandered their property, and caused their father much trouble and anxiety. Major Phillips lost his wife several years before he left the South. She was said to have been a woman of much natural ability and culture ; was an excellent wife, and a kind and indulgent mistress. The major was a man of more than ordinary talent. He had once been president of a bank in New Orleans, and was several times elected to the State Legislature. In the war of 1812 he was a major under General Jackson. He possessed a high reputation and much influence in that part of the South where he was known, and was regarded as a man of honor and respectability. There were many excellent qualities in his character. He was a kind master, and would not allow his overseers to whip his slaves cruelly, or otherwise abuse them. He and his first wife—a short time before her death—came to the conclusion to liberate all their slaves, and made out deeds of emancipation for them. The Legislature of Miss-

issippi was then in session, and passed a law prohibiting the liberation of slaves in that State.

Major Phillips and his wife went to the county
seat to acknowledge the deeds and have them
recorded, but when they arrived in town they heard
of the law that had just been passed, and were
obliged to abandon their good intentions. Phillips
had the reputation of being kind to the poor, and
in several instances instituted lawsuits to secure
the rights of orphan children, who were being
defrauded of them, and succeeded in his benevolent efforts, at a heavy expense to himself.

This information was given me by one of his
neighbors, who added that he thought no other
man could have succeeded in such cases, but the
major had great influence and was very benevolent.
After his first wife died, the major remained a wid-
ower for several years, then contracted a second
marriage, which, unfortunately, did not prove to
be a happy one. His wife was unfaithful to her
marriage vows, and he put her away, treating her,
however, with kindness and consideration.

The two entered into a legal contract of separation, in which they bound themselves to live unmar-
ried the rest of their lives. The major gave her
one of his cotton farms, besides other property,
and allowed her to retain her own servants. To
aid her in cultivating the plantation, he left thirteen
of his own slaves on it. He gave her no title to
these slaves, and it was understood that they should
only remain there until he called for them.

Soon after this separation, the major bought from

a drove of slaves offered for sale in Yazoo City, a young mulatto girl, who was recommended to be a good house servant, and who proved to be a most excellent one. A short time afterward the major had a stroke of paralysis, and was rendered almost entirely helpless for several months. He lost the use of his right arm, and his power of speech was for a time impaired. He never recovered the use of his right arm, and ever afterward signed his name with his left hand. During his illness, the new house servant was very kind to him, and nursed him tenderly through all his suffering. He became much attached to her, and afterward kept her as his wife. She became the mother of several children. After his stroke of paralysis, Major Phillips was not able to carry on the business of his plantation, and he resolved to sell out and come to the North, in order to educate his little yellow children, to whom he was much attached, and have them brought up in a free State. He had given his profligate sons about seventy-five thousand dollars and they had squandered most of it; he now wished to secure the rest of his estate to his young children.

He sold his plantation, with more than one hundred slaves on it, to a wealthy planter, binding the purchaser not to separate families, and then moved to Cincinnati, bringing with him his yellow children, their mother, and a few favorite servants, as I have before mentioned. The mulatto woman he now professed to keep as a hired servant—but she dressed richly, and her extravagant expenditures showed that she was not a mere servant.

The major's house was large and well furnished. He kept a span of horses and a fine carriage, and he and his grandson often rode out to take the fresh air. He employed an intelligent colored woman, nearly white, to act as matron in his establishment, and her daughter, who was a fine scholar, a graduate of Oberlin College, to teach his yellow children. This young woman was a good pianist, and the major bought a fine piano for her use in teaching his grandson and elder children music.

On his arrival in Cincinnati, Major Phillips deposited in the Trust Company Bank ten thousand dollars, a similar amount in Ellis and Company's bank, and a third ten thousand in Smead's bank, besides paying eleven thousand dollars for his house. He also loaned several thousand dollars to a merchant who had managed to gain his confidence. This man appeared to be a person of wealth; he lived in a good house, on which he gave Phillips a mortgage, and sold Phillips other property which he professed to own—receiving cash for it, and making the deeds in the name of Phillips' children, as he requested. The major was old, and not being able on account of his failing strength to attend to his business, he intrusted the care of it largely to his friend, the merchant, whom he supposed to be perfectly honest. Among other things, the major intrusted Wilcox, the merchant, with making deposits for him in bank, collecting checks, and drawing the interest for him on his deposits in bank. At one time, when Phillips was ill, he sent for Wilcox, and told him that he wished his illegitimate children and their mother to have the benefit of his money in bank; he wished real estate to be purchased for them, and gave other directions for the disposition of his money, in case he should not live.

Wilcox agreed to attend to the business and carry out his wishes, but told him that he must sign some blank checks in order that he—Wilcox— could draw the money. He said to the major: "If you should not live I will fill them out, draw the money and carry out your wishes, but if you recover, I will return the checks to you, blank."

The old man was very feeble, and evidently not in his right mind, and after signing one blank check on the Trust Company Bank with much difficulty, he seemed to lose his consciousness, and signed no other—very fortunately for him, as it afterward proved. After a tedious spell of sickness he recovered his usual health, but had no recollection of signing the blank check. When informed of it by his matron, or housekeeper, he sent immediately for Wilcox, to inquire about the check and have it returned.

Wilcox said: "I destroyed it, when I found that you were getting well."

Phillips now began to lose confidence in Wilcox, and in another shrewd man who had managed to gain his confidence so far as to be appointed his agent to go to New Orleans and Yazoo City, and other places in the South, to collect money for him. This man had also transacted some business for him

here. Phillips believed that both of these men
were dishonest, and that they had deceived him.

One morning a messenger from the major came
to my store, and said that he requested that I
should come to see him, as he had some special
business about which he wished to talk with me
that morning.

He had lived in Cincinnati several years, but I
had had no acquaintance with him. I had frequently seen him passing along the street in his carriage, but had never spoken to him. My knowledge
of him had been confined to what I heard from
others concerning him—that he had brought some
slaves to Ohio and had liberated them, and that he
had some colored children—which was not very
reputable in this State, but I concluded to go and
see what special business he had with me—an entire
stranger. When I arrived at his house, I found the
old man quite feeble; he was just recovering from a
spell of sickness. He appeared to be very much
of a gentleman in his manners, and impressed me
favorably. He told me of his troubles—how he
had been deceived by dishonest men since he had
been paralyzed and not able to attend to his own
business. He said: "I know you by reputation,
Mr. Coffin, but have never had the pleasure of a
personal acquaintance. I have several times been
advised to call on you and consult with you about
my business." He then went on to mention his
deposits in different banks, and said that he wished
me to draw the interest for him at the Trust Company Bank, where he had ten thousand dollars

deposited. I agreed to do this, and taking his bank-book and check, went to the bank and told the cashier that I wished to draw the interest due on Major Phillips' deposit.

He said: "Major Phillips has no funds here."

I spoke with surprise, and said: "He told me that he had ten thousand dollars here."

"He did have," replied the cashier, "but Wilcox drew it all out, both principal and interest."

"When?" I asked.

He turned to his books, and said: "Last August." It was now December.

When I returned and informed Major Phillips that he had no money in the bank, that Wilcox had taken it all out on his check, he seemed astounded, and was very angry. He sent for Wilcox immediately, and begged me to remain until he came, which I did. Wilcox stepped in, but seemed to be in great haste and would not be seated. He said he had but a moment to spare, that he had left some men at his store who had special business with him, and he must return immediately. Phillips inquired about the money.

Wilcox acknowledged that he had drawn it, and said, hurriedly, "I will make it all right, but can't stop to talk now."

Then without giving any satisfaction, but promising to call again soon, he stepped out. I was sent for again to meet Wilcox at Major Phillips' house, but he failed to make his appearance, and failed in all his promises to secure Phillips from loss.

Suit was entered against him, but his property

42

proved to be covered with mortgages and nothing could be realized from it, to reimburse the major. There were judgments of older date against the property on which the major held a mortgage, and the property which Wilcox had sold to the major for his children was covered with mortgages.

Altogether, Major Phillips lost by him over eighteen thousand dollars. After this the major seldom transacted any business without consulting me. He seemed destined to sustain heavy losses. A money panic came; several banks failed, and stopped payment, among them Goodman and Company's and Smead and Company's banks, where his money was deposited. He made a compromise with Goodman and Company, agreeing to take half of the amount of his deposit, which they paid him. Smead and Company secured him in full, by giving him good notes for the principal, and paying the interest in gold.

By failures in New Orleans Phillips lost about forty thousand dollars. Thus his means seemed to be fast diminishing, and no property was secured to his yellow children and their mother. Knowing that they were illegal heirs and could not inherit their portion of his estate when he was gone, I advised Phillips to buy real estate and have the title made in their names. He agreed to do this, and hearing of a valuable farm for sale in Shelby County, Ohio—near Sidney, the county seat—he visited that place and bought the farm, having the title made to his children. He then sold his property in Cincinnati and purchased a valuable house and lot in Sidney for his own residence, the title of which he also secured to his colored children, and another house and lot for their mother, the mulatto woman, making the title to her. He then removed to Sidney, and there spent the remainder of his days. I had much to do in these transactions, feeling an interest in these helpless children, and being anxious that they should be provided for and their rights secured while the old man lived.

Before Major Phillips moved to Sidney, he expressed a wish to get from Mississippi the thirteen slaves whom he had left there with his wife, from whom he had separated, and bring them to Ohio and emancipate them. I encouraged him to act in this matter at once, and to secure their liberty without delay. I wrote letters from him to his attorney at Yazoo City, who had charge of his business in Mississippi, and whom Phillips represented to be a worthy man and his particular friend. This attorney had previously informed him that his former wife had married a reckless young man, contrary to law and to their contract, and that he could legally take possession of the slaves.

It was advisable that the major should be there in person to take possession of them, and he asked me to go with him and assist him in bringing the company to Ohio. He said he had many warm friends at Yazoo and in the neighborhood of his former home, but they were slaveholders, and might oppose his bringing the slaves to a free State.

The major was quite feeble, and having lost the use of his right arm from the effects of paralysis in

that side, he had to have a servant to wait on him
and to dress and undress him, consequently he
could not have the oversight of the thirteen
slaves on their journey up the river, and he
wished me to see that they were properly cared
for on their way to Cincinnati. I agreed to accompany him, and we made the journey down the river
together. I had some business in New Orleans
which I wished to attend to, and the major also
had some business matters there, which he wished
me to look after for him, as he expected to be
detained at Yazoo City a week or two, having other
business to engage his attention, besides getting
possession of his slaves. So we parted at Vicksburg; I went on to New Orleans and Phillips to
Yazoo City, where he was to await my return.

I had a power of attorney to enable me to transact
the major's business in New Orleans, and at other
points on the river. I expected to be detained two
or three weeks, and the major thought that he
could have his business transacted at Yazoo City
and his negroes in readiness by the time I returned.

At Vicksburg, several passengers were added
to our company, among whom was a gentleman
who lived on a cotton plantation near that place,
and had another plantation in Louisiana. He
owned a large number of slaves. Our list of passengers represented almost every class of society.
The boat was a large and popular steamer, and
passengers had come aboard at nearly all the principal towns on the Mississippi River. They were
all strangers to me, and being nearly all Southern

slaveholders were not congenial companions for me. There was much drinking, card-playing and loud, profane talking in the cabin, and I frequently seated myself out on the guard-deck where it was more pleasant, and took out my pocket Bible, my daily companion. Here I could read, undisturbed, and be away from the smell of whisky, and the sound of the card-players' profane language.

Several passengers having often noticed me sitting alone, reading my Bible, introduced themselves to me, professing to be religionists. They said they inferred from my dress and address, that I was a Quaker, and they wished to make my acquaintance. I told them that I was a member of the religious Society of Friends, called Quakers—a name given in derision by our persecutors in the early rise of the society. The name Quaker did not appear on our records. They asked many questions in regard to Friends. I endeavored to explain our principles and testimonies, dwelling most on our testimony against slavery. I told them that a Friend could not own a slave anywhere, and retain his right of membership in our society. This generally brought on a discussion about slavery. I discussed the subject mildly but candidly, and they treated me with much kindness and respect; often telling me, however, that if I lived in the South, I would change my notions about slavery.

I informed them that I had been brought up in the South, in the midst of slavery; that I was well acquainted with the system, and its deleterious

effects and influences. Quite a company had gathered around to listen to the conversation, and
though I spoke freely of my abhorrence of slavery,
I used mild and respectful language, and no one
appeared to be offended.

After this interview I was treated with marked
respect by several of the professors of religion who
had taken part in the conversation. They seemed
to want to know more about the Quakers, and made
many inquiries concerning them. I answered their
questions to the best of my ability, and endeavored
to explain Friends' testimonies on the subject of
war and spirituous liquors, our manner of worship,
our views in regard to outward forms and ceremo-
nies, types and shadows of Christ, the substance,
etc., and generally ended by referring to slavery as
contrary to the teachings of the gospel which they
professed to believe.

One day the cotton planter, who lived near
Vicksburg, came and took a seat by me, and commenced talking on the subject of slavery. He said
he was a member of the Methodist Church, and he
believed there was not much difference between the
Methodists and Quakers on doctrinal matters, except on the subject of slavery; then he undertook
to justify slavery by the Bible, referring to the Jew-
ish servitude, and quoting many passages from the
Old Testament in support of his views.

I heard him through patiently, and then replied
that Methodists differed on that subject. John
Wesley was an anti-slavery man, and some of the
Methodists in the North had strong anti-slavery

sentiments. I told him that the Bible was the best anti-slavery book we had, and turning to it, I read several passages to him, and asked him how he could reconcile slavery with them.

He seemed confused and evaded direct answers to my questions, saying "Ah, Brother Coffin, if you lived in the South you would soon change your opinions about slavery."

I told him that the longer I lived in the South the stronger were my convictions of the sin of slavery, and then referred to the separation of husbands and wives, parents and children, and other evils contrary to the teachings of the gospel.

The planter replied that he thought it was wrong to separate husbands and wives. He owned a good many slaves, but had tried to keep husband and wife together. "But sometimes," said he, "they separate of their own accord. I have a man and his wife who had lived together many years, but some time ago they quarreled; the man became jealous of his wife and refused to live with her. I took them out into my orchard, and cut two bundles of peach-tree sprouts, and made them wear them out on each other. They both got severely whipped, and it cured them; they lived together very peaceably after that." He laughed heartily at the recollection.

I said: "Perhaps the woman was innocent. I have known instances where the master or the overseer was the guilty one. A slave woman has no power to protect herself; according to your law, her body belongs, not to herself, but to some one else, and is subject to the will of the master or overseer. It may be that thou hast punished the innocent. This good book which I hold in my hand says that we should do to others as we would have others do to us. Now, suppose that thou and thy wife should have some difficulty of the kind, and I had it in my power to compel you to whip each other in the same way—wouldst thou not think that I was a cruel tyrant?"

He said again: "Ah, Brother Coffin, if you were to come down South and live there a few years, you would soon get over these tender notions."

"Yes," I replied, "and deny the teachings of this precious book—a result to which slavery leads."

He replied: "I see that we do not agree on the subject of slavery," and left me, but continued to be friendly as long as we traveled together. He left the boat, some distance above New Orleans, opposite his plantation.

Before reaching New Orleans, I inquired of some of the passengers with whom I had become acquainted, whether there was a temperance house of entertainment in the city, saying that if there was, I wished to patronize it, as I intended to stay a week or two. One gentleman said that there was a respectable boarding-house, called the Farmer's Hotel, where there was no bar, a place where country merchants often stopped, and which was kept by a worthy man. He gave me the number and street, and on my arrival in the city I went directly to that house. Finding it to be a comfortable house, I took my quarters there during my stay in New Orleans.

I had corresponded with Judge Cage, the gentleman previously mentioned, who had sent a colored boy to my care, some years before, and had informed him of my prospect of being in New Orleans some time that spring. He lived some distance from the city, but desiring to see me in regard to the boy, and other matters concerning the rest of his brother's children, he requested me, as soon as I arrived in the city, to call on his nephew, a lawyer, whose address he gave me. This nephew, he said, would inform him at once, and he would come to the city to see me.

Accordingly, I called at the lawyer's office, and gave him his uncle's—the judge's—letter to read. He appeared pleased to see me, and treated me with much cordiality and kindness. He said that he had often heard me spoken of, and knew that his uncle was very anxious to see me, and would come to the city as soon as he learned of my arrival. He then introduced me to several gentlemen, prominent citizens of New Orleans, and kindly tendered his services in looking after Major Phillips' business. I availed myself of this offer, and received much aid from him. Having to examine the records of the court, in regard to some of Major Phillips' business, he accompanied me to the Court-House, introduced me to the clerk and other officers of the court. All of these gentlemen treated me with kindness and respect, so that I felt at home among them. This state of things was quite different from that which

43

my friends in Cincinnati had pictured for me, when they heard of my intended trip to New Orleans. They had tried to discourage me from going down the river with Major Phillips, saying that it would be at the risk of my life. I was extensively known in the South as a notorious abolitionist, and I might be taken by a mob and shot or hanged to a tree— as the slaveholders had often threatened to hang abolitionists. I told these foreboders of danger that I was not troubled with fears on that score—I was a Southern man and understood Southern character. I had always traveled in the South, or in any other section of the country where I had tangible business, without fear, and had always been kindly treated. I never carried weapons, and never visited saloons or theaters, but associated with the better class of people, who would not allow a man of peace to be maltreated. I told them that my wife had not tried to discourage me from going to New Orleans. This was no new advice ; I had often been cautioned about going South, but when duty or business called me, I never hesitated, and though in all my travels in the Southern States, I had spoken my mind freely on the subject of slavery, I had endeavored to speak in the spirit of love and kindness, and had never been molested.

As soon as Judge Cage received information of my arrival at New Orleans, he came to see me. This was our first meeting. I found the old man to be noble looking, and a perfect gentleman in his manners. He was a man of wealth and high standing in that part of the country. He manifested a great deal of interest in the boy he had sent to me some years before, to be educated, and spoke of the rest of the family of his unfortunate brother, as he called him.

This brother had died some years before, leaving a large family of children, who were slaves, according to the law of Louisiana. They followed the condition of their mother who, though nearly white, and a perfect lady, was a slave. I have referred to this case previously. The judge told me that his brother, who had been his partner in business, left a considerable estate when he died, which he wished his children to have. As they were not legal heirs in Louisiana, and could not inherit his property there, he had intended to send them to the North, have them educated, and buy property for them there. He intended to have his sons taught trades, and had sent the older ones to the East before he died. The whole family came into the judge's hands as property when their father died, and he told me he intended to carry out the wishes of his brother.

The younger girls were then in school in New Orleans. The judge furnished me some means to continue the boy, in my care, at school, and requested me to put him to a trade when he came out of school. After our business was finished, the judge introduced me to several of his friends, bankers and other prominent business men.

While in New Orleans I called at the banking-house of old Jacob Barker, and introduced myself to that well-known financier and remarkable man, having had some knowledge of his reputation and history. He was formerly of Nantucket, but had lived a number of years in the city of New York, where he was engaged in an extensive trading and shipping business—owning a fleet of trading vessels.

He accumulated an immense fortune, and during the war of 1812 he loaned to the Government a large sum of money. He met with some reverses, and having in some of his trading operations taken a large tract of land in Louisiana, to secure a debt, he moved to that State and settled in New Orleans, in the year 1834. He had lived there twenty-four years, when I visited him.

On learning that my name was Coffin, and that I was of Nantucket descent, he seemed much pleased to meet me, and invited me to his house. He was quite an old man, but full of life and activity, being blessed with the preservation of his mental and physical faculties to a greater degree than is usually accorded to persons of his age. He was still engaged in banking business. He owned a number of slaves and had tried various experiences with them—had settled some on his lands and had several families living in houses that he owned in the city—yet he professed to be opposed to the system of of slavery. He had sent several of his slaves to the East to be educated, and two to Europe—one to England and one to Germany. The law of Louisiana would not permit slaves to be educated in that State. Barker took me to visit several families of his slaves, who lived in com-

fortable houses provided with all the furniture necessary.

They all appeared glad to see the old man. He
told me that he had bought many of his slaves, out
of pity, and with a hope of bettering their condition.

Barker was thoroughly versed in the law, and
had rescued several slaves that were illegally held
in bondage, but notwithstanding his kindness and
humane endeavors, I could not sanction his holding
property in human beings, and advised him to
secure their liberty to them while he lived. I do not
know that he acted on my advice, but he and all
other slaveholders were relieved of responsibility
in the matter, a few years later, by the proclamation of President Lincoln.

One morning Jacob Barker took me to the slave
pen, or auction room, where a large drove of slaves
were to be sold that day. There were men and
women, of various shades, from the complexion of
ebony black with woolly hair, flat nose and thick
lips, to the fair complexion, with light wavy hair
and delicate features. Several handsome young
women were in the company, and these were
arranged on raised benches to show to the best
advantage.

The auction had not yet commenced, but a number of men who wished to purchase were examining
the stock. They selected such slaves as they
thought would suit them, and took them through a
close and critical examination—as I would a horse
which I wished to purchase. Their limbs, bodies,

and teeth were examined, and many questions were asked in regard to the quality of the article under notice. The purchasers gave utterance to many profane and indecent expressions, plainly evincing that their natures were rough and coarse and low— that they had lost the higher and more refined sentiments of humanity. This company of slaves—I was informed—were from Virginia and Kentucky, and were considered quite valuable, as they all had the appearance of being sound and healthy. Their countenances were sad, and while they were under examination, they looked with expressions of aversion and dread upon those who wished to buy them. Many of them, no doubt, had been separated from wives or husbands or children, and were now to be sold and taken to rice swamps or cotton fields or cane plantations, there to toil beneath the lash of a cruel task-master, until life left their suffering bodies. When I gazed upon them and pictured to myself the fate in store for them, I longed to give them passage on the Underground Railroad to Canada. I turned from the scene in sorrow and disgust, before the bidding commenced, and made my way back to my boarding-house. There I again met my Methodist friend, the planter from Vicksburg, who had stopped at his plantation, some distance up the river. After completing his business there, he had come on to New Orleans, and had taken quarters in the house where I was staying. He accosted me as an old acquaintance, calling me "Brother Coffin," and seemed to be glad to meet me again. He introduced me to a merchant from Arkansas—who was stopping in the same house—as Brother Coffin, of Cincinnati, who also was a merchant and produce dealer, but who would not deal in negroes. He added that I was a Quaker and opposed to slavery.

I replied: "That is true—I have been opposed to slavery from my childhood to the present day. I was brought up in the South in the midst of slavery, and when I was a little boy learned to hate it. I saw a coffle of slaves driven past my father's premises on their way to the South, to be sold like cattle in the public market, and my childish sympathy and indignation were aroused. Just such a scene have I witnessed in the slave market in this city to-day."

I then described what I had seen, and told how it operated on my feelings to see human beings—the image of God—chattelized and sold like brutes, or put upon the auction block and sold as common articles of merchandise, and added: "I can not see that any one who professes to be a Christian can sanction such things."

My Methodist friend, addressing himself to the Arkansas merchant, said: "Brother Coffin and I do not read the Bible alike. As we came down the river I tried to convince him that the Bible sanctioned slavery, but he does not appear to be convinced."

The merchant said: "The Quakers are good honest folks; I like to deal with them. I go to Philadelphia every spring to buy goods—have just now returned from there, and come here to buy sugar and molasses. I tell you, Mr. Compton, they are good folks, but they have queer notions about slavery. I don't agree with them about that, but think they are nice people. I like to hear them say 'thee' and 'thou.' I can tell a Quaker by his dress, and I always love to meet one. The Quaker women, Mr. Compton, wore the prettiest bonnets I ever saw—the young women wore silk bonnets without any feathers or flowers about them, and they looked so nice and plain. I really think I would like to have a Quaker woman for a wife. I have lost my wife since I moved to Arkansas—I want another one, and think that a Quaker woman would make a good mistress over my negroes."

I said: "Quaker women are generally abolitionists and opposed to slavery, and if one is worth having for a wife, she would not marry a slaveholder."

"Oh, they would soon lose their notions about slavery if they lived down here," the merchant replied, then went on to say that he had formerly lived in South Carolina, and had known some Yankee girls who came down there to teach. They were abolitionists in sentiment, but soon lost that notion and married slaveholders and made first-rate mistresses."

I became tired of his palaver and turned the conversation to business matters, then soon withdrew. That afternoon I went into a large commission store or warehouse, where I had some business. This firm received large consignments of produce from up the river, and also sold large quantities of cotton for the planters. While I was in the office a country planter, who appeared to be one of their customers, came in. It seemed that he had been at the slave auction, for as soon as he entered one of the firm said:

"Well, Mr. S——, did you buy all the women you wanted?"

"No," he replied, "I intended to buy five, but I bought only three. I have five men who have no wives, and I intended to purchase a wife apiece for them, but the women sold so d——d high, I bought only three."

"You ought to have bought one apiece for your men," rejoined the merchant.

"I intend to get two more," replied the planter; "but I think I can do better nearer home."

The next day while I was alone in the sitting-room of my boarding-house, reading, my friend the Vicksburg planter, accompanied by his friend the merchant, came in, and, seating themselves near me, broached the subject of slavery again. They spoke in a friendly, persuasive manner as if they wished to convince me of my error of opinion, and represented the happy condition of the slaves, saying that all their wants were provided for by their masters—they were fed and clothed, doctored when sick, and had no care assigned to them. "Yes," I said; "they even have wives assigned to them by their kind master, whether they want them or not. It is a matter of profit to the master, and the slave can·have no choice in the matter; he must take the

woman assigned to him." I then related what I had
heard the day before, of the planter buying wives
for his men, and went on to say: "No doubt these
five men, whom the planter had recently bought
out of a drove of slaves, from Virginia or Kentucky, had been sold away from their wives and
children, whom they loved, and the women he
bought for them had probably been forced away
from husbands and children that were near and dear
to them. While their hearts were weighed down
with grief, they were brought to this market and
sold for wives for men whom they had never seen
or heard of, and for whom they could not possibly
have any affection. How can these men and
women fix their affections upon each other under
such circumstances? But it is not a question of
choice with them; they are doomed by their master's will to live together in violation of their own
feelings and of God's command—to live in a state of
adultery, for marriages among slaves are not legalized. To whom will this sin be charged?" They
evaded the question but seemed to feel the force
of my argument. I continued to speak of the horrors and evils of slavery, giving instances that had
come under my observation, while living in a slave
State, speaking of the separation of families, etc.
This phase of slavery they admitted to be wrong,
but still justified the system. Notwithstanding our
discussion of the subject from different standpoints,
these two slaveholders manifested kind feeling
toward me as long as we continued together, frequently introducing me to others as their Quaker

friend. Thus, instead of being mobbed or hung, as some of my friends had feared, I was treated with kindness and respect by all with whom I came in contact—although I often expressed my sentiments freely on the subject of slavery.

After closing my business in New Orleans, I took passage up the river, stopping at Baton Rouge, Natches and Vicksburg, to attend to business for Major Phillips. At Vicksburg I took boat up the Yazoo River to Yazoo City, one hundred and twenty miles distant, where I was to join Major Phillips.

On my arrival in Yazoo City I went to the hotel where I expected to meet the major, but to my surprise found that he was gone, and learned that the thirteen slaves he had come to take away were in jail, awaiting a decision of the court. Major Phillips had left a note with the hotel-keeper, directing me to call on his attorney, who would give me all necessary directions regarding his business. I went immediately to the office of the attorney, who received me very cordially and said that he was glad I had arrived. He had been anxiously looking for me, hoping that I would come in time to take possession of the major's slaves as soon as the decision was made in court—which decision he had no doubt would be in the major's favor. He then gave me an account of what had occurred.

The major's former wife, as has already been mentioned, had married again—a reckless young man, whose object, no doubt, was to get possession of her property. When the major arrived in Yazoo, and sent out an order for the thirteen slaves he had left on her plantation, she and the young man she called her husband refused to give them up, although they had no right or title to them, and the young man swore that he would kill any person who attempted to take them away.

Then Major Phillips got out a writ of replevin for his property. This was placed in the hands of the sheriff, who took a posse of men, went out to the farm—several miles distant—and brought the slaves into Yazoo City, and put them into jail for safe-keeping.

The young man who claimed the slaves as the property of himself and wife followed them into town, and employed lawyers to defend his claim. He was a desperate fellow, was in the habit of drinking freely, and, on this occasion, raved about the streets, displaying his pistols, and threatening to shoot Major Phillips the moment he got sight of him. Knowing the character of this desperate fellow, and knowing also that the major was brave and could not be intimidated, the major's friends managed to keep him out of sight, for they were sure somebody would be killed if the two came in contact. Hearing that this young man had been hunting for Phillips all day, with intent to shoot him, and that in the evening he had gathered a posse of ruffians, they feared that he intended to mob the house where Phillips was stopping and kill the old man, so they contrived to get the major away privately. He went to Vicksburg, and would await my arrival there, with the negroes. He left an order for the sheriff to deliver the slaves to me.

The day after I arrived in Yazoo City, the case of the right of property in the negroes was brought before court. The lawyers employed by the young man to oppose Phillips' claim picked a flaw in the proceedings. The sheriff had neglected to do his duty; the writ had not been served in due time, according to law. It was returnable, according to date, the day before it was served, therefore it was out of date when served. This caused a long debate between the lawyers. Major Phillips' lawyers contended warmly against the quibble raised by the other lawyers, but the judge decided that the sheriff had neglected his duty and that the proceedings were illegal. He then dismissed the case.

Phillips was gone, and there was no one to renew the writ, so the slaves were brought out of jail and delivered to that wicked young man who claimed to own them. They looked sad and disappointed; they had hoped to go to Ohio and be free, but found themselves doomed to return to bondage. The man mounted his horse, cracked his whip, and started them back to the farm, as though he were driving a drove of cattle. I felt sorry for them, and regretted that it was not in my power to rescue them from the hands of that tyrant. I now felt anxious to leave Yazoo City, which was said to be one of the worst sinks of iniquity in the State of Mississippi, but there was no boat. The Vicksburg packet had passed up the river that day and I must await its return, the next morning, so I reluctantly made up my mind to pass another night in the midst of the drinking, swearing, and dissipation of every kind that abounded.

That evening, while sitting on the sidewalk, under the awning, talking to the hotel-keeper, two colored ladies passed by us, dressed in rich silks, and adorned with jewelry. I said to the hotel-keeper: "I suppose that those persons are free?"

"No," he replied, "they are both slaves, but are kept as mistresses by two of our wealthy merchants."

I asked: "Is such a state of society permitted here?"

He answered, "Oh, yes; most of our merchants, and other gentlemen of wealth and high standing, keep such women. The practice is quite common in our community."

He then spoke of a wealthy gentleman living a few miles out of town, who had a wife and a family of children. He owned several plantations, and on one of them he kept a black wife, who had several children.

"And does his white wife know it?" I asked.

"Yes," was the reply, "but she can't help it, and I don't think she makes any fuss about it. One of his colored sons is his carriage driver. That gentleman stands fair in this community."

I spoke of the demoralizing effect of such examples upon the lower classes and upon the young. I felt depressed in spirit when I reflected upon such a state of society and the wickedness that abounded in the South. It appeared to me that the cup of iniquity was about full; that a dark cloud was hanging over that land and must soon burst.

I was anxious to get away from that Sodom of debauchery. It was known in Yazoo City that I was there as the major's agent to take possession of his slaves, if the court decided in his favor, and conduct them to Cincinnati. I had been treated with kindness and respect by the officers of the court and all others with whom I came in contact, but as the mob spirit had been manifested toward Major Phillips, I knew not what the feeling of his enemies might be toward his agent, or what demonstration might be made against me.

I was favored, however, to rest quietly and peacefully through the night, and the next morning I took passage on the Vicksburg packet. There were several passengers who had come aboard at other points up the river, among them a Baptist minister who introduced himself to me. He said he always liked to meet a Quaker, and asked many questions, which I answered briefly. He informed me that he was a Baptist clergyman, and said that he was always glad to meet with a professor of religion. I told him that I was also glad to meet with such, but I had seen very little of the fruits of true religion in that part of the country, He admitted that the fruit was not very abundant. The boat was delayed an hour or more after I went aboard, taking on bales of cotton and other freight. The deck-hands were all slaves, and the mate was hurrying them and swearing at them at a fearful rate, though they appeared to be doing all that they could.

The preacher and I were sitting on the guard-deck in front of the cabin, and I said to him that the mate appeared to be a cruel tyrant.

He replied: "Oh, those lazy niggers must be hurried."

When the freight was nearly all aboard and a number of passengers had come, one of the deck-hands, a slave man who lived in that town, asked the mate to let him run up to his house and get a clean shirt, as the one he wore was torn and very dirty. He said that he would be gone only a few minutes, but the mate cursed him and refused to let him go. Shortly afterward the mate went on the boat with some of the hands to move some of the freight, and while he was aboard, the slave man started on a run to his house to get his shirt. The mate saw him and hallooed to him to come back, making use of dreadful oaths and threats. The man replied that he would return in a few minutes and ran on toward his home. The mate rushed after him, calling on some of his acquaintances among the passengers for assistance. They sprang out and joined in the chase.

The slave reached the hut where his wife and children lived, but before he had time to get his shirt, he was knocked down by the mate, who had a club in his hand, and was bound. He was brought back to the boat with his arms tied behind him and a rope around his neck, while the blood trickled over his body from a gash that had been cut in his head when he was knocked down. The mate had picked up a piece of barrel hoop with which he struck him at nearly every step, using at the same time the most abusive language in reply to the begging and crying of the poor slave. It was, to me, a most heart-sickening spectacle.

The mate was a younger man than the slave he was beating so cruelly, but what of that? The negro was a poor chattel whom no law protected; he had no rights that a white man was bound to respect. The mate and his company dragged the poor fellow aboard and tied him to a post on the lower deck.

The freight and passengers were now all on·board, and the boat started down the river.

All seemed quiet for a mile or two, until we had got fairly under headway, then I discovered that the cabin passengers were all in a stir and going down stairs to the lower deck. I asked the Baptist minister what was going on, and he replied:

"Oh, nothing; only that nigger is to be whipped and they are going down to see the fun. Will you go down?"

"No, indeed," I replied; "it is the mate that ought to be punished, and I hope that he will not be allowed to punish that poor man any more."

"He needs a good thrashing for his impudence," said the preacher; "he even tried to resist, and they had to drag him on the boat."

He then followed to see the fun, as he called it, leaving me alone in the men's part of the cabin; a few ladies remained in the ladies' apartment.

44

The whipping soon commenced and continued for— what seemed to me—a long time. I could hear the blows but was too much agitated to count them, for the cries of the poor slave pierced my ears and stirred every feeling of humanity in my breast. Toward the last his cries and moans became faint and weak. I could not sit still, nor get out of hearing of the dreadful sounds, and in my agitation I walked the room, thinking: "How long, O Lord, how long will such cruelty be permitted on the earth?" Soon after the whipping was over, dinner was announced, but my feelings were so wrought upon that I could taste little. I retired to my room and sought comfort in prayer. I had often been in the South, but never before had been so sensible of the Egyptian darkness that overhung the land. I was deeply impressed with the belief that the day was not far distant when the fetters of slavery would be broken.

Some time in the afternoon the boat stopped to take on wood, and the deck-hands were hurried ashore. The poor, tortured slave was driven out, among them, and my heart bled afresh in sympathy. His shirt was soaked with blood all over his back, and he appeared weak and exhausted; it was with difficulty that he could carry a stick of wood. I learned that his shirt had been taken off before the whipping, and that his back had been gashed and cut to pieces, then washed with salt and water. The Baptist preacher was a slaveholder, and justified the whipping; he said that slaves must be made to obey, otherwise there was no managing them. I protested against such inhumanity and cruelty, but felt that it was most prudent to avoid entering into a discussion on the subject of slavery. I felt no freedom in conversation with any one on board, and was truly thankful when we reached Vicksburg, and I was able to get out of hearing of the profane language to which I had been obliged to listen on that boat. Major Phillips was much chagrined with the way matters had terminated in Yazoo City, and seemed determined to renew his efforts to get possession of his slaves and bring them to Ohio. We took passage on a boat for Memphis, where we stopped one day, as I had some business to attend to, and then went aboard the Memphis and Cincinnati packet. I reached home in safety, and I was thankful that I was permitted to breathe again the free air of Ohio. Major Phillips made further efforts, through his attorneys at Yazoo City, to obtain his slaves, but he grew more feeble, and died before it was accomplished.

CHAPTER XV.

THE MOB SPIRIT IN CINCINNATI—DESTRUCTION OF THE
PHILANTHROPIST PRESS IN 1836—DEMONSTRATION
OF PRO-SLAVERY FEELING IN 1841—A DISGRACE-
FUL RIOT—THE SCANLAN MOB.

THE mobs caused by the pro-slavery element
in Cincinnati occurred before I moved to the
city, but the following accounts of them are compiled from authentic records and narratives.

I first refer to the demonstration of the mob
spirit, exhibited when the office of the *Philanthropist* was broken into by a crowd of men, and the
press destroyed.

"The 'Philanthropist' was the organ of the Ohio Anti-Slavery
Society, and was edited by James'G. Birney, a stanch abolitionist.
It was first published at New Richmond, twenty miles from Cincinnati, but in April, 1836, after a few numbers had been issued,
the establishment was removed to Cincinnati.

"The pro-slavery spirit was strong in the city, but no demonstration was made against the paper at first.   The subscription list
of the 'Philanthropist' numbered 1,700, and was rapidly increasing at the time of the disturbance.   Testimony was given almost
daily of the fair and manly and respectful conduct of it.   From
the time of its removal to Cincinnati, there was not the least show
of molestation till the 12th of July.   At midnight a band of men,
amounting to thirty or forty in number, including those who stood
as sentries at different points of the street, made an assault on the

premises of Achilles Pugh, the printer, scaled a high wall by which the lot was inclosed, and with the aid of a ladder and plank mounted the roof of the press office. They then made their way through a window on the roof into the room below—intimidated into silence, by threats of bodily violence, a boy who was asleep there—covered his head with the bed-clothes to prevent him from seeing who were the perpetrators—tore up the paper that was prepared for that week's number of the 'Philanthropist,' as well as a larger part of the impression of an omitted number that had not yet been mailed, destroyed the ink, dismantled the press and carried away many of its principal parts. Whilst the depredation was going on within doors, a watch of the confederates was stationed in the street, near the door of Achilles Pugh's dwelling-house, to prevent him from giving the alarm. A remarkable feature in the transaction is this—notwithstanding so long time (nearly or quite two hours) was occupied in doing the mischief, and that Pugh's premises lay on one of the principal streets of the city, and that the noise and confusion made by the rioters were loud enough to wake many of the neighbors (who were mysteriously admonished to be quiet), still no interference was offered by the night watch of the city to prevent the outrage.

"Although the names of the actors in this scene were not ascertained sufficiently to authorize their publication, yet there is reason to believe that some of the leaders were persons of wealth and reputed respectability who would never, before this, have been suspected of engaging in such a transaction. The work was done, as it is supposed, by their dependents and hirelings. Next morning, as soon as the damages could be repaired, the business of the office went on as usual. Whatever the character and designs of those committing the trespass were, it was plainly to be discerned that there was a plan to intimidate those concerned in the press."

This act of depredation seemed to be the expression of a state of popular feeling existing in the city. Placards were posted on the corners of the streets warning the abolitionists to beware, and several of the city papers expressed the same sentiments, though in more guarded terms. The excitement appeared to increase, instead of diminishing, and many threats of violence were made against the editor and publisher of the *Philanthropist*.

A public meeting was held at the Lower Market House, and a series of resolutions was adopted expressing abhorrence of the principles advocated by the abolitionists, and warning those connected with the *Philanthropist* to desist from publishing it in the city of Cincinnati. These resolutions were formally presented to the Executive Committee of the Ohio Anti-Slavery Society, and the members composing that committee returned a formal answer, stating their resolve to continue the publication of their paper, and giving their reasons.

This answer appeared in the city papers on the morning of July 30. The following account from the Cincinnati *Gazette* relates the disturbances that took place that night.

"DESTRUCTION OF PROPERTY.

"On Saturday night, July 30, very soon after dark, a concourse of citizens assembled at the corner of Main and Seventh Streets, in this city, and, upon a short consultation, broke open the printing-office of the 'Philanthropist,' the abolition paper, scattered the type into the streets, tore down the presses and completely dismantled the office. It was owned by Achilles Pugh, a peaceable and orderly printer, who published the 'Philanthropist' for the Anti-Slavery Society of Ohio. From the printing-office the crowd went to the house of Achilles Pugh, where they supposed there were other printing materials, but found none, nor offered any violence. Then to the Messrs. Donaldsons, where ladies only were at home. The residence of Mr. Birney, the editor, was then visited; no person was at home but a youth, upon whose explanations the house was left undisturbed. A shout was raised for Dr. Colby's, and the concourse returned to Main Street, proposing to pile up the contents of the office in the street, and make a bonfire of them. Joseph Graham mounted the pile and advised against burning it, lest the houses near might take fire. A portion of the press was then dragged down Main Street, broken up and thrown into the river. The 'Exchange' was then visited and refreshments taken; after which the concourse again went up Main Street to about opposite the 'Gazette' office. Some suggestions were hinted that it should be demolished, but the hint was overruled. An attack was then made on the residences of some blacks in Church Alley; two guns were fired upon the assailants, and they recoiled. It was supposed that one man was wounded, but that was not the case. It was some time before a rally could be again made, several voices declaring that they did not wish to endanger themselves. A second attack was made, the houses were found empty, and their interior contents destroyed. It was now about midnight, when the party parading down Main Street was addressed by the Mayor, who had been a silent spectator of the destruction of the printing-office. He told them that they might as well now disperse. A dispersion to a considerable extent followed; but various other disturbances took place through the night, of the magnitude and particulars of which we are not advised."

There were some demonstrations of the public feeling next day—Sabbath—but no serious disturbances.

Several mobs collected on Monday night, but were prevented from violence and dispersed by the city authorities, and the volunteer companies acting under their orders.

The excitement died out without any more serious demonstrations. The publication of the *Philanthropist* was afterward resumed and continued for many years.

THE MOB OF 1841.

The next outbreak of violence, which disgraced the city of Cincinnati, occurred in the early part of of September, 1841. The *Daily Gazette*, of September 6, gives the following account of it :

"This city has been in a most alarming condition for several days, and from about eight o'clock on Friday evening until about three o'clock yesterday morning, almost entirely at the mercy of a lawless mob, ranging in number from two to fifteen hundred.

"On Tuesday evening last, a quarrel took place near the corner of Sixth Street and Broadway, between a party of Irishmen and some negroes, in which blows were exchanged and other weapons, if not fire-arms, used. Some two or three of each party were wounded.

"On Wednesday night the quarrel was renewed in some way, and some time after midnight a party of excited men, armed with clubs, etc., attacked a house occupied as a negro boarding-house, on McAlister Street, demanding the surrender of a negro who they said had fled into the house and was there secreted, and uttering the most violent threats against the house and the negroes in general. Several of the adjoining houses were occupied by negro families, including women and children. The violence increased and was resisted by those in or about the houses. An engagement took place, several were wounded on each side, and some say guns and pistols were discharged from the house. The interference of some gentlemen in the neighborhood succeeded in restoring quiet, after about three-quarters of an hour, when a watchman appeared. But it is singular that this violent street disturbance elicited no report to the police, no arrest— indeed, that the Mayor remained ignorant of the affair until late in the day, when he casually heard of it.

"On Thursday night another rencounter took place in the neighborhood of the Lower Market, between some young men and boys, and some negroes, in which one or two boys were badly wounded, as it was supposed, with knives.

"On Friday, during the day there was considerable excitement, threats of violence and lawless outbreaking were indicated in various ways, and came to the ears of the police and of the negroes. Attacks were expected upon the negro residences in McAlister, Sixth and New Streets. The negroes armed themselves, and the knowledge of this increased the excitement.

But we do not know that it produced any known measure of precaution on the part of the police to preserve the peace of the city.

"Before eight o'clock in the evening, a mob, the principal organization of which, we understand, was arranged in Kentucky, openly assembled in Fifth Street Market, unmolested by the police or citizens. The number of this mob, as they deliberately marched from their rendezvous toward Broadway and Sixth Street, is variously estimated, but the number increased as they progressed. They were armed with clubs, stones, etc. Reaching the scene of operations, with shouts and blasphemous imprecations, they attacked a negro confectionary on Broadway, and demolished the doors and windows. This attracted an immense crowd. Savage yells were uttered to encourage the mob onward to the general attack upon the negroes. About this time the Mayor came up and addressed the people, exhorting them to peace and obedience to law. The savage yell was instantly raised, 'Down with him.' 'Run him off,' was shouted, intermixed with horrid imprecations, and exhortations to the mob to move onward.

"They advanced to the attack with stones, etc., and were repeatedly fired upon by the negroes. The mob scattered, but immediately rallied again, and again were in like manner, repulsed. Men were wounded on both sides and carried off, and many reported dead. The negroes rallied several times, advanced upon the crowd, and most unjustifiably fired down the street into it, causing a great rush in various directions. These things were repeated until past one o'clock, when a party procured an iron six-pounder from near the river, loaded it with boiler punchings, etc., and hauled it to the ground, against the exhortations of the Mayor and others. It was posted on Broadway, and pointed down Sixth Street. The yells continued, but there was a partial cessation of firing. Many of the negroes had fled to the hills The attack upon houses was recommenced with firing of guns on both sides, which continued during most of the night, and exaggerated rumors of the killed and wounded filled the streets. The cannon was discharged several times. About two o'clock a portion of the military, upon the call of the Mayor, proceeded to the scene of disorder and succeeded in keeping the mob at bay. In the morning, and throughout the day, several blocks, including the battle-ground, were surrounded by sentinels, and kept under

45

martial law—keeping within the negroes there, and adding to them such as were brought during the day, seized without particular charge, by parties who scoured the city, assuming the authority of the law.

"A meeting of citizens was held at 'the Court-House, on Saturday morning, at which the Mayor presided. This meeting was addressed by the Mayor, Judge Reed, Mr. Piatt, Sheriff Avery and Mr. Hart. They resolved to observe the law, to discountenance mobs, invoked the aid of the authorities to stay the violence, and pledged themselves to exertion in aid of the civil authority to arrest and place within reach of the law the negroes who wounded the two white boys on Columbia Street; that the Township Trustees enforce the law of 1807, requiring security of negroes, pledging themselves to enforce it to the very letter, until the city is relieved of the effect of 'modern abolitionism,' assuring our 'Southern brethren' to carry out that act in good faith—and to deliver 'up, under the law of Congress, forthwith' every negro who escapes from his master and comes within our borders. They requested the Mayor, Sheriff, and the civil authorities to proceed at once to the dwellings of the blacks and disarm them of all offensive weapons—and recommended search for offenders against the laws, immediate legal proceedings against them, and an efficient patrol to protect the persons and property of the blacks, during the existence of the present excitement, and until they give the bonds required by the act of 1807, or leave the city. They requested the parents and guardians of boys to keep them at home, or away from the scene of excitement. They resolved, 'That we view with abhorrence the proceedings of the abolitionists in our city, and that we repudiate their doctrines, and believe it to be the duty of every good citizen, by all lawful means, to discountenance ever man who lends them his assistance.' These resolutions adopted unanimously, and signed by the Mayor. They were afterward printed in handbills and posted in all parts of the city.

"The City Council also held a special session and passed resolutions invoking the united exertions of orderly citizens to the aid of the authorities to put down the violent commotion existing in the city, to preserve order and vindicate the law against the violence of an excited and lawless mob—requesting all officers, watchmen and firemen to unite for the arrest of the rioters and violators of law, and the Marshal to increase his deputies to any number required—not exceeding five hundred—to preserve life and protect property; requiring the Mayor and Marshal to call in the aid of the county militia to preserve order, and the captain of the watch to increase his force. These proceedings were posted in handbills. Intense excitement continued during the day, the mob and the leaders boldly occupying the streets without arrest, or any effort to arrest them, so far as we have heard.

"The negroes held a meeting in a church, and respectfully assured the Mayor and the citizens that they would use every effort to conduct themselves as orderly, industrious and peaceable people—to suppress any imprudent conduct among their population, and to ferret out all violation of order and law. They deprecated the practice of carrying about their persons any dangerous weapons, pledged themselves not to carry or keep any about their persons or houses, and expressed their readiness to surrender all such. They expressed their readiness to conform to the law of 1807, and give bond, or to leave within a specified time, and tendered their thanks to the Mayor, watch officers and gentlemen of the city, for the efforts made to save their property, their lives, their wives and their children.

"At three o'clock in the afternoon the Mayor, Sheriff, Marshal, and a portion of the police proceeded to the battle-ground and there, under the protection of the military, though in the presence of the mob, and so far controlled by them as to prevent the taking away of any negroes, upon their complying with the law, several negroes gave bond, and obtained the permission of the authorities to go away with sureties—some of our most respectable citizens—but were headed even within the military sentinels, and compelled to return within the ground. It was resolved to embody the male negroes and march them to jail for security, under the protection of the military and civil authorities.

"From two hundred and fifty to three hundred negroes, including sound and maimed, were with some difficulty marched off to jail, surrounded by the military and officers; and a dense mass of men, women and boys, confounding all distinction between the orderly and disorderly, accompanied with deafening yells.

"They were safely lodged, and still remained in prison, separated from their families. The crowd was in that way dispersed. Some then supposed that we should have a quiet night, but others, more observing, discovered that the law-less mob had determined on further violence, to be enacted immediately after nightfall. Citizens disposed to aid the author-ities were invited to assemble, enroll themselves, and organize for action. The military were ordered out, firemen were out, clothed with authority as a police band. About eighty citi-zens enrolled themselves as assistants of the Marshal, and acted during the night under his direction, in connection with Judge Torrence, who was selected by themselves. A portion of this force was mounted, and a troop of horse and several compa-nies of volunteer infantry continued on duty till near midnight. Some were then discharged to sleep upon their arms; others remained on duty till morning, guarding the jail, etc. As was anticipated, the mob, efficiently organized, early commenced operations, dividing their force and making attacks at different points, thus distracting the attention of the police. The first successful onset was made upon the printing establishment of the 'Philanthropist.' They succeeded in entering the establish-ment, breaking up the press, and running with it, amid savage yells, down through Main Street to the river, into which it was thrown.

"The military appeared in the alley near the office, interrupt-ing the mob for a short time. They escaped through by-ways, and, when the military retired, returned to their work of destruc-tion in the office, which they completed. Several houses were broken open in different parts of the city, occupied by negroes, and the windows, doors and furniture totally destroyed. From this work they were driven by the police, and finally dispersed from mere exhaustion, whether to remain quiet or to recruit their strength for renewed assault, we may know before this paper is circulated.

"Mortifying as is the declaration, truth requires us to acknowl-edge, that our city has been in a complete anarchy, controlled mostly by a lawless and violent mob for twenty-four hours, tramp-ling all law and authority under foot. We feel this degradation deeply—but so it is. It is impossible to learn the precise number killed and wounded, either of whites or among the negroes; prob-ably several were killed on both sides, and some twenty or thirty variously wounded, though but few dangerously.

"The authorities succeeded in arresting and securing about

forty of the mob, who are now in prison. Others were arrested, but were rescued or made their escape otherwise.

"Monday morning, three A. M.—No disturbances have occurred in our city during the night. The different military companies were stationed at various points through the city. Captain Taylor's troop of horse, together with a large number of citizens, formed themselves into companies of about thirty each, and kept up a patrol until about two o'clock, when the citizens generally retired, leaving the military on duty.

"Governor Corwin issued a proclamation on the 5th of September (the day on which the mob demonstrated), calling upon and commanding all people who might be in the city, to yield prompt obedience to the civil authorities engaged in the preservation of the peace, and enjoining upon all persons to abstain from all unlawful assemblages, or any act of violence against the persons or property of the citizens.

"There was no further disturbance ; and thus ended the disgraceful outbreak."

Some particulars not given in this account may be mentioned here. While these demonstrations were in progress it was reported that a number of negroes had fled to Walnut Hills, and were concealed at Lane Seminary. The mob expressed their intention to ferret them out, and breathed many threats against those who protected them. The students of Lane Seminary heard of this, and began preparations for defense. They formed a military company, under command of E. M. Gregory, and collected all the available weapons in the neighborhood. Governor Corwin, hearing of their organization, sent them a supply of fire-arms from the State Arsenal. The mob mustered a company two hundred strong, and started to make an attack on the "d——d abolition hole," as they called the seminary, but hearing of the warlike preparation of the students, they concluded that prudence was the better part of valor, and relinquished their purpose.

THE SCANLAN MOB.

Slaveholders from the South often brought their families to the North to spend the summer months, and the vicinity of this city was a favorite stopping place. In the summer of 1843, a man from New Orleans, named Scanlan, was spending the time here with his brother-in-law, whose name was Hawkins. He had with him his family, part of which consisted of a slave girl, nine or ten years old, named Lavinia. The mother of this girl, who was a slave in New Orleans, knew that, according to the law of Ohio, a slave brought to this State by his master was free as soon as he touched the soil; and she wanted her daughter to profit by this law. She told Lavinia to make her escape while in Ohio, and go to some of the Northern people who would protect her, adding that she would whip her severely if she allowed the opportunity to pass and came back to New Orleans with her master. She said that she intended to escape herself some time, and in order to identify her daughter, if the two should meet, years afterward, in Canada, the mother put around Lavinia's neck a small gold chain, with a pendant ornament, which she superstitiously regarded as a charm, and gave her other little keepsakes. Lavinia remembered all her mother's advice when she reached Ohio, and looked wistfully into the face of every stranger, longing to find some one who "looked kind," to whom she could apply for help in making her escape. She soon made the acquaintance of a colored man and woman who lived near the place where the Scanlans were staying, and to them she confided her hopes and fears, and asked their assistance. They promised to aid her, and one night they dressed her in a suit of clothes belonging to one of their sons, and took her to the house of Samuel Reynolds, a Quaker, who lived at the head of what was then called Spring Street, near the foot of Sycamore hill.

Here she was concealed and remained several days undiscovered, though Scanlan had offered a reward and a strict search was made.

The wife of Edward Harwood, whose residence was near Reynolds', called one day, and being interested in Lavinia took her home with her. All the members of Harwood's family, including, then, John H. Coleman and his wife, were strong abolitionists, and they were ready, in case of danger, to defend the slave girl to the last. The rest of the story shall be told in the graphic language of Mrs. Elizabeth Coleman, who was a participant in the scenes that followed:

"We kept Lavinia closely in the house all day, but at dusk we let her out to play in the yard, for exercise and fresh air. There was a steep grade of perhaps twenty feet in front of the house, so that the street below was entirely hidden from our view, and we could not see any one approaching until he reached the top of the stone steps that led up from below. On the sides and in the rear, however, the house could be easily approached, as the land was high and sloped directly to the back part of the house. At night when the lamps were lit, any person concealed outside could see directly into the house.

"One night as Lavinia was playing in the yard, the big watch dog, Swamp, kept growling as though there were intruders on the premises. Mr. Harwood and Mr. Coleman went out several times to examine, but could see no one. They said: 'That child had better come in, there may be parties about watching for her.' So I put my head out of the window and called, 'Come in, Lavinia, some one might see you.' She came in, and we heard no more growling from Swamp that night.

"The next day she was not very well, and at dinner time was lying asleep up stairs, so we did not call her to come down. Shortly after dinner, when we were sitting in the front room with the doors and windows open, a man suddenly appeared at the top of the steps leading from the street, and without any ceremony walked right into the house. Mr. Harwood and Mr. Coleman had gone down town, and there was no one there but Mrs. Harwood, myself, and a gentleman who was an invalid. We thought at once that the intruder was Scanlan, looking for Lavinia. He looked round hurriedly, and exclaimed in an excited manner: 'Where's my child? I want my child!'

"I replied: 'Your child is not here.'

"He turned toward me and exclaimed 'She is here, my slave girl Lavinia. I saw her last night, and if it hadn't been for you and that cursed dog I would have got her. I had my hand almost on her shoulder when you called her in. Where is she? I want her!' The flight of stairs descended into the sitting-room, and the stair-door stood open. He went to it, saying, 'If my child hears my voice she will answer,' and he called, 'Lavinia, Lavinia!' I trembled lest she should wake suddenly out of sleep and answer him, but, as soon as she recognized his voice, she crawled between the beds and hid herself.

"Mr. Scanlan raved round the room awhile, threatening divers things if his property was not delivered to him, and finally said: 'I'm going down town to get a warrant to search this house, and I'll set a guard to watch you while I am gone;' then stepping to the door, he said: 'Mr. Hawkins, come in here,' and a man whom we had not seen—Mr. Scanlan's brother-in-law, we afterward learned—appeared at the top of the steps and came into the house. 'Just guard this family while I am gone,' and Mr. Hawkins took a seat in the room, looking embarrassed and ill at ease, while Mr. Scanlan started down town. Half way down the hill he recognized Mr. Harwood coming up in his buggy, and, beckoning to him to stop, he informed him in a few words that he was in search of his slave whom he knew to be then concealed at his (Mr. H.'s) house; that he had left a guard there to await his return, and was going for a search warrant, thinking to intimidate Mr. Harwood, and force him to give up the girl. Mr. Harwood replied, with some warmth, that he would have no one guarding his house, and, leaving Scanlan, he drove on quickly, and, reaching the house, accosted Mr. Hawkins: 'I understand that you are here to guard my family; we need no such service and can dispense with your presence; leave my house immediately, or I will pitch you over that bank. Leave, sir!' Mr. Hawkins stood not upon the order of his going, but went.

"Scanlan in the meantime had proceeded on his way down town, breathing out threatenings and slaughter, and going to the "Alhambra," then a popular saloon on Third Street, gathered a crowd of roughs around him, gave orders for an open bar, and, after dispensing liquor freely to all, made a speech to them relating his grievances. He then invited them all up to the hill that evening, to help him obtain his slave and to see the 'fun.' A great many promised to support him, and the excitement ran high, as they exchanged threats against the nigger thieves.

"Mr. Harwood went down town to alarm our friends, telling us to allow no one to enter whom we did not know.

"A strong, trusty person—a stone-cutter in the marble yard of Mr. Coleman—started up to the house as soon as he heard of the state of affairs, and on the way noticed numerous small flags stuck up at intervals to 'blaze the way' for the mob. He threw them down wherever he found them. By the time Mr. Coleman arrived, a crowd of people had collected in the street below, and he saw among them an officer who was notorious for his sympathy with slave-hunters, and his willingness to send fugitives back to bondage for the sake of a few dollars. Mr. Coleman went up to him, said, 'How do you do, O'Neal?' and shook hands with him, then said, 'I understand that you have a warrant to search my house.' 'Is this your house, Mr. Coleman?' 'Yes, sir, I live here and claim this as my home, and wish to see what kind of a paper authorizes you to search my house.' He knew that no warrant to search the house could be legally issued, for only in case of murder or stolen property could a house be searched, and the law of Ohio did not recognize human beings as property. 'Oh, there's some mistake, Mr. Coleman, I did not understand the nature of the case,' said the other, apologetically. 'Let me see the paper, sir.' 'No,' said the other, backing away, 'it is of no consequence,' and went off down town, looking cowed and ashamed.

"Mr. Harwood returned with some friends, and saw an increasing throng in the street. No one had yet tried to enter the house, though several had started up the steps. Mr. Harwood stood at the top, with his big dog by his side, and when any one started up the steps, he said, 'Watch him, Swamp,' and the brute growled and showed his teeth till those below returned.

"Mr. Coleman, premising that there would be trouble that night, went, accompanied by young Alf. Burnet, to a Dutch armory near by, and procured powder, shot, and an arm-load of guns. The weapons were rusty with disuse and had to be cleaned before they could be used. We took up the carpets in the parlor, and gave that room to the men for their preparations. Mrs. Harwood and I bundled our valuables—silver, papers, etc.—and sent them to a neighbor's. All this time the crowd grew larger, and there were howls and oaths and cries to bring out the girl. One ruffian kept exclaiming: 'If my property was in there, I'd have it or I'd have those villains' heart's blood.'

"Alf. Burnet went and came frequently to and from town, and reported matters from there. He said Scanlan was still making speeches, the liquor was flowing freely at the saloons, and new recruits were joining the mob, though some said, 'They have shooting irons up there, and we are not going.' Earlier in the day Mr. Coleman had applied to the Sheriff to protect his house, but received the reply: 'If you make yourself obnoxious to your neighbors you must suffer the consequences.' Toward evening the street was packed with a howling mob, but they had no leader, had no interests at stake, and were too cowardly to make any attempt that would place themselves in danger, for, they knew that those in the house were armed, and that they were determined.

"Between thirty and forty abolitionists, about all there were in the city at that time, had gathered to our aid, and a council was held as to what should be done with the girl. It was decided that she·must be taken away from the house. The suit of boy's clothes that she wore when she escaped were put on her, and Mr. Harwood, Mr. Coleman, Albert

Lewis, and others, conducted her out of the house without arousing the suspicion of the mob. She was taken to the house of Mr. Emery, at the foot of the hill. The mob remained some time longer, without, however, making any attempt to enter the house, overawed by the preparations for defense they saw. An armed guard marched at the top of the steps, and strangely enough the crowd never thought of obtaining access to the building by any other way.

"The mob afterward went to the house of Mr. Burnet, Alf. Burnet's father, on Fifth Street, and stoned it, breaking in all the windows and damaging the whole front of the building. Mr. Burnet collected all the stones in barrels, and kept them for years as specimens of pro-slavery arguments.

"Scanlan detailed his grievances in notices printed in the city papers, but could not, forcibly or otherwise, gain possession of his slave girl, and, hearing that he was to be arrested for trespassing, left suddenly and returned to New Orleans.

"Lavinia remained at Mr. Emery's a week or two, then, dressed in the suit of boy's clothes she had worn before, she followed some boys who drove cows out of town to pasture on the hills, and was conducted by them to the house of a trusty friend. She was afterward sent to Oberlin, where she received a good education, and proving to be a woman of good ability and much intelligence, she was sent as missionary to Medina mission in Africa. A few years since she came back on a visit to see her friends, and, while in Cincinnati, she was taken sick and died."

CHAPTER XVI.

TRIALS UNDER THE FUGITIVE SLAVE LAW—THE WASH.
MCQUERRY CASE—THE SERVICES OF JOHN JOL-
LIFFE—ESCAPE FROM A COURT-ROOM—THE RO-
SETTA CASE—MARGARET GARNER—THE STORY OF
A HAT.

THE first fugitive case that occurred in this
district, after the passage of the fugitive slave
law of 1850, was tried before Judge McLean, of the
Supreme Court of the United States, on the 16th
and 17th of August, 1853. The following account
is culled from reports of the trial :

"The fugitive, Wash. McQuerry, was a bright mulatto, about
twenty-eight years old, well-built and intelligent looking. Four
years before he and three other slave 'boys,' had escaped from
their master, Henry Miller, who lived about fifty miles back of
Louisville, in Washington County, Kentucky. Their flight was
soon discovered, and they were closely pursued. One of the four was
captured in Louisville, but afterward made his escape ; the other
three, including Wash., crossed the Ohio River just above Louisville, in the night. They found a skiff tied to a raft and took it ;
there were no oars, but they managed to row across with pieces of
bark. After getting into Ohio, they traveled by night and lay
concealed during the day. One of them had two or three dollars
with him, which was used to purchase food. They would watch
until the men had left the farm-houses for their daily work, then
go in and buy something to eat from the women. Whether

Wash.s' companions went on to Canada or settled in this State I do not know; Wash. himself, thinking, no doubt, that he would be safe here, settled near Troy, Miami County, Ohio. He was industrious and upright, and was well respected in the neighborhood. He married a free colored woman and became the father of one or two children. His prospects for the future were bright. He had escaped from the thralldom and curse of slavery, and, in the enjoyment of those 'inalienable rights,' liberty and the pursuit of happiness, he felt the dignity of manhood—felt that he was no longer on a level with the brutes. He was a peaceable and law-abiding citizen, and in every way proved himself worthy of the boon of freedom. But this state of tranquillity and happiness did. not last long; Wash. was destined to be torn from his family and dragged back to slavery, and that not surreptitiously, but with the sanction of the law of the United States, as pronounced by one of its highest officers. A white man named John Russell, living not far from Piqua, learned in some way that McQuerry was a fugitive, and having also ascertained the name and locality of his master, basely, and perhaps actuated by a desire for gain, wrote to Miller, informing him where his slave could be found. Miller had offered a reward of one hundred dollars each for the four slaves when they escaped, and Russell no doubt expected to receive this amount as his reward for betraying McQuerry to his master.

" As soon as he received this information, Miller, accompanied by four other Kentuckians, came to Miami County, and, having engaged the services of an officer, sought McQuerry, who was at work on a canal boat, arrested him and conveyed him to Dayton, where he was placed in the hands of Deputy United States Marshal Trader. A writ of habeas corpus was taken out against the sheriff of Montgomery County, but the judge of the Probate Court, before whom the case was brought, decided that the colored man was in the custody of the United States Deputy Marshal. This officer had McQuerry ironed and brought him to this city.

" The party took quarters at the Galt House, about which a large crowd of colored people soon collected, having heard of the case of the fugitive. They made some demonstrations of their sympathy with McQuerry, but were held in check by the police force. At two o'clock in the morning an application was made by Peter H. Clark, a prominent colored man of this city, to Judge

McLean for a writ of habeas corpus requiring those persons who held McQuerry in custody to bring them before him—the judge—and show cause why they deprived him of his liberty. This application was carried to the residence of Judge McLean, in Clifton, some three miles from the city, and he granted the writ, and appointed ten o'clock A. M. for the hearing of the same. In the meantime Miller, the claimant of the fugitive, made application to S. S. Carpenter, United States Commissioner, who appointed seven o'clock A. M. for a hearing. The fugitive was brought before the Commissioner in irons, which he humanely ordered to be taken off. At that hearing the Commissioner postponed further proceedings untll two P. M. at the Criminal Court-room, and ordered the United States Marshal to receive the fugitive into his custody and safely keep him until discharged by due course of law.

"At ten o'clock, the time appointed by Judge McLean to hear evidence on the habeas corpus writ, Deputy Marshal Black, to whom the writ had been directed, made return that McQuerry was not in his custody, and informed the judge that he had been taken by the claimant and Deputy Marshal from Dayton, before United States Commissioner Carpenter, who had postponed the hearing of the case before him until two P. M., at the Criminal Court-room, until which time he had committed him to jail. Upon which the case was referred to the Commissioner to proceed with, but he, inasmuch as the matter had thus come before Judge McLean, and as it was the first case under the fugitive slave law in Ohio, said that he was willing and would prefer that the hearing should proceed before him (Judge McLean) as it was important as a precedent that it should be determined by the highest authority. Judge McLean thereupon ordered the two Deputy Marshals, Black and Trader, to bring the prisoner before him at two o'clock P. M., at the Criminal Court-room, as appointed by the Commissioner.

"At the time appointed, the court-room was crowded by whites and blacks, the jury box being filled by ladies. The Mayor was present, and had ordered a large police force to station themselves in and around the Court-House.

"T. C. Ware appeared for the claimant, and Messrs. Jolliffe and Birney for McQuerry. The testimony for the claimant went to prove that the prisoner was his property, and was a 'fugitive from service and labor,' due to him as his master. The counsel for the prisoner moved for a continuance of the case until absent witnesses could be produced to prove that he had resided for more than four years in Ohio, during which time he had been reputed and taken by his neighbors to be a free man and had borne an irreproachable character, but as the counsel for the claimant was willing to admit all that, the judge ordered the case to proceed. When the testimony closed, Ware opened the argument, very briefly, for the plaintiff. He said that when he came into the court-room he had no doubt but that he should be able to prove, as he had done, that the man Wash. McQuerry was the fugitive property of his client. 'We have proved,' said he, 'that he and his mother before him were the slaves of Mr. Miller—that the whole family belonged to Miller. It is in evidence that he was always well treated, and it is probable that the good character he has proved in this State is the result of his good training by Mr. Miller. May it please the Court, I am free to say that aside from our constitutional obligations, as an abstract question, I can agree with the counsel for the defense, as to the abstract rights of his client and the wrong of slavery. But I came up here to assist in supporting the constitution and the laws—to do this peaceably and with dignity, and without the excitement of the natural sympathies.' He then alluded briefly to the admission made by McQuerry that he ran away from Miller, and waived further argument for the present.

"Mr. Jolliffe followed for the defense. He concurred entirely with the opposite counsel in loyalty to the constitution and readiness to support it. But not alone the constitution, not alone the laws. Human justice and human right were also to be regarded.

"'Our only evidence,' said he, 'is that of the hunters of this man, that he has been four years a resident of this State; that he has been a sober industrious man, a good husband, a respected neighbor. Four years in Ohio, and reputed to be a free man. But now comes a man from the State of Kentucky, demanding a process by which this defendant—this intelligent and upright human being—may be dragged from his home, from the wife of his bosom, from the graves of his children, and, bound hand and foot, hurried forever away from them and from all he holds dear, into a bondage by the side of which Egyptian thralldom was a mercy! Nor is his home to be in the Kentucky of his youth.

46

Already the wielder of irresponsible power—the awful power over a human soul—has warned the heart-broken husband that he is to be sold; the last drop of his blood may be scourged out on far Southern plantations, till his soul is freed by the Great Emancipator and goes to its God.

" ' The question upon which your Honor is now to pass is one of extraordinary interest; it is the first time it has been brought before so distinguished a tribunal. The question is still open; it has not yet been decided by any binding authority.' Mr. Jolliffe then proceeded to a powerful constitutional argument, taking the broad ground that the fugitive slave law of 1850 was unconstitutional and void. On this point the defense rested. Why was it assumed that Washington McQuerry was a slave? What was the evidence that Miller had a right to his body, which God made, and to his soul, for which Christ died? No statute of Kentucky could be found to establish that right. He quoted a number of authorities to support his position, and asked the consent of the Court for a friend—Dr. Brisbane, of South Carolina—to read an argument on the point, which he had adopted as his own. The request was granted. After Dr. Brisbane had read an elaborate argument, Mr. Jolliffe concluded his own by a powerful review of the fundamental principles of human law, and the nature of human rights. There was a difference between rightful legislation and tyranny; was not that legislation which struck down all the rights of a man tyranny? Suppose one man should be placed aside, and all the millions of earth's population passed by him, and as they passed, each one cast a vote that this one man should be a slave—would that divest him of a single natural right? There was no such thing as constitutional slavery in the United States. The one fact that the slave act of 1850 denies the right of trial by jury made it unconstitutional.

" Mr. Birney, the other counsel for the fugitive, deferred his argument until the next morning and the court adjourned. On the return of the prisoner to the jail, strongly guarded by the police, some demonstrations were made by the crowd of colored people, but they were checked by the police.

" The next morning Mr. Birney made an able argument in behalf of the fugitive. He was followed by Mr. Ware for the claimant, after which the judge gave his decision. After reviewing the evidence, he referred to the law bearing on such cases and said,

'I can not here be governed by sympathy; I have to look to the law and be governed by the law, and to guard myself with more than usual caution in such a case, when judgment might be warped by sympathy.   *   *   *   *   This is not a case for sympathy; the evidence certainly is complete, that the fugitive had a kind master; of this matter we on the north bank of the Ohio River have no concern. The law has been enacted by the highest power—that none is higher is acknowledged by all men. Sooner or later a disregard for the law would bring chaos, anarchy and widespread ruin; the law must be enforced. Let those who think differently go to the people who make the laws. I can not turn aside from the sacred duties of my office to regard aught but the law. By the force of all the testimony and the law I am bound to remand the fugitive to his master.'

"After this decision, Mr. Jolliffe moved for a writ of certiorari to the Supreme Court. The Court said that there could be no appeal from the decision of a judge of the Supreme Court of the United States made at chambers. The point had, he was quite certain, been decided by the Supreme Court. He was willing, however, to give any reasonable time for counsel to investigate the question. At the suggestion of the Court it was finally arranged that the claimant, Mr. Miller, should enter into a bond for two thousand dollars, conditioned upon his returning McQuerry to this State in case it should be decided that the case could be taken to the Supreme Court.

"At the conclusion of his argument, Mr. Ware stated that Mr. Miller would emancipate his slave for the sum of one thousand two hundred dollars, and donate fifty dollars himself toward that purpose, or he was willing to take the appraisement of disinterested parties in Lexington.

"Wash. McQuerry was then delivered up to his claimant by the United States Deputy Marshal, and was at once taken across to Covington on his way back to slavery.

Those of us who were deeply interested in the fugitive's case made zealous efforts to raise the sum required by his master and to buy his freedom. Money was sent in by various individuals, and a number of subscriptions were obtained, but we did not succeed in raising the amount required.

THE SERVICES OF JOHN JOLLIFFE.

In connection with the cases tried under the Fugitive Slave law in this city, that noble anti-slavery lawyer—John Jolliffe—was especially prominent. He has gone to his reward, but the record he left is imperishable. His heart was quick to respond to the needs of the fugitives, and no sacrifice of time, strength, talent, or business reputation was too great to be willingly and cheerfully rendered in behalf of the oppressed. He pleaded the cause of the fugitive slaves with all his skill as a lawyer and all his eloquence as an orator. In those days when to be an abolitionist or in sympathy with the hapless victims of bondage was to be shunned and to lose one's reputation and chances of success in one's business or profession, it required a heart true to the principles of right, a self-forgetful devotion to the cause of humanity, to pursue the course followed by John Jolliffe. The talents and the knowledge of law that might have won for him a wide and richly remunerative practice, he devoted to an unpopular cause, receiving for his services no reward but the plaudits of his own conscience, and the highest respect and esteem of all who were not blinded by prejudice.

ESCAPE FROM A COURT-ROOM.

A slave man, named Louis, escaped from the interior of Kentucky, and came to Cincinnati, where he found employment, and remained for some time, but finally made his way to the neighborhood of Columbus. After he had lived there several years, his master learned of his whereabouts and went in pursuit of him. A writ was obtained and placed in the hands of the marshal of Columbus, who arrested Louis and brought him to Cincinnati, on his way back to slavery. In the meantime friends of Louis at Columbus telegraphed to Lawyer Jolliffe, notifying him of the case. He at once came to see me, and we immediately got out a writ to arrest the master for kidnapping. The sheriff of Cincinnati awaited the party from Columbus at the Little Miami Railroad depot, and when the train arrived, he took the slaveholder in custody.

Lawyer Hays united with Jolliffe in defending the fugitive. They endeavored to prove that Louis had formerly accompanied his master to this State to aid him in driving a drove of horses back to Kentucky, and that under the law of Ohio, which liberated every slave who came into the State by his master's consent, Louis was free. The slaveholder was allowed to go home to get evidence and secure witnesses that Louis was his property, and the negro was placed in jail to await his trial. The case was tried before Commissioner Carpenter, and as it was among the first in this district that came under the Fugitive Slave law of 1850, it attracted much attention. The trial lasted several days, and after all the evidence had been given and the lawyers closed their arguments, the Commissioner deferred judgment until next day at two o'clock, wishing to deliberate on the case. When the time set for the decision arrived, the court-room was crowded with interested listeners, white and black. It was during the building of the new Court-House, and the court was held in the second story of Wilson's building on Court Street. The room was long and had a table or counter through the center. On the west side of this there was a crowd of colored people, standing; the judge and lawyers were sitting at the table. Opposite them sat the slave, between his master and the marshal of Columbus, and just behind him stood a crowd of white people, composed of friends of the slave, and others who had been drawn to the spot by matters of curiosity. The judge was slow and tedious in reviewing the evidence, and as he spoke in a low tone, and the auditors were anxious to hear they leaned forward much absorbed, trying to catch every word, as they expected every moment to hear the negro consigned to slavery.

Louis was crowded, and to gain more room, slipped his chair back a little way. Neither his master nor the marshal noticed the movement, as they were intently listening to the judge, and he slipped his chair again, until he was back of them. I was standing close behind him and saw every movement. Next he rose quietly to his feet and took a step backward. Some abolitionist, friendly to his cause, gave him an encouraging touch on the foot, and he stepped farther back. Then a good hat was placed on his head by some one behind, and he quietly and cautiously made his way around the south end of the room, into the crowd of colored people on the west side, and, through it, toward the door. I and several other abolitionists had our eyes on him, and our hearts throbbed with suppressed excitement and anxiety lest he should be discovered. The door and passage were crowded with Germans, through whom Louis made his way, and passing down stairs gained the street. He was well acquainted with the different streets, and made his way quickly, though with not enough haste to attract attention, through an alley, across the canal, through the German settlement, and by an indirect route to Avondale, where he knew the sexton of the colored burying ground. About five minutes after he left the court-room his absence was discovered, and created a great sensation. The marshal cried, ''Louis is gone!'' and made a rush for the door and down stairs, followed by his supporters to search for the fugitive who had slipped through their fingers. Louis' friends were all delighted, of course, and there was an extensive display of grinning ivories among the crowd of colored people. The Commissioner adjourned court till the following Tuesday (but it has never been convened from that day to this), and the crowd dispersed, some jubilant over the unexpected course things had taken, some equally chagrined. A vigorous search was made for Louis by the marshal and the pro-slavery party, but he could not be found.

I, and other abolitionists, learning of his whereabouts, decided that he was not safe on the outskirts of the city, and the following night we dis-

guised him in woman's apparel, brought him into
the city, and took him to the house of one of his
colored friends, on Broadway, near Sixth Street.
He was placed in an upper room and the door
locked, and here he remained about a week. Only
two or three persons knew of his hiding-place, but
as several policemen were seen frequently in the
vicinity, we feared that he was in danger, and for
greater safety decided to remove him.

I had an interview with the trustees of a popular
church known to be friends to the slave, and arrangements were made for Louis' removal. He was
again dressed in woman's apparel, and, obeying
directions previously given him, he walked down
Broadway, one Sabbath evening, to the corner of
Eighth Street, when he saw me. I passed on to
Vine Street and joined the throng of people going
to evening service. Louis followed, at a short distance, and was conducted to the church previously
mentioned. I passed in at a side gate and went into
the basement of the church. Louis followed me
and was soon safely secreted in one of the committee rooms, where he remained for several weeks.
The officers of the law made vigorous efforts to find
him, but gained no clue to his hiding-place. It was
said that the Columbus marshal disguised himself as
a Friend, and went among the Friends' settlements
in Ohio, under a fictitious name, inquiring for Louis.
He professed to feel great anxiety and concern for
Louis' safety, as there was so much search for him,
but he gained no intelligence of the fugitive.

To mislead his pursuers, a telegram was sent to

Cincinnati from Columbus, and published in the *Gazette*, saying that Louis had passed there on the train bound for Cleveland, and another dispatch from Cleveland, saying he had arrived there and taken the boat for Detroit. All this time, Louis remained in his comfortable quarters in the committee room, where he heard the preaching every Sabbath, in the room above. Finally, a Presbyterian minister and his wife, who were in Cincinnati for a short time, with their horse and carriage, offered to convey him out of the city. Arrangements were accordingly made, and they drove to the church door one morning about nine o'clock. Louis, disguised as a woman with a vail over his face, entered the carriage and sat on the back seat by the lady. They took him about thirty miles out of the city, that day, to a noted depot of the Underground Railroad, and he was duly shipped to Sandusky, where he arrived in safety and took the boat for Canada.

There afterward appeared an ironical article in a Cincinnati paper, giving the intelligence that all the time Louis' pursuers were searching for him, he was comfortably ensconced in the committee rooms of a popular church, and inquiring "What is to become of the rights of slaveholders, and the divinely appointed institution, if ministers will connive at such plans to defraud owners of their property?"

Louis' master claimed his full value—one thousand dollars—from the marshal of Columbus, who had him in charge at the time of his escape, and who was responsible for his safe-keeping, but it was reported that the marshal effected a compromise with him, and closed the case satisfactorily to the claimant, by paying eight hundred dollars.

The whole occurrence excited much attention and was widely commented upon at the time. It is probably the only instance on record of a prisoner escaping from a court-room in broad daylight, and eluding the grasp of a watchful marshal, and the surveillance of the officers of the court. As soon as court adjourned several persons came into my store, which was in the adjoining building, laughing and appearing much pleased with what had happened, and asked me if I had a trap-door by which I could let fugitives down to the Underground Railroad. I replied, "Yes," and showed them the hatch-way into the cellar.

I afterward asked Commissioner Carpenter what his decision in the case would have been. He said that he had decided that the Fugitive Slave Act conferred, or purported to confer, powers of a judicial character on him as Commissioner, which, in his opinion, he could not constitutionally exercise. The case of Louis occurred in October, 1853. In the following June, Carpenter resigned his office as Commissioner, giving his reasons for doing so in an able and lengthy article that appeared in the Cincinnati *Gazette.*

THE ROSETTA ARMSTEAD CASE.

The Rosetta case, or the trial of the slave girl Rosetta Armstead, created much excitement in this city at the time, on account of sympathy with the girl, and attracted much attention on account of the principles involved. It occurred in March, 1855. The outlines of the case are as follows:

"Rosetta, a light mulatto girl of sixteen, was the property of Rev. Henry Dennison, of Louisville, Kentucky, who had owned her all her life. The family had formerly lived in Wheeling, Virginia, and had removed to Louisville about three years before the opening of our story. Dennison placed Rosetta in the care of one Miller, one of his friends, to take her back to Wheeling. Miller started by river, but on account of heavy ice running could proceed no farther than Cincinnati. Here he left the river, intending to go straight through by rail, but finally decided to pay a visit to some friends in Columbus. He went to that city, taking Rosetta with him. By this act of Miller's—acting as agent for the master—Rosetta was made free, but she did not know the law governing such cases, and probably would not have taken advantage of the facts in the case, had not the colored people of Columbus interested themselves in her behalf and informed her that she was now free. She was taken from the custody of Miller by a writ of habeas corpus, and brought before the Probate Court of Columbus for a hearing. She was declared free, and being a minor, a guardian was appointed to look after her rights, Louis Van Slyke, Esq., of Columbus. A paper of that city says: 'The Rev. Mr. Dennison, of Louisville, the owner of the girl Rosetta Armstead, arrived in this city yesterday, and held an interview with her at the house of Mr. Van Slyke, to whose care she was committed by the court. Mr. Dennison told the girl that he had come for the purpose of taking her home with him if she wished to return, but as she was in a free State, she had the liberty of going or remaining at her option. The girl, after deliberating about a minute, said she should prefer remaining in a free State, rather than return to slavery. Mr. Dennison bade her good-by, shook hands with her and parted, evidently much grieved at the loss of a favorite servant. The girl is now in the employ of Dr. Coulter, at whose house she will doubtless meet with the kindest treatment.'

"Dennison, the master, was not satisfied, and thinking that he still might obtain possession of the girl, got a warrant for her arrest and placed it in the hand of the United States Marshal, for the Southern District of Ohio, who brought Rosetta to Cincinnati, intending to have her tried before Commissioner Pendery, under the Fugitive Slave law. Van Slyke accompanied her to look after her rights. Before she could be brought before Commissioner Pendery, a writ of habeas corpus was sued out by her friends, and she was brought before Judge Parker to show cause for detention. The judge decided that she was free, that the warrant for her arrest was defective, and that the marshal had no right to hold her in custody.

"In the meantime Dennison had made an affidavit before Commissioner Pendery, that Rosetta was a fugitive from labor and service, and the case was set to be tried before the Commissioner. S. P. Chase, who was counsel for Rosetta's guardian, before Judge Parker, feared that she would be rearrested to go before Pendery, and asked that she might be protected to a place of safety; he wished the Court to grant an order authorizing the sheriff to conduct her to a place of safety before delivering her out of his hands. The sheriff asked her guardian where he wished Rosetta delivered to him, and Van Slyke said: 'At the Woodruff House.'

"This was accordingly done, but as soon as she was released from the custody of the sheriff, Robinson, the United States Marshal, who brought her from Columbus, stepped in and presented a warrant for rearrest. Van Slyke complained to the Court before which the case had just been decided, and Judge Parker issued a summons to United States Marshal Robinson, to answer for contempt, for rearresting Rosetta after the Court had pronounced her free, and the warrant defective.

" We will not follow this side issue, as it involved only technical points of law, but turn to Rosetta again.

" F. Ball appeared for Rosetta, and after the testimony had proved that she had been placed in Miller's charge by Dennison, and that Miller, acting as his agent, had brought her into a free State, he plead that she was entitled to her freedom—that such an act made her free—that Dennison's offering her her choice to stay or return (when in Columbus), amounted to tacit manumission, and that she had already been pronounced free by two courts of law. The claimants refused to recognize the jurisdiction of those courts in the premises, and claimed the right to take her as a fugitive from service and labor, under the Fugitive Slave law.

"Rosetta's counsel claimed that she could not be returned under the Fugitive Slave law, for that only provided for the escape of a slave from a slave State to a free State, and Rosetta had done nothing of the kind, she had been brought here. After argument by opposing counsel, the Commissioner deferred decision until the following Tuesday—this was on Saturday. The marshal took Rosetta to the county jail for safe keeping during the interval. A large concourse of people who were interested in the case followed them along the street to the jail.

"On the following Tuesday, the Commissioner decided that the claimant, Dennison, was bound by the act of his agent Miller ; that there was no escape on Rosetta's part; that bringing her to Columbus and there offering her her freedom was equivalent to emancipating her. He then declared Rosetta free.

"Hearty demonstrations of applause followed this announcement. Van Slyke received many congratulations on the issue of the trial, then, with Rosetta in his charge, he took carriage for the railroad depot, and returned to Columbus. A deep interest there had been felt in the trial, and a concourse of. five hundred people met them at the depot.

MARGARET GARNER.

Perhaps no case that came under my notice, while engaged in aiding fugitive slaves, attracted more attention and aroused deeper interest and sympathy than the case of Margaret Garner, the slave mother, who killed her child rather than see it taken back to slavery. This happened in the latter part of January, 1856. The Ohio River was frozen over at the time, and the opportunity thus offered for escaping to a free State was embraced by a number of slaves living in Kentucky, several miles back from the river. A party of seventeen, belonging to different masters in the same neighborhood, made arrangements to escape together. There was snow on the ground and the roads were smooth, so the plan of going to the river on a sled naturally suggested itself. The time fixed for their flight was Sabbath night, and having managed to get a large sled and two good horses, belonging to one of their masters, the party of seventeen crowded into the sled and started on their hazardous journey in the latter part of the night. They drove the horses at full speed, and at daylight reached the river below Covington, opposite Western Row. They left the sled and horses here, and as quickly as possible crossed the river on foot. It was now broad daylight, and people were beginning to pass about the streets, and the fugitives divided their company that they might not attract so much notice.

An old slave man named Simon, and his wife Mary, together with their son Robert and his wife Margaret Garner and four children, made their way to the house of a colored man named Kite, who had formerly lived in their neighborhood and had been purchased from slavery by his father, Joe Kite. They had to make several inquiries in order to find Kite's house, which was below Mill Creek, in the lower part of the city. This afterward led to their discovery; they had been seen by a number of persons on their way to Kite's, and were easily traced by pursuers. The other nine fugitives were more fortunate. They made their way up town and found friends who conducted them to safe hiding-places, where they remained until night. They were then put on the Underground Railroad, and went safely through to Canada.

Kite felt alarmed for the safety of the party that

had arrived at his house, and as soon as breakfast was over, he came to my store, at the corner of Sixth and Elm Streets, to ask counsel regarding them. I told him that they were in a very unsafe place and must be removed at once. I directed him how to conduct them from his house to the outskirts of the city, up Mill Creek, to a settlement of colored people in the western part of the city, where fugitives were often harbored. I would make arrangements to forward them northward, that night, on the Underground Railroad. Kite returned to his house at once, according to my directions, but he was too late; in a few minutes after his return, the house was surrounded by pursuers—the masters of the fugitives, with officers and a posse of men. The door and windows were barred, and those inside refused to give admittance. The fugitives were determined to fight, and to die, rather than to be taken back to slavery. Margaret, the mother of the four children, declared that she would kill herself and her children before she would return to bondage. The slave men were armed and fought bravely. The window was first battered down with a stick of wood, and one of the deputy marshals attempted to enter, but a pistol shot from within made a flesh wound on his arm and caused him to abandon the attempt. The pursuers then battered down the door with some timber and rushed in. The husband of Margaret fired several shots, and wounded one of the officers, but was soon overpowered and dragged out of the house. At this moment, Margaret Garner, seeing that their hopes of freedom were

vain, seized a butcher knife that lay on the table,
and with one stroke cut the throat of her little
daughter, whom she probably loved the best. She
then attempted to take the life of the other children
and to kill herself, but she was overpowered and
hampered before she could complete her desperate
work. The whole party was then arrested and
lodged in jail.

The trial lasted two weeks, drawing crowds to the
court-room every day. Colonel Chambers, of this
city, and two lawyers from Covington—Wall and
Tinnell—appeared for the claimants, and Messrs.
Jolliffe and Getchell for the slaves. The counsel for
the defense brought witnesses to prove that the
fugitives had been permitted to visit the city at
various times previously. It was claimed that Margaret Garner had been brought here by her owners
a number of years before, to act as nurse girl, and
according to the law which liberated slaves who
were brought into free States by the consent of their
masters, she had been free from that time, and her
children, all of whom had been born since then—
following the condition of the mother—were likewise free.

The Commissioner decided that a voluntary return
to slavery, after a visit to a free State, re-attached
the conditions of slavery, and that the fugitives
were legally slaves at the time of their escape.

Early in the course of the trial, Lawyer Jolliffe announced that warrants had been issued by
the State authorities to arrest the fugitives on a
criminal charge—Margaret Garner for murder, and

the others for complicity in murder—and moved that
the papers should be served on them immediately.
Commissioner Pendery wished that to be deferred
until he had given his decision, and the fugitives
were out of the jurisdiction of his court, but Jolliffe
pressed the motion to have the warrants served—
"For," said he, "the fugitives have all assured me
that they will *go singing to the gallows* rather than
be returned to slavery." He further said that it
might appear strange for him to be urging that his
clients should be indicted for murder, but he was
anxious that this charge should be brought against
them before they passed from the jurisdiction of the
Commissioner's Court, for the infamous law of 1850
provided that no warrant in any event should be
served upon the fugitives in case they were remanded to the custody of their owners. Not even
a warrant for murder could prevent their being
returned to bondage.

Jolliffe said that in the final argument of the case
he intended not only to allege, but to demonstrate,
conclusively, to the Court, that the Fugitive Slave
law was unconstitutional, and as part and parcel of
that argument he wished to show the effects of carrying it out. It had driven a frantic mother to murder
her own child rather than see it carried back to the
seething hell of American slavery. This law was of
such an order that its execution required human
hearts to be wrung and human blood to be spilt.

"The Constitution," said he, "expressly declared
that Congress should pass no law prescribing any
form of religion or preventing the free exercise

thereof. If Congress could not pass any law requiring you to worship God, still less could they
pass one requiring you to carry fuel to hell." These
ringing words called forth applause from all parts of
the court-room. Jolliffe said: "It is for the Court
to decide whether the Fugitive Slave law overrides
the law of Ohio to such an extent that it can not
arrest a fugitive slave even for a crime of murder."

The fugitives were finally indicted for murder, but
we will see that this amounted to nothing.

Margaret Garner, the chief actor in the tragedy
which had occurred, naturally excited much attention. She was a mulatto, about five feet high, showing one-fourth or one-third white blood. She had
a high forehead, her eyebrows were finely arched
and her eyes bright and intelligent, but the African
appeared in the lower part of her face, in her broad
nose and thick lips. On the left side of her forehead was an old scar, and on the cheek-bone, on the
same side, another one. When asked what caused
them, she said: "White man struck me." That
was all, but it betrays a story of cruelty and degradation, and, perhaps, gives the key-note to Margaret's hate of slavery, her revolt against its thralldom, and her resolve to die rather than go back
to it.

She appeared to be twenty-two or twenty-three
years old. While in the court-room she was dressed
in dark calico, with a white handkerchief pinned
around her neck, and a yellow cotton handkerchief,
arranged as a turban, around her head. The babe
she held in her arms was a little girl, about nine

months old, and was much lighter in color than herself, light enough to show a red tinge in its cheeks. During the trial she would look up occasionally, for an instant, with a timid, apprehensive glance at the strange faces around her, but her eyes were generally cast down. The babe was continually fondling her face with its little hands, but she rarely noticed it, and her general expression was one of extreme sadness. The little boys, four and six years old, respectively, were bright-eyed, woolly-headed little fellows, with fat dimpled cheeks. During the trial they sat on the floor near their mother, playing together in happy innocence, all unconscious of the gloom that shrouded their mother, and of the fact that their own future liberty was at stake: The murdered child was almost white, a little girl of rare beauty.

The case seemed to stir every heart that was alive to the emotions of humanity. The interest manifested by all classes was not so much for the legal principles involved, as for the mute instincts that mold every human heart—the undying love of freedom that is planted in every breast—the resolve to die rather than submit to a life of degradation and bondage.

A number of people, who were deeply interested in the fugitives, visited them in prison and conversed with them. Old Simon, his wife Mary, and their son Robert, while expressing their longing for freedom, said that they should not attempt to kill themselves if they were returned to slavery. Their trust in God seemed to have survived all the wrong and cruelty inflicted upon them by man, and though they felt often like crying bitterly, "How long, O Lord, how long?" they still trusted and endured. But Margaret seemed to have a different nature; she could see nothing but woe for herself and her children. Who can fathom the depths of her heart as she brooded over the wrongs and insults that had been heaped upon her all her life? Who can wonder if her faith staggered when she saw her efforts to gain freedom frustrated, when she saw the gloom of her old life close around her again, without any hope of deliverance? Those who came to speak words of comfort and cheer felt them die upon their lips, when they looked into her face, and marked its expression of settled despair. Her sorrow was beyond the reach of any words of encouragement and consolation, and can be realized in all its fullness only by those who have tasted of a cup equally bitter.

Among those who visited Margaret in prison was Lucy Stone, the well-known eloquent public speaker. It was reported that she gave Margaret a knife, and told her to kill herself and her children rather than be taken back to slavery. Colonel Chambers, the counsel for the claimants, referred to this rumor in court, and Lucy Stone, coming in shortly afterward, was informed of it. She requested to say a few words in reply, and when the court had adjourned, the greater part of the crowd remained to hear her. She said: "I am only sorry that I was not in when Colonel Chambers said what he did about me, and my giving a knife to Margaret. When I saw that poor fugitive, took her toil-hardened hand in mine, and read in her face deep suffering and an ardent longing for freedom, I could not help bid her be of good cheer. I told her that a thousand hearts were aching for her, and that they were glad one child of hers was safe with the angels. Her only reply was a look of deep despair, of anguish such as no words can speak. I thought the spirit she manifested was the same with that of our ancestors to whom we had erected the monument at Bunker Hill—the spirit that would rather let us all go back to God than back to slavery. The faded faces of the negro children tell too plainly to what degradation female slaves must submit. Rather than give her little daughter to that life, she killed it. If in her deep maternal love she felt the impulse to send her child back to God, to save it from coming woe, who shall say she had no right to do so? That desire had its root in the deepest and holiest feelings of our na-ture—implanted alike in black· and white by our common Father. With my own teeth I would tear open my veins and let the earth drink my blood, rather than to wear the chains of slavery. How then could I blame her for wishing her child to find free-dom with God and the angels, where no chains are? I know not whether this Commissioner has children, else I would appeal to him to know how he would feel to have them torn from him, but I feel that he will not disregard the Book which says: 'Thou shalt not deliver unto his master the servant which is escaped from his master unto thee: he shall dwell with thee, even among you, in that place which he shall choose in one of thy gates, where it liketh him best.'"

But in spite of touching appeals, of eloquent pleadings, the Commissioner remanded the fugitives back to slavery. He said that it was not a question of feeling to be decided by the chance current of his sympathies; the law of Kentucky and of the United States made it a question of property.

In regard to the claim, plainly established by the evidence, that the fugitives had previously been brought to this State by the consent of their masters, he said: "Had the slaves asserted their freedom, they would have been practically free, but they voluntarily returned to slavery. In allowing them to come to Ohio, the master voluntarily abandoned his claim upon them, and they, in returning, abandoned their claim to freedom."

By a provision of the law, previously referred to, they could not be tried on the warrant for murder, and their indictment on that charge was practically ignored. Jolliffe said, indignantly, that even a savage tribe reserved to itself the right to investigate a charge for murder committed within its border, but the sovereign State of Ohio allowed itself and its laws to be overruled by the infamous Fugitive Slave law, made in the interests of slaveholders. The question of bringing the case before a superior court, and trying the slaves for murder was agitated, and Gaines, the master of Margaret, promised to have her in safe-keeping on the opposite side of the river, to be delivered up to the authorities of the State of Ohio, if a requisition for her was made.

The fugitives were then delivered to their owners, who conveyed them in an omnibus to the wharf of the Covington ferry-boat. A crowd followed them to the river, but there was no demonstration. The masters were surrounded by large numbers of their Kentucky friends, who had stood by them and guarded their interests during the trial, and there was great rejoicing among them, on account of their victory.

The masters kept their slaves in jail in Covington, a few days, then took them away. When the requisition was made for Margaret, Gaines said that he had kept her in Covington for some time according to the agreement, then, as the writ was not served, he had sent her down the river. This was a violation of the spirit of the agreement, and much indignation was manifested by Margaret's friends in Ohio, but nothing further was done. Margaret was lost, in what Jolliffe called, "the seething hell of American slavery." It was reported that on her way down the river she sprang from the boat into the water with her babe in her arms; that when she rose she was seized by some of the boat hands and rescued, but that her child was drowned.

After the trial of the fugitives, a committee of citizens presented a purse to Jolliffe, accompanied by an address, in token of their appreciation of his services. He returned thanks in an eloquent letter, setting forth his views on the unconstitutionality of the Fugitive Slave law.

THE STORY OF A HAT.

During the time of the Margaret Garner trial, the popular vocalists and anti-slavery singers, the Hutchinson family, of New England, were in Cincinnati. They had given several concerts here which had attracted large audiences, as their anti-slavery concerts generally did. They felt a deep interest in the trial and offered to give a concert for the benefit of the fugitives. A meeting of the friends of the fugitives was held, and a committee, of which I was a member, was appointed to secure a suitable hall and make all the necessary arrangements for the concert. Smith and Nixon's hall, on Fourth Street, the best public hall in the city at that time, was kindly offered by the proprietors for the occasion. A part of the committee met next morning, but as not all the members were present, it was agreed to hold a meeting at three o'clock that afternoon to complete all the arrangements, and in the meantime to notify the absentees of the hour agreed upon. It was laid upon me to notify Samuel Alley, who was absent. About two o'clock in the afternoon, while looking for him, I was informed that he was in the court-room listening to the proceedings in the fugitive case. The trial had then been going on for several days, and a large number of special marshals had been summoned as guards to fend off the abolitionists—a few unarmed, inoffensive men, who felt it right to plead the cause of the oppressed, and to endeavor, by moral suasion, to convince the people of the evils of slavery.

These special marshals were mostly brought from the Kentucky side of the river—all at the expense of the United States—to see that the infamous slave law of 1850 was executed. These Kentuckians, invested with a little brief authority, were stationed in and around the Court-House, and often assumed authority to prevent colored people and the particular friends of the slaves from entering the court-room. One of these marshals was stationed at the door. When I was about to pass in, he inquired, abruptly:

"What are you going in for? Are you a witness?"

I replied: "That is my business, not thine—we live in a free State on this side of the river," and passed by him into the court-room. It was a long room—where the Commissioner's Court was held—and was densely crowded. The seats had all been moved behind the bar, in order to give standing room.

The weather was extremely cold, and the only provision for warming the apartment was a stove at each end. The southern part of the room was occupied by the Commissioner and his Court; in the northern part every foot of standing space was occupied by spectators. I saw Samuel Alley standing near the stove in the end of the room, and made my way through the crowd to him, but neglected to take off my hat.

The Kentucky-marshal at the door, noticing this, spoke in a loud commanding tone, and said: "Take off your hat!" several times. I paid no attention

48

to him.   He then made his way through the crowd to me, and said, loudly and angrily: "I command you to take off you hat, sir!"

I spoke in a low tone, and asked: "What is the matter with my hat?   I suppose that it will not hurt anybody."

He spoke as before, and said: "Why, sir, you are in the United States Court.   I have authority; I command you to pull off your hat."

I replied: "I shall not pull off my hat to accommodate thee.   It is not my habit nor the habit of my people to make obeisance to men."

He repeated, angrily, "You are in the United States Court, sir, and I command you to pull off your hat."

I replied, mildly, "It is not the first time that I have been in the United States Court.   I have served on juries in different courts, and in various States, and was never commanded to pull off my hat; and I am not aware that a Commissioner's Court, trying a fugitive slave case, is a more sacred place than other courts."

The attention of the crowd seemed to be drawn to us; they turned their eyes in our direction to watch the marshal's movements, and listened to the words that passed between us.

The marshal, seeing that I was not disposed to obey his commands, seized my hat rudely and jerked it off my head.   He then offered it to me, but I did not take it, or pay any attention to it further than to say, "I thought thou wanted my hat."

Turning quietly toward my friend Alley, I resumed conversation with him, in a low tone, regarding the business of our committee meeting that afternoon. The marshal stood a short time holding my hat, and looking quite foolish (others said); then seeing that I paid no attention to him, and was not disposed to relieve him of the care of my hat, he began to look around for some place on which to lay it.

He espied a table or bench in one corner of the room, and kindly laid my hat upon it, then made his way back to his station at the door. A member of our city police who knew me came to me and said, "You had better go and get your hat; it might get lost." I replied: "I did not put it there and I shall not go after it." The policeman then went after it and brought it to me. I thanked him, and put it on my head. The marshal at the door soon discovered it, and began to cry out, as before, "Pull off your hat!" Seeing that I paid no attention to him, he made his way through the crowd toward me, and again commanded me to take off my hat, saying that he had authority; that I was in the United States Court, etc. I replied again that I had often been in courts before, and had never been commanded to pull off my hat. "I have been in the Queen's Court," I said, "and was allowed to wear my hat there without molestation. Friends have been permitted to approach kings and emperors with their hats on; I told thee before that we did not make obeisance to men; I generally take off my hat, for my own comfort, when seated in a house; but I do not wish to take it off now; it is not uncomfortable this cold day."

Again he seized my hat and pulled it off in a rude manner. He offered it to me, as before; but I appeared not to notice it, and went on talking with Alley as though nothing had occurred to interrupt our quiet conversation. The marshal started across the room to lay my hat where he had laid it before, but on the way he met our city officer, who took hold of it and said, "Let the gentleman's hat alone." I could not hear the marshal's reply, as he spoke in a low tone on that occasion, but I heard the city officer say, sharply, "I have as much authority as you have, sir." He then took my hat from the marshal, brought it to me and kindly placed it on my head.

The Kentucky marshal went back to his place at the door, and did not trouble me further about my hat, although I remained for some time with it on my head.

When the marshal took off my hat the second time, his action seemed to arouse a feeling of indignation among the people standing near me. When he started away with it, some of them manifested a spirit of fight; one said: "Let him try that again;" another said: "I can't stand that;" and a third exclaimed, with an oath: "I won't stand that." I did not turn my head to see who these men were, nor pay any attention to what they said, but continued my conversation with Samuel Alley.

A *Gazette* reporter was present when this occurred, and next morning an article appeared in that paper giving an account of the marshal's rudeness in reference to my hat, and remarking that it did not appear to throw me off of my usual equanimity.   One error occurred in this account; the reporter said that the marshal knocked my hat off— he pulled it off with his hand.

The committee met according to agreement, and completed the arrangement for the concert.   I then returned home, and finding there Jonathan Cable, a stanch abolitionist and Presbyterian minister, from College Hill, I related to him my adventure with the marshal in the court-room.   Cable immediately picked up his hat and said: "I will try him."   He hastily made his way to the court-room, and passed in, by the marshal at the door, keeping his hat on his head.

The marshal cried out several times: "Pull off your hat!" but seeing that his order was not obeyed, he pressed through the crowd to the place where Cable stood, and in an authoritative manner commanded him to take off his hat.   Cable made no reply nor paid any attention to him, and the marshal jerked his hat from his head, as he had done mine.   He then offered it to him, but Cable declined to take it and said to him:

"Are you a United States officer?"

"Yes, sir," replied the marshal.

"Well, then," rejoined Cable, "you are a servant of ours; you may hold my hat;" adding, in a sharp, commanding tone, "don't carry it off."

The officer seemed perplexed and stood for a short time, holding the hat.   Court adjourned, at that juncture, and Cable, taking his hat, returned to my house in a very good humor, and related his experiment.

The story of my adventure with the marshal, respecting my hat, soon became extensively known. The accounts given of it in the Cincinnati papers were copied by other papers in various parts of the country. The editor of the *Gazette* told me that he had seen it in sixteen of his Southern exchanges.

For several days I could not walk the streets without being accosted by some one who would assert that I had whipped the marshal. My general reply was: "I didn't hurt a hair of his head."

CHAPTER XVII.

AN UNDERGROUND RAILROAD DEPOT—THE PURCHASE
OF SLAVES BY THEIR RELATIVES—OTHER SERVICES
FOR THE COLORED PEOPLE—THE CASE OF CON-
NELLY—"SAMBO IN A TIGHT BOX."

IN the year 1856 I sold out my store, but continued to do more or less commission business,
receiving consignments of country produce, etc.,
until a few years later, when I engaged in the
work for the Freedmen. After disposing of my
store, I leased a large, convenient house on the
southwest corner of Franklin Street and Broadway,
near Woodward College. It had been built for a
boarding-house by William Woodward—who established the school and donated a large amount of
property to sustain it—and was well adapted for
such a purpose. It was in a quiet location, and de-
tached from other buildings, having a large open lot
on the south, with shade trees, and the college lot
on the west. The building contained over thirty
rooms, most of them large and well ventilated.
Here we opened a private boarding-house, receiving
only such as we thought would be agreeable company, for regular boarders, and in a short time had

a large and pleasant circle around our table. The members were mostly professors of religion, of different evangelical denominations, and the majority were strongly anti-slavery in sentiment. Several of the principals and teachers of the public schools boarded with us, as well as those of the Woodward High School, and we also had ministers of different denominations in our family. In addition to all these, we had many transient boarders. Our house was a resort for Friends who came to the city on business, and other of our acquaintances from the country, so that for a number of years it was similar to Friends' Institute in London, where members of the Society from different parts of the kingdom lodge and dine together when in that city on business or other errands.

The building and locality on the corner of Franklin and Broadway made a very suitable depot of the Underground Railroad, and rarely a week passed without bringing us passengers for that mysterious road. There was no pecuniary income from that class of boarders, but a constant outlay for them. I kept a horse and wagon always on hand to convey fugitives to the next depot. My wagon was made to order for this express purpose; it was a strong spring-wagon, neatly curtained so that it could be tightly closed, having a curtain in front, just behind the driver, and had seats for six passengers. On one occasion eight grown persons were crowded in, besides the driver; this was a heavy load for my horse, but when out of the city and beyond Walnut Hills, the men got out and walked, which they

could safely do, as it was in the night. Some of
my friends called my wagon the Underground Railroad car, and my horse the locomotive.

THE PURCHASE OF SLAVES BY THEIR RELATIVES.

In addition to this work I was often called upon
to aid persons who had obtained their liberty, to
buy their wife or husband or children out of slavery.
Many such cases were brought before me where
there appeared to be little probability of success.
I discouraged the effort, but in other cases I did
what I could to aid in accomplishing the desired
object. When the matter was presented in some
tangible form and the money contributed passed
into the hands of some responsible person who had
agreed to transact the business, I felt like I could
take hold of the case, and recommend it to others.
There were some very touching stories of distress,
of a wife, a husband or a child to be sold to a trader
and taken to the far South, perhaps to be forever
separated from all they loved. In such instances
when some near relative started out to solicit money
to buy the person from bondage, it was hard to
refuse, almost impossible if one brought the case
home to himself.

OTHER SERVICES FOR THE COLORED PEOPLE.

Besides aiding fugitives, I often assisted the poor
and-destitute among the free colored people of our
city, visiting the sick and afflicted among them who
seemed to be neglected by the white people, and
was often accused by those who were prejudiced

49

against colored people, of thinking more of the colored race than I did of the white. To such accusations I generally replied that I was no respecter of
color or race, that the negroes had souls equally as
precious as ours, that Christ had died for them as
well as for us, and that we were all alike in the
divine sight. The poor and destitute among them
were not looked after as such classes were among
the whites, and on that account I felt it my duty to
seek them out and help them. I often gave them
employment in preference to whites, not that I felt
any greater attachment to them on account of their
color, but because I knew that they were often
unjustly refused and neglected.

Sometimes I heard people say that they would
not have a negro about them ; they had never hired
one that did them any good, etc. I replied that
my experience had been different ; the best servants
I had ever employed belonged to that despised race.
"But," I added, "it is quite natural that they
should not work with much zeal for those who dislike and hate them."

In addition to these attentions to the colored
people in our city, I was frequently called upon to
look after the welfare and proper settlement of families that had been set free, and brought here, because the laws of the slave States would not allow
them to remain there and be free.

Such charges and cares seemed to accumulate on
my hands for several years preceding the war. I
was burdened with them because others could not
be found to take them, and because, out of compas-

sion, I could not refuse. I devoted much time to looking after the interests of negroes who were brought here and liberated, without receiving any pecuniary compensation for my time and services.

. At one time a company of slaves, consisting of several families, were willed free by their master— living in the interior of Kentucky—and brought to Cincinnati by an agent, and left to shift for themselves. They had difficulty in getting houses to live. in, and several families finally huddled into an old tenement, which was so uncomfortable that some of them soon became sick from exposure. Not being used to city life they were unable to find work, and soon became dissatisfied and discouraged. They wished to go into the country but knew not where to go. I was informed of their case and went to visit them. Finding them situated so uncomfortably, and learning that the money which had been given them was nearly gone, I advised them to go into the country at once. The father of one of the families was quite an intelligent man, and appeared to be the leading spirit among them; he had been the manager of his old master's plantation. I agreed to accompany him to hunt homes for the company in the country, and we started next morning to Springfield, Ohio, taking several of the young men with us. Arriving at Springfield, I called on several of my friends there and roused their interest in behalf of these people. Next day the young men found good situations among the farmers—it being the spring of the year—and the old man found a comfortable house for his family and employment on a farm, at good wages. We returned to Cincinnati rejoicing at our success, and the whole company removed at once to Springfield, where they did well.

I was not allowed much rest from such demands upon my services and sympathy, though the cases differed in some respects. I think that it was in the fall of the same year, that I was called upon by an old gentleman from the State of Tennessee, named McKnight, who told me that he had brought a large family of slaves to Cincinnati, whom he wished to liberate and locate in a settlement of Friends, where they would be properly cared for. He said he could recommend them as being honest, industrious, and trustworthy. The family consisted of the father, mother, and eight or nine children, among whom were several boys nearly grown. McKnight said that the children had all been born in his house and brought up as part of his family, and had never known what it was to be treated as slaves. He and his wife had not been blessed with children of their own, and they had reared these children carefully, and were quite fond of them; it was a trial to part with them. The man had had the entire charge of the farm and was a good manager, and the woman was an excellent housekeeper, and looked after all the affairs of household work.

McKnight and his wife were old and feeble, and felt that they must make some provision for their faithful servants. They intended that their slaves should never belong to any one else, and as the law did not allow them to be set free and remain in the

State, they concluded to locate them in a free State. He had accordingly brought them to Ohio, and, having been advised to consult me, had called on me for advice. After hearing the old man's story, I felt deeply interested in his case, and began to think over the places that would be suitable for the purpose. In weighing the matter my mind seemed to settle on Harveysburg, Warren County, knowing it to be a good anti-slavery neighborhood, and I advised him to go there.

The old man insisted on my going with him, as he was a stranger to that part of the country, and I finally agreed to accompany him. Next afternoon we took the train to Corwin—the nearest station to Harveysburg—taking with us the slave family and all their freight, consisting of household furniture, cooking utensils, etc. They seemed to be well supplied with clothing and bedding. At Corwin we obtained a comfortable room at the depot for them to lodge in, using their own bedding, and having an opportunity to prepare their food there. McKnight and I procured conveyance to Harveysburg, four miles distant. We arrived there after dark, and were kindly received and entertained by my friends Jonathan and Jane Clark. Next morning several Friends, both men and women, were called in to counsel with us in regard to the slave family; among the women were Martha Antrim and several others, who were noted sympathizers with the oppressed. All present appeared to listen with deep interest to McKnight's story about his family of slaves and his desire to settle them among Friends.

Jonathan Clark kindly offered a house for their present use. Teams were sent to Corwin for them, and they were soon located in their new quarters. I then returned home, but the old man remained a few days longer, to see them comfortably settled. They manifested great regard for their old master, and appeared very loth to part with him. He petted the little children, and they evidently loved him.

McKnight stopped at my house on his return home, and seemed happy and thankful that he had been spared to get this great burden off his mind and to see his slaves free. He spoke of his kind treatment at Harveysburg, and of the council held at J. Clark's the morning after we arrived there. Alluding to the Quaker women that were present, he said: "I never felt so much like I was surrounded by a company of angels," and burst into tears. Some of those dear Friends he spoke of with so much tenderness have since gone to their reward.

The slave family proved to be equal to the old man's recommendation. They soon rented a large farm, which the father and sons managed well, and as the whole family were industrious and frugal, they accumulated in a few years sufficient means to buy a farm of their own. Here they lived, when last I heard from them, comfortably situated and respected by all their neighbors.

The following occurrence took place not long before the breaking out of the war:

Two slaves, man and wife, belonging to a man who lived in Covington, Kentucky, escaped to Cincinnati, and went to the office of James Connelly, at that time engaged on the local staff of the *Commercial*. Having anti-slavery sympathies, he received the fugitives and promised to aid them. I was absent from the city at that time, and while waiting my return, to ship the two fugitives on the Underground Railroad, Connelly put them in a room back of his office, where he kept them several days, and fed them. At night, when he left the office, he locked them in. The search for them was so vigorous that it was not considered safe for them to move, and they remained in this place for more than a week. By some means their master learned of their whereabouts, and came with a posse of officers and men to take them.

Connelly was absent at the time, and the door was locked. The pursuers succeeded in making their way into the office, and demanded entrance at the inside door. The negro man, declaring he would not be taken, refused to open it. They broke the transom over the door, and he attempted to shoot them. They fired at him, inflicting a mortal wound, then, breaking in the door, they secured him and his wife. Notwithstanding his wound he fought desperately, but was soon overpowered and bound. The fugitives were then taken across the river to Covington, where the man died shortly afterward.

The master got out a writ to arrest Connelly for harboring fugitive slaves, but Connelly heard of it, and immediately fled from the city. He went to New York, where he obtained a position on the staff of the *Sun*, and remained several months.

Learning of his whereabouts, the Cincinnati marshal went East, and arrested him, brought him back to Cincinnati and placed him in jail. As soon as I heard of this I went to see Connelly, and it was arranged that he should be released on bail till court convened. I went to work, and interested a number of prominent men, who agreed to sign the bond. The sum required was large, but such business firms and persons as Harwood and Marsh, Allen and Co., Dr. W. H. Mussey, and others, soon subscribed it. Connelly was brought before Judge Leavitt, of the United States Court, to have the bond executed. In the court-room, S. M——, prosecuting attorney, came to me, and said: "Levi, you have rallied a set of good-looking men to sign Connelly's bond."

"Yes," I replied; "first-class men."

"Well," continued the attorney, "how is the Underground Railroad prospering?"

"Oh, finely, finely, we have a great many passengers; scarcely a week without more or less. But you seem to get hold of very few cases. How is it, Friend M., that I see thee engaged in this case? Thou used to be on our side."

"I must see that the law is executed. But how was it about this case? It seems to have been badly managed."

"I was away from home," I replied, to which he rejoined, "Ah! that explains the whole matter;" then I went on: "Now, if I were to get into a scrape of this kind, I would not dodge as Connelly did. I would submit myself and abide the consequences; and I know thou wouldst dislike to prose-

cute me for doing what thou knowest to be right,
and according to the dictates of humanity. Thou
wouldst not like to face me in court in such a case
as this."

He patted me on the shoulder and said: "I
guess there is no danger of your getting into
trouble, Mr. Coffin."

I continued: "How is it that you do not get
hold of cases at my house? We often have rich
cases there that would be worth considerable to
you. Only last week we had one of this kind. A
young woman as white as any of our wives or
daughters, who was held as a slave in Kentucky,
made her escape and came to this city. She found
a position as a servant girl among white people, and
no one suspected that she belonged to the colored
race. When she had been here a month or two
her master learned of her whereabouts and came in
pursuit of her. With two other men whom he had
called to his assistance, he undertook to capture her
one evening as she was returning from church with
several ladies, but she showed fight, and her companions did also. Some policemen saw the struggle
and interfered, and while the master was trying to
explain that the person he sought was his slave, the
girl slipped away and came to my house. We kept
her several days and prepared her for traveling,
then I bought her a ticket to Detroit and took her
in my carriage, in broad daylight, to Cumminsville,
where I put her on the train."

With a few more remarks, the conversation closed
and would soon have been forgotten, but a reporter

was present listening with professional ear, and next morning there appeared a lengthy article in a morning paper, giving an account of it, with much added and the whole embellished.

Connelly resumed his place on the *Commercial* staff, and came to board at our house, where he was joined by his family, who had removed to Pittsburg during his absence.

At this time there was a large anti-slavery element in Ohio. Abhorrence of the Fugitive Slave law and its penalties was rapidly increasing among the better class of citizens, and the feeling had become very strong against making Ohio a hunting ground for Southern slaveholders; consequently the public sentiment was largely in favor of Connelly. Ex-Governor Corwin, Judge Stallo, and other prominent lawyers volunteered to defend him.

When the United States Court convened and his trial came on, the court-room was crowded. The trial lasted several days and was the subject of unabated interest. After able arguments by the prominent lawyers who had volunteered to defend Connelly, and a ' lengthy charge by the judge, the jury retired to deliberate and finally brought in a verdict of guilty. The penalty was as light as the law allowed—imprisonment for twenty days and a fine of ten dollars.

Connelly was immediately taken to jail, by the deputy sheriff, to serve out his sentence. As they passed me where I was standing on the sidewalk, I said: "Friend Connelly, I hope thou wilt have a pleasant time in jail."

"Shut your mouth," said the officer; "you are not allowed to speak to the prisoner."

"Stop, my good fellow," said I, "thou art a servant of ours, not a master, and not clothed with so much authority."

"It will not be long before I will have you in jail, too."

"Perhaps that would be a difficult and costly job."

I and others of Connelly's friends made arrangements with the jailer to give him a good room and allow us to furnish it with a bedstead, bedding, a table, chairs, writing utensils, and other articles of comfort and convenience. We also stipulated that he should have good fare, and agreed to pay his board.

A number of people visited Connelly every day during his imprisonment. Ladies carried him strawberries, pastry and other dainties; the teachers of the public schools formed a procession and visited him, and ministers of the different churches called to see him. The Methodist Conference was in session in this city when he was imprisoned, and the members of it visited him in a body.

The next week the Unitarian Conference met here, and the members composing it formed a procession, headed by Horace Mann, and went to the prison to see Connelly. All these demonstrations showed sympathy with Connelly and made the time of his imprisonment pass quickly and pleasantly.

The jailer grew tired of locking and unlocking the door of his room so often, and finally left it open, that visitors might pass in and out as they pleased. The fine of ten dollars, which was a part of the penalty, was never exacted.

Connelly's term of imprisonment expired at noon, but as the Turners and other societies wished to form a torchlight procession, and escort him from jail, the jailer allowed him to remain till night. The arrangements were all made, and at the appointed hour, the procession, headed by a band of music and several carriages, containing Judge Stallo and other prominent citizens, proceeded to the jail. A committee appointed conducted Connelly from the jail to the carriage reserved for him, then the procession paraded through the principal streets, and went to Turner Hall, where Connelly delivered a speech.

A short time afterward a large public hall was engaged, and Connelly was advertised to deliver a lecture on the Underground Railroad, the proceeds, after deducting expenses, to be applied for the benefit of the road mentioned.

A large and interested audience filled the hall at the time appointed, and listened attentively to the address, in which Connelly took the ground that the Underground Railroad was a Southern institution, and explained the different principles on which it was conducted.

"SAMBO IN A TIGHT BOX."

This story may be related in letters. The following appeared in the Nashville (Tennessee) *Union and American*, in April, 1860:

A NIGGER-STEALING QUAKER.

The Cincinnati *Commercial*, of April 18, contains the following:

"SAMBO IN A TIGHT BOX.

"EDITORS COMMERCIAL,—In this morning's issue of your paper I find under the above head a caution administered to me to be careful, after informing the public that a box was forwarded from Nashville, Tennessee, by Adams Express, to my care, and all went well until the train reached Seymour, Indiana, when the box burst open, and out dropped a nigger, etc. You go on to state that yesterday morning Mr. Coffin called for the box, and the clerk questioned him closely as to its contents, but he 'didn't know a thing; couldn't guess what was in it.' Then you say: 'Be careful, Friend Levi; thee [thou] musn't tell fibs.' Your caution is fully appreciated, and in return permit me to suggest to you to be careful to make no improper insinuations to lead the public to believe a fib in regard to my complicity in the matter.

"About twelve o'clock on Seventh day, the 14th inst., I received through the post-office a letter, post-marked Nashville, Tennessee, dated Nashville, April 11, signed Hannah M. Johnson, stating that a box would be forwarded by Adams Express to my care, and wishing me to go to the express office and take charge of it, stating that the express would arrive at half past ten o'clock, Saturday night, but did not say what the box contained. I learned that the express would not arrive till First day morning, nine o'clock. I went to the office at that time and handed the letter to the clerk or agent. He informed me that they had just got a dispatch informing them that a box marked Hannah M. Johnson, care of Levi Coffin, Cincinnati, had burst open at Seymour, Indiana, and a nigger rolled out. I informed them that I did not know Hannah M. Johnson; never heard of her before; had no knowledge of any box or anything else being shipped to my care from that direction, until I received that letter which was before them.

"No questions were asked me. My statements were voluntary.

They requested the letter to copy. I gave it to them with the promise that it be returned to me. They have the letter. The public is welcome to its contents. Previous to receiving this letter I have had no correspondence with any one in Tennessee for more than a year past; did not know of any person, male or female, traveling in that direction; knew nothing of the matter in any shape.

"My name and address are well known in the South. It is no new thing for me to receive consignments of slaves from the South, generally gentlemen's children to be educated; but this is the first case in a tight box, and no instructions whether they wished him sent to school or not. I am sorry that Sambo did not get through safely after suffering so long in a tight box. I would have received him kindly, though I would object to that mode of traveling as dangerous and decidedly uncomfortable.

"LEVI COFFIN.

"Cincinnati, April 16, 1860."

After copying the above from the Cincinnati *Commercial,* the editor of the Nashville *Union and American* made the following scurrilous comment, trying to use Quaker language :

"Friend Levi, thee ought to have studied thy subject a little better, and then perhaps thee would not have involved thyself in such palpable contradictions. Thee never heard of Hannah M. Johnson, yet thou wert quick to 'run after the strange woman,' to pay the express charges upon her box, the contents of which thee knew nothing about unless thy instinct told thee. Verily hath it been said that the man given to prevarication ought to have a good memory, and be able at least to tell a straight story.

"Thee ought to have conned this lesson over well, Friend Levi, before thee did pen thy communication to the editor who gave thee such good advice. Thy worst enemy could not desire thee to write a book after reading thy communication. Thee knew too much about that strange woman and her mission among thy Southern friends, and never did criminal more surely betray his guilt. Thee knew that the box shipped thee by the strange woman contained a chattel, which the law, both human and divine, declared to be stolen, and which could not be received by thee without making thyself a party to the crime.

"We fear from thy avowal of sorrow that 'Sambo did not get through safe,' that thou art a most hardened reprobate, and that a lecture upon the evil tendency of thy practice would accomplish about as much as a moonbeam falling upon an iceberg. But there is one thing, Friend Levi, to which we wish to call thy especial attention. It is clear from thy confession that thou didst have an intrigue with this Hannah M. Johnson, and as that 'kind-hearted individual' charged and received from Sambo, seventy dollars in cash and a double-case silver watch, according to his statement, we put it to thee whether it is not thy duty to make Sambo whole again in his purse? The sincerity of thy compassion for the nigger is now put to the test."

To which I wrote the following reply:

"To THE EDITORS OF THE NASHVILLE UNION AND AMERICAN—I find in your paper of 20th ult., after publishing my card or statement of facts as published in the Cincinnati 'Commercial,' a scurrilous comment in which you make some very grave charges. Absence from home has prevented me from noticing them sooner, but your Southern honor can not deny me the right to be heard in reply. It seems that thou hast found it in thy heart to call in question my plain statement of facts, and to accuse me of contradictions, prevarications, etc. Then thou proceeds to make positive assertions without the slightest foundation to build upon, unless thy instincts told thee, and they are not apt to dictate untruth. I am not aware of my veracity being questioned by those who are acquainted with me; hence thy comment will have about as much effect as a moonbeam falling upon an iceberg, as thou supposed. And thou hast blundered into another truth, perhaps not intentionally. Thou sayest: 'Thy worst enemy could not desire thee to write a book.' True; thou didst not desire Helper, of North Carolina, to write a book, and I should not suppose for a moment that thou wouldst desire me to write a book. I am a Southern man, born and raised in the State of North Carolina; have traveled in most of the Southern States, and have connections and acquaintances in several of them; and, if I were to write a book, I might expose some of the abominations of slavery, that would not be pleasant to thy ear. The extent of the evils of slavery, and its demoralizing effects upon the white population of the South, can not be written even by a Southerner. I am opposed to the whole system of slavery, in all its heinous forms, and conscientiously believe it to be a sin against God and a crime against man to chatelize a human being, and reduce God's image to the level of a brute, to be bought and sold in the market as cattle or swine. I am also opposed to amalgamation, and the whole system of concubinage, which are the legitimate fruits of slavery, and prominent evils growing out of it. It is also well known in the South, as well as in the North, by all who are acquainted with me, that I am opposed to any interference with slavery, or the institutions of slave States, except by moral suasion. I am a firm believer in the doctrines and precepts of the gospel, which teaches us to do unto others as we would that they should do unto us; and to feed the hungry, clothe the naked, etc.; but does not make any distinction of color. Now, if the editor of the Nashville 'Union and American' should be so unfortunate as to be reduced to slavery (for color is no protection in the South), and should he employ Hannah M. Johnson, or somebody else, to put him in a tight box and consign him to me, he may be assured that I will receive him kindly, and feed him if he should be hungry; for it is not in my nature to be unkind to the least or the poorest of the human family. But I would advise some other mode of conveyance as more safe, and that Hannah should pay express charges, as I suppose she did in the case of Sambo; for I heard no account of express charges until I saw thy false assertion, that I was quick to run after the strange woman to pay express charges, etc.

"Thou hast said that Hannah received of Sambo seventy dollars in cash, and a double-cased silver watch, for her services; and thou hast no doubt relieved thy mind of a burden by suggesting that I should make Sambo whole again in his purse. But, as I presume that Hannah M. Johnson is a citizen of Nashville, or was a delegate to the Charleston Convention, and entirely unknown to me, it does not strike me very forcibly that I should be accountable for her misconduct, for if her motives had been purely benevolent, she would not have charged Sambo anything. But there is one thing, my dear friend, to which I wish to call thy especial attention. I am very often called upon by slaveholders from the South, who come to Ohio, to liberate a portion of their slaves, generally their own children and sometimes their slave mothers, for assistance and advice in regard to locating them, etc., all of which I have given cheerfully without charge, and in addition to this, there have been quite a number of slave children from several different Southern States placed under my care to be educated, generally by their white fathers or their agents, and in some instances by judges and lawyers—men of honor and high standing in their own country; and as I am left minus in several cases, and in one case from Tennessee where the bill is not paid, does it not strike thy mind very forcibly that it would be just as fair and right for thee to make me whole in my purse for money that I have paid out of my pocket for some of your own citizens, as for me to make Sambo whole in his purse? Thy generosity is now put to the test.   LEVI COFFIN.

"Cincinnati, 5th mo. 12, 1860."

50

CHAPTER XVIII.

LAST WORK ON THE UNDERGROUND RAILROAD—THE
PRINCE OF WALES — BEGINNING OF THE WAR —
KIRBY SMITH'S THREATENED RAID—RESCUE OF A
SLAVE GIRL BY TWO UNION SOLDIERS—THE KEN-
TUCKY POLICY AND COLONEL UTLEY'S ACTION.

BUSINESS on the Underground Railroad continued brisk up to the time of the breaking
out of the war, and for a year afterward—before
slaves were received and protected inside our military lines. The friends of the fugitives had increased
in number, and though my time and attention were
still heavily taxed, I had less difficulty in raising
.means to pay their passage, or in 'finding safe shelter for them among the white people when it was
necessary to divide the companies, as was frequently
the case. I often raised money, bought tickets, and
forwarded the fugitives by rail to Detroit, Sandusky,
or some other point on the lakes, when it was not
likely that hunters were ahead of them. I generally started them on the evening train, that they
might make the greater part of their journey in the
night, and in every instance they arrived safely at
their destination. I had friends at the other end of

the line who generally notified me of the safe arrival
of passengers by way of the Underground or Upper-
ground Railways.

THE PRINCE OF WALES.

It will be remembered that when the Prince of
Wales was in America he visited a number of our
principal cities, after he had been to Canada. When
in Cincinnati, he was escorted about the city to see
the most important and interesting places, and in
his progress through the streets, he and his suite
were conducted up Broadway to Franklin Street,
and west along Franklin, in front of Woodward
College, to Main Street. This course gave them
two front views of my house, which stood on the
southwest corner of Broadway and Franklin. The
piazzas fronting on Broadway, and all the windows
in both fronts of that large house, were filled with
our boarders and the neighbors who had come to
get a good view of the Prince. My wife and I
stood in front, on the piazza. The Prince, who was
riding in an open carriage, took off his hat and
made a graceful bow as he passed our house.
Some of our company wondered why he should be
brought through our quiet locality, for it was quite
unusual for public guests to be conducted through
that neighborhood of family dwelling-houses.

Others replied: "It is not at all strange; the
Prince has been to Canada and seen the terminus
of the Underground Railroad, and of course he
wished to see this end of it, and as this house is
the principal depot, he wished to take a fair view

of the premises so that he could make a correct report to the Queen."

This explanation seemed satisfactory to the company, and caused a hearty laugh among us.

THE BEGINNING OF THE WAR.

With the excitement that attended the breaking out of the rebellion in the spring of 1861, there came a new feeling, in the free States, in regard to slavery. The odium that had been attached to abolitionism began to die away; there was no longer such disgrace in professing its sentiments or danger in aiding the fugitives. Much of my work for them was now done boldly and above board— or, I might say, above ground.

When the first news of the war reached me, I said: "This war will never end while slavery lasts," but I was told that the rebellion would soon be put down, leaving slavery untouched. The popular religious denominations were still under the influence of that pro-slavery power which had so long had the ascendency. Prayer-meetings were held in all the churches to pray that the rebellion might be put down and the awful calamities of war averted. Acknowledgments were made of our sins, such as intemperance and Sabbath-breaking, and the forgiveness of God was implored, and He was asked to restore peace and brotherly love to our land; but the sin of slavery was not mentioned, not a prayer for the poor suffering slaves was heard in these meetings in Cincinnati. The exciting subject of slavery must not be touched.

A union prayer-meeting for business men was established in a central church on Fourth Street. The sessions were held from eight o'clock to nine every morning, and, besides prayers, there were brief exhortations. These meetings were largely attended. They were led, in turn, by prominent religionists who acted each in his appointed time as presiding officer, and with the tap of his mallet timed the speaker or stopped him if he touched upon any controverted point or exciting question. The subject of slavery must not be alluded to; it might hurt the feelings of some good·brother in the meeting.

About this time that noble friend to the slave, John G. Fee, of Berea, Kentucky, came to the city on business and stopped at our house, as he generally did when in Cincinnati. He asked me if I had attended those morning prayer-meetings. I said, "I have attended but one; I have very little faith in those meetings. The real cause of the war is not alluded to; the poor slaves are not remembered in their prayers, and the sin of slavery is not mentioned. The same pro-slavery spirit that has ruled the church so long still exists. This war has been permitted by the Almighty to come upon us as a judgment and the North must suffer as well as the South, for we are partners in the national sin. I believe that this war will not end until the great sin of slavery is removed·from our land."

Friend Fee heartily united with me in these sentiments. He had preached and prayed and labored for many years in Kentucky, in behalf of the poor slave, and had suffered mob violence and persecution of every kind, for doing what he believed he had been appointed by his Divine Master to do.

The next morning we went together to the business men's prayer-meeting. It was largely attended; many prayers and short speeches were made, and every sin but that of slavery was mentioned. Toward the close of the meeting John G. Fee rose and spoke of the real cause of the war —slavery, that great and crying sin of the nation, to which no one had alluded. The chairman of the meeting at once brought down his mallet, as a signal for him to stop, but Fee continued to speak, for a few moments, with great earnestness and power. His words seemed to create a stir and uneasiness with many in the meeting. When a few more sharp taps of the mallet had been given, he took his seat, but immediately kneeled in prayer, and prayed with such earnestness and power that he was not interrupted, although he brought before the Lord the great sin of slavery and alluded to it as the cause of the terrible judgment that was hanging over us. At the close of the meeting, Horace Bushnell, a minister and a warm friend to the slave, came up and taking Fee by the hand said: "Brother Fee, you drove in the nail and then you clinched it, and they can't get it out."

The war excitement still grew stronger, and party feuds and distinctions were for awhile forgotten in the all-absorbing subject. The rebellion in the South increased, one State after another seceded, except Kentucky, which professed to occupy neutral ground, and all loyal or Union men were united

on the same platform. By the South, all Northern
men were termed Yankees or abolitionists, and
among us much of the odium formerly attached to
abolitionism died out. It was now "Union" or
"Rebel," but there was still a class of men in the
North who were connected in business with the
South, or had interests in slaves, who sympathized
with that section and threw the weight of their influence with the rebellion. This troublesome. element
in the North doubtless served to prolong the war.

KIRBY SMITH'S THREATENED RAID.

The war excitement was greatly increased when
the news came that the rebel General Kirby Smith
had approached near Cincinnati with a large army,
and great preparations were at once made for
defense; the city was at once put under martial law.
The wires flashed the news all over the country and
special trains were bringing in soldiers from all parts
of the State. The Mayor of the city issued a proclamation requiring every man, without distinction
of age, color, or country, to report at the voting
places in the various wards, to be organized into
military companies for the protection of the city.
The Governor of the State had also issued a proclamation requiring all volunteer military companies to
rally at once to our assistance. Arms and ammunition were ordered here from other points. Cannon
were placed on Mount Adams, and the high hills
above and below the city, in position to rake the
river if the rebel army attempted to cross. It was
feared that they would shell the city, and that a

general conflagration would be the result. The excitement pervaded all classes of society. A number of women and children were sent out of the city for safety, and money from the vaults of the banks was transferred to banks at other points. General Wallace, of Indianapolis, arrived in the city, with a number of Indiana soldiers, and took command. Companies of volunteers were arriving almost every hour. Wherever the telegraph had spread the alarm, men of all classes dropped their business and rallied to the defense of their State. Judges, lawyers, preachers, professors, and students of colleges, were in these companies, as well as farmers armed with their squirrel-guns and other weapons that were at command. We soon had an army of over one hundred thousand men in Cincinnati—many of them raw, untrained soldiers, without any preparation for camping or supplies of provisions. These were called "Squirrel Hunters," but they were fully in earnest, and determined to protect the city against the rebel army that threatened our destruction. Preparations were at once made to feed our protectors, and the ladies of each ward did their duty nobly. Tables were spread in the market-houses and parks, and (in some wards) on the public side-walks, and bountifully furnished with provisions by the ladies—many of whom attended as waiters. Public halls and other places were used as headquarters and lodging places for the soldiers. In our ward a table was spread on the side-walk of Franklin Street, from Broadway to Sycamore—in front of our house and

Woodward College—where five hundred could be fed at one time. It was supplied with provisions for several days by the ladies of the ninth ward. Our basement kitchen was made the depository for the victuals between meals; and our large cooking-stove was used to furnish hot coffee and tea. At that table were fed the Oberlin students, and other abolitionists from the northern part of Ohio, many of whom we knew. After meals, they frequently formed in line in front of our house and sang "John Brown," and other anti-slavery songs—the whole company joining in the chorus. Nearly every night, while this great excitement lasted, we had sick soldiers to care for. Many of our acquaintances from the country were among the new volunteers, or "Squirrel Hunters," and not being used to soldier life, a number of them became sick. We took them in and cared for them; although we did not believe in war and fighting, we always considered it right to take care of the sick and feed the hungry, and in this way we did our full share by the soldiers. To some of the young men who had none, my wife gave blankets for use in camp.

One morning one of our city officers, with a posse of men, came to my house and demanded to know why I had not reported for service at the place designated by the Mayor in his proclamation. He said he was instructed to visit all in that ward who had not reported, and if they refused to comply to compel them to report. I told him that I should not comply, and he said: "Then I shall be obliged to compel you to do so."

51

I replied: "Thou might find that to be a difficult job. I am a non-resistant, and thou would have to carry me to the place, and that would look ugly."

The officer laughed, and said he guessed I would go without carrying.

I said: "If thou wast to get me there it might be very difficult to compel me to report for service in the army. I could not take a gun and go out to shoot anybody; that is contrary to the spirit and doctrines of the gospel. Christ instructed us to love our enemies and to do good to them that hate us, and I am a full believer in his teachings. I can not comply with the Mayor's proclamation. General Wallace is now in command in the city, and he will not require such service of me, for he knows my principles."

The officer left me, and I was not again troubled. Soon after this a certain boundary was set in the city that none were allowed to pass, without permission, for some time. Pickets were stationed along the line to enforce the restriction. I happened to have business across the line, and was permitted to pass and repass when I wished to do so.

When the alarm first came that the rebel army was advancing toward Cincinnati, and a number of frightened women went, with their children, to the country, a few of our lady boarders partook of the panic, and packed their trunks and left the city. They, together with others of our friends, seemed anxious for us to close our house and go out of the city for safety. Some of them said that our house would be the first one destroyed, for many of the

Kentuckians knew where it was, and that it was a depot of the Underground Railroad. I laughed at their fears, and told them that I felt no alarm; I had never run from danger, and if our friends and neighbors were to suffer I would stay and suffer with them. "Besides," I said, "we may be needed here to help care for the sick and wounded; though I do not believe the rebel army will cross the river. There is a large army gathered here, and they will not run into the lion's mouth."

It proved to be not very long till the rebels, having discovered the formidable force here, and the great preparations for defense, fell back some distance from the river. Neither was it long till our services were needed in caring for sick and wounded soldiers brought here from various Southern battle-fields, for whom sufficient hospital room could not be provided.

During the excitement our house was more like a military post than a depot of the Underground Railroad. We had a number of boarders, and all the men armed themselves and reported for service, in obedience to the Mayor's proclamation. They placed their guns by their bedsides, and when an alarm was sounded on the fire-bells in the night, they sprang up, seized their weapons and hurried to their posts. These signals were to be given when the rebel army attempted to cross the river, and the city was kept in a state of constant excitement, though the alarms proved false. They were sounded, no doubt, to call the people together quickly, and to try their metal.

The German element was strong in our city. Many of the men were veteran soldiers who had seen service in their own country, and well understood military tactics.

The negro element, on the contrary, was utterly ignorant of all kinds of drill. Many of the colored men did not understand why they should be called upon, having never before been recognized as citizens, and neglected to report; some of them were alarmed and hid themselves. The police hunted them out and forced them into the ranks. One day a posse of men came to our house and asked if there were any colored people about the place who had not reported for service. I said, "Yes, there are several colored persons about our house," and invited the captain to come in. He followed me through the hall into the kitchen, where we had two or three colored women employed. I introduced them to the officer, saying, "These are all the colored people we have at present." He laughed and said he did not want women, and asked if these were Underground Railroad passengers. I said: "No, but if they were you would not let the rebels have them, would you?"

He replied: "No, sir," and left the house.

My wife reproved me for being mischievous.

Judge Dickson, who was the colored people's friend and in whom they had entire confidence, organized a separate company of colored men. They rallied willingly to him. A pontoon bridge was made across the Ohio River, between Cincinnati and Covington, and a large army marched over into Kentucky. A few miles back of Covington they went into camp and made great preparations for defense, throwing up breastworks and extending their lines so as to prevent the approach of the enemy to the city. Colonel Dickson's colored regiment was marched over to aid in making the fortifications, and was said to be the most orderly and faithful regiment that crossed. After they were released and marched back to the city, the men contributed money to buy a fine sword, which they presented to Colonel Dickson as a testimonial of their regard for him, accompanied by an able speech from one of their company selected for the occasion.

The rebel army had retreated southward, and the excitement that had been so high in this city seemed to die away, but we were constantly reminded that war was going on. Regiments of volunteers, regularly organized and equipped, from Indiana and other Northwestern States, passed through this city on their way to the South and East. Among the Indiana companies were many noble young men of our acquaintance—some of them our relatives—and our feelings were continually harassed with the thought that they might never return. It was not long till the terrible battles of Fort Donelson, on the Cumberland River, and Pittsburg Landing, on the Tennessee River, were fought. Steamboats from this place, with doctors and surgeons on board, hastened to the scenes of carnage to aid in caring for and removing the wounded. They were brought to Cincinnati, but sufficient hospital room had not been provided for them. A meeting was held by the citizens, and a committee appointed to call on families and ascertain how many would be received in private houses. We were called upon and agreed to take eight of the wounded soldiers in our house and care for them. Many others volunteered to take a greater or less number, and next morning the names of those who thus volunteered, and the number they agreed to receive, were published in the morning papers. The committee succeeded, however, in renting a large house for a hospital, and only two soldiers were brought to our house. We nursed them carefully until they were able to go to their homes. At various times we took in sick soldiers and cared for them until they were able to travel, feeling that it was our duty to do so.

RESCUE OF A SLAVE GIRL BY TWO UNION SOLDIERS.

Among the regiments that collected at Cincinnati, during the time of Kirby Smith's threatened raid into Ohio, was one from Racine, Wisconsin, which, from the well-known anti-slavery sentiments of the commander, Colonel Utley, and the men composing it, had received the name of the Abolition regiment. While they were in camp near Nicholasville, Kentucky, a young mulatto slave girl, about eighteen years old, of fine personal appearance, was sold by her master, for the sum of seventeen hundred dollars, to a man who designed placing her in a house of ill-fame at Lexington, Kentucky. As soon as the poor girl learned of the fate in store for her, she fled from her master, and making her way to the camp of the Twenty-Second Wisconsin volunteers—

the regiment referred to—told her story, and asked protection. The true-hearted men, to whom she applied for help, resolved to aid her, though the law did not then allow Northern troops to protect fugitive slaves who came within their lines.

Her master soon came to the camp in pursuit of her, but the men secreted her, and he did not find her. The colonel now wished to send her to a place of safety, and two soldiers volunteered to conduct her to Cincinnati. One of their officers told them that he knew me personally, and recommended them to bring the fugitive to my house. She was dressed in soldier's clothes and hidden in a sutler's wagon, under some hay. The two men dressed themselves in citizen's clothing, and having learned the password that would open a way for them through the picket lines, took their seats in the wagon, and drove out of camp about one o'clock at night. They traveled almost without stopping until the distance—more than a hundred miles—was traversed, and they reached Cincinnati in safety.

They came immediately to my house, and were ushered into the sitting-room, accompanied by their charge, who presented the appearance of a mulatto soldier boy. As there was other company present, they called me to one side and related their story. The "soldier boy" was given into my wife's care, and was conducted up-stairs to her room. Next morning he came down transformed into a young lady of modest manners and pleasing appearance, who won the interest of all by her intelligence and amiable character.

The party remained a day or two, to recover from
the fatigue of their journey, and during the interval visited a daguerrean gallery, where they had
their pictures taken, the lady sitting, the soldiers
standing, one on either side, with their revolvers
drawn, showing their readiness thus to protect her,
even at the cost of their own lives. Not content
with escorting her to a free State, these brave young
men telegraphed to Racine, Wisconsin, and made
arrangements for their friends there to receive her,
and I took her one evening in my carriage to the
depot, accompanied by her protectors, and put her
on board the train with a through ticket for Racine,
via Chicago. She was nicely dressed, and wore a
vail, presenting the appearance of a white lady. I
conducted her to a seat in a first-class car, her soldier friends having previously taken leave of her in
the carriage. As the train moved off they lifted
their hats to her, aud she waved her handkerchief
in good-by. They afterward remarked to me, that
it seemed one of the happiest moments of their
lives when they saw her safely on her way to a place
beyond the reach of pursuers. They had done a
noble unselfish deed, and were rewarded by that
approval of conscience which contains the most
unalloyed joy of life.

After their return to camp, I received the following letter from one of them:

"IN CAMP, NEAR NICHOLASVILLE, KENTUCKY,
"November 17, 1862.

"FRIEND L. COFFIN: As the Lord prospered us on our mission to the land of freedom, so has He prospered us in our

return to our regiment. At five o'clock on Friday evening, after a ride of three days, we arrived at our camp near Nicholasville; and you would have rejoiced to hear the loud cheering and hearty welcome that greeted us on our arrival. Our long delay had occasioned many fears as to our welfare; but when they saw us approach, the burden of their anxiety was gone, and they welcomed us by one hearty outburst of cheers. The colonel was full of delight, and when he heard of the Friend L. Coffin, who had so warmly welcomed us to the land of freedom, he showered a thousand blessings on your head. The way was opened, and we were directed to you by an unseen but ever-present Hand. The Lord was truly with us upon that journey.

" Your humble friend,
" JESSE L. BERCH."

The name of the other soldier was Frank M. Rockwell. Both were young men of true principles and high character, and, as representatives of the solid worth of Wisconsin's noble sons, were men that their State could regard with pride.

I received a letter from Jesse L. Berch, a few months ago, making inquiries in regard to a book which he had heard I had published. When I replied, stating that my book was not yet published, I asked for news of the slave girl whom he had aided to rescue. He responded, giving information of her safe arrival in Racine, and of her residence there for a few months, concluding by saying, ''Afterward she married a young barber and moved into Illinois, and I have never been able to ascertain her whereabouts since I came from the army, though Mr. Rockwell and myself have tried repeatedly.

This young man has kindly loaned me a book entitled ''The Star Corps,'' by G. S. Bradley, chaplain of the Twenty-Second Wisconsin Volunteers, from which I cull various extracts relating to Colonel Utley, the commander of that regiment, and his combat with the slave power in Kentucky.

THE KENTUCKY POLICY, AND COLONEL UTLEY'S ACTION.

"Colonel Utley, the commander of the Wisconsin abolition regiment, was the chief actor in an occurrence which, though seemingly not very important at the time, had the effect of producing a radical change in the attitude of the Government toward contrabands. At the beginning of the war the policy of Northerners disclaimed any intention to disturb the 'peculiar institution' of the South. It was not a war against slavery, said all the representatives of the Government then. The commanders of Union troops, when they first entered the South, would not receive or protect fugitive slaves who sought refuge in their lines; some sent them back; others allowed their masters to come and take them. But this policy was very repugnant to some true-hearted Northerners who had all their lives sympathized with the slaves and hated the bondage that held them in thralldom; and they scorned the half measures dictated by policy."

The following order was issued just before Colonel Utley's command left Camp Wells:

"HEADQUARTERS, DIVISION ARMY OF KENTUCKY,   }
"North Williamstown, Kentucky, October 15, 1862. }

"GENERAL ORDER NUMBER FIVE.—All contrabands except officers' servants will be left behind when the division moves forward to-morrow morning. Public transportation will in no case be furnished to officers' servants. Commanders of regiments and detachments will see this order promptly enforced. By order of
"BRIGADIER GENERAL Q. A. GILMORE,
"W. L. M. BURGER, Captain and Acting Assistant General,
"P. B. PARSONS, Lieutenant and Acting Assistant Adjutant General, Second Brigade.
"[Official.]"

A few days afterward, while at Camp Jones, Colonel Utley received the following:

"JONES, October 18, 1862.

"COLONEL,—You will at once send to my quarters the four contrabands, John, Abe, George and Dick, known to belong to good loyal citizens. They are in your regiment, or were this morning.

"Your obedient servant,

"Q. A. GILLMORE, Brigadier General.

"To Colonel W. L. Utley, Commanding Twenty-Second Wisconsin Volunteers."

To this order the colonel returned the following reply:

"HEADQUARTERS TWENTY-SECOND REG'T WISCONSIN VOLS., {
"October 18, 1862. {

"GENERAL Q. A. GILLMORE:

"DEAR SIR,—I have just received your orders to deliver up certain contrabands said to be in my regiment. Permit me to say that I recognize your authority in all matters pertaining to the military and to the movements of the army; but I do not consider this as belonging to that department. I recognize no authority on the subject of delivering up contrabands, save that of the President of the United States. You are, no doubt, conversant with the proclamation of the President of September 22, 1862, and with the law of Congress on the subject. In conclusion, I will say that I had nothing to do with their coming into camp, and I will have nothing to do with sending them out.

"Very respectfully your obedient servant,

"WM. L. UTLEY."

"The colonel was immediately summoned to headquarters. He went, and the interview between him and the general was short and spicy. Said the general: "I sent you an order this evening."

"The colonel replied: 'Yes, sir, and I refused to obey it.'

"The general thought he must be obeyed, and said he should dispose of the matter at once.

"The colonel thought it would not be settled in a remarkably summary manner.

"The general finally said that he should repeat the order in the morning.

"To this the colonel replied: 'General, to save you the trouble and folly of such a course, let me say I shall refuse to comply in the same positive manner.'

"The morning came, but the order was not received. Instead of an arrest, the colonel was put in command of .the brigade, with orders to protect the supply train to march to Georgetown.

" The colonel afterward call on the general, and was informed that the act of Congress and the proclamation of the President had been more carefully examined since the affair at Camp Jones, and that a different policy would be instituted. No more contrabands would be returned, and those coming into our lines would be organized into a brigade by themselves for appropriate services.

"Regiments from Ohio and Michigan, in camp near the same place, sustained Colonel Utley in the position which he took. The affair created considerable excitement, occasioned much discussion, and proved a triumph of principle."

The following account of Colonel Utley's conflict with a slaveholder, I take from the book referred to :

"When we left Lexington, we comforted ourselves with the hope that the slavery question, which had proved a constant and grievous annoyance from the time we entered the State, would trouble us no more, but in this we have been sadly disappointed. The slave catchers follow us day and night, and seem determined to crush us, if in their power to do so. It is not, however, so much the desire for the 'nigger' himself, which drives them to desperation, as the necessity of breaking down the principle upon which we stand. The negro is a personal and comparatively trifling matter, and probably we have a smaller number of them than any other regiment in Kentucky, but the principle involves the position of the State.

"On the very day after arriving at this place—Nicholasville— the colonel was informed that a gentleman, outside the lines, wished to see him.

"The colonel remarked : 'Another negro catcher, I presume.'

" On approaching the lines, a large portly old gentleman appeared, lying back in an elegant carriage, with a negro servant for driver in front. He informed the colonel that he was in pursuit of a boy, who was in his regiment, at the same time presenting an order from General Gillmore, directing that he be permitted to enter the lines and get the boy.

"The colonel coolly informed him that such orders were not current in his regiment. The old gentleman then went on to say that he, too, was opposed to slavery; that he was the only survivor among the 'honorables' who voted for the famous Missouri Compromise, and that he had written an essay against slavery and in favor of emancipation, which was eagerly sought after by the President at the present time. Said the colonel: 'If you had done these things honestly, and from principle, it would certainly have been very commendable; but, sir, your mission here to-day gives the lie to all of these professions. I do not permit nigger-hunters to ransack my regiment. If you will drive back into town, and return at three o'clock P. M., I will look through the regiment, and if I find such a boy and he is willing to go with you, I pledge you my honor that you shall have him.' He reluctantly consented, and turned his horse toward the village.

"After he left, the colonel found the boy, who frankly acknowledged that he belonged to the old gentleman.

"The little fellow then gave us a tale of sorrow, and that with such an air of truthfulness and intelligence as astonished those that listened to it. And when at last, he drew up his diminutive little figure, called upon us to see what beating and starving had done for him, and cried: 'See me; I am almost nineteen years old—what am I? and now they beat me because I am no larger, and can do no more;' moisture was seen to gather in the colonel's eyes, and he left the tent with a significant determination on his brow. Before reaching his tent, he met the old slave-hunter returning long before the appointed time, so eager was he for his prey.

"'Have you found the boy?' were the first words to tremble on the old man's anxious lip.

"'Sir,' said the colonel, fixing his 'wicked look' upon him, 'I have found a little yellow boy who says he belongs to a man in Lexington, who hired him out to a brutal Irishman for fifty dollars per year. The Irishman, never having seen him, was dissatisfied, he being so much smaller than he anticipated for a boy of nineteen, and as his master would not take him back, he declared, with an oath, that he would lick it out of him—that the man beat him for anything and for nothing—that he had been to his master many times, and told him he could not stand it. His master would say: "Go back, you dog."

" ' He also says he showed his master his neck, with the skin torn off, where the Irishman had tied a rope around it, and dragged him about. And yet his master would give him no protection — had commenced hiring him out when only five years of age, and had left him there ever since, taking all his wages. He says that he has been beaten and worked and starved till there was nothing left of him, and that he was then beaten for not being bigger. He also says that he endured it till he could no longer, and fled. He lived on black walnuts till the snow came, and he was obliged to seek shelter somewhere. He sought protection from several regiments, but could gain no admission till he came to this. Now, sir, is that your boy? Are you the fiend of a master of whom he speaks? You, who came to me boasting of your wonderful works in the cause of the oppressed? I say, sir, is that your boy? Are you that master?'

"These declarations fell with terrible force upon the old gentleman's trembling nerves. It was some time before he could answer, but finally faintly replied: 'It is my nigger, but niggers will lie.'

"The colonel then told him that they would go and see the boy. When we arrived at the quarters, the little fellow, instead of shrinking away from his presence, walked out with a firm step, and meekly but boldly said:

" ' How do you do, massa?'

"The colonel said to him: 'This man claims you as his property, and says you ran away and left him.'

" ' Yes, sah,' said the little fellow, and then he proceeded to rehearse the whole story in a calm, respectful, but decided manner. The master struggled in vain to resist the force of the simple tale. The following questions and answers passed between the master and the slave:

" ' Have I not always treated you well?'

" ' No, massa, you have not.'

" ' How so, sir?'

" ' When I went to you for protection from those who beat me, you refused to give it, and drove me back like a dog.'

" ' But did I not tell you that I would take you away?'

" ' Yes, massa, but you never did it.'

"Ah! it was a beautiful sight to see that little abused slave confront so nobly that proud, bloated, aristocratic slaveholder. The Lord was with the weak, and gave him power to confound the mighty.

"The colonel then asked the boy if he was willing to go home with his master. He replied: 'No, sir,' and that 'no, sir,' went to the heart of every loyal man who heard it. There he stood, that boy who came into our lines cold, barefooted, ragged and hungry, amidst a dreary snow-storm, asking food and shelter and raiment, after having spent days and nights in the woods, living upon black walnuts. Was he to be returned to slavery?

"Turning to Judge Robertson, the colonel said: 'I don't think you can get that boy. If you think you can, there he is, try it. I shall have nothing to do with it.'

"This gentleman slave-hunter was no less a person than the Chief Justice of the State, said to be the most learned jurist in Kentucky. He will be likely to remember the scathing which he received from a Wisconsin colonel for some time. I regret that the whole North could not have heard it.

"The colonel was threatened with Kentucky laws, but he thought it might be profitable to his country, and the cause in which he was engaged, were he even sacrificed, did that rend the delusive vail and permit the nation to look in upon Kentucky as she is.

"The colonel intimated to the judge that he preferred that he should leave the camp, lest an excitement should be created among the 'boys.' The idea of leaving without his nigger was evidently a painful one, and he was inclined to argue the case. State subjects were dropped, and the conversation became at once rich and animating. To an intimation from the judge that we were a set of 'nigger stealers,' the colonel replied: '*You* talk about negro stealing! *You,* who riot in idleness, and who live on the sweat and blood of such little creatures as that! *You,* whose costly mansions, and churches even, are built out of the earnings of women and children, beaten out of them by brutal overseers! *You,* who hire out little children to brutes who beat and starve them, stealing from their backs and mouths their small earnings! *You,* who clothe them in rags, and when, at last, they can stand it no longer, and flee from that protection which you denied them, you hunt them down like a ravenous beast, to drag them back to their chains, toils and sufferings, that you may eke out a few more pennies from this last life drop ! *You* talk about our stealing, when all the crime which we have committed was to feed, clothe and shelter that poor, half-starved suffering little boy ! Sir, I would rather stand in the place of that slave to-day than in that of his proud oppressor. It will be more tolerable for him in the day of judgment than for you.'

"Said the judge: 'If that is the way you talk and feel, the Union can never be saved. You must give up our property.'

"The colonel replied: 'If the perpetuity or restoration of the Union depends upon my delivering to you, with my own hands, that poor little over-worked creature, dwarfed by your own avarice, the Union may be cast into hell, with all the nations that forget God.'

"He then told him, in his own peculiar scathing style, what kind of 'Union men' he had found in Kentucky. Said he: 'I have not seen half a dozen who did not damn the President. You may put all the pure Unionism in Kentucky into one scale, and a ten-pound nigger baby in the other, and the Unionism will kick the beam.'

"Before leaving, the old jurist condemned the President's proclamation; declared that it had no bearing upon Kentucky, and that it was the policy of generals commanding our armies to ignore both the action of Congress and the proclamation.

"From our lines the old gentleman drew a very straight line to the 'general's headquarters' and to this place the colonel was soon summoned, where he enjoyed another interview with the persevering judge, and several other Kentucky gentlemen.

"Colonel Coburn, now in command of this brigade, arose and stated in a very gentlemanly manner the policy of comanding generals in Kentucky, which is simply this: 'To look at a slave in an encampment as in the same condition precisely that he would be were there no regiment there—that any person has a right to enter the encampment and take out a fugitive at his pleasure.'

"The judge corroborated the statement, and added: 'The proclamation of the President is to have no consideration in Kentucky.'

"Colonel Utley commenced by saying that he regretted to be under the necessity of differing from his commanding officer.

Said he: 'I reverse the Kentucky policy, and hold that the regiment stands precisely as though there was no slavery in Kentucky. We came here as freemen from a free State, to defend and support a free government. We have nothing to do with slavery, and we will never be made nigger-catchers. We came at the call of the President, and still recognize his authority.'

"It is useless to think of stating all that was said, but you may be assured that the old slave-catching Felix trembled as he listened to such bold declarations upon the Union-neutral soil of Kentucky.

"But he could not leave without making one more effort to obtain the dwarfed human property now in danger of being transformed into a man. Turning to the colonel he said: 'Are you willing that I should go and get my boy?'

" ' Yes, sir,' said the colonel, 'you may go, and I will remain here.'

" ' Do you think I shall be permitted to take him?'

" ' I think not, but I can not tell.'

" ' Will you send him into some other regiment?'

" ' No, sir!' said the colonel; 'I would see you in hell first.'

"The colonel has since been indicted by a Kentucky court at Lexington for man-stealing; but he has not yet been arrested. It will be remembered that there is now a little spot from Wisconsin down here in the center of Kentucky. How long a more serious collision with the insulting and heaven-daring slave power can be avoided, it is difficult to calculate. It is my clear conviction that Judge Robertson's principles correctly and fairly represent the Unionism of the State."

The following, which I copy from a letter written to me by my worthy Wisconsin friend, J. L. Berch, when he sent the book from which this extract is taken, will inform the reader how this affair terminated:

"The sequel of the whole matter was, that while Colonel Utley was in the front, beating back the rebel from off the soil of Kentucky, this negro-cripple's owner, Judge Robertson, sued him (Colonel Utley) in the United States Court for Kentucky, and obtained an exparte judgment against him for one thousand five hundred dollars and costs, which judgment being duly certified to the United States Court for Wisconsin, stood against the colonel's property as a lien thereon, which he would some day have been compelled to pay, had not Congress, in 1873, passed a bill appropriating money enough to pay the principal of the judgment, leaving Colonel Utley still the costs to' pay—some seven hundred dollars—which he has paid."

CHAPTER XIX.

WORK AMONG THE FREEDMEN—VISIT TO CAIRO AND OTHER POINTS SOUTH—SCENES AND INCIDENTS AMONG THE CONTRABANDS—CONDITION AND SUFFERINGS OF THE COLORED PEOPLE—EFFORTS IN THEIR BEHALF.

IN the fall of 1862 the terrible civil war had fully opened west of the mountains. Two large armies had gathered in Kentucky and Tennessee; many bloody battles were fought. A different policy in regard to the slaves was adopted. They flocked within the Union lines, as the armies advanced through Tennessee to Memphis, and other points in the southwest, and were protected. Many of the slaveholders fled farther South, taking their able-bodied slaves with them, and leaving the women and children, aged and sick ones, to take care of themselves. In many cases there was nothing for this helpless class to live upon. The two vast armies that had swept over the country had consumed all the provisions, and the poor slaves were left in a suffering condition. Thousands gathered within the Union lines, and were sent to various points up the river. Some were brought on boats to Cincinnati, and left on the wharf without food and shelter, or means of obtaining them. I was frequently called upon for aid and assistance. The colored people here acted nobly, taking as many as they could and caring for them. Several thousand contrabands, as the slaves were then called, were sent to Cairo, Illinois, and placed under charge of J. B. Rogers, chaplain of the Fourteenth Wisconsin Volunteers. Hearing of the great destitution and suffering at that place and other points, I resolved to visit the quarters of the contrabands, and learn what their real condition and wants were.

Cairo is at the mouth of the Ohio, five hundred miles from Cincinnati. To shorten the distance and make greater speed, I took the Ohio and Mississippi Railroad, by way of Vincennes, Indiana. I left home on the fifth of the twelfth month—December. At Odin, Illinois, the next morning, I met with my friends, Job Hadley and his wife, from Hendricks County, Indiana, who were on their way to Cairo, on a similar mission. We were greatly rejoiced to meet, and proceeded on our way together. We arrived at Cairo that evening, and took quarters at the Commercial Hotel. Job Hadley and his wife had left home with the intention of opening a school among the colored people, if privilege could be obtained, and remaining with them through the winter. No schools had yet been opened among the contrabands; they were not yet called Freedmen, as it was before the emancipation proclamation of President Lincoln. We called that evening on General Tuttle, who had command at that military post. He received us cordially, and, when he understood our mission, seemed to be pleased and offered us any privilege we might wish. In regard to opening a school, he referred us to J. B. Rogers, the superintendent, who had charge of the contrabands' camp. On the morning of the next day, which was the Sabbath, we visited the old military barracks where the contrabands were located. We first went to the office of J. B. Rogers, the chaplain and general superintendent, who gave us a very cordial reception. Although an entire stranger, he appeared much rejoiced to meet us, and gave us a general account of the conditions and wants of the contrabands under his care. He went with us to visit some of them in their crowded huts and sick rooms. We found their condition to be even worse than it had been represented to us before leaving home. The deepest emotions of pity and sympathy were called forth as we witnessed their extreme destitution and suffering. Many were sick from exposure and for want of sufficient clothing; they had no bedding nor cooking utensils, none of the comforts and few of the necessaries of life. The scanty rations issued by Government were their only subsistence. The weather being quite chilly, many of them were suffering with coughs and colds; that dreadful scourge—small-pox—was quite prevalent among them, and added to the horrors of their situation. A large part of the contrabands collected at this point were women, children, and old people. Superintendent Rogers—a noble Christian worker—

was doing all in his power to make them as comfortable as the scanty means at his command would allow.

To give them better shelter than their poor huts afforded he was fitting up the old barracks—stopping the cracks to keep out the cold wind, and making other repairs.

We believed friend Rogers to be the right man in the right place, and felt much sympathy with him in his arduous work. He evinced a deep interest in the welfare of the contrabands, in every sense, and was fitting up a large room in which to hold religious meetings. This apartment was also to be used as a school-room, but the school had not yet been organized. It seemed to be a great relief to friend Rogers when Job Hadley and wife offered to take charge of the school. The assistance of Job Hadley in other work would also be of great service to him. We visited Dr. Reynolds, the physician in charge of the contrabands, at his office, and received a hearty welcome. He told us there were about one hundred and fifty cases of small-pox among the colored people in camp.

At two o'clock in the afternoon I attended their religious meeting, which was held in the large shelter prepared for that purpose. The weather being fair and the sun shining brightly, a large multitude of the poor ragged slaves crowded together for devotional service. All the rough seats and every foot of standing room were occupied, and the doors and windows were crowded with anxious listeners.

J. B. Rogers opened the meeting with prayer and

singing. He was a Baptist minister and had, I believe, not only been baptized with water but with
the Holy Ghost. He seemed to speak with the
power of the Holy Ghost. The singing of the colored people was characterized by fervor and whole-
souled abandonment, such as I never before heard.
I thought of the day of Pentecost, when the disciples being all of one accord in one place, there came
a sound from heaven as of a rushing mighty wind
that filled the house where they were sitting, and
filling them with the Holy Ghost so that they spoke
as the Spirit gave them utterance. Their hearts
seemed filled to overflowing with praise to God for
their deliverance from slavery. J. B. Rogers deliv-
·ered a short gospel sermon, well adapted to their
understanding, after which a Presbyterian minister,
who was present, delivered a few remarks. Friend
Rogers then informed the colored people of my
presence and mission among them. His introduction was somewhat embarrassing to me, but I felt
fully prepared to talk to them and encourage them.
After I closed my remarks, singing and prayer were
continued by the colored people for some time,
many of the old men and women giving utterances
to expressions of praise and thanksgiving. Friend
Rogers gave them full privilege to take part in the
meeting, which they seemed to enjoy greatly.

After the meeting was concluded, friend Rogers
and I spent some time visiting the sick and afflicted,
and making notes of the articles of bedding and
clothing most needed. The next morning I started
home, leaving my friends, Job Hadley and wife, to

open a school among the colored people. It was
continued successfully during the winter. I will
here introduce an extract from J. B. Rogers' book,
" War Pictures: "

"On one beautiful Sunday morning of December, 1862, there
came into our office (at Cairo) three unpretending strangers
whom I recognized at once as Friends or Quakers. The name
of one of them, Mr. C——, was familiar to me as I had often
heard of him as one of the truest and most active philanthropists
of the day. He was accompanied by two friends, a gentleman
and a lady. The three had fallen in company on their way to
Cairo to look after the wants and conditions of the colored people
there in that place under my charge. I soon found that though
called by a different name than my own, they were none the less
devoted Christians, disciples of Jesus. They spent the whole
of the Lord's day with me.

"This visit, while affording me great encouragement in my
work, left with me some thoughts on the subject of Christian
association, which I found sweet and profitable after my friends
had left. It had never fallen in my way to make many acquaintances among that class to which they belonged; but I am prepared now to recognize the distinctive traits of the genuine
Christian spirit in some, at least, if not all, of that interesting
people whose unpretending name is significant of the gentleness
and kindness and wide benevolence for which they have always
been remarkable. These Friends, of whom I speak, seemed to me
divested of everything like denominational or sectarian prejudice.
I saw the difference, too, between talking Christianity and acting
it; between devotion to creeds and formularies and love for
Christ and for souls.

"And this 'godly simplicity'—what an engaging trait of Christian character! It is the transparent medium through which we
look in upon the heart and discover there the spirit of the dear
Lord himself. Nor does a Christian need any kind of ostentation
to commend him either to God or his fellow-men. When such
Christians meet, they soon know each other. 'Christ in them the
hope of glory,' becomes a means of mutual recognition; for, 'as in
water, face answereth to face, so the heart of man.'"

After my return I wrote to friend Rogers, and will here insert his reply, as it gives some account of the freedmen's school:

"CAIRO, ILLINOIS, December 21, 1862.

"LEVI COFFIN:

"DEAR BROTHER—Your very kind favor I received in due time, for which I am under very strong obligations to you. I have thought very much of the precious visit I enjoyed with you while here, and hope it was not without profit to myself. These social interviews, if rightly enjoyed, can but be a source of great usefulness to us in producing greater spirituality of mind, and leading us closer to the man Christ Jesus. The school under the charge of our good friends Hadley and wife more than answers our highest hope. It has been in progress five days and a half, and I think I may be safe in asserting that over fifty have learned the alphabet entire, and most of them are in the a b ab, and perhaps half, if not more, can spell words of three letters. Those who visit the school are greatly astonished at their progress. Where is there a parallel case among the whites? Talk as much as you may about their dull and blunt parts, we can not find an equal number of whites that will excel them in the avidity with which they try to learn. Old and young come together— the majority, however, are children. They are seen all about after school hours, with books in hand, learning their lessons. May we hope, my dear brother, that from this small beginning there may be great and important results growing to bless the colored race? Brother Hadley and lady are excellent folks; I have begun to appreciate their services very highly, and think their influence to be very salutary indeed. May they not go unrewarded for their self-sacrificing labors to benefit the despised of our country. As our school advances I will keep you informed from time to time, and hope I may hear from thee, true yoke-fellow.

"Your most humble and obedient servant, and brother in Christ,   J. B. ROGERS."

After my return from Cairo I devoted my whole time and energy to the work for the freed slaves. I wrote many letters to my friends in the country—

53

in Ohio and Indiana—and they began at once to collect bedding, clothing, and money, and forward them to me. We had no facilities for sending them to the various camps of the freedmen, or for properly distributing them. It seemed necessary to have some regular and responsible organization here on the border, to receive and forward the supplies.

A meeting was called, and the Western Freedmen's Aid Commission was organized, comprising many prominent members of the different religious denominations of our city. I was appointed general agent of this commission. We went to work at once and opened an office and wareroom where the supplies sent for the freedmen could be received, and stored until forwarded to their destination.

The members of the Society of Friends in various parts of the country had become deeply interested in the subject, and were actively at work. Miami Quarterly Meeting had appointed a committee, the members of which had issued a printed circular, to Friends, on the subject of the sufferings and wants of the freedmen. The response to this appeal came in the shape of supplies from various parts of Ohio and Indiana.

The Aid Commission was organized in January, 1863. It will be remembered that President Lincoln's emancipation proclamation took effect the first day of that year.

General Grant, who at that time had command of the Southern division of the army, gave us free transportation for all supplies for the freedmen and for our agents and teachers. We sent efficient agents to attend to the proper and judicious distribution of the clothing and other articles, and a number of teachers, well supplied with books, to open schools among the colored people. Notwithstanding the hardships and dangers to be encountered in going into the enemy's land, several noble young men volunteered their services. Among the first that accompanied the supplies were Isaac Thorne; John L. Roberts, and Franklin Coggeshall. Boats passing down the river were often fired into by guerrillas concealed in the trees and shrubbery along the bank, and the trip was a hazardous one on other accounts.

To Nashville and other points in Tennessee, then in possession of the Union forces, the freedmen had gathered by thousands, in great destitution and suffering. The work constantly increased, and the demands upon us far exceeded our supplies. During the winter and spring I frequently took hasty trips into the country to endeavor to arouse a deeper interest on this subject among the people, and attended many of the Quarterly Meetings of Friends in Ohio and Indiana, to encourage increased action in behalf of the freedmen. These efforts were blessed with success, and our supplies largely increased.

Other denominations began to take a lively interest, and as our organization was anti-sectarian, all were united in this work of benevolence, and labored together harmoniously.

Our field of labor had now become so large that it seemed necessary for me to visit it again, and in

the latter part of May I left home to engage in this
mission. It necessitated a trip down the Mississippi
River, and to various points in the South. Most of
the freedmen formerly at Cairo were now stationed
at Island Number Ten, where they were cultivating
the land, under charge of Chaplain B. Thomas. My
first call was at Columbus, Kentucky, twenty miles
below Cairo, where there was a large colony. I
went next to Island Number Ten, and thence to
Memphis, Tennessee. I arrived at the latter place
on Sabbath morning, and was very cordially received by Chaplain Eaton, who had been appointed
by General Grant general superintendent of contrabands on the Mississippi, and to whom we had
forwarded large supplies of clothing, farming utensils, and school-books.

At Memphis there were three large colonies or
villages of the freed people, who were cultivating
the ground with farming implements which we had
sent them. Chaplain Eaton made me welcome at
his quarters during my stay in Memphis, and gave
me all the assistance in his power, and every facility
I needed to accomplish my mission. I found him
to be a very intelligent and agreeable man and
Christian worker, and much interested in the welfare of the freedmen, but greatly overworked with
so heavy a charge upon him. On my expressing a
wish to visit the camps on the day of my arrival,
and attend the meetings of the colored people, he
procured two cavalry horses, well equipped, and we
rode out to the camps.

As Eaton held the rank of colonel, we had no

difficulty in passing the picket lines. We arrived at Camp Holly Springs in time to visit the teachers in their tents before the hour of worship. Their meeting-house was a long shelter, covered with clapboards. The services were conducted by friend Conner, of Ohio, a missionary sent to this place by the United Presbyterians. The meeting.was very large and interesting, and before the crowd dispersed I had the privilege of addressing the lately emancipated slaves.

We dined in a large tent with the missionary, his wife, and two young lady teachers, and afterward attended a meeting on President's Island, where a large colony had lately been established. All of the colored people here lived in tents ; their church and school-house was a shelter made of brush. S. J. Wright was located there under the auspices of the American Missionary Association. Franklin Coggeshall and other teachers were laboring there. In the evening we paid a short visit to the teachers at Camp Shiloh. Each of these camps had a strong picket guard of colored men, who kept a sharp lookout ; raids were often made by the rebels, and it was necessary to guard against surprise.

A strong Union force was stationed in this vicinity at the time of my visit, and several gunboats were lying on the river ready for service. I visited both the colored and white hospitals at this point. In the latter there were a large number of wounded soldiers, who had been brought in from various battle-fields, and among them I found some young men from Indiana and other Western States, with whom I was acquainted, and who seemed glad to see me. To witness the sufferings of the wounded was enough to move the stoutest heart. I never before so fully realized the horrors of war.

I was admitted into the old fort where a regiment of colored soldiers was being organized and drilled, and met with the teacher and missionary who labored among them. His name was Norton, and he was a member of the Presbyterian Church. Notwithstanding the efforts that were made to relieve and care for the lately emancipated slaves, I found many of them in a suffering condition. Those who were in the camps outside of the city were in charge of the superintendents, and their wants were provided for as well as the means at command would allow, but more than two thousand had taken refuge within the city limits, and their condition was truly deplorable.

As the slaveholders fled before the advancing Union forces they took with them their able-bodied slaves, and when these tried to escape and reach the Union lines, they were pursued and fired upon by their masters, who had rather shoot them down than let them go free. The slaves came into Memphis every day, many of them wounded, and all of them suffering for lack of food and clothing. While I was visiting one of the colored hospitals, a large brick house—the residence of an aristocratic Southerner—in the suburbs of the city, which had been appropriated to the use of the sick and wounded freedmen, a company of slaves was brought in, some of them suffering from gunshot wounds. They said they had attempted to escape from their masters, and had been pursued. Two of their number were shot dead, and the others were so disabled that they were lying helpless by the roadside when a company of Union soldiers discovered them and brought them in.

After remaining two days at Memphis, I obtained a pass to Corinth, Mississippi, by way of La Grange, Bolivar, and Jackson, Tennessee. The railroads were all under military control, but Chaplain Eaton had been authorized by General Grant to give free transportation to all agents visiting the freedmen, also to our teachers and supplies. There was much red tape in the rules and regulations of the military department. I had to report to the provost-marshal and obtain a permit to go South—then report to the various military posts, and have it indorsed.

At La Grange, some fifty miles south of Memphis, there was a contraband camp in charge of Chaplain Joel Grant, of the Twelfth Illinois Infantry. I had previously forwarded boxes of school-books, clothing, blankets, and farming utensils to this place and to Corinth. Of the two thousand contrabands gathered at this point, many had no shelter but cast-off army tents; there was much destitution and suffering among them. One of our teachers, John L. Roberts, had prepared a long shelter of brush, and was about to open a school. A strong Union force was stationed here, under command of General Smith, of Ohio. A college building was used as a hospital for sick and wounded soldiers, and a large private residence, in the suburbs of the city, was occupied as a hospital for the contrabands. Many of the freedmen here were in Government service as waiters, cooks, washers, teamsters, etc., and a colored regiment was being organized.

Superintendent Grant accompanied me to visit the farm grounds which the freedmen were cultivating within the picket lines, and to see the soldiers in camp and in the hospitals. I found here a number of our Ohio boys. In the evening I attended religious service in the contrabands' camp, and at night found comfortable quarters in the mansion that had been deserted by its owner, and was now used as a hospital for the colored people.

Next morning I returned to the large double tent which constituted the headquarters of Chaplain Grant. He told me that during the night a large number of contrabands had come in—mostly women and children—for whom no shelter could be provided, as the tents were already crowded full. A few blankets were all that could be furnished them, and they remained exposed to the heavy dews during the night and the hot sun during the day, unless they made a shelter of green brush. I visited them as they sat in their rags and dirt, and listened to their accounts of the privation and suffering they had undergone before reaching the Union lines. Although their destitution was extreme, I heard no murmurs or complaints. Their hearts seemed full of praise to God for their deliverance from slavery; they regarded it as an answer to the prayers they had sent up so often in their days of cruel bondage.

I was touched by their simple expressions of thanks-giving, and felt my eyes fill with tears.

I attended the opening of John L. Roberts' school, under the shelter of green brush, and was much interested to see the eagerness with which his pupils pressed forward to have their names regis-tered and receive the school-books. When this was done they retired in good order to their seats, formed of rough slabs, holding carefully in their hands the precious books, of which they knew no word or letter. The parents of many of them looked on with deep interest.

While at La Grange I witnessed the arrival of a company of contrabands, thirty-one in number, mostly women and children. They were brought in by a company of cavalry scouts, and rode, part in a wagon to which four mules were attached, part in an elegant carriage, drawn by a span of bay horses. The cavalry had been out in pursuit of a band of guerrillas, and had gathered up these negroes from the plantation of a rich planter, whose house had been the headquarters of the guerrillas. The contrabands were quite jubilant at the prospect of liberty, and collected in a semicircle around the superintendent's tent to have their names and ages registered. One old woman, whose head was as white as wool, stood first, and when she was asked her age, she replied: "Don't know, massa; dey tole me I was twenty-one and made me do de work of a gal. I s'pose I's seventy-five or eighty."

The chaplain put her down as seventy-five, then proceeded to put the same question to the others.

They could not tell how old they were, and he had to register their names and guess at their ages. When this was done the old woman made a speech to us, part of it amusing and part quite pathetic.

She said: "Yesterday when de sogers come I was out milkin' de cows and prayin' dat de Lord would send de Yankees here.. Massa had tried to scare us; he told us if de Yankees got hold of us dey would work us mos' to death, then send us off to Cuba and sell us, but de Lord didn't tell me so, and I kep' prayin' dat dey would come. While I was milkin' I happened to raise my head, and bless de Lord, dere was de Yankees' heads poppin' up above de fence. Oh, my heart almos' jumped out of me for joy. Dey come right up and surrounded de house; de rebs was gone but massa was dere. I quit milkin' and walked right by de captain. He said for us all to get ready, he was going to take us out of slavery. Oh, dat made me feel good. I took de bucket of milk into de kitchen and set it down, and went out into de yard and tole de captain how dey had used us and how dey had 'bused us, all right before massa's face and he dasn't cheep. De boys was plowin' in de field and de captain sent sogers to tell 'em to unhitch de mules and hitch 'em to de wagon, and I tell you dey done it mighty quick. Dey put four mules to de wagon, den dey fetched out de fine carriage and fine horses and made 'em ready. Den we fetched out our old bags and old beds and put in de wagon, and de captain tole us to put in provisions to eat. I tell you it was all done mighty quick, and we drove off, some of us riden' in.de fine carriage and de rest in de wagon. De sogers went before and behind us, and here we all is, bless de Lord!"

All listened with intense interest to the old woman's story, told in her own simple language. She pointed to several of the company, and said: "Dese are my children and grandchildren;" then turning to us, she continued: "Gent'men, dis is all de work of de Lord. I has been prayin' many years dat He would send deliverance to us poor slaves, and my faith never failed me dat He would hear my prayer, and dat I would live to be free." She then broke forth in a song of praise and thanksgiving, in which others joined her, singing in that peculiar, plaintive manner characteristic of the musical utterances of slaves—those who sing from the depths of heart experience. I was renewedly convinced that many of the Lord's children were to be found among the poor untutored slaves.

At La Grange I took the train for Corinth, Mississippi, going by way of Bolivar and Jackson, Tennessee; the road by way of Grand Junction having been destroyed by the rebels. Our route to Corinth lay through the enemy's country, where there had been much fighting and great destruction of property. The road was strongly guarded, squads of soldiers being posted, at short distances, along the entire route. Breastworks had been thrown up here and there, and rifle-pits were to be seen every few miles. The desolation wrought by war was visible on every side. Fences were gone, houses burned, and plantations deserted; everything seemed to be going to destruction. Two large armies had passed over the land, leaving ruin in their track. The rebel army had taken away or destroyed the property of Union men in the South; the Federal army had done the same with the property of the rebels, and nothing remained for the poor slaves to live upon. The women and children, and the aged and feeble were often found on the ruined plantations suffering for the means of life. Our soldiers frequently shared their rations with them, but could do little to alleviate the sudden and general distress.

A large military force was stationed at Corinth, but having proper credentials, I found no difficulty in passing the picket lines. Colonel Alexander, superintendent of contrabands at this place, received me cordially, and gave me lodging in his tent. I found about six thousand contrabands within the picket lines. Several teachers and missionaries were stationed here, and about three hundred children attended school. The cabins and tents of the contrabands were kept clean, and were visited often by the distributing agents and teachers. It was truly an arduous field of labor; numbers of newly emancipated slaves arrived every day, and there was much destitution and suffering. Colonel Alexander and I rode out to view the farm and gardens cultivated by the freedmen—about one thousand acres were under cultivation, one hundred and twenty-five being in garden. The soldiers were supplied with vegetables from these gardens. A regiment of colored soldiers was organized and equipped at this place. It was called the Alabama Regiment, because most of the men composing it were from that State. They were all able-bodied, and presented a fine appearance on dress parade. Their colonel told me that they were the most orderly and best behaved regiment in camp; it was the first time that their manhood had been recognized, and they were anxious to prove that they were worthy of the confidence reposed in them. A second regiment of colored soldiers was nearly full. There were many stanch abolitionists among the Northern soldiers stationed here, and when off duty they spent much time teaching the colored soldiers to read. The latter appeared to be making fine progress; there was a great demand for school-books among them. I mingled with them in their quarters, and endeavored to encourage them in their efforts to learn, promising to forward some books to them when I returned to Memphis.

I spent about three days at Corinth, visiting the schools and teachers, attending the religious meetings of the freedmen, and visiting many of them in their tents and hospitals. I also visited many of the Northern soldiers in their tents. The evening before I left Corinth I witnessed the arrival of a large company of contrabands, many of them clothed only in rags, and suffering for want of food. They were provided for as well as the means at command would allow. On my way back to Memphis I made short visits at Bolivar and Jackson. Between Corinth and Jackson we stopped at a way station, and took on a company of contrabands who had been gathered together and brought to this place by a company of soldiers.   They were taken on to Jackson, where a camp was being organized.

At Jackson a strong guard of soldiers mounted to the top of the cars, and accompanied us the rest of the way, as guard.   The day before there had been a raid of guerrillas on the road between here and Memphis, and a number of rails had been torn up, but the destruction had been discovered in time to save the train.   A brave Union citizen, at the risk of his life, flagged the approaching train and warned the engineer of the danger.   A company of soldiers aboard soon repaired the track, and there was only a detention of a few hours, where there might have been a frightful accident.   We reached Memphis in safety, without having seen guerrillas on our route. I stopped again with my friend Colonel Eaton, and resumed my labors of visiting the schools, hospitals and camps of the freedmen and soldiers.   A number of wounded soldiers had just been brought up from Vicksburg, where desperate fighting was going on.   Among them were several from Ohio, but none with whom I was acquainted.   It was a painful sight to see their mangled bodies, and to know that they must soon die, or, if they survived, to be maimed and crippled all their lives.

On Sabbath morning I went over to President's Island, and attended a large and interesting meeting of the freedmen, which was held in the shade of the trees.   Afterward I dined with our teachers and with Superintendent Barnes, of Illinois, an excellent man, who died not long afterward while engaged in this work.   In the evening I returned to Memphis, expecting to start down the river to Helena, Arkansas, and other points where contrabands were congregated. The next day I obtained a permit and a free pass, and went on board the sanitary boat, Alice Dean, from Cincinnati. It was used to bring sick and wounded soldiers up the river from points below, to hospitals where they could be cared for. Two large boats, the Jacob Strader and the Tycoon, went in company with us, one before and the other behind us. They were loaded with troops, having four thousand soldiers on board, who were going down to join Grant's army at Vicksburg. A larger number had gone down the day before. It was not considered safe for boats to pass up and down the river without troops on board, or unaccompanied by a gunboat, for several had lately been fired into; on board of one a woman, who had been laboring among the freedmen, was killed by a shot from the bank. I felt that I was in the midst of war and danger, but was favored to rest in peace and to arrive safely at Helena. After reporting at the office of the provost-marshal and showing my credentials, I called on Chaplain Sawyer, the superintendent of contrabands at this post, who received me cordially. He was from Grant County, Indiana, and we had previously had some acquaintance. I met another person here whom I had known before—William Shugart, son of one of my old neighbors. He was captain of the First Indiana Cavalry. General Prentice was commander of this post at the time of my visit. I found here three thousand six hundred contrabands, about one-half of whom earned their support in Government service, and by cultivating the ground; the others—mostly women and children—were entirely dependent. Eight hundred had come in the night before I arrived, having been ·brought up the river in boats from points below.

Three large churches were filled with colored people, and many found shelter in other houses and in tents. Beside those in Helena, quite a number were in camps two miles out of town. In company with Chaplain Fisher, assistant superintendent, I visited Camp Deliverance, containing four hundred and eighty, Camp Wood with four hundred and ninety, and Camp Colony, with two hundred and fifty. They were all within the picket lines of the army, but were, I thought, in an unsafe position, for a large rebel army was camped not far away, and it was feared that an attempt would be made to retake the town.

On our return to Helena we heard the roar of cannon some distance down the river; it continued, with intervals of cessation, for several hours, and we surmised that a severe engagement was taking place. Next morning we learned that the boats which were conveying troops down the river to Vicksburg were fired into by guerrillas on the bank, and that a gunboat which accompanied the transports had shelled the woods for some distance, and dispersed the guerrillas.

I had intended to start down the river the following day, to visit the camps of contrabands between Helena and Vicksburg, but was advised not to risk my life by undertaking such a journey. I concluded to return to Memphis, and while waiting for an up-river boat visited the freedmen in the churches. The chaplains in charge had gathered them into these buildings for instruction, and were teaching them the alphabet from charts hung in front of the pulpits. It was interesting to watch them, to see their eagerness to learn. No schools had then been established at Helena; school-books and teachers were much needed.

One devoted Christian woman, M. R. Mann, was laboring there, distributing clothing among the freedmen. Here, as elsewhere, there was much destitution and suffering.

I took passage on a boat that was conveying some wounded soldiers to Memphis, and reached that place in safety. There was some difficulty about getting passage farther up the river, for all the boats had been pressed into service by the Government, for the purpose of conveying soldiers and supplies to General Grant's army. Some of the boats had taken passengers and freight aboard, and were ready to start up the river, but the order was imperative, and we were kept in suspense for some time. It was finally decided that one large boat should take the passengers and freight of the other smaller ones and proceed on her way, and about dark we started. The Tillman was a large, handsome boat, but we were much crowded. I stopped one day at Island Number Ten, where there were more than a thousand contrabands in camp, and where several of our teachers were located, and, proceeding on my journey, reached Cairo early Sabbath morning.

54

The boat that brought me to Cairo was much crowded, having eight hundred passengers on board. There were some sick and wounded soldiers, a number of rebel prisoners, and a company of white refugees from the South—mostly women and children. This company was landed on the wharf, in charge of a Government officer, to be sent out by railroad, and scattered among the people in Indiana and Illinois, to find sustenance. They numbered about three hundred, and were the most wretched, forlorn-looking company of people I had ever seen. All appeared to be in deep distress. They had been ruined by the war; being Unionists in sentiment and opposed to secession, their property had been destroyed or taken by the rebels, their houses burned, and the men forced to flee for their lives or enter the rebel service. The husbands and fathers of some of these families had been shot down before their eyes; others had succeeded in escaping and joining the Union army. These refugees had been gathered together by Union soldiers, and sent, at Government expense, to the free States, to be provided for by the more fortunate Northern people, whose homes had not been destroyed by war. I spent some time walking about among them and listening to their stories of suffering and distress. The deepest sympathies of my heart were stirred in their behalf. Their situation was indeed pitiful. Some were sick and lying on the wet ground, with but a scanty supply of bed clothing. Others were moving about in a dejected and spiritless manner, trying to prepare something to eat. Army rations had been issued to them, but the food was coarse and unfit for delicate women and children and sick persons. One aged grandmother, ninety-five years of age, was munching a piece of cold corn bread.

I had witnessed many scenes of destitution and suffering among the contrabands in the South, but this surpassed them all. The colored people were hopeful; they had gained their liberty, and in the midst of privation and hardship were praising the Lord for their deliverance from bondage. The refugees were despondent, and many of them wept bitterly as they related their sad stories. Many of them had been in comfortable circumstances; they were now ruined and dependent upon the charity of strangers. Before I left this pitiful group, some of the ladies of the town came among them to minister to their wants.

There were still a number of contrabands in the old barracks. I attended their meeting in the forenoon, and spent most of the Sabbath with them. In the evening I took passage on the Evansville packet, and stopped the next day to visit the contraband camps at Smithland and Paducah, Kentucky. The day following, I arrived at Evansville, and called to see Major A. L. Robinson—with whom I was acquainted—to consult with him regarding the best plan of taking up a collection for the aid of the freedmen of the South. He was an influential man and a popular attorney at law, and I knew that his action in the matter would have weight with the people. We concluded to call together the ministers of the different churches and other prom-

inent citizens, endeavor to get them interested in
the subject, and consult with them whether it would
be better to call a public meeting or make individual
appeals. The latter course was decided upon, and
after heading the list with a subscription of fifty
dollars, Major A. L. Robinson went around with
me to solicit contributions. We spent that evening
and the most of next day in canvassing, and succeeded in collecting six hundred and forty-five dollars. I then took leave of my kind friend, who had
so efficiently aided me in making collections, and
took passage on the steamer Gray Eagle for Louisville. Most of the waiters, cooks, and deck-hands
on the boat were colored people belonging to
Louisville. Some of them knew me, and when they
learned my mission they took a collection, voluntarily, among themselves which amounted to more
than seven dollars, and which they placed in my
hands to be expended for the relief of their colored
brethren in the South. When the boat stopped at
Louisville I crossed over to Jeffersonville, and spent
the night with my friend, Dr. Field. Next morning I collected thirty dollars for the freedmen.

I afterward visited New Albany, where I called
on J. G. Atterbury, pastor of the Second Presbyterian Church. After making known to him my
mission, he went around with me to see the ministers of the other churches. Their interest was
aroused, and it was decided .to call a meeting for
the afternoon of the next day—Sabbath—and to
present the subject to the people. Notices were
given in all the churches that such a meeting would

be held in the Methodist Episcopal Centenary Church, and a large company gathered at the time appointed. I gave them an account of the condition and wants of the freed people in the South, and spoke of my recent visit among them. Several speeches were made by others, and much interest was manifested. Two prominent men were appointed to assist me next day in making collections. In the evening I attended—by invitation—the African Methodist Episcopal Church, and gave a brief account of the scenes I had witnessed among the lately emancipated slaves. A liberal collection was taken up, and the next day we collected two hundred and thirty-seven dollars. At Louisville I received contributions from Elder Adams, pastor of the colored church, and several other colored persons.

On my return to Cincinnati I had the satisfaction of reporting to our board the amount of about one thousand dollars, the sum of the various collections. The members of the board seemed quite encouraged with my success; new fields of labor were opening, and there was a constant demand for assistance. The work increased constantly, and I found little time to rest. Boxes of clothing, bedding, books, and other articles came in large numbers from the country, to be shipped to the suffering freedmen. They were consigned to me, and this entailed a great deal of labor. Their receipt must be acknowledged and inquiries answered; I often spent the greater part of the night writing letters.

I often received pressing appeals from our teachers and agents, representing the extreme destitution and suffering of the freed people, and begging for more help. Having visited the camps I could easily picture to myself the scenes they drew, and my feelings were constantly harrowed up, and my deepest sympathies excited. I often made short tours to the country to solicit contributions and to endeavor to arouse the sympathy of the people. I was successful in making collections wherever I went, and this enabled us to extend our labors; to send more teachers, and more relief to the sufferers.

The field of operations was constantly widening; colonies of freedmen were being organized at various points in Tennessee, Mississippi and Kentucky. Each day brought new tales of suffering and incited us to fresh effort. Vicksburg had fallen, and of the thousands of slaves collected in that vicinity many were dying for want of the common necessaries of life. A terrible battle was fought at Helena about a week after I left there, and the freedmen's camps outside the town were destroyed by the rebels. The cabins were burned, and many of the aged and sick ones perished in them. It was reported that the rebels were driven back with great loss, and the final victory won by the valor of a regiment of colored soldiers who had been kept in reserve till the last, and who fought with desperation when ordered into action. The contrabands at that point were now left without shelter, and suffered greatly.

The army at Corinth, Mississippi, had been called to Vicksburg, and the large and prosperous colony of freedmen at that point, whom I had visited so short a time before, were obliged to leave hastily and seek refuge at Memphis and President's Island. Their gardens and farms were abandoned to the rebels, and they were deprived of the fruit of their labors. Other similar misfortunes, and the inhuman massacre of colored troops at Fort Pillow, tended to increase our sympathy for the freedmen.

In addition to the work in the South, there were many demands made upon us here. I have mentioned that companies of contrabands were frequently brought on boats to this city, landed on the wharf, and then left to shift for themselves. The number increased, and we petitioned Government to establish a home for the freedmen on this side of the river and issue rations to them until places could be found for them in the country. This was eventually done. A tract of land was leased in the suburbs of the city, and a large building erected at the expense of Government. The quartermaster at this post was ordered to issue rations and furnish fuel and medical attendance. The Western Freedmen's Aid Commission agreed to furnish clothing, bedding, books, etc., and take the general oversight of the institution. We employed several teachers, and a large school was kept up as long as Government sustained the home—a period of three years.

In the autumn of 1863 the subject of establishing a Freedmen's Bureau was agitated by the various freedmen's associations. President Lincoln had been consulted on the matter; he favored having the subject brought before Congress, and suggested, unofficially, that a strong delegation from the different associations should meet in Washington and endeavor to influence the members of Congress.

This suggestion was acted upon, and delegations from the associations of Boston, New York, Philadelphia, Cincinnati and Chicago met at Washington in December.. I was one of the delegates from our association. We had interviews with the heads of the different departments, and found Secretary Stanton and Secretary Chase warmly in favor of the establishment of the Bureau. President Lincoln promised to send a message to Congress on the subject. We appointed a committee to draft an address to the members of Congress; several prominent members who were interested in the matter agreed to have a bill brought before their body, and do all they could to promote its passage. We felt assured that our labors would result in success.

After spending about a week at Washington, I visited the freedmen's associations of Philadelphia, New York and Boston, to invite them to turn their attention, in part, to the great field of labor opening in the Southwest. I did not wish to divert their supplies from their own field; it was not my purpose to collect in their districts, but to explain to them the extent and increase of the work west of the mountains and encourage them to help us. I was cordially received wherever I went, and assured of co-operation and assistance.

Women Friends of Philadelphia had an organization for aiding the freedmen by collecting clothing, and material for clothing, which their sewing circles made into suitable garments. I was in Philadelphia when one of their regular meetings was held in Arch Street Meeting-House, and was invited to attend and give information regarding the freedmen in the Western field. I complied with the request and gave an account of my experiences, and the scenes I had witnessed while visiting the contraband camps. Several large boxes of clothing and blankets were afterward forwarded to our association from this society. Numerous liberal contributions were handed to me. Besides the associations of New York·and Boston, I visited also those of Lynn, Massachusetts, and Providence and Newport, Rhode Island, receiving contributions at each of those places, and the promise of other supplies, clothing, shoes and blankets, which were afterward sent.

I attended, on New Year's day, the meeting of the old anti-slavery society at Plymouth, and stood on the famous Plymouth Rock, with Samuel J. May, Wendell Phillips, and others of my old co-laborers in the anti-slavery cause. This was a jubilee meeting of the old abolitionists.

After visiting William Lloyd Garrison and others of similar principles in Boston, I returned home, having received during my travels the sum of two thousand dollars—contributions voluntarily handed to me by individuals, to be devoted to the relief of the freedmen in our district of labor. I felt encouraged to persevere in the work, feeling that my efforts had been blessed.

The American Missionary Association of New York aided us materially in our work, not only send-

55

ing large boxes of clothing, but supplying teachers to assist those already in the field or to open new schools.

After my return from the East, I was actively engaged in receiving supplies and forwarding them to our agents and teachers, to be distributed at the most needy points.

CHAPTER XX.

MISSION TO ENGLAND—LABORS IN BEHALF OF THE
FREEDMEN—INCIDENTS OF THE WORK—CONTRI-
BUTIONS FROM ALL CLASSES OF SOCIETY—PUBLIC
MEETINGS.

IN March, 1864, I made another visit to our field
of labor in the South, to see that a judicious distribution of alms was made to the sufferers, and to
look after the welfare of our numerous teachers,
who, at the cost of much privation and self-sacrifice,
were doing a noble work among the freedmen.

On my return home my mind was impressed with
the thought that if our friends in England could
understand the conditions and wants of these suffering thousands of lately emancipated slaves, many
of them would willingly help us in this great work.
I was personally acquainted with several prominent
ministers of our society, and others who had visited
this country, and knew something of the sympathy
and state of feeling that existed there in regard to
the freedmen. I thought that it might be right for
me to lay the subject before the philanthropists
of England, but in meditating on the matter I felt
many misgivings. I was inclined to plead excuses,
to say, as Moses did, that I was not eloquent, but

slow of speech and of a slow tongue, but I remembered that the Lord said to Moses: "Go, and I will be with thy mouth, and teach thee what to say," and told him that Aaron should meet him and go with him, and the thought occurred that I might meet an Aaron on the other side of the water, who would assist me. After much thought and earnest prayer, the path in that direction seemed clear. I brought the subject before my dear wife and she encouraged me to go. My health seemed to be failing under the pressure of my labors here, and she thought that rest and a change of work would be of great benefit to me. I then presented the matter to the board of directors of the Freedmen's Aid Commission, under whose auspices I proposed to go. They appeared to be much pleased with my prospective mission, and gave me their united sanction and encouragement. They asked me what salary I would require, or what per cent. of my collections I would be satisfied with; to which I replied that I had never collected money for benevolent purposes in that way, that my mission might not be a successful one—I might not collect enough to pay expenses—but if they were willing to bear my expenses I would engage in the mission and do the best I could. I wished to go entirely untrammeled by any pecuniary considerations, or any limitations of time. They at once agreed to furnish means for my expenses, leaving the other matters to my choice. Preparations were then made for the journey, and I was furnished with numerous credentials.

In addition to the commission as general agent

of the Western Freedmen's Aid Commission, given
me by the board of directors, a number of official
documents were voluntarily offered; one from the
board of directors of the Western Tract and Book
Society—of which I had been a member for many
years—and one signed by the mayor of the city and
some prominent judges and lawyers of the courts
of Cincinnati. I was also presented with a recommendation signed by the faculty of Lane Seminary
—a theological school on Walnut Hills—and another
signed by the ministers of the different religious
denominations in the city. Most of these documents were prepared without my knoweledge, and
though they expressed more than I felt I merited, I
received them, with gratitude for my friends' kindness, knowing that they would be of much service
to me in my mission. I obtained also from the
Monthly Meeting, of which I was a member, a certificate of membership in the Society of Friends,
indorsed by the correspondents of the Yearly Meeting. Thus equipped with all necessary documents
I took leave of my family and friends at Cincinnati,
the first of 5th month, May, and started on my
mission. I remained a day or two at New York,
where I received from Secretary Chase, at Washington, the passport to Europe which was then
required, and for which I had previously applied.
I received, besides, a general letter of recommendation from the secretary; also one of similar character from Henry Ward Beecher.

I then took passage on the steamship *City of
Edinburgh*, for Liverpool, arriving at that port in

safety after a voyage of thirteen days, during which time we encountered strong head winds and some very rough weather. From Liverpool I went to London, and stopped at a hotel. Here I met William Blaine, of Liverpool, a Friend whom I had once met in America. It was pleasant to recognize a familiar face among so many strangers, and we greeted each other as old friends. London Yearly Meeting of Friends was then in session. The next day, first day (Sabbath), I rode out to Tottenham and attended the morning meeting. Here I met with Josiah Forster who had been at my house in America—this place was the home of the noted Forster family. I dined with this dear old friend, and then returned to my quarters in London. The next morning I went, accompanied by William Blaine, of Liverpool, to the Devonshire House, that old and spacious edifice where London Yearly Meeting is held, where it was established, two centuries ago, in the days of George Fox and William Penn.

From all parts of the kingdom, Friends were gathered here to attend the great annual assembly of this once despised and persecuted people, now a wealthy and influential body of Christians. Many of them held high positions in the Government; John Bright, Samuel Gurney, William Edward Forster, Henry Pease and others being members of Parliament. The apartments of both men and women in this large building were well filled. It is a plain structure, comfortably and conveniently arranged, and will accommodate a large assembly of people. Two sessions of the Yearly Meeting were held in a day, one in the forenoon and one in the afternoon. I took my seat with William Blaine near the center of the building, having not yet made myself and my mission known to the prominent members of the meeting, or to those ministers whom I recognized—John Pease, Benjamin Seebohm and John Hodgkin. These eminent Friends had visited America several years before on a mission of gospel love, and I had some acquaintance with them.

After the adjournment I made myself known to these persons; they gave me a hearty greeting and introduced me to other prominent Friends. I was invited to dine with John Pease and others at their boarding-place; here I had an opportunity of showing them my credentials and informing them of my mission. They appeared to be much interested, and John Pease proposed to introduce the subject before the meeting the next day. After the devotional services closed, the next morning, and the clerk opened the business meeting, John Pease rose and informed the meeting of my presence, and my mission to that country. He then requested me to come forward and occupy a more prominent place; I was sitting where I had sat the day before. In this he was joined by other Friends, and the clerk invited me forward and I was placed by the side of John Pease, Benjamin Seebohm and others, on the upper seat. Such a prominent position, before such a large body of people, was embarrassing to me; I felt my inability to do justice to the cause that I had come to advocate. The clerk read my certificate of membership and standing in the

Society of Friends and my commission from the Western Freedmen's Aid Commission of Cincinnati, and alluded to the documents of recommendation given me by Secretary Chase and others. I was then requested to give an account of the condition and wants of the Freedmen in America. I rose and said that I felt diffident about occupying much of the time; knowing that much business would come before the Yearly Meeting, I would endeavor to confine my remarks to the outlines, and not enter into the details of the subject—an evening meeting, called for that purpose, would perhaps be more appropriate for an extended statement. John Pease spoke up and said: "Don't be afraid of occupying too much time." All diffidence seemed to vanish, and I was favored to give a comprehensive account of the condition and wants of the lately emancipated slaves in America and of our labors among them. I stated that my mission to England was not intended to be confined to the Society of Friends, but was to philanthropists in general; our association was anti-sectarian, but evangelical, and all denominations of Christians could labor together harmoniously in this great work of benevolence. The meeting seemed to be deeply interested in the matter, and gave me much encouragement. Next day a note was sent in from the women's meeting, requesting me to come in their apartment and give them an account of the freed slaves in America, similar to that which I had given the men's meeting. The clerk informed me of this request, and asked me if I was willing to comply

with it. I said that I would give the women Friends
the desired information at any time that was suitable to them. The clerk sent in a note to that
effect, and a message soon came back that they
were ready to receive the visit. The meeting then,
as is the custom in such cases, nominated two
Friends to accompany me, and Robert Alsop and
William Satterthwaite—both ministers—went with
me into the women's apartment. Here we occupied
the upper seat, and faced a large and intelligent
audience of English women. I felt that this was a
fit place to present an account of the extreme destitution and suffering which I had so lately witnessed among the thousands of women and children
whose chains had so recently been stricken off. I
felt that the cause I had come to plead would find
quick sympathy in the benevolent hearts of the
mothers and wives and sisters before me. I gave
them a brief account of my visits among the freedmen, and spoke of their wants and sufferings. After
a few appropriate remarks from some of the women
we returned to the men's apartment.

The object of my mission was now well understood by both men and women Friends of London
Yearly Meeting, and as representatives were there
from all parts of the kingdom, I felt that the way
was prepared for me inside the limits of our religious society. But as I have said before, my mission
was not to be confined to the Society of Friends.
It was anti-sectarian, and my appeal in behalf of the
freedmen was intended for the British public. I
had letters of introduction to prominent men of

other denominations, and to John Bright, Richard Cobden and other members of Parliament.

During the session of the Yearly Meeting I became acquainted with many influential Friends from various parts of the kingdom, who invited me to visit their neighborhoods, kindly offering their assistance in my work in those localities, and cordially inviting me to their homes. They suggested that public meetings should be called and the subject in that way be introduced to the notice of the people. I thanked them for their kindly manifested interest, and said I had not yet decided what course to pursue in bringing the matter before the public. I had by this time moved my quarters to Friends' Institute, near the meeting-house, where an excellent boarding-house was kept for the accommodation of traveling Friends, and where a large number of Friends congregated to take dinner. This gave me the opportunity of extending my acquaintance among them.

Great harmony and brotherly love prevailed during the transaction of business in the meeting; the great Head of the Church appeared to rule and reign, and the wing of divine goodness seemed to overshadow the asssembly.

When the meeting was over, and Friends had gone to their homes, I felt lonely and depressed in spirit. I reflected that I was a stranger in the great city of London, and knew not what course to pursue in order to effect the object of my mission. I had been a worker and not a speaker in the anti-slavery cause; I had always avoided public speaking or prominence of any kind, yet the work before me seemed to demand the very qualifiacations which I felt I lacked.

A sense of the great responsibility resting upon me weighed me down. I felt that I was unequal to the task, and feared that I had mistaken my call to the work; I might make a failure in my attempt, and injure the cause I had come to promote. These serious discouragements engrossed my thoughts the most of the night, so that I slept little. I prayed earnestly for divine guidance and direction in all my movements, and toward morning the cloud seemed to pass from my mind; I became quiet and peaceful, believing that some way would open for me to plead the cause of the suffering freedmen.

Sleep then came to me, and I awoke in the morning refreshed and hopeful. Soon after breakfast Robert Alsop, of Stoke-Newington, called to see me and said that his wife had sent him to take me to their house—that I must make my home with them for awhile. I thanked him for his kind invitation and said that I would pay them a visit. At his house I found kind friends and congenial spirits who sympathized with me in my arduous mission, and wished to give me all the aid and encouragement in their power. Robert Alsop and his excellent wife Christine were both prominent ministers in our society. I also met here his sister, Christiana Alsop, of Malden, a minister, who expressed much interest in my work. Several friends were invited to the house to take tea with me, among whom were Stafford Allen and his amiable wife

Hannah; they seemed to sympathize deeply with the cause I had at heart, and afterward invited me to make my home with them. I received much encouragement; new light and hope brightened my pathway; plans of procedure were suggested for consideration, and liberal contributions were made by Stafford Allen, Robert Alsop and others.

Joseph Bevan Braithwaite, a minister and barrister, had manifested much interest in my mission. He came to see me to counsel with me and encourage me in the work. As he was a man of much influence I found his advice and assistance to be of great service to me. He went around with me to deliver some introductory letters which I had, addressed to prominent men of his acquaintance. I was told by him and other influential Friends that my success would depend largely upon the encouragement that I received and the start that I made in London. They suggested that we should get up an invited meeting, as they called it—invite prominent men, ministers and members of Parliament to meet me at the house of some well-known Friend; I would thus have an opportunity to bring to their consideration the needs and sufferings of the freed slaves and confer with them as to the best plan for prosecuting my mission. I had become satisfied that if I succeeded in unlocking the heart of the British public I must get the key in London, and that much depended on the character and standing of those who gave countenance to and took part in the work. I submitted the matter of the invited meeting entirely to my friends. Dr. Hodgkin agreed to call such a meeting at his house, and sent out letters of invitation indorsed by the prominent Friends I have mentioned, and by others. On such occasions it was known beforehand what the principal proceedings were to be, who would serve as chairman, and who would take part in the meeting.

A well-known public man had consented to take the chair, and John Bright, William Edward Forster and other members of Parliament had agreed to participate in the proceedings of the meeting.

While these arrangements were being made I received a letter from Liverpool inviting me to attend a public meeting at that place—which had been appointed to consider the subject of the freedmen in America. The writer informed me that they had an organization at Liverpool which had been collecting funds and forwarding to the Boston Freedmen's Association, and they did not propose to change the channel through which their contributions had been sent. Several speakers were to address the meeting, and I was invited to speak; my expenses would be paid if I accepted the invitation. I felt, on reading the letter, that I could not fill their expectations, and was disposed to decline the invitation, but my friends urged me to accept it, and I went.

My friend William Blaine welcomed me to his hospitable home and entertained me during my stay in Liverpool. I had letters of introduction to several prominent men in that place, which proved of service to me.

We had a large and interesting meeting, and I was favored to speak without embarrassment on the subject of my mission. A liberal contribution was made, and fifty pounds were awarded to me for our Western field of labor. I also received other contributions from private individuals, and returned to London feeling well satisfied with my visit to Liverpool.

The invited meeting at Dr. Hodgkin's was largely attended, about seventy-five people being present. Among them were prominent ministers of various religious denominations, members of Parliament, such as John Bright, Richard Cobden, William Edward Forster and Samuel Gurney, and several noted speakers; Newman, Hall, Dr. Massie, Dr. Tomkins and others. Representatives of the principal London papers were also present. The meeting was opened with prayer. The chairman then made a pretty long introductory speech, giving some account of my life and labors in the anti-slavery cause, then introduced me to the audience with eulogies which I felt I did not merit.

When I rose to speak I said that I had not come to England to speak of what I had done, but of what I hoped to do. I had come to tell them a plain, simple story of facts in regard to the freedmen whom I had recently visited, and to endeavor to arouse their sympathy. I said: "You were lately engaged in a noble work of philanthropy— during the time of the Irish famine and Lancaster distress—and we had the privilege of aiding you in it. We are now engaged in a work that has no parallel in history; there has been nothing like it since the children of Israel were led out of the land of bondage." I then explained the condition and wants of these people; the extent of our field of labor and the daily increase of the number of sufferers. I said that the work for the freedmen commenced east of the mountains—in Maryland, Virginia, and the Carolinas—that associations were organized in Boston, New York, and Philadelphia, composed of excellent men who had done a noble work, and we had aided them before the work opened in the West, and that I knew they had received some aid from this country, and that these noble philanthropists were still doing a good work among the freedmen, and worthy of their patronage and aid. But that these camps and colonies in the East were now nearer self-supporting than they were in this great new field now opened west of the mountains which I represented. I stated that nearly three-fifths of all the slaves in the United States were located west of the range of Allegheny Mountains, and that the Eastern cities were the money centers of our country; the people there were more wealthy than those of the West; that I would ask that a part of their contributions should go to this great new field.

However, I did not plead for these alone. Although I was an agent of the Western Freedmen's Aid Commission, the first organization established west of the mountains, I had no personal or local interests to promote. I plead for the thousands of suffering freedmen in the United States, and when the most needy cases were met through the most economical channel, my mission would be completed. I told them that I had not come to England to beg, but to lay the matter fairly before them ; it was not simply an American question, but one of Christian philanthropy the world over. I did not wish to dictate to them what course they should pursue in regard to collecting and forwarding funds, but I would suggest that they organize a freedmen's association, appoint their own treasurer and banker, and transact their business through a bank. I did not wish to take the responsibility of receiving and forwarding money.

John Bright followed me in a short speech commending my suggestion, then William Edward Forster, Newman Hall, Dr. Massey and others spoke. A resolution to organize a London Freedmen's Aid Society was then adopted, and the work was fairly begun. Samuel Gurney, M.P., suggested that they should not complete their organization then; there were a number of prominent men not present whom he wished to interest in the subject, and he proposed to invite a similar meeting at his house. This was agreed to, and the company separated.

The London papers of the next morning contained accounts of our meeting, giving the names of those who were present, and a synopsis of the speeches, so that my mission to England was soon known all over the kingdom. The meeting at Samuel Gurney's was quite aristocratic in character, being largely composed of lords, dukes, bishops, and members of Parliament. Several prominent ladies were also present. J. B. Braithwaite accompanied me to this meeting. A servant dressed in livery met us at the carriage and conducted us into the hall—where we registered our names—then into an adjoining room, where a table was spread with fruits, pastry and other dainties, and supplied with coffee, tea and wine. After partaking of some refreshments, the guests were conducted to the large elegant parlor on the floor above, where the meeting was to be held, by a servant of higher grade, who announced our names as we entered the door. Here we were met by Samuel Gurney and wife, who introduced us to the ladies and gentlemen present. When this was over, and I was seated near the lord who was to preside over the meeting, I thought "This is quite a contrast to the scenes I so recently witnessed among the refugee slaves of the South, whose cause I have come to plead," and a secret prayer arose in my heart that I might be able to do justice to their cause.

The meeting was opened by prayer, from one of the bishops, after which the secretary read several letters from those who had been invited, expressing regret that they could not come, and sympathy with the object of the meeting. My credentials were then read, and Secretary Chase's letter of recommendation, which was short and to the point. The chairman mentioned that I had other letters from various sources, but said that he was sure what had been read would be sufficient—that I was known to many present by reputation, and to some

56

personally. He then went on to give, in an introductory speech, a brief sketch of my life and labors, concerning which some one had informed him. When I rose to speak, I disclaimed any merit for what I had done, and proceeded to give an account of my late experiences among the freedmen, and to speak of their needs and sufferings. My remarks were the same, in substance, that I had made at the previous meeting. In referring to the war, I said: "I had no sympathy with war under any circumstances. I believe that the terrible conflict now raging in our country was permitted by the Almighty to come upon us as a judgment for the great sin of slavery, and that the North is guilty as well as the South, and must also suffer. The people of the North have connived at and sustained the system of bondage—neither is England innocent in this matter. She was guilty of introducing slavery into America, and has done much to sustain it by purchasing the products of slave-labor. She, too, has suffered, in a degree, in consequence of this war." I alluded to the Lancaster distress, occasioned by the lack of cotton. After speaking of the work as being one of Christian benevolence the world over, and explaining the extent of the field of labor that in the providence of God had been opened before us, I took my seat.

Charles Buxton, M. P., followed me in an able speech; after which several other gentlemen spoke. I was asked a number of questions concerning the freedmen, among the rest was the inquiry, " Do they manifest a disposition to help themselves?" I replied that we had been agreeably surprised in that particular; in general they were inclined to support themselves when they had an opportunity. They did not wish to become paupers. "However," I said, "there is quite a difference among them; some are nearly as trifling and worthless as white people." This remark caused laughter all over the room.

A prominent bishop of London inquired about prejudice against color in America, saying that he understood colored people were not permitted to sit at the table with white folks, or ride with them in public conveyances, and were often refused admittance at hotels.

I replied that a great deal of that kind of prejudice still existed in our country, but that it had lessened since the war commenced.

The bishop said: "In this country we respect people according to their merits. I had the honor of dining with this brother to-day," placing his hand on the woolly head of a very black man who sat near him—a bishop from Sierra Leone, Africa.

The subject of organizing a London Freedmen's Aid Society was next introduced; an account of the proceedings of the meeting at Dr. Hodgkin's was read and united with, and the organization completed. Sir Thomas Fowell Buxton was appointed president; Samuel Gurney, M.P., treasurer; and William Allen, sub-treasurer. Frederick Tomkins, Esq., M.A., D.C.L., Rev. Samuel Garratt, B.A., Rev. John Curwin, and F. W. Chesson, Esq., were made honorary secretaries. A large and influential committee was then appointed to promote the object of the association, consisting of the following names:

Charles Buxton, Esq., M.P. ; W. E. Foster, Esq., M.P. ; Henry Pease, Esq., M.P. ; John Bright, Esq., M.P. ; Hon. and Rev. Baptist W. Noel; Rev. W. Brock, D.D. ; Dr. Hodgkin; Rev. Dr. Worthington, F.R.G.S. ; Rev. J. W. Massie, D.D., LL.D. ; Rev. J. C. Gallaway, M.A. ; Rev. W. Tyler; Rev. Newman Hall, LL.B. ; Rev. R. L. H. Wiseman ; J. B. Braithwaite, Esq. ; Robert Alsop, Esq. ; Thomas Norton, Esq. ; Richard Smith, Esq. ; Thomas Hughes, Esq., B. A. ; Andrew Johnston, Esq. ; J. M. Ludlow, Esq. ; J. C. B. Potter, Esq. ; W. J. Probyn, Esq.; Mr. Serjeant Parry ; Gerard Ralston, Esq. ; William M. Wood, Esq. ; Stafford Allen, Esq. ; William Binns Smith, Esq., Benjamin Scott, Esq., Chamberlain; Rev. John Shedlock, M.A.

The association held its first meeting a short time after in the Devonshire House—where the Yearly Meeting of Friends is held—to make arrangements for forwarding the cause to which I was devoted. The London papers had published the proceedings of the meeting at Samuel Gurney's, thus again giving prominence to my mission. I frequently received letters inviting me to attend meetings at various places. I proposed to labor under the auspices of the London Association, making reports to them of all collections, and paying into the hands of their treasurer all the money I received—leaving them to dispose of it as they thought proper—thus relieving me of the responsibility of forwarding it. I informed them that our treasurer, J. F. Larkin, was a banker, and I suggested that all funds awarded to the Western Freedmen's Aid Commission by the London Association should be forwarded to our treasurer through bank. This suggestion was approved of, and we were informed that the banking-house of Barclay, Bevan, Tritton and Company would receive and forward all contributions for the freedmen without charge. It was proposed to publish a special appeal to the people, and hold meetings in the various towns and cities.

This arrangement would lead me at once into public speaking, to which I was not accustomed; I felt that I was not fitted for it; my voice was weak and my health feeble. I had been a successful collector for the freedmen in my own country, and this had generally been accomplished by holding meetings of a mere private character, calling ministers and prominent men together in the various towns and cities, and arousing their interest, and having some prominent citizen selected to accompany me in making individual calls. In this way I had been successful in accomplishing much for the freedmen; feelings of discouragement and misgivings perplexed me for a time. I feared that I could not succeed so well in addressing large assemblies; that I could not extend my voice over an audience in a large church or public building. That was my only fear. I felt no diffidence or embarrassment; I was fresh from the field of suffering, and could talk about it any length of time, giving a plain statement of facts.

When I made these statements to the committee, several responded that is all we want, and you can be heard to satisfaction. I told them that when the thought of going to England to plead the cause of the slave was first presented to my mind, I felt dis-

posed to plead excuses, as Moses did, but I remembered that he was told that Aaron would meet him
and go with him, and I thought, perhaps, I would
meet Aarons on this side of the water who would
speak for me.   Dr. Massie volunteered to be my
Aaron and go with me; Dr. Tomkins also volunteered to aid me in the work, and to attend as many
of the meetings as his other engagements would
permit.   They were both clergymen and prominent
speakers.   Dr. Tomkins and Dr. Massie had both
taken a deep interest in promoting the object of my
mission.   The way now seemed to open pleasantly
before me.   I frequently received invitations to
breakfasts and dinners and teas, to meet other
guests.   J. B. Braithwaite often accompanied me
to these gatherings, where I was introduced to
members of the higher classes of society, and after
the repast must necessarily make a speech on the
subject of my mission, and answer many questions
in regard to American affairs.

I found a great deal of misconception and prejudice to combat among some of those occupying
high positions.   I endeavored to correct the false
impressions made by Southern agents and copper-
head papers as to the real cause of the war, and in
answering questions I had to talk a great deal on
the various subjects connected with our struggle in
America.   I felt deeply sensible of the necessity of
great care and watchfulness in all that I said, and
earnestly craved to be guided by best wisdom in
all my movements.   Duties began to crowd upon
me.   Among the letters I received relative to my

mission were several from Birmingham inviting me to visit that place and hold meetings. An association had been organized there, called the Birmingham and Midland Counties Freedmen's Aid Association, and it was proposed to load a ship with clothing and other material most needed by the freedmen. Arthur Albright and Benjamin Cadbury had written to me on the subject, making inquiries in regard to the articles needed, and asking other questions, which I answered by letter. I received a letter from the widow of Joseph Sturge, that noble philanthropist of Birmingham, proposing to have an invited meeting for me at her house. I attended it at the time appointed, accompanied by William Allen. The following account of the meeting is taken from the Birmingham *Daily Gazette*, of July 1st, 1864:

"AID FOR ESCAPED SLAVES.

"MEETING AT MRS. JOSEPH STURGE'S.

"Yesterday evening a meeting was held at the house of Mrs. Joseph Sturge, in Wheeley's Road, for the purpose of hearing an address from Mr. Levi Coffin, a member of the Society of Friends, who has come over from America to seek aid for the thousands of escaped slaves who are now to be found within the Federal lines. What Mr. Levi Coffin himself has done will be best told by quoting an extract from a letter written by him in answer to some inquiries that had been made about the middle of June:—'The number of fugitive slaves that I have had the privilege of assisting in their escape from slavery is over three thousand. The most of these I have had the satisfaction of sheltering under my roof, and feeding at my table. This has been through the course of more than thirty years past, and mostly before this cruel war commenced. I claim no merit for simply doing my duty in feeding the hungry and clothing the naked ; I desire not to speak of it boastingly, but to feel humbly thankful that I had the privilege of aiding these poor sufferers in the time of their distress, when fleeing from the land of whips and chains, and seeking a land of liberty in Queen Victoria's domains. I am glad to hear of your exertions to load a ship of useful articles for the poor refugees ; you can hardly go amiss, as they need everything, coming as they do bare and destitute, not only of clothing but of cooking utensils, farming tools, etc. ; tools of every description ; without knife, fork, spoon, plate or cup, you can well imagine that all things would be acceptable.' A large number of ladies and gentlemen assembled at the hour appointed, and after partaking of tea proceeded to the large room where the meeting was held. Mr. Edward Gem took the chair, and there were present Messrs. John Yates, James Baldwin, ʻJohn Palmer, William Allen, Frederick Giles, Thomas Aston, Howard Lloyd, J. C. Woodhill, James R. Boyce, George Hunt, W. W. Allford, John Reynolds, G. B. Kenway, Benjamin Hudson, William Morgan, Arthur Albright, Edmund Sturge, Thomas Aston, F. Pigott, Thomas Crawley, William Barwell, Henry Heaton, Alexander Forrest, S. A. Goddard, Charles Felton, R. A. Husband, G. Glossop, Thomas Gibson, J. Mitchell, Brooke Smith, Rev. F. Watts, John Cadbury, James Stubbin, J. S. Wright, William White, Charles B. Partridge, T. Simons, Charles Pumphrey, B. H. Cadbury, W. S. Atkins, William Blews, Rev. P. Reynolds, Joseph Blakemore. Among those who sent apologies were the Rev. Dr. Miller, Dr. Newman, Captain Warlow, Rev. J. J. Brown, Rev. J. H. Burges, Rev. W. B. Benison, Mr. John Goodman, Rev. J. H. Scowcroft, Mr. G. F. Muntz, and Mr. G. Dixon.

" The Chairman, in opening the proceedings, said the practical but pleasant gatherings held under the hospitable roof of Mrs. Joseph Sturge were made still more pleasant because they knew they were always for something connected with the improvement of the spiritual and temporal interests of their fellow-creatures. They had that evening a most interesting subject to look into, and one which he felt convinced would meet with the sympathy of all. There were in all one hundred and six answers to the invitation to attend the meeting. Some of the answers inclosed promises of subscriptions, among which were £10 from Mr. R. L. Chance, 10s. from Mr. John Onions, £5 from Mr. Avery, and

£2 from Mr. Barwell. The Rev. Mr. Marsden had also written, allowing the use of his name in forwarding the objects of the meeting, and the Rev. Dr. Miller said that he was greatly pressed by business, and therefore prevented from being present. The immediate object of the meeting was to make the acquaintance of a gentleman who had been during the whole of his life interested in the great question of the emancipation of slaves. Mr. Coffin brought with him a letter from Secretary Chase, who said that Mr. Coffin was well known to him as a conscientious and faithful member of the Society of Friends, as one anxious and diligent in benevolent labors for the fugitive slaves, and as one worthy of the confidence and esteem of all good men. He also brought with him testimonials signed by Mr. Harris, Mayor of Cincinnati, by Judge Storer, the members of his Monthly Meeting, and many others, including the authorities of the American Reform Tract and Book Society. During the whole of his life Mr. Coffin had not aided and abetted slaves in leaving their masters, but when he found them, after they had escaped, hungry and naked, he fed and clothed them. In doing this he had set an example for their imitation, and although they could not do as he had done directly, they could do it indirectly by giving contributions toward the ship-load of goods to be sent for the relief of freed colored men, or by giving money with which the necessaries of life might be purchased for them. In conclusion the Chairman read the following letter he had that morning received from Mr. Adams, the American Ambassador:—

"'LEGATION OF THE UNITED STATES, LONDON, 29th June, 1864.

"'SIR—I shall take great pleasure in transmitting a copy of your note to me to my Government. I have no doubt that everything possible will be done to facilitate the reception of goods destined for so benevolent a purpose, and the feeling of kindness the act will create will be worth far more than all.

"'I am, very truly yours,
"'C. F. ADAMS.

"'Edward Gem, Esq., Birmingham.'

"Mr. Levi Coffin was then introduced by the Chairman, and said that having had the satisfaction once, some years ago, of a very pleasant acquaintance with their dear friend Joseph Sturge, in America, and having had the pleasure of corresponding with him both before that time and afterward, it was very pleasant to him to have the privilege of meeting that company at his former residence. There had been some mention made of his anti-slavery labors, and it might not be improper for him to explain what his labors really were in connection with the Underground Railroad. The phrase itself was first made use of by slaveholders, who, not being able to capture those who had fled from their plantations, said there must be an underground road to Canada. Well, he dared say, many people in this country, as well as in America, did not understand exactly the position he occupied toward those poor slaves who were seeking their liberty in the domains of Queen Victoria. Soon after he removed to the town of Newport, in Indiana, he found that many fugitive slaves were passing that way, and were often captured and taken back. Those who were disposed to give them facilities in their escape were afraid of the penalty attached to the harboring of fugitives, but he thought he ought to do what was right and what was taught in the New Testament, by feeding the hungry and clothing the naked. He was not fearful of the penalty, and it soon got to be known among the slaves that he was ready to feed and shelter those who came to him. The result was, that during the twenty years he remained at Newport he had the privilege of sheltering under his roof an annual average of one hundred and six. When he removed to Cincinnati the work became heavier, and he had in one year as many as one hundred and eighty-nine. In all, he had had the privilege of relieving 3,300. He wished to be understood that in speaking on this subject he claimed no merit; what he had done was his duty, and he trusted he felt humbly thankful that he had had the opportunity of rendering some assistance to those poor sufferers in the time of their distress. He had always taken the ground that everybody had a right to liberty who had not forfeited it by crime, but that it was no part of his business to interfere with what was law in the slave States. He did not incite or assist any slaves to make their escape, what he did for them was done after they had run away, and then he was disposed to give them all the aid and comfort he could. He often told slaveholders that it was no part of his business to interfere with slaves on their estates, but that if a slave had run away and he found him needing assistance he would help him. He added, that on the same principle he would feed the slaveholders if they came to him hungry, but that he would not help them in the capture of escaped slaves. After the American war broke out, a great number of slaves came within the Federal lines in a destitute and suffering condition, and his attention was turned in that direction before they had any association organized west of the mountains. He visited the camps and colonies formed on the Mississippi, and he found the poor people in a state of destitution far exceeding anything he had anticipated. He felt that something must be done on their behalf, and he could not remain still. He had now come to this country as the representative of the Western Freedmen's Aid Commission, which was organized in Cincinnati in 1863, and was the first organization for that object in the West. His concern was not local, but was for the general body of suffering thousands and tens of thousands, gathered in different parts of his country. In the camps on the Mississippi there were now fifty thousand, all destitute, and in Tennessee, Alabama, and Georgia, there was an equal number, and one which was rapidly increasing. In the course of this year it was expected the whole number would reach half a million. Of the poor people who were destitute, three-fourths were women and children, the able-bodied men being mostly employed in some position connected with the army. Everything was needed by them, and everything that the people of Birmingham might give would be thankfully received, and would be of great benefit.

"Mr. Albright and Mr. William Allen afterward addressed the meeting, and on the suggestion of Mr. Morgan a number of new names were added to the Birmingham and Midland Counties Freedmen's Aid Association.

"A subscription in aid of the objects for which the meeting was held was commenced in the room, and numerous donations were announced."

"To the above, extracted from the ' Gazette,' the committee of the Birmingham and Midland Counties Freedmen's Aid Association desire to add, that the concluding result of the meeting, in numerous addresses from gentlemen present, in spontaneous important contributions of both goods and money, and in hearty offers of other aid, was most cheering, and strongly encourages the belief that their prime object of loading a ship with manufactures and commodities for the freed refugee negroes will be promptly accomplished.

> " W. MORGAN, ⎫
> " B. H. CADBURY, ⎬ *Secretaries.*"
> " C. FELTON, ⎭

After my return to London, I was engaged in attending parlor meetings by invitation, and public breakfasts, dinners and tea parties among the higher classes of society, where the subject of my mission and American affairs in general were freely discussed. These were pleasant occasions, and productive of good results. The ladies were organizing sewing societies and making up new clothing for the freedmen, also collecting second-hand clothing. The firm of Johnson, Johnson and Company had kindly offered to receive and forward to Liverpool, without charge, all packages of clothing and other articles for the freedmen.

Goods for shipment were now rapidly accumulating, and knowing that duties were very high at that time, I called on our Minister, Charles F. Adams, to consult with him in regard to getting the duties remitted on all goods shipped for the benefit of the freedmen. He manifested a deep interest in the subject, and agreed to write to Washington at once, requesting me also to write. I accordingly wrote to Secretary Chase, requesting immediate action on the part of our Government in the matter, and informing him that I would probably ship a large amount of clothing and other goods for the relief of the freed slaves. It was but a short time until Minister Adams was informed that the duties would be remitted on all goods shipped for the benefit of the freedmen, and bearing certain designated marks. The way was now clear to ship the goods free of expense. The railroads charged no freight to Liverpool, a commission house there received and forwarded all packages for the freedmen without charge, and the regular lines of steamships from Liverpool to New York agreed to give them free transportation to that city. I had the goods consigned to C. C. Lee, Secretary of the National Freedmen's Aid Society of New York, to be forwarded to our association at Cincinnati. When all these arrangements were completed I felt great relief and encouragement. I had found many warm friends, and received efficient aid, and valuable contributions of money and clothing were now being forwarded for the relief of those whose cause I had come to plead. All this was a source of great satisfaction to me; I felt that my efforts were being blessed.

The London and Birmingham societies were now actively at work. The London committee had arranged for public meetings at various towns and cities round about, and issued handbills and other advertisements announcing my name at the head of the list of speakers. I felt my inability to meet the expectation of the people as a public speaker, but I looked to a higher power for guidance, and the fear of man was taken away. I was enabled to tell a plain story of facts to large audiences, apparently to their satisfaction, and was often embarrassed by applause. Dr. Massie traveled with me to these appointments at Manchester, Bradford, Leicester, Sheffield, Rochester, Newcastle-on-Tyne, Kendal, and numerous other places. Dr. Tomkins also attended a number of these meetings, and gave us efficient aid. Both these gentlemen were able speakers, and in full sympathy with the North; they had traveled in America, and were strong advocates of the Federal cause. Our meetings were largely attended; much interest was manifested, and committees were organized to carry on the work. In addition to newspaper notices and printed circulars, the following appeared in the *Anti-Slavery Reporter*, the organ of the British and Foreign Anti-Slavery Society, August 1, 1864:

"LEVI COFFIN'S MISSION TO ENGLAND.

"Levi Coffin, of Cincinnati, a member of the Society of Friends, has come to England for the purpose of advocating the cause of the refugees in the United States, who have been emancipated in consequence of the war, either by running away, or by being abandoned by their former masters. We have already given prominence in our columns to the condition of these unfortunate people, and therefore need not now further dwell upon the subject. Mr. Coffin comes highly recommended, and has himself been instrumental in rescuing many slaves, while the Fugitive Slave law—now happily repealed—was in full force. After a preliminary meeting, held at the close of June, at Dr. Hodgkin's, another was held at the house of Mr. Samuel Gurney, M.P., President of the British and Foreign Anti-Slavery Society, when a committee was organized to promote the objects of Mr. Coffin's mission. The committee of the British and Foreign Anti-Slavery Society passed the following resolution, at their last general meeting, on Friday, the 1st of July:

"RESOLUTION.

"'The committee, having examined the credentials of Levi Coffin, of Cincinnati, and being satisfied that the object of his mission to England is most worthy, and that he is himself in every respect deserving of confidence, have great pleasure in commending the cause of the freedmen of the United States, as advocated by him, to the prompt and kind consideration, and especially to the liberality of the friends of the colored race in this country.

" ' (Signed)

" ' SAMUEL GURNEY, President,

" ' EDMUND STURGE, Chairman of Committee.

" ' L. A. CHAMEROVZOW, Secretary.' "

The London Freedmen's Aid Society issued the following circular in letter-form, which was largely circulated:

"FREEDMEN'S AID SOCIETY.

" Levi Coffin, from America, well known on the other side of the Atlantic for the part which he has taken in aiding the fugitive slaves (several thousands of whom he has personally assisted in their escape to Canada), is now in this country for the purpose of enlisting the sympathies of philanthropists on behalf of the refugee negroes, who, as is well known, have fled in great multitudes from bondage, in consequence of the war, many of them in a state of deplorable destitution and ignorance.

"As the accredited agent of the Western Feedmen's Aid Commission his labors in this cause are altogether disinterested. And having kindly arranged to act in concert with the Freedmen's Aid Society in this country, the committee are glad to avail themselves of his advocacy, and cordially commend him to the confidence and sympathy of the friends of the negro in this important crisis of the history of the colored race.

" As a member of the Society of Friends, he can as little sympathize with war as with slavery, and, in urging the claims of these poor fugitives, he desires that his advocacy may be maintained upon simple Christian grounds, apart from all political considerations.

" (Signed)

" T. FOWELL BUXTON, President of the Freedmen's Aid Society.

" SAMUEL GURNEY, Treasurer of the Freedmen's Aid Society.

" LONDON, July 20, 1864."

After attending the series of meetings arranged by the London committee in many of the principal towns in England, I returned to my pleasant home at Stafford Allen's, Stoke-Newington, London, to rest awhile from my arduous labors. The unusual exertion of addressing public assemblies, generally evening meetings that held to a late hour, and raising my voice so that it could be heard over large audiences, told upon my health, and I felt the need of recruiting my strength. It was laid upon me, at these meetings, to make the first speech, and I endeavored to tell a plain and concise story, leaving it to others to make eloquent appeals and rhetorical displays. It became an easy matter for me to talk on the subject of the freedmen; I was never at a loss for words to express myself. The subject lay near my heart and I could talk, concerning it, to any class of people, as I could not have done, perhaps, on any other subject. It mattered not to me what title they held, or how high a position they occupied in the Government. It was the wealthy, influential class whom I wished to interest in the subject of my mission, and my letters of introduction and credentials had introduced me to the higher classes of society. I had been received with much kindness and respect, and felt at my ease among them.

After spending several days with my kind friends in London, Stafford Allen and his amiable wife Hannah, who always cheered and comforted me with their kindness, I again engaged in active service, feeling much refreshed. My time was largely

spent in holding parlor meetings, which often resulted in the organization of sewing societies to
make up clothing for the freedmen. J. B. Braithwaite and wife, and Stafford Allen and wife, with
many other kind friends in and about London, rendered me much service in my labors. I was again
invited to Birmingham, and attended a public meeting in the town-hall, and several other meetings
more private in their character.

The Birmingham and Midland Counties Association was doing a noble work for the freedmen.
Arthur Albright had taken a deep interest in the
cause, and gave me efficient help in many ways.
He traveled with me in that part of the country,
and wrote and circulated documents relating to the
freedmen. He was a man of wealth and influence,
and his untiring energy and perseverance in the
work did much to promote the cause in which I
labored.

In September I visited Dublin, Ireland, accompanied by Dr. Massie and wife, who had friends
and relatives there. Samuel Bewley had been notified of my expected visit, and met me at the
quay, and conducted me to his house, where I had
a pleasant home during my stay in that part of the
country. An invited meeting, or rather a public
breakfast, was gotten up by Samuel Bewley and
Jonathan Pim, at Friends' Institute, where a number
of the most prominent men in Dublin were invited
to meet me and confer on the subject of my mission.
This conference resulted in holding a public meeting, at which the Lord Mayor presided. After the

reading of my credentials and a short introductory speech by the chairman, I addressed the assembly at some length on the subject of my mission. Several short speeches followed, and much encouragement was given. The proceedings of the meeting were published. The following is taken from the Dublin *Daily Express:*

"CONTRIBUTIONS IN AID OF THE COLORED REFUGEES IN NORTH AMERICA,

"At a meeting held at the Friends' Institute, Molesworth Street, on the 12th inst., called for the purpose of enabling Mr. Levi Coffin, of Cincinnati, Ohio, to give information as to the present state of the fugitives from slavery in the valley of the Mississippi, and of the exertion made for their relief,

"ALEXANDER PARKER, Esq., in the chair,
the following resolutions were adopted:—

"I.—Moved by the Rev. Dr. Massie; seconded by John L. Blood, Esq., and resolved—

"That the exertions of the Western Freedmen's Aid Society of Cincinnati, and of the other associations in America, for the relief and instruction of the colored fugitives from slavery, are deserving of our warm sympathy, and that we commend those associations to the liberality of the Christian public.

"II.—Moved by the Rev. Dr. Kirkpatrick; seconded by John Bagot, Esq., and resolved—

"That the following gentlemen be appointed a committee to take such steps as they may think desirable for bringing this subject before the notice of the public:—

"Thomas Drury,	David Drummond,
"William Todd,	Henry Wigham,
"Maxwell M'Master,	John L. Blood, Esqrs.
"John Sibthorpe,	

"III.—Moved by Maxwell M'Master, Esq.; seconded by James Haughton, Esq., J.P., and resolved—

"That Alexander Parker and Samuel Bewley, Esqrs., be requested to act as treasurers to receive any funds that may be subscribed, and to remit the same to America.

"ALEXANDER PARKER, Chairman.

"Alexander Parker, Esq., having left the chair, and John Barrington, Esq., the Lord Mayor Elect, having been called thereto, it was moved by the Rev. Dr. Massie; seconded by John Bagot, Esq., and resolved—

"That the thanks of this meeting are due, and are hereby given to Alexander Parker, Esq., for his kindness and courtesy while presiding at this meeting, and for the valuable assistance which he has given to this cause.

"JOHN BARRINGTON, Chairman.

"JONATHAN PIM, ⎞
"WILLIAM FRY, ⎠ Secretaries."

Over two hundred pounds (£200) was paid into the hands of Samuel Bewley, treasurer, and forwarded to our treasurer at Cincinnati before I returned to England.

The work was now fairly commenced in Ireland; much interest was manifested. Dr. Massie returned home from Dublin, and I visited Cork, Waterford, and other towns in the south of Ireland. The Dublin papers had given a favorable notice of my mission. Letters and circulars preceded me to those places, and meetings were appointed. Wherever I went in this part of the kingdom, as in England, homes were provided for me. Some kind friend met me at the depot, and conducted me to his house, so that I never felt I was among strangers. The meetings were satisfactory and the contributions liberal. After making this hasty tour to the south of Ireland, I went back to England, where I had engagements to fill; I expected to return to Ireland in a few months.

I attended, by invitation, the Methodist General Conference at Bradford, and the Baptist Union at Birmingham, also the semi-annual Conference of the Congregationalists at Lyons. I then visited Scotland, accompanied by Dr. Massie. We had appointments at Kendal, Carlisle, and other places on our way to Edinburgh, having large and interesting meetings and warm receptions. I formed many pleasant acquaintances at Kendal, and our call for the freedmen was nobly responded to.

We held meetings at Edinburgh, Glasgow, and nearly all the principal towns in Scotland, having hearty receptions and good audiences wherever we went. Liberal contributions were made, and public interest was manifested in various ways. The daily papers published our speeches and the proceedings of the various meetings. I met with many warm sympathizers in Scotland, and made many pleasant acquaintances there whom I still hold in loving remembrance. The following account of our labors in Scotland was given in the *British Friend,* a periodical published at Glasgow:

"FREEDMEN'S AID SOCIETY.

" We presume most of our readers are aware that a society under the above name has recently been established in London, 'Sir Thomas Fowell Buxton, Bart., being President, and Samuel Gurney, M.P., Treasurer. In promotion of its object, our friend, Levi Coffin, of Cincinnati, Ohio, who is well known to Friends as the General Agent of the Western Freedmen's Aid Commission, has been laboring in many of the large towns in England, in conjunction with Dr. Massie, of London.

" Arriving in Edinburgh on the 1st ult., they held a public meeting in that city, besides some of a more private and social character; also in Glasgow, Paisley, Ayr, Port-Glasgow, Greenock, Perth, and Dundee. At Glasgow a meeting of ladies was convened, when a committee was named to co-operate with the gentlemen's committee, and both have since been engaged in endeavoring to interest the public in the cause; obtaining contributions in money, clothing, etc. All the associations thus formed, it is understood, are to act in concert with that of London, and other similar organizations having the same benevolent end in view—the shelter, feeding, clothing, and educating of the colored refugees from slavery, in consequence of the war in America.

"Dr. Massie left Glasgow on the 19th ult., since which time Levi Coffin has been holding parlor meetings, mostly in the city. While we write he is at Helensburg, one of the watering-places on the Clyde. After meeting the ministers of the various denominations in Glasgow, he is to pay a second visit to Dundee; soon after which he expects to proceed to Belfast, and other towns in the north of Ireland.

After closing my labors in Scotland, I crossed over the Channel to Belfast, Ireland, where I was cordially received and entertained at the pleasant home of Richard Bell. I had letters of introduction to Dr. McCosh and other prominent men, which were of great service to me. After holding a conference with them, the following letter of invitation to a public meeting was sent out:

"Levi Coffin, of Cincinnati—a member of the Society of Friends—with unquestionable credentials and letters of introduction, is desirous to hold a meeting with the benevolent public of Belfast and to make an appeal to them on behalf of the liberated slaves in America, for whose spiritual and temporal interests large means are now required.

"The Mayor of Belfast has kindly granted the use of the Town-Hall, and has consented to preside at a meeting, appointed to be held there on Second day (Monday) the 12th instant, at one o'clock, and we respectfully invite you to be present on the occasion.

"BELFAST, 12th month (December) 9, 1864.

"John Owden,	Henry Cooke, D.D., LL.D.,
"Joseph Richardson,	John Edgar, D.D.,
"Richard Bell,	James McCosh, LL.D.,
"Joshua Pim,	Thos. H. Purdon, M.D.,
"E. H. Thompson,	C. D. Purdon, M.D.,
"Charles Seaver, Incumbent,	Joseph W. McKay,
St. John's Church,	Wesleyan Minister,
"Robert Hannay, Incumbent,	James Donnelly,
Christ Church,	Wesleyan Minister."

The public meeting was well attended by eminent men, and several short speeches were made, which were all published in the daily papers. The following account of the meeting, with an appeal, was printed in letter-form, and addressed to prominent persons in the north of Ireland, who were not at the meeting, and liberal contributions were received:

"CONTRIBUTIONS IN AID OF THE COLORED FREED-MEN IN AMERICA.

"At a meeting held in the Town-Hall, Belfast, on the 12th instant, for the purpose of enabling Levi Coffin, of Cincinnati, Ohio, to give information respecting the colored freedmen in the valley of the Mississippi,

"The Mayor of Belfast in the chair,

the following resolution was adopted—

"RESOLVED—'That this meeting has heard with much satisfaction, the simple, luminous, and convincing statements of Levi Coffin respecting the condition of the emancipated slaves in America, and the extreme necessity of immediate efforts to meet their great spiritual and temporal wants. We return him our very sincere thanks; and for the purpose of carrying out effectually this benevolent object, we appoint the following committee to use immediately the most effective means of securing the co-operation of the benevolent in Belfast.'

" The Mayor,	Professor Macdouall,
" John Owden, Esq.,	Dr. Thomas H. Purdon,
" Richard Bell, Esq.,	John Young, Esq.,
" Rev. R. Hannay,	John Simms, Esq.,
" Rev. Hugh Hanna,	Rev. James Donnelly,
" Rev. Dr. M'Cosh,	Rev. M. M'Cay,
" Rev. Dr. Morgan,	Joshua Pim, Esq.,
" Rev. Charles Seaver,	William Mullan, Esq.

Rev. Dr. Edgar, }
E. H. Thompson, } Secretaries.

———— o ————

"APPEAL.

" Since the commencement of the fearful war in America, it is calculated that upward of a million of those who were held in bondage have made their escape, or have been deserted by their masters. The greatest part of these are aged people, women, and children. In the freedmen's camps of the Mississippi valley alone there are more than 50,000 dependent persons, and this number is daily increasing. A very large proportion have arrived in a state of utter destitution, the clothing of the men and women being literally in rags, and many of the children completely naked. They have been most kindly received and cared for by a large number of philanthropic persons of all denominations; but it is a serious consideration how their wants are to be met, especially during the present winter. The Government supplies them with rations, but every other need must be provided from private sources. It is fully expected that if they are now furnished with clothing, tools, etc., they will in a short time be able to maintain themselves. Books, slates, and every article of school use have to be supplied to them, and their eagerness to learn to read, and willingness to work, have been most cheering.

" The work is great, and one in which the Christians of this country, without reference to political or sectarian considerations, may gracefully manifest a deep interest. The American people responded nobly to our call for aid during the Irish famine, and have the strongest claims on our sympathy and assistance at the present time. We inclose subscription list, and respectfully, but earnestly, request you will add your contribution thereto, and return same promptly.

"JOHN EDGAR, D.D.,
"E. H. THOMPSON.
"Richard Bell & Co., have consented to act as Treasurers.
"BELFAST, 12th month, December 19, 1864."

I attended the Quarterly Meeting of Friends at Belfast, where I had the opportunity of presenting the subject of my mission, and explaining the extent of the work in America. I visited Lisburn and other neighborhoods in the north of Ireland, receiving encouragement and liberal contributions. Wherever I went, I met with many kind friends.

From Belfast I went to Moyallen, county Down, where I was kindly received by John G. Richardson and wife, and entertained for several days, during which time I was visiting and attending meetings in that neighborhood. I met with good success in collections. I then returned to Dublin, where I again had a pleasant home with my kind friends, Samuel Bewley and his interesting family, while I remained in Dublin, where I had formed many pleasant acquaintances during my former visit, and whom I shall ever remember with kind regard. I found the committee had been actively engaged, and a considerable amount of money and clothing had been collected and forwarded. The work was still in progress, and the ladies' sewing societies were rendering efficient aid. I attended several meetings in Dublin, and other neighborhoods of Friends, and finding a general interest manifested in the work for the freedmen, I felt much encouraged.

It was now the first of the year 1865. I thought that *the labors* of my mission were nearly at an end, and that I might look forward to returning home in the second month (February). I felt that my labors had been much blessed; I had succeeded beyond my most sanguine expectations. Freedmen's associations had been organized in nearly all the principal towns in England, Ireland and Scotland. A noble response had been made to my appeal in behalf of the suffering refugee slaves. A large amount of money, clothing, hardware, cutlery, shoes, blankets, etc., had been forwarded to our association in Cincinnati. After spending a week or two very pleasantly in that part of Ireland, attending several meetings in Dublin and visiting other neighborhoods of Friends, and receiving liberal contributions, I took leave of my kind friends at Dublin, and crossed over the Irish Channel to Holyhead, and took the train to Birmingham, where I had been requested to meet Dr. Haynes, who had just arrived in England, being sent as an Agent of the National Freedmen's Aid Society of New York. They were encouraged, no doubt, by hearing of my great success in Europe.

After attending some meetings in Birmingham and vicinity, I returned to London, where I met with a cordial welcome at my pleasant home at Stafford Allen's. My headquarters, however, were at Friends' Institute, of which I have spoken before. I found little time for rest. The work of

58

my mission seemed to be increasing upon me every day. My correspondence was large; I was frequently receiving remittances and letters of invitation to attend meetings and to visit various places. The demands upon me were so numerous that I could not comply with them all. The way did not seem clear for me to quit the work and go home, as I had intended. Letters from home encouraged me to continue longer in the work if my health permitted, as the result of my labors was quite beneficial to the cause I represented. My friends in England also encouraged me to remain, and I decided to stay until some time in the spring. During the winter I attended a number of Quarterly Meetings of Friends in different parts of the kingdom, where I had the opportunity of pleading the cause of the freedmen.

John Hodgkin had written an admirable address to the Society of Friends, and others, on the subject of the freedmen. It was printed in pamphlet form and read in all the Quarterly Meetings, and widely circulated. Friends everywhere were fully informed on the subject, and earnestly engaged in the work. At a public meeting held in Friends' Meeting-House at Leeds, after the business session of the York Quarterly Meeting was over, about a thousand pounds were subscribed.

The committee of the London Freedmen's Aid Society had arranged for a general meeting to be held in Exeter Hall on the evening of February 15th, on the subject of the conditions and wants of the freedmen in America. It was advertised in the principal London papers, and large bills were posted in all the most public places giving the names of those who would address the meeting. I was surprised to find my name placed at the head of the list,· and would have objected had it not been too late. I had taken a deep cold and was suffering with sore throat and hoarseness, so that it appeared impossible for me to speak as advertised, but my friends were anxious for me to be present, and though I had been confined to my bed for several days previous, I managed to attend the meeting. My hoarseness had measurably left me, but I still felt feeble and unable to address an audience. I was seated on the platform near the chairman and surrounded by many of the prominent men of London. All the space in the large hall appeared to be occupied, the ladies' apartment and all the galleries being filled. The number of people present was estimated at five thousand. I thought that I should not attempt to speak, but after the chairman had spoken and the meeting was fairly opened, my feelings became warmed up, and I now felt more like speaking. When I was introduced to the meeting and began to speak, my voice, to my astonishment and that of my friends, seemed to grow stronger and clearer, so that it could be heard all over the hall. J. B. Braithwaite came to me when the meeting was over and said that he had never heard me speak so well—that I had been distinctly heard all over that large assembly. The following account of the meeting is taken from the *Evening Star*, of February 16, 1865:

"THE FREEDMEN'S AID SOCIETY.

" A public meeting in support of the objects of this admirable society was held in Exeter Hall last night. There was a large attendance, and the proceedings were of a peculiarly enthusiastic and unanimous character. The following gentlemen were among those present:—Sir T. Fowell Buxton, Bart. ; the Rev. Dr. Haynes, President of the National Freedmen's Relief Association, and Mr. Levi Coffin, the representative of the Freedmen's Aid Commission of Cincinnati; Mr. W. E. Forster, M.P.; the Rev. Dr. Massie; the Rev. J. H. Hinton, M.A. ; the Rev. James Davis, Secretary of the Evangelical Alliance; the Rev. Samuel Garratt, B.A.; the Rev. Henry Richard; the Rev. Newman Hall, LL.B.; the Rev. James H. Wilson; Mr. M. D. Conway, of Virginia; Mr. J. Bevan Braithwaite; Mr. J. Morgan, of Birmingham; Mr. William Allen; Mr. Stafford Allen; the Rev. Crammond Kennedy, late United States Army Chaplain; Mr. F. W. Chesson, and Mr. R. Alsop.

" Sir T. F. Buxton was called to the chair.

" The Rev. Samuel Garratt opened the proceedings with prayer.

" The Chairman, who was received with cheers, rose and addressed the meeting. He said that the present meeting was, to some extent, connected with the great anti-slavery struggle which took place in England more than thirty years ago. In 1834 slavery was abolished throughout the British colonies; and now they could assert that more than two millions of the slave population of the United States had gained their freedom. (Cheers.) But while they rejoiced in this great change they should not forget the misery and destitution which this change involved. They knew how difficult it was to meet the distress caused by the cotton famine in Lancashire; and they could conceive how this would be aggravated by the fact that those freedmen who were suffering from the destitution were without that education which every free man must have acquired for himself. These men were not taught from their youth, they were not able to supply their own needs and wants, and were undergoing the greatest misery. They were escaping in thousands, partly from their plantations and partly left by their owners, who were driven southward. They considered that they had a right to appeal to the people of this country in behalf of these freedmen, not merely on the ground of charity, but as a debt due by this country to those who were suffering. They could not forget on this occasion how much they had profited by their enforced labor, and that it was to their labor that they owed the prosperity of their northern counties. (Hear, hear.) They appealed to them with the more confidence that the destitution was of a transient character, because in the course of a short time those freedmen would become absorbed into the working population of the United States. (Hear, hear.) In order to show them that the abolition of slavery had been of advantage to their colonies he would state that in their West India Islands they grew in 1831, when there was a high protective duty, 8,920,132 cwt. of sugar; while, in 1862, with no protective duty, and no extraneous help, they grew 9,800,000 cwt—or nearly 1,000,000 more than when slavery existed. (Cheers.) It might be said that the property of a country ought to be met by the property and the wealth of that country itself. That in some measure was true ; but it was not an argument which they could cast in the teeth of their kinsmen across the Atlantic who had helped to relieve their starving Irish and the destitution of their artisans in Lancashire. (Cheers.) They should embrace this opportunity of showing their good-will and friendship to their kinsmen in America. (Hear, hear.) There were, unhappily, people in both countries who were willing to excite feelings of hostility between the two countries, and they ought therefore to take every means in their power to frustrate these efforts. (Cheers.) Might they not hope that if they showed their hearty sympathy with their American brethren in their efforts, and cultivated their good-will it would tend to the pros-perity of both countries ? If they wished for the welfare of their own country, the prosperity of the whole British Empire, and of the whole English speaking community, they should take every means of cementing all branches of the Saxon race together. (Cheers.) If they cared for the progress of liberty, the extension of self-government, and the happiness of the world, they should desire to unite together those two nations which enjoyed in the highest degree those blessings. (Cheers.) It was with this object that they brought this society before the public, and they trusted that its claims would be heartily responded to by London, and by the country generally. (Cheers.)

"The Rev. Dr. Massie then read letters of apology from a num-ber of gentlemen who were unable to attend the meeting.

"The Chairman then called upon Levi Coffin, Esq., the dele-gate of the Western Freedmen's Aid Society, who, he said, had come to this country with letters of introduction from Secretary Chase and many other gentlemen occupying high positions on the other side of the Atlantic.

"Mr. Levi Coffin then came forward, and was received with loud cheers. He said that he was suffering from such an attack of illness that had it not been for the deep interest he took in this cause he should not have come forward to say anything on the present occasion. Mr. Coffin then proceeded to say that he wished it to be distinctly understood that his mission was simply one of Christian philanthropy, and had nothing whatever to do with the political bearings of either side of the North or South. As a member of the Society of Friends he could have as little sympathy with war as he could have with slavery. In traveling over this country he found a misconception existed in many per-sons' minds with regard to the number and location of these poor refugees. The impression seemed to be that they had come to the North, and were scattered about the free States. This was an incorrect view. The freed slaves were principally gathered in the Federal lines in the seceded States. As both armies had swept over the country, nothing was left for the poor negro. They therefore came in the deepest distress—in fact many of them were in such a state of destitution that it beggared description. They came in by thousands and tens of thousands until the number was now swelled to two millions. (Cheers.) Two years ago, last autumn, this work commenced west of the mountains; in the East it commenced earlier. As the Federal army advanced down the Mississippi thousands came within the lines, many of them almost in a state of nudity. He heard of their condition and paid a visit to that part of the country, and he found the destitution greater than he had anticipated. On his return the Western Feedmen's Aid Society was organized at Cincinnati, and measures were taken at once to relieve the poor refugees with articles of clothing, etc. Great exertions were made, but the means at their disposal were nothing to the wants of the people. The following year he paid a second visit and found that the work had largely increased. On his return more extensive efforts were put forth, but thousands perished for lack of the means of helping them. In all his travels he had never met with a single case where there was a single wish to return to slavery. (Loud cheers.) They looked upon their deliverance as the intervention of a special Providence. He found them to be patient in suffering, disposed to die rather than return to their former condition. Schools had been organized in the camps and colonies, and great progress had been made by those who had attended these schools. Tools were put into the hands of those able to work, in order to make them self-supporting. In one district of the Mississippi, where there were 113,650 registered during the past year, they had had 74,981 acres under cultivation in cotton, besides their potatoes and other vegetables. (Cheers.) Out of the number of slaves he had mentioned there had been over 13,000 under instruction. Above 4,000 had learned to read fairly, over 2,000 to write, and many were supporting themselves by working; but there were so many aged, crippled, and orphan children, that a considerable time must elapse ere they could relax their efforts. Most of the slaves showed great willingness to work, and this was an encouraging fact. Mr. Coffin having urged these points upon the meeting, said he must refrain from proceeding further, as his voice was failing him, and he then resumed his seat amidst loud applause.

"The Rev. Dr. Massie bore testimony to the great amount of good that Mr. Levi Coffin had accomplished. He said the slave planters had got to call him the 'Underground Railway.' (Cheers.) For thirty-three years he received into his house more than one hundred fugitive slaves every year. (Loud cheers.) These slaves he housed, clothed, and when sick attended them, and when they died buried them. (Cheers.)

"The Rev. H. Haynes was called on, and received with cheers.

He expressed the pleasure which he felt in making his first appearance in Exeter Hall, and said that although he had his opinion as to the trouble in his country he did not come here in any partisan spirit. He himself had collected from men of all opinions $100,000 for their freed slaves, and the society with which he was connected had raised $500,000. They were engaged in a purely charitable work, but they found that all their efforts were unable to meet the immense tide of destitution, and they therefore now appeal for aid to those in England who felt it to be their duty and privilege to aid them. Whatever differences might exist as to the war they were all agreed about the freedmen. The freedmen had been the most misused of men. It was no wonder that John Wesley, who lived in Georgia, pronounced slavery to be the 'sum of all villainies,' and that Thomas Jefferson said that he trembled for his country when he thought of slavery. Then they could not forget how much Britain owed to the productions of slave labor, nor would they forget how much British eloquence and remonstrances had to do with the freedom of these slaves. The influence of their Clarksons, their Wilberforces and their Buxtons had been felt in America, and George Thompson was not forgotten there. (Cheers.) And, when appealing to a British audience, he thought it right to tell them that now the laws against the slave-trade in America were executed: that one man at least had been hung—(A voice: 'Sarve him right")—that two millions of slaves had been emancipated by the war; that Congress had abolished slavery in Columbia and prohibited it in the Territories; that Missouri, Tennessee, West Virginia, and Maryland had constitutionally voted the abolition of slavery; and now to-day they had the news that the House of Representatives had passed an act of general emancipation. (Loud cheers, which were again and again renewed.) Already two millions of slaves had been made free by the war, and the other two millions were a dissolving view. (Cheers and a laugh.) He then referred to the sufferings undergone by those freed negroes, and said that no tongue or pen could describe them. They were coming in in hundreds and thousands, most of them without proper clothing, and destitute of all means of assisting themselves. [At this stage a gentleman who had taken up a place on the platform, here stood forward, and interrupted the speaker, and declared with great vehemence, 'I am a Southern." He was greeted with loud hisses and groans, and in a few minutes was ejected by some of the gentlemen on the platform.] Dr. Haynes proceeded to say that unless they received the aid of British philanthropy many of these people would have to undergo great suffering, and said he believed that these charities would promote international harmony and good-will. (Cheers.) One of their papers said the other day that it would not suit the North to go to war with England at present. He said that it would not suit them to go to war at any time. (Cheers.) The people whom he represented were the people who would see to it that no war was created between the two countries. (Cheers.) The speaker concluded by referring to the peace news from America, and said he believed in it.

"Mr. W. E. Forster, M.P., was then called upon. He said: I rise for the purpose of moving a resolution expressing the approval of this meeting in the objects of this association, and I do so not merely because these negroes are in great distress, though that would be a reason why Englishmen should be asked to aid them, and not merely because we owe a debt of gratitude to the Americans, though we do. Have they not helped our people when in distress, and how have we repaid it? Have we repaid the debt we owe them? There was great misery in Lancashire of late; the misery was brought on by this terrible war, which we may say was not only caused in America, but in England, by what we did originally in planting this seed of slavery among them. But miserable as was the state of Lancashire, the misery of America was far greater; but not losing sight of our suffering they sent over help. What have we done to repay them? The ship which came with the food which was for our starving operatives was seized by the privateer that issued from our shores. I say we owe something to them for what they did; but it is not only that debt we owe. We forget what they did for us in the time of the Irish famine. (Hear, hear.) It is curious how some people seem to completely forget this. I saw not long ago an article in the 'Times'—(hisses)—in rather more generous terms than is usually used, acknowledging the assistance the Americans gave to the Lancashire operatives; but, said the writer, their contributions were £100,000 less than those given during the Irish famine. But the sum sent over for the Lancashire distress was a handsome sum, for it amounted to £55,000, though £170,000 was sent during the Irish famine. But it is not merely because it is an act of humanity or gratitude, but I consider it to be an act of duty that we owe, especially, if we are, as I hope and believe all here are, thoroughly anti-slavery men. (Cheers.) In fact it would be almost impossible to think of any other meeting than the present being held in Exeter Hall— (hear, hear)—with its associations. Being in this hall takes me back to the time when many years ago I was here, before I personally took any part in meetings of the kind, and I must be allowed to congratulate my relative who is in the chair on this occasion. I can recollect what the feelings of his revered grandfather (my uncle) was upon this subject, and I am quite sure if he had wished the best possible wish for his grandson it was that he should take the chair in this hall at a meeting held on behalf of the negro, on the very day when this news comes from America. (Cheers.) The ruling powers of that county have irrecoverably pledged themselves to the abolition of slavery. (Cheers.) Let us look back at the position of the negro, and then consider what it is now. It is now nine years ago since the hopes of the negro were very dark. I take that time, for I think it was the blackest period for those who were the friends of the negro. That was the time when it was declared in an American court of justice that the negro had no rights. That was the time when these four millions of slaves seemed condemned to hopeless bondage, for that great republic, though free in name, was not so in fact, for it was ruled by the slave power. That was the time when every Territory which was opened out by Anglo-Saxon enterprise seemed to be merely conquered for slavery. Even in their pride the slaveholders were not content. They defied the principles of freedom—they defied every one, including England—and the 'Times' did not protest against that. (Hear, hear.) There appeared to be no hope for the negro at that time, and the friends of freedom were a simple minority. In the heart of the slaveholder there was pleasure and profit in carrying on the system, and the negro could expect no hope from him. Only nine years have passed, and what is the present condition of affairs? Why, close upon two millions of negroes (and having tested these figures, I believe them to be correct) are already free, and the power that rules the Federal Union, instead of being a slavery one, is now opposed to slavery; State after State has abolished slavery. That very State of Missouri, over whose borders went those ruffians who endeavored to take possession of Kansas and make it slave soil, has declared itself for the abolition of slavery. With the State of Tennessee I am in some way connected. Nine years ago my father went out to America to represent the evils of slavery, and he died in Tennessee, believing that in no State in America was slavery more deeply rooted than there. Yet Tennessee has abolished it. Maryland has also done so, and now we have the news this morning that Congress has taken the first step toward declaring that slavery is illegal. Doubtless much prejudice exists against color, but just in proportion as they cease to be slaves in the South, will the prejudice of the North against color cease. (Hear, hear.) We hear of one item in the news this morning which, though little in itself, is yet most important. In New York, where the feeling against color is strong, a colored man has been admitted to the bar. (Cheers.) With this good news also comes the other good news alluded to by Dr. Haynes respecting the peace rumors. It is rather a curious coincidence that just when comes the statement that the Federal Government have irrecoverably pledged themselves to abolish slavery, so that no compromise of slavery is now possible—(loud cheers)—there should come the peace rumors, coming with more force and credibility than they have done before. How difficult it does appear for men in England to take any sensible view of this question. The 'Globe,' which generally in its articles takes a sensible view of this matter, says to-night that the peace news is most important, and that the anti-slavery news is also important; but that they can not help thinking that the anti-slavery action will destroy the peace prospects, for the men of the South, when they find that the Government of the United States is irretriev-

59

ably pledged to the abolition of slavery, will feel that there is no reason to return to the Union. Now, how could a sensible man write such an article as this? Why, the men who have gone on this deputation as well knew that that act would be passed, and that that vote would take place, as did the men who voted for it themselves. They know that all hopes of compromise have disappeared. (Cheers.) They are perfectly aware of that, and they know very well that no terms can be made with the men of the North except upon abolition. Is it not strange that just when they have arrived at the certainty of that knowledge they come forward with their peace embassies, and, for aught I know, with their peace propositions. I am not surprised. It is just what I expected. It does not often do for political men to make predictions, but I will venture to make one prophecy, and that is, that soon after slavery is abolished the American war will cease. (Cheers.) And why? Because there will then be nothing to fight about. But we must not be contented with congratulating ourselves on this matter, we must consider whether we have not something more to do. We can not forget how heavy is the price which has been paid for the change; and shall we fold our arms and say that we are contented to see what has been gained for the cause of humanity but will bear none of the price? Are we not in some measure responsible? It was we who originally planted slavery there, and we have tempted the American slave-owners to the continuance and increase of the system by buying their cotton. (Hear, hear.) We may say that we were not responsible for the mode in which it was grown. Still, if that be so, is it not incumbent upon us to do everything that we can so that cotton shall be grown according to the principles of humanity? (Cheers.) But there is a greater responsibility even than that, especially upon old anti-slavery men. Who was it that incited and excited the anti-slavery men of America to take the stand which they have against slavery, and to make that resistance to the slave power which led to this war? Why, the anti-slavery men of England. (Hear, hear.) The war had been one of the most terrible and sorrowful of all wars; but I confess, for my part, I see only one way in which that war could have been avoided. Considering what the facts of the case were, and what human nature is, I do not believe that the war could have been avoided, except by the men of the North consenting to be ruled—to be themselves enslaved by the men of the South—(cheers)—consenting that the great and free republic should continue to be the greatest conspiracy against freedom in the world—consenting that the party which ruled by an oligarchy of color should continue to control the destinies of America. (Cheers.) But who was it that made that curse impossible? Why the anti-slavery men of England, who, whenever a free American came to our shores, exhorted him, preached to him, taunted him, and ridiculed him if he did not do his part to free his country from that stain. (Hear, hear.) The Republican party then joined with the abolitionists so far as to say that 'we will no longer allow the power of this Union to be used for the purposes of slavery—we don't see that we can can destroy, but we will allow it to go no further, and are resolved that the Territories shall be conquered for freedom.' If they once took that stand, every one who considered the facts of the case dispassionately must have felt that war was a necessity. The slave-owners would not give up their power without a struggle, and they said that if they were not to rule they would break up the Union. Now the Americans, if the majority of them had not a strong conscientious principle against war under all circumstances, had a habit which was, after all, an Anglo-Saxon habit—they would fight for their country. But they have had to pay a heavy price for the glorious change in the progress of humanity, and in the progress of the world, which this war has brought about; and shall we not assist them to bear this heavy burden? We can not suffer anything like to the extent which they have done, nor ought we; but we can in some slight degree assist them to bear the burden which has been imposed upon them. (Cheers.) I will say just one word as to the misunderstandings between us and the Americans as bearing upon this particular question. There is a good deal of ill-feeling in America which no speeches and no acts of ours can remove, because it springs from most unworthy motives; but it is a sorrowful fact that those who have been our best friends in America seem to misunderstand us, and who, if they have no ill-will to us, greatly regret that we have done as we have. I think that arises in a great measure from the fact that the anti-slavery men have been disappointed with our attitude in this matter. They feel that we have incited them, and then when they imperil their country in the cause of freedom they naturally complain that we look coldly on, and advise them to sacrifice their country. (Hear, hear.) I can not help feeling that they have some ground for entertaining that view, and therefore I rejoice that we have now an opportunity of coming forward and endeavoring in some measure to remove this impression. (Cheers.) You all must know that the freedom of these two millions of slaves can not have been attained without great sufferings and privations on their part, and I hope that we in England will do everything we can to assist those who are endeavoring to meet the wants of these liberated thousands. The honorable gentleman concluded by proposing 'That this meeting approves of the object of the Freedmen's Aid Associations in America which, while ministering immediate temporal relief, seek to give such aid, physical and educational, and to apply such moral and religious culture as shall, under the Divine blessing, enable the once down-trodden and degraded slave to act for himself and to give evidence of his capacity for the blessings of freedom and equality in the eye of the law.'

"The Rev. Newman Hall next addressed the meeting, and he urged various grounds upon which the people of this country ought to support the present society. The inevitable result of the present war would be the destruction of slavery—(hear, hear)—and it was for the benefit of the slave that this enormous cost was being borne by the Government and the people of the United States. England had wisely determined to be neutral respecting the war, but she could not be neutral as respected slavery, and now an opportunity presented itself for her to show her sympathy with the anti-slavery movement, and she ought not to neglect it. In the interests of peace they ought to support it. There had been many public men in England, and some of the public journals, that had said and done things calculated to deeply imbitter the American feeling against this country. Cruisers and blockade-runners had been fitted out in England, and the question had been mooted of the possibility of a war between England and America when the present civil war was ended. When he thought of the possibility of this war he trembled. Both nations were equally brave—both were the champions of freedom, and the resources of America were equal, if not superior, to those of England—and if they got to war with each other how the tyrants of the world would chuckle. (Loud cheers.) Such a war would be more terrible than any history had ever yet recorded. (Hear.) He therefore earnestly hoped every man would do his best to preserve peace. Never let an unkind sentiment be broached against America without reproof, and let every allowance be made for her while the present war raged. If they helped the fugitive slave they would show their sympathy with a nation that had already done so much on behalf of the slave. In conclusion, the reverend gentleman suggested that five millions of working men in England should make a penny subscription on behalf of these fugitive slaves, and this would yield no less than £20,000, which would be a welcome contribution. (Cheers.) The reverend gentleman seconded the adoption of the resolution, and sat down amidst loud applause.

" The resolution was put and carried unanimously.

" Mr. F. W. Chesson, moved the next resolution, 'That this meeting cordially commends the delegates from the Cincinnati and New York Freedmen's Association, Mr. Levi Coffin and Dr. Haynes, to the liberal consideration of all friends of the slave in Great Britain, by contributions in money and clothing, or other means of relief, for the support and improvement of the freedmen within the United States of America.'

" Mr. Morgan, who is connected with the Freedmen's Aid Society of Birmingham, seconded the resolution. He stated that that society had commenced operations in May last, and that the value of their contributions in money and clothing already amounted to £3,000.

" The resolution was carried with acclamation.

" A working man here got on the platform and attempted to address the meeting. He avowed that he was a Southern sympathizer; but as soon as he made this announcement he was met with a storm of hisses. He vainly endeavored to gain a hearing, and then left the platform apparently in a high state of indignation.

"Rev. Mr. Curwen moved a vote of thanks to Sir Thomas Fowell Buxton for his conduct in the chair.

"The Rev. Dr. Massie seconded the motion, which was carried with loud cheers.

"The meeting then separated."

About the middle of April I visited Paris and other cities in France, accompanied by Dr. Massie, who had acquaintances in Paris and understood the French language sufficiently to be of service in holding intercourse with the people. We arrived in Paris on Sabbath morning, and took quarters at the Hotel de Ville de Albion, where we met R. A. Chamerovzow, secretary of the British and Foreign Anti-Slavery Society; his home was in London, but he was spending some weeks in the French capital. His mother being a French woman and his father a Russian, he spoke several languages fluently. Being well acquainted in Paris and much interested in my mission he was very useful to us. We attended the American Church, of which Dr. Sunderland, of Washington, was pastor, and received a hearty greeting. Dr. Sunderland knew Dr. Massie personally and me by reputation, and gave us all the aid in our work that lay in his power. The next day we spent in making calls and being introduced to Protestant ministers and others, which resulted in the appointment of a meeting at the house of M. Laboulaye. This was attended by thirty-three of the most prominent Protestants in Paris, and by a few Catholics. I was introduced by the chairman, in French, and addressed the meeting through an interpreter, which was not so difficult as I had anticipated. Several short speeches were made, in French, and much interest was manifested. This resulted in the appointment of a committee to address the French people through the press, and to carry on the work for the freedmen in connection with the London society. We held several other meetings in Paris, where I addressed the people and received liberal contributions.

In company with R. A. Chamerovzow I visited Versailles, having letters of introduction to several noble French philanthropists of that place. One of these letters was written by Christine Alsop, of London; she was a French wòman, and a minister of the Society of Friends, well known iń France. I had a hearty reception at Versailles, and received several contributions. My intercourse with these acquaintances was none the less cordial because we did not understand each other's language, but had to speak through an interpreter.

We found some earnest working Christians in Paris, and received several invitations to parlor meetings where their friends had been invited.

After remaining a week in the French capital we returned to London, feeling that our time had been well spent. I was then looking forward earnestly toward the time when I could be released from this arduous work and return to my family and friends in my native land.

I had written to our board of directors at Cincinnati, some weeks before, requesting them to send Dr. Storrs, or some other suitable person, to take my place and continue the work through the summer, leaving me at liberty to return home. The London committee advised me to remain or to have some suitable agent to represent our association in my stead.

On my return from Paris, I received a letter informing me that Dr. Storrs expected to arrive in the early part of May, and wished me to remain until I introduced him to the work. The time of holding London Yearly Meeting of Friends was now drawing near, and I concluded to stay in England until it was over.

Dr. Storrs arrived a few days before the opening of that great annual assembly of Friends. A meeting of the London Freedmen's Aid Society was called to welcome him as agent in my stead. He informed the society that he wished to labor as I had done—under their auspices—and report to them. At Yearly Meeting I had the opportunity of introducing him to Friends from various parts of the country where I had labored.

I now felt that I was prepared to leave England, and secured passage on the steamship Scotia, to sail from Liverpool on the 3d of June. The Yearly Meeting closed on the 2d, about noon. Notice had previously been given, that a meeting on the subject of the freedmen in America would be held at four o'clock in the Yearly Meeting-House; all were - requested to attend. It was stated that I would be present, and that I would sail the next day for America, having completed my mission. When the appointed hour came that large house was crowded. The occasion was to me a solemn but a happy one. My heart was filled with thankfulness to my Heavenly Father for his great mercy in preserving my life through danger and exposure on land and sea, and endowing me with ability and strength to plead the cause of the suffering, and, finally, for crowning my labors with great success. I expressed my heartfelt thanks to the people for their kindness and hospitality, and for their liberal contributions, and then bade them an affectionate farewell. John Pease, Benjamin Seebohm, and others, responded on behalf of the meeting. After shaking hands with those near me, I endeavored to pass out, but many rose on each side of the aisle to bid me good-by, and my progress was slow. A friend was waiting to accompany me to Liverpool, and see me started on my homeward voyage.

I sailed the next day for America, having been absent more than twelve months. I left England with a thankful and cheerful heart; it had been one of the happiest years of my life. I could reflect upon my labors with satisfaction; they had been blessed beyond my expectation. Over a hundred thousand dollars in money, clothing, and other articles for the freedmen had been forwarded to our association in Cincinnati during the year, and there was a prospect that other fruits of my labor would follow.

I had a pleasant voyage across the Atlantic, and arrived at home in good health, receiving warm welcome and greetings from my family and friends.

A short time after my return the following testimonials were received from England—they had been prepared by a committee appointed by the London Freedmen's Aid Society:

"TO MR. LEVI COFFIN,

'AGENT FOR THE WESTERN FREEDMEN'S AID COMMISSION,
CINCINNATI, UNITED STATES.

" *Dear Friend,*—After taking our leave of you after almost a year spent in this country, in co-operating with us in seeking aid for the relief of the freed slaves of America, we feel that it is due to you and the cause you represent and have at heart, thus to express our personal esteem, and our satisfaction with the manner in which you have conducted your arduous mission. You arrived in this country when in consequence of misrepresentation, or want of knowledge, public opinion was wavering or unformed upon the state of the slave question on your side. We feel that, by your circumspect walk and truthful utterances, you have aided in the formation of more correct sentiments in reference to what is now known as the American question generally, and the claims of the freedmen in particular. In the midst of circumstances that might have disheartened a less devoted and patient friend of the slave, you have in kindly words pointed to the condition and sad necessities of four millions of men, gradually shaking off their fetters and rising to the hopeful condition of freedom. This, too, has been done whilst your health has been feeble, and your heart humbled for the sufferings entailed upon your country by the death and desolation of a cruel war. We rejoice with you that this war is now at an end. When you left your noble country, the whirlwind of civil rebellion afflicted and distressed the people. Now, we trust you will be spared to witness the soil of your loved home regenerated from the crime and curse of slavery, and the people at peace with all mankind! Nor can we forget the noble service of your past life. Long may it be told that Levi Coffin, in the darkest days of slavery, assisted to rescue three thousand three hundred bondsmen and bondswomen from their abject and degraded condition, and placed them in the serene and joyous atmosphere of freedom. And now, thou Apostle of Liberty, we bid thee farewell! Thou hast secured the blessing of him that was ready to perish, and consequently the favor of Him who said : 'Inasmuch as ye have done it unto one of the least of these my little ones, ye have done it unto Me.' We hope and believe that you will behold this people, for whose welfare you have labored, elevated to the rank and position of good citizens of your Republic, and ever advancing in moral and religious culture.

" We remain, dear and honored friend, on behalf of the Freedmen's Aid Society of London,

" T. FOWELL BUXTON, Bart., Chairman.
"SAMUEL GURNEY, M.P., Treasurer.
" WILLIAM ALLEN, Sub-Treasurer.
"FRED. TOMKINS, M.A.D.C.L., ⎫
"SAMUEL GARRATT, M.A., ⎬ Honorary Secretaries.
" F. W. CHESSON, ⎭
" JOHN CURWEN.
"LONDON, June, 1865."

———— o ————

"TO THE PRESIDENT AND COMMITTEE OF THE
WESTERN FREEDMEN'S AID SOCIETY OF
CINCINNATI, OHIO, UNITED STATES.

" Our friend, Levi Coffin, having informed us of his intention to return to his native land on the 3d of next month, we think that a few words testifying to his unselfish and prudent efforts on this side of the Atlantic, in the cause of the colored race, will not be unacceptable to you, and are felt by us to be due to him. He has prosecuted his labors among us under much bodily weakness ; but we are thankful to say has been preserved from an actual break down of his health. He has traveled over a great part of England, also in Scotland and Ireland ; he has visited Paris— everywhere giving the first place to the interests of your association, and making his way among strangers by his sterling integrity and consistent conduct. He has been very materially assisted by Dr. Tomkins and Dr. Massie, of our association, in combating the mass of prejudice and misconception, respecting American affairs, held by many occupying positions of influence in our country. Nevertheless, success has attended their placing the claims of the down-trodden colored men in America before the view of our countrymen, and he has been spared to see the dawn

of a brighter day, and we trust his life may be sufficiently pro-
longed to witness the triumph of right in both hemispheres, and
that in yours especially he may in process of time behold the
colored race in the full enjoyment of their rights as men and
citizens, and that in his latter days he may be favored to review
the labor of his hands on their behalf in peace.

"Signed on behalf of the Society,

"T. FOWELL BUXTON, Bart., Chairman.

"SAMUEL GURNEY, M.P., Treasurer.

"WILLIAM ALLEN, Sub-Treasurer.

"FRED. TOMKINS, M.A.D.C.L.,
"F. W. CHESSON,   } Honorary Secretaries.
"SAMUEL GARRATT, M.A.,

"JOHN CURWEN."

I felt thankful for these testimonials of approbation of my humble efforts on the other side of the
ocean in behalf of the poor colored race, though I
felt that more was expressed than I merited.

Our board was much pleased with my work and
encouraged by its results. They voted me a satisfactory compensation for my labor, though I made
no charge.

In the autumn following my return from England, I attended the Iowa, Western and Indiana
Yearly Meetings, accompanied by my dear wife and
daughter. At the first of these I met my dear
friends, J. B. Braithwaite and James Crossfield, from
London, who had come to this country on a gospel
mission.

At Indiana Yearly Meeting, held at Richmond, I
met Dr. Massie, of London, who had traveled with
me in England and France, and rendered me so
much service in advocating the cause of the freedmen. He had come to America as a delegate to

the Congregational Conference in Boston, and desired, besides, to visit our field of labor among the freedmen in the South. He returned with me to Cincinnati, and attended a meeting of the Board of Directors of the Western Freedmen's Aid Commission, when I had the pleasure of introducing him, and where he received a hearty reception. Shortly afterward I accompanied him through our field of labor among the freedmen in the Southern States, visiting most of our schools and institutions in Kentucky, Tennessee, Alabama and Georgia, holding meetings among the lately emancipated slaves, and preaching to them. It was a deeply interesting visit to both of us. We had the satisfaction of seeing many of the school children dressed in English clothing, which had been contributed through our agency. Their faces brightened, and they listened intently when I told them of the many kind people on the other side of the water who were friendly to them, and had sent them these nice clothes and shoes and school books. I asked: "What shall Dr. Massie tell these good people for you?" The answer was unanimous: "We thank them!" These were happy occasions to us. I parted from Dr. Massie at Augusta, Georgia; he visited Savannah, Charleston, Richmond, and Washington, and I returned home. I had noted the most needy points, and engaged at once in forwarding supplies.

We were constantly receiving clothing and other goods from England, in addition to our home contributions. During the fall and winter we received several thousand pounds, and our friends across the channel continued to remember us for several years. I frequently received drafts from the Treasurer of the London Aid Society. I continued to act as general agent, and devoted my time to the freedmen's cause until the summer of 1867, when I was appointed a delegate from the Western Freedmen's Aid Commission to attend the International Anti-Slavery Conference in Paris, to be held on the 26th and 27th of August. Delegates were expected from every civilized country in the world. The Secretary of the British and Foreign Anti-Slavery Society had sent me a notice of the conference, and invited me to be present.

I left home on the last day of July, and sailed from New York three days afterward on the steamship City of Boston. I was accompanied on this journey by my son, Henry W. Coffin. We reached Liverpool on the 14th of August, and the next day went to London, where we took quarters at Friends' Institute. Many of my old friends and former acquaintances called to see me and welcomed me back to England. I attended a meeting of the London Freedmen's Aid Society, and received a most cordial reception. In compliance with their request I gave them an account of the progress of our work among the freedmen, and went on to speak of the great good accomplished by their liberal contributions. After spending a week in London very pleasantly, we left for the continent, accompanied by my dear friend Stafford Allen and his daughter. We arrived in Paris on the 23d of August, and spent several days visiting the great International Exposition then in progress. Here I met many acquaintances from England and America. The Anti-Slavery Conference convened on the morning of the 26th, and lasted two days. Delegates were present from various countries, and the proceedings were deeply interesting. Speeches were made in different languages, and most of them were translated by interpreters into English.

After the conference ended we remained in Paris several days, visiting the Exposition and other places of interest, and then went to Switzerland, by way of Strasburg and Basle, to Zurich. I had acquaintances in this country and in Germany, who had been at my house in America, and wishing to present the cause of the freedmen in their localities, I accepted the invitations which they had so often extended to me. We had a pleasant and instructive visit, and received a number of liberal contributions for the freedmen. I had letters of introduction to prominent men in Zurich and Winterthur, where we were kindly treated and entertained.

From Switzerland we crossed Lake Constance into Germany, and went to Stuttgart, the capital of Wirtemberg, where we were met by our friend and acquaintance, Louise Weil. She was once a teacher in Cincinnati, and had boarded at our house. She conducted us to her father's house, in the village of Pliedshousen, near Tubingen, where we spent several days very pleasantly with her family and friends; she acted as our interpreter in conversation. I was well known, by name and reputation, in that locality. In a book which she had written concerning her travels and experience in America, Louise Weil had given an account of my anti-slavery labors and Underground Railroad operations, and her German friends greeted me as though they had known me before.

We returned to London, by way of Rotterdam, and attended the Quarterly Meeting of Friends at Devonshire House, and several other meetings among Friends. We then went to Birmingham to attend an anniversary meeting of the Freedmen's Aid Society, and gave them an account of the progress of our labors in that cause, and thanked them for their continued liberal aid. After visiting my dear friends, Benjamin Cadbury, Arthur Albright, and others, we passed over to Dublin, and, after a short stay with my friends in that part of Ireland, we went to Queenstown—accompanied by Samuel Bewley—and took passage for home, on the steam ship City of Baltimore. We reached our destination safely about the middle of November, having been absent nearly four months.

Our educational work among the freedmen had increased every year, and large supplies of clothing and books were still needed. My time was devoted to this cause; there was no longer need for the Underground Railroad work in which I had so long been actively engaged. When the colored people of Cincinnati and vicinity celebrated the adoption of the Fifteenth Amendment of the Constitution, I thought that it was a fitting time to resign my office as President of the Underground Railroad. Many of our prominent citizens took part in the celebration, and able speeches were made both by white and colored speakers. Judge Storer, Judge Hagans, Judge Taft, and other public men, were on the platform, and made able speeches. Near the close of that great meeting I was introduced by the chairman. I said that I had held the position of President of the Underground Railroad for more than thirty years. The title was given to me by slave-hunters who could not find their fugitive slaves after they got into my hands. I accepted the office thus conferred upon me, and had endeavored to perform my duty faithfully. Government had now taken the work of providing for the slaves out of our hands. The stock of the Underground Railroad had gone down in the market, the business was spoiled, the road was of no further use.

Amid much applause, I resigned my office and declared the operations of the Underground Railroad at an end.

FINIS.